The New Woman Driver

THE NEW WOMAN DRIVER

All a Woman Needs to Know
About Cars to Buy One,
Drive It, Have It Maintained

DON SHARP

Houghton Mifflin Company   Boston   1984

A Robert Wool Book

Copyright © 1984 by Don Sharp and Premier Cru Books, Inc.
Line drawings by Sarah J. Drews and Stephen Wilcox

Library of Congress Cataloging in Publication Data

Sharp, Don, date
    The new woman driver.

    "A Robert Wool book"—T.p. verso.
    Includes index.
    1. Automobiles—Purchasing. 2. Automobiles—Main-
tenance and repair. I. Title.
TL162.S5 1984   629.2′222   83-12812
ISBN 0-395-33971-5
ISBN 0-395-33972-3 (pbk.)

Printed in the United States of America

S 10 9 8 7 6 5 4 3 2 1

ACKNOWLEDGMENTS

John Donne wrote well that "No man is an island, entire of itself." We are never alone, and we owe our prodigies to others as much as to our own genius.

I did not write this book by myself. I owe many for the substance hereof—a lanky truck driver met in Boise City, Oklahoma, over twenty years ago who gave me a roadside lecture on the function of a condenser and, thus, enabled me to reactivate a dead '46 Ford; a grizzled veteran of Skid Row met on the Monahan wheat ranch near Derby, Colorado, who showed me (between swigs of Virginia Dare wine) how to set Chevrolet-six valve clearances by touch and feel; an eldern mechanic, minus the middle fingers of his right hand, who showed me the value of patience when dealing with precise mechanisms—these and many others helped with this work. Though I do not remember their names, they are here, nonetheless.

To extract substance from my jumbled experience also required help. Hence, thanks to Lewis H. Lapham, who, while editor of *Harper's*, brought me into contact with Robert Wool; to Robert Wool, who knew what I had not learned in twenty-five years of automotive diversions—that this book needed to be written—and who supplied the organization my experience needed; and to Nan Talese, of Houghton Mifflin, who agreed to both the need and the organization.

Organizing from random experience, though, requires monitoring—a nudge this way, a pull that way—to keep the scribbler to the point; thanks here to Debbie McGill, associate editor at *The Atlantic* magazine, whose remarks on my general progress told me when I was doing right; also, to Natalie Wilens, marketing consultant, whose remarks on particulars told me when I was doing wrong.

Substance, though, must ultimately have a form, so thanks also to Helen Weeks Baker, of Conway, Massachusetts, who prepared the first draft of the manuscript, and to my neighbor, Terry Cassidy, who put the final manuscript in order (and provided many a lunch and dinner to the improvident author in the process).

For what is faulty in this work, I owe to my own limitations; for what is good, I owe to these others.

Don Sharp
Emmet Road
Ashfield, Massachusetts

CONTENTS

Part II MAINTENANCE AND REPAIR

Part III DRIVING

ILLUSTRATIONS

PHOTOGRAPHS

following page 240

BMW—1982 320i
Ford—1981 Fairmont
Saab—1979 model 99
Mercedes—1954 190 SL
Mercedes—1983 380 SL roadster
American Motors—1983 Jeep Cherokee
Peugeot—1983 505 sedan
Mercedes—1983 300 TD wagon
Mercedes—1968 250 S sedan
International Harvester—1971 1010 series Travelall
Chevrolet—1962 Chevy II sedan

INTRODUCTION:
WHY FOR WOMEN?

Since the early 1900s, the automobile industry, in its own post-Victorian way, had encouraged women to drive, despite recalcitrant engines that had to be cranked by hand and tires that were more likely to go flat than not. "Any woman can drive a 'Winton' the first time she tries," declared the Winton Motor Carriage advertisement in 1905, and "She can start it speeding up to 60 miles an hour with the same foot she might run a sewing machine with." The Northern Runabout ads, also of 1905, show a woman and two children gathering flowers while the automobile waits in the background—and not a man in sight, thus to suggest the reliability of the machine and the propriety of a woman's using it for her own purposes. The Dunlop-Hartford tire ads of the same era show four women in an open touring car (a Peerless, from the look of it), to demonstrate that women might well go motoring without taking a man along to fix flats. When the electric self-starter appeared in 1912, it was promptly called the "Lady's aid," and advertisements for the Lambert automobile predicted that, "with the advent of the Self Starter, thousands of women will take up the driving of motor cars." In its first thirty years, the automobile industry openly encouraged women to buy and drive cars.

According to some social psychologists, women had to stay home after WWII to repair the psychosocial damage of their having taken men's places in the production line while the men were off to war. It was a period of the cult of motherhood and dependence. Whatever the reason, they certainly did get shut away and did not get out again until around 1960. I mark women's escape from domestic imprisonment by the earliest miniskirts and by the number of Volkswagen Beetles I saw them driving—alone. They escaped, but with a definitely warped perspective about how they thought they were *supposed* to feel about cars.

While confined to hearth and home, women heard fathers and uncles and snot-nosed little brothers crack jokes about women drivers. They also saw cartoons such as the one in *The Saturday Evening Post* that showed two women pouring gasoline into the radiator of a stalled car as one says to the other, "Those men don't think we know anything about cars," the cartoon being by a man who apparently didn't realize the women couldn't pour gasoline into the radiator because it would already be full of coolant.

As the automobile became a standard family possession, her brothers could prove their coming of age by acquiring a car and strewing its greasy innards about the yard. Women were not allowed to participate, except as handers of tools and bringers of iced tea, because for a woman to have smeared her virginal hands with grease would have been unladylike.

Of course, she would have a driver's license of her own, but her uses for the family car remained subordinate to those of her brothers. They *had* to have the car because they had a date. The idea that she and her friends might do something together— why, that was just a waste of the car on a perfectly good Friday night.

What I call the "daughters of the sixties" have come of age. No longer do they drive the family car to do errands for their fathers, brothers, and spouses—to say nothing of chauffeuring children hour upon hour—they are now buying the cars.

These are the new women drivers; they buy cars alone, they also drive alone and are alone when they confront the mechanic.

The vast majority of men are equally alone in these circumstances, but the big-boys-don't-cry syndrome prevents them from freely admitting it. When the car sputters to a halt beside the road, they raise the hood with great authority but get surly and defensive when their wives ask what's wrong. By contrast, since women aren't "supposed" to know anything about cars in the first place, they often are more expeditious about seeking a solution when the car breaks down.

Many women have sought to resolve this problem by taking community college and night school classes in auto mechanics. I have reservations about such classes, for I know that one evening a week for a dozen weeks does not get you far into the complexities of a car. However, I endorse such classes despite my reservations, and for several reasons.

First, because to enroll in an auto mechanics class is to make a positive assertion concerning your own intelligence about cars. To enroll is to declare, "I *can* understand a car—even if its complexities can not be fully understood in one course." Also, to enroll is a way of confronting and resolving fear of cars. "I may not learn all your secrets," the student says to her car, "but I'm damned if I'm going to be afraid of you." In sum, enrolling in an auto mechanics course is but one element in the way modern women assert their self-confidence and self-determination.

This book, from a one-time college teacher who simply can't quit lecturing, is my contribution to the matter. Like the night classes, this book won't make you an expert on all elements of a car, but it will pull away some of the mysterious wrappings of jargon and technicality and show you the simplicity of what lies underneath.

Although I cannot make you an expert—not in one book— I can promise, in the context of cars, that a modest understanding will go a long way in the dealer's showroom, in the mechanic's garage, and on the road.

This is a much grander promise than it might seem, as you will see. You will have to help, for much of what follows will be new and the going will not always be easy. However, it will be rewarding (and if it's entertaining, so much the better).

PART I

Buying

AUTOMOTIVE DESIDERATA: WHAT DO YOU WANT?

The public needs to be educated as to the different types of motor carriages, but a fair understanding can only be attained by the interested person looking carefully into the matter and making a personal trial of the different types. If a person desire to purchase a motor vehicle, he should consider carefully just what conditions are to be met and just what work the machine has to do. It is very probable that any person purchasing an automobile from a reliable concern will have success, provided he operate the machine carefully and give it proper attention.

—J. A. Kingman, "Automobile-Making in America," *American Monthly Review of Reviews*, September 1901

Most of us remember a time when we were young when we stood in front of the candy counter at the corner store, a lone five-cent piece in a sweaty palm, and tried to make up our minds which of all those wonderful goodies to buy. Choosing a car is simply an adult version of the same experience. If you list all the different brand names—makes, as people say—such as Ford, Pontiac, Datsun, and so forth, and then all the different models of a particular make, the result is a total of about 150 models from over a dozen different makes. If you add specialty vehicles, such as pickup trucks, vans, and four-wheel-drive vehicles, which include Jeeps, the grand total equals about 175 different models. How shall you discriminate among all the possibilities?

Car salesmen will be delighted to help you discriminate. They will assure you that the make of car they sell is absolutely the best in the world. A Chevrolet Celebrity and a Pontiac 6000 are identical cars under the nameplate, but the Pontiac dealer will give you all sorts of reasons why you should buy the Pontiac rather than the Chevrolet. The question gets messier when the choices are more distinct: the Ford Escort salesman will tell you that Chevrolet Chevettes are made by the workers who were fired from Ford, the Chevette salesman will tell you that Dodge Colts are made of the steel that General Motors rejected, and the Colt salesman will say Datsuns are made on the graveyard shift when the supervisors are half asleep. These assurances leave you satisfied that all salesmen are liars, but that hardly helps you choose a car.

Choosing a car entangles you in a host of variables that ultimately reduce to money. The BMW 318i is a nice, smaller car, but so is a Ford Futura at two-thirds the price. Which should you buy, and why?

That "why" is the determining factor. What do you want *to do with* the car? What do you want *from* the car? Do you want the car to enhance the convenience of your errands and trips, or do you want it to improve your (putative) social status? These are honest questions and they deserve honest answers. Suppose you do want a status symbol but can't afford one, so you buy a Datsun 210 coupe—and ever after, you despise the Datsun and criticize it unfairly.

Or, you want a status symbol and *can* afford it, so you buy a Cadillac De Ville and discover it's too big to park without knocking the fenders. Well, don't blame the car—you picked it, and maneuverability was not among the things you bought it for. You should have bought a BMW or Mercedes-Benz that will turn in a much smaller circle.

Back to the basic issue: Why do you want the car in the first place? What do you expect of it?

Let's say you're an urban apartment dweller who has never owned a car before. You've finished a college degree, got a good job, and now you are ready to buy a car. You make a list of what you want from the car:

- go grocery shopping
- commute to work
- good mileage
- reliability

The list clearly indicates a small car, so you go forth to buy. You find, for example, Dodge Colt, Plymouth Horizon, Ford Escort, Mercury Lynx, Chevrolet Chevette, Pontiac 1000—plus

Saab, Datsun, Toyota, and, just recently, Isuzu and Mitsubishi. Now, what do you do? How do you choose?

Following the oft-quoted Charlie Wilson statement that "What's good for General Motors is good for the U.S.A.," you buy the Chevette. You enjoy it immensely. It is nimble in traffic, fits into tight parking spaces, and holds one passenger and two bags of groceries nicely. As the experience of owning a car becomes more familiar, you begin to drive more. You grow bold and begin to make long trips.

As soon as you make a long trip, you discover that the Chevette was not intended for people over five feet six inches tall. Driving around town, you didn't notice the lack of room for your legs, but on a long trip, you get so cramped you try to figure out how to drive from the back seat. When summer comes, you discover that you can't get enough air through the vents and you suffocate, but if you roll the windows down the noise and buffeting drive you insane.

Now, once again, don't blame the car. It didn't change — you did. Of course, you didn't know you were going to change. However, in making your list, you have to anticipate changes. For example, my friend Elaine, a political scientist at the University of Kansas, was happy with her Chevette — until she bought a trailerable sailboat. Then she needed more space to carry the sailing gear, so she traded in for a Datsun 210 station wagon — and promptly discovered camping.

Your list, therefore, must include your anticipations.

Besides use and anticipated use, the car should suit your driving style. If you zealously observe speed limits, the cheapest car on the market will serve nicely (and to observe legal speeds will conceal its inherent deficiencies). You do not need Mercedes-Benz or Jaguar engineering in your suspension system if you drive at posted limits, although you will certainly notice an incredible sense of security from the stability of the suspension and the precision of the steering of the Jaguar and Mercedes. Also, the rear suspension and weight distribution will help you avoid getting stuck in snow in the winter. However, how often do you come near to getting stuck, anyway? If the probabilities are remote, then you can't exploit that virtue.

Even if you drive on interstate highways at the speeds the interstate highways were designed for, you will not find a domestic car incapable. In fact, as you drive along, at, say, 70 mph, you may well wonder why people spend the money for a BMW 528e when an ordinary Dodge Aries seems tractable at the same speed. A few panic stops or a few lane changes at 85 mph will show you the relevant differences, but how often do those things come up in your driving?

If you drive aggressively, as people do in Boston and New York (Los Angeles traffic is a convent picnic compared to the vicious barbarism of Boston), you can get a lot of use out of the suspension, steering, and brakes of an ultra-quality European car. However, a prudent financial adviser might question the wisdom of putting a $25,000+ car at hazard in such traffic.

Similarly, if you drive the narrow, twisty secondary roads such as you find in virtually all rural areas east of the Mississippi, you will find that an expensive European suspension system gets you around the curves with alacrity and security. Of course, if you drive such roads in sedate reserve, you have no need of such a suspension system.

Suppose you spend the $40,000 for a Porsche 928 and go hustling through curves with great élan and satisfaction—and then, here comes some daredevil teen-age kid in a rusty '72 Toyota Corona, with its engine turbocharged up to 150 hp and a high-class "handling package" in the suspension, and he passes you. Now, you may wonder, what did you spend all that money for?

Porsche fanatics will wax apoplectic at this suggestion that a modified Toyota could outperform their chosen marque. Their paroxysms obscure a basic truth; viz., that to possess the price of the car does not automatically confer the driving skill needed to get the most out of the car. If you can't get the performance out of the car, then you certainly needn't buy the built-in performances.

Several years ago, before that fateful morning in December 1973, when then-President Richard M. Nixon awoke in a grumpy humor and, disdaining to give his dog a sound kick, instead persuaded the Congress to impose the 55-mph speed limit, several Western states had speed limits of 75 mph and Nevada state police typically looked the other way when the Hollywood set came through in their Maseratis and Ferraris at 100+ mph. People west of the Mississippi, therefore, could find good reasons for paying the price for Jaguar, Lamborghini, *et al.* suspension systems. No more. Today, only naughty, naughty people (and those who can afford the fines or the lawyers to handle the tickets) drive over 55 mph—so who needs or can use a high-class suspension?

You see where this leads: on a rational basis alone, we can find little reason for buying a car with ultrasophisticated engineering. Of course, our approach to the matter has been largely practical and that may be its flaw, for the choice of a car involves other elements, both emotional and quasi-spiritual.

Back in the 1950s, the driver of a Volkswagen Beetle always honked when encountering another Beetle, a habit practiced among people who drove International Travelalls in the 1960s and which persists today among Saab owners who flash their headlights. These signals are gestures of recognition among the members of an elect society; those who exchange such signals feel privy to special secrets that are denied to the common multitude.

Now, what on earth could they be so smug about? Well, use the Saab 99 owner as an example: When faced with a flat tire, the owner finds the spare tire readily accessible and so located that it can never be buried under luggage. Under the hood, the owner sees a lot of machinery packed into a tight space, but yet with everything accessible for service. The owner marvels at the road manners of the car, especially on rough roads, but finds utter simplicity in the suspension. Before long, the driver thinks, "Whoever designed this car was not only intelligent, but also cared about whoever would drive it."

Now, how many cars can provoke a statement like that? (Well, actually, quite a few, which is one reason foreign cars reached 30 percent of new car sales in 1982.)

The experience of owning a car comes to involve more than the mere satisfaction of getting around. Interest quickens. People who never read a car magazine in their lives buy a car, then begin buying car magazines. More serious devotees join marque clubs and spend $50 or so for "coffee-table" books full of glossy pictures of their chosen car. Marque club members enjoy a sense of having joined a special society blessed with special sensitivities and insights and that consciousness is not to be disparaged; it is as real as religion and the members usually pay more than a tithe for the car that goes with membership.

If you have some spiritual inclination to join a marque club—

an automotive sect devoted to a particular car—you should indulge yourself. You will enjoy association with people who share a common intimacy, and if the marque happens to be one that costs far more than you can rationally justify, the members of the marque club will reassure you that you spent your money well (if not wisely).

REPUTATIONS AND DIFFERENCES

My immediately older brother, William, bought a 1936 Chevrolet as his first car. Sibling individuality being what it is, he thus dictated that my first car had to be other than a Chevrolet; so, my first car was a 1946 Ford (that had a broken rear axle when I bought it—a real mess to change). My high school associates owned other cars—Hudsons, Nashes, Studebakers, etc.—and we had long, vehement, and fruitless arguments about which was the "best" car.

In those days, such arguments had some merit. Fords had good acceleration, gas mileage, and top speed, while Chevrolets had a "softer ride" and didn't develop as many rattles. Plymouths were notably civilized—quiet and smooth, and the doors would shut without being slammed. A Hudson was fast and stable at high speed, a 1949 Oldsmobile 88 coupe would accelerate faster than any other car, and you could stuff five hulking teen-age boys into the trunk of a Buick and sneak them into a drive-in movie. The back of a Chrysler front seat was high enough that couples on a double-date could enjoy (and exploit) a high degree

of privacy, and for those more socially advanced the Nash Ambassador had seats that folded down into a decent bed.
Alas, those days are gone. To apply George C. Wallace's words to current cars, I hardly see "a dime's worth of difference."

The distinctions began disappearing in the late 1950s, largely because the cheaper cars got better. For example, General Motors produces five cars—Chevrolet, Pontiac, Oldsmobile, Buick, and Cadillac—and these five marques cover a price range from highest to lowest. At a time when cigarettes cost a dime a pack, a gallon of gasoline cost 15 cents, and a working man earned less than $100 per month, the 1941 Chevrolet convertible cost around $750 while a Buick convertible cost around $1600 (measured against cigarettes, gasoline, and wages, cars don't cost any more today). In those days and up toward 1970, each of the GM divisions designed and built its own engines and the quality of the engines was reflected in the cost of the car, as was the quality of other components.

In time, the qualitative differences largely disappeared due to improved manufacturing methods. Chevrolet engines became as good as Cadillac engines, so GM decided to eliminate the duplication of effort in the five divisions and reduce the total number of engines offered in the GM family. Thus, Cadillac, Oldsmobile, Pontiac, and Chevrolet all use the same 350-cubic inch (5.7-liter) V-8 diesel, and both Chevrolet and Pontiac use the same 305-cubic inch (5.0-liter) V-8 gasoline engine. This sort of sharing is nothing new. Ford and Chrysler have long done the same thing and for the same reason: to reduce costs. Similar sharing also exists with differentials and transmissions, so much so that differences in marques from the same manufacturer almost no longer exist. To be a trifle snide about it, the car bearing the Cadillac name is, nowadays, just the most expensive Chevrolet you can buy: the distinct Cadillac of old is gone.

Thirty years ago, a car with 50,000 miles was assumed to be ready for an overhaul and a car still running after 75,000 miles was a rarity. In those days, a Buick would last twice as long as a Chevrolet, so the price difference meant something. Now, both cars have equal longevity and the price differences are based almost entirely on gadgets and upholstery.

As GM cars came to be clones of each other, so did they come to resemble the Ford and Chrysler products, the era of greatest similarity being roughly 1968–1972. The bodies of the full-size cars of that era resemble each other and you can find little that is different about the way they drive. (The Ford Falcon, Plymouth Valiant/Dodge Dart, and Chevrolet Vega were distinct, of course, but they were not definitive.) And, as the cars came to resemble each other in shape and behavior, so did they achieve such high degrees of reliability that arguments about the "best" ceased to mean anything.

High school students still argue, though, and old loyalists will say, "I bought a new Buick in '55, bought another in '67—a six, that one was—and a new one last year, and I'll always buy Buick." No need to tell such people that their last two Buicks were really Chevrolets, although the Chevrolet die-hards might be flattered.

In sum, I don't believe anybody can point to genuine qualitative differences in the domestic cars of today. The Chevrolet Vega of several years ago and the Cadillac V-8-6-4 of 1981 (see page 330) were aberrations. In the 1976–79 era, Chrysler did have more than its share of trouble with the slant-six Dodges and Plymouths, but these difficulties arose from the pollution-control system and have since been ironed out by the use of electronic devices.

The issue we're grappling with here is whether qualitative differences exist among domestic cars. I can't find any. True, a Chevette is not the same as a Cadillac, but the difference is *quantitative*, not *qualitative*. The Cadillac is not better; it is simply bigger and has more gadgets (most of which have nothing to do with getting you down the road).

A lot of ink has been spread around in the search for qualitative differences; for example, the *Consumer Guide* and *Consumer Reports* people try to find them in repair records. Presumably, the readers of *Consumer Reports* report their experience with their cars, and the *CR* staff organizes these reports into tables that, presumably, indicate something about the frequency of repairs made to certain cars.

Frankly, until I see the data itself, I don't believe a word of the *CR* stuff on repair records. For assorted reasons, particularly bias and error in the data, I don't think the *CR* reports on repairs can reliably predict anything. So *CR* reports that the 1978 Ford Fairmont automatic transmission has a "worse than average" repair record? Yet, my neighbor Raymond Cassidy drove his '78

Fairmont with automatic transmission over 120,000 miles with no transmission trouble at all. *CR* gives this same car an "average" rating for brakes, but Raymond Cassidy got 90,000 miles out of his original brake linings. So what does this tell us? What is the rule, and what is the exception?

If you try to cut out many, many paper dolls to the same pattern, you will inevitably spoil some of them. This spoilage is your "failure rate" and it is inherent in every assembly-line production system. Detroit has always accepted a fairly high failure rate—2 to 3 percent—as the price of mass production and traditionally corrected failures at the dealer level. Thus, the ultimate quality of the product came to depend on the conscientiousness (and honesty) of the dealers.

By contrast, the Japanese and Europeans have long held to much lower failure rates—about one half of one percent. Their lower failure rate did not arise from ethical rectitude; rather, it arose from differences in the total production system. Also, neither the Japanese nor the Europeans ever produced at, say, the level of General Motors. Where Toyota produces a total of 1,000,000 vehicles, General Motors produces 5,000,000, and these different levels of production affect failure rates.

Detroit's worst rates of failure seem to have occurred during those careless years from 1968 to about 1973, when Detroit was mainly devoted to selling as much body sheet metal as possible (at a profit on every pound). The failures of that era were compounded by the hassles of developing pollution-control systems, and those hassles were further compounded by the fact that mechanics were extremely slow to face up to pollution control. Mechanics spent a lot of time by-passing or disabling pollution-control systems, but virtually no time learning how to fix them. These several circumstances produced a lot of grief in the 1970s, but, in my observation, the problems have settled down here lately. Detroit has reduced its failure rate, and more fail-safe elements, especially electronic devices, have improved the performance of pollution-control systems. Look as hard as I can, I can't see qualitative differences in domestics; you get the same quality from all manufacturers.

Do not misread here: the differences at issue are differences that would lead you to choose one car over another, and the emphasis is on the mechanical elements. That is, I am not addressing matters of style here—just mechanical quality.

You may feel a Ford is prettier than a Plymouth or may feel a Chrysler is nicer to drive than a Buick, but these are not qualitative differences so much as matters of personal taste. The bottom line is that if you like Ford appearances or Chrysler handling, you don't really have to worry about the quality of the machinery underneath.

Qualitative differences can be found more easily when comparing foreign and domestic cars. Domestic cars seek to insulate you from the road, to give you the illusion that you are not driving at all, a design philosophy that goes back to the 1930s. By contrast, foreign cars keep you in much more intimate contact with what you are doing, as do the smaller domestics (which largely derive from foreign models). To sample the differences, drive a 1983 Chevrolet Malibu and a 1983 BMW 528e, then compare the original price tags of $8200 and $23,000, respectively, and see how you feel about the differences. Next, drive a Plymouth Horizon ($5800) and a Volkswagen Rabbit ($6000); the differences will not be so striking, and neither will the price difference.

To summarize: no domestic car can claim qualitative superiority over another, for mechanical quality is effectively uniform; and foreign cars differ in handling qualities and in mechanical quality, but that quality has a price tag (quality always does).

DOWN TO CASES

So far, the discussion seems to be leading to a place where few differences exist and where those that do exist hardly matter. While Ecclesiastes the Preacher, with his pronouncements on "vanity and vexation of spirit," might concur, this nihilistic conclusion is not what we're looking for; we've still got to find some reason for choosing one car over another.

Existentialism, the philosophy that young rebels and old cynics wear like a hairshirt, holds that every act includes a moral element, that every act constitutes a participation in a particular sense of values. Hence, a crucial step in choosing a car is to review your sense of values.

Some people choose a certain car because they believe it will ensure the realization of their dreams. Such expressions of a simple faith, read in the scriptures of advertising, obviously motivate a lot of car sales. Our emphasis here, though, is on use, which is not a simple matter of whether the car will get you down the road; rather, "use" involves whether *you and the car* will get down the road together and how happily you will do so.

Let us reflect on some hypothetical cases:

- Mail carrier with a route in northern Idaho; on the road half the day, six days per week.
- Executive who lives in Manhattan; goes to work by subway, goes to Florida by car in December, goes to Vermont to ski every two weeks during January and February, and in August drives to Peoria to visit her grandmother.
- Civil engineer who lives in Skokie and commutes to work in Chicago by car; uses the car for grocery shopping but makes long trips by air.
- Person who car-pools with three others and makes one long trip per year by car.
- Person who car-pools with three others and makes no trips.
- Person who car-pools with one other and makes many long trips.
- Widow with three children who marries a widower with four children.

These cases point to certain considerations of size, handling, roadworthiness, economy, comfort, and cost. The mail carrier needs an all-weather vehicle, such as a four-wheel drive (4WD; see page 355) AMC Eagle, Jeep Wagoneer, Subaru, or the latest, the Toyota Tercel 4WD. (Dana Kirkpatrick, who delivers the mail where I live, recently traded in her 4WD pickup for a 4WD Subaru.) The executive needs a car that will make long trips and which minimizes her repair risks, for example, perhaps a Ford

Fairmont or Dodge Aries such as most service station mechanics can handle. The engineer needs maximum convenience in traffic and parking, plus maximum economy; hence, a Honda Civic, Datsun 210, Chevrolet Chevette, or one of the other domestic cars of similar type such as the Omni/Horizon or Escort/Lynx. Car-pooler Four needs less economy; however, if the car-pool trip is not long, even comfort for passengers is not a serious concern, so the one long trip per year may dictate the type of car, whether a handy, bouncy little Volkswagen Rabbit or a behemoth such as a Lincoln Continental. Car-pooler Five, having no trips to consider, might seek to serve passenger comfort, which automatically means a full-size, four-door sedan. Car-pooler Six will be influenced by the dominant personal interest, the long trips, and will prefer a car with optimum long-trip ability, say a Mercedes-Benz or BMW at one end of the scale or a Peugeot at a lesser extreme. The widow obviously needs a station wagon with an extra seat or, perhaps, a van.

The car must suit its purposes, but it must also fit its people.

My 1972 Toyota Corona station wagon had ample leg room for a six-footer, but I could not wear a furry winter cap when driving it. My head hits the headliner of the current model Datsun 210, even with the seat well back. On the International Travelalls (see page 348), I could not reach across to lower the window on the passenger side. I can do so in the Chevrolet Suburban, but only a gorilla could reach the Suburban's windshield-wiper switch; I must lean forward, half-hunched, to turn the wipers off and on in moderate rain and in that position I can't see the high-beam indicator because it is masked by the steering wheel. And, consistent with Chevrolet practice in pickups for the past forty years, the headlight dimmer switch is in an awkward location under the clutch pedal. The Saab 99 has a lump for the left front wheel right where my left foot wants to be, though it is not as bad in this respect as the Chevrolet Citation. The seat in a Ford Fairmont is just wrong (for me); it encourages me to slump. A Toyota Celica is a pure joy of its type, but it would never do if my two dogs were St. Bernards. A Chevrolet Vega is like crawling into a padded bathtub—one of the most impossibly awkward cars to enter and escape from. By contrast, the Dodge Dart/Plymouth Valiant of recent years is one of the most convenient; however, in manual-shift form, the Dart/Valiant has an awkward off-on, no-middle-ground clutch and a clumsy, notchy shifting system.

I find a BMW 320i comfortable but am conscious of being hemmed in by the central console, a feeling I also get from the current Mercedes-Benz SL models. A CJ-model Jeep has an honest, elementary quality, but it does not provide leg room for a tall person and needs sound insulation for anyone who is not deaf. In the 1955 Sunbeam-Talbot, I had to turn my foot lengthwise to get it between the seat and the door jamb (á la Vega). The 1947 Lincoln club coupe had virtually no vision out the rear window, a design deficiency still in vogue nowadays. Partly because the rear overhang was short, the 1936 Ford four-door had excellent visibility (though its mechanical brakes were erratic). The 1955 Buick Riviera hardtop I drove in Honolulu was a gas hog, but since I only paid $50 for it (in 1967), and sold it for $45 when I left, I couldn't complain. The 1959 Triumph Herald was immensely handy, but would not allow legs to be stretched; i.e., it was the worst possible car for a long trip.

The intention here is not to present a malcontent's catalog of automotive deficiencies, but to point out factors that affect satisfaction with a car. No car is perfect, so what can/will you put up with? Also, the point here is to call attention to details that get overlooked in the enthusiasm of a car purchase. The front seat feels great in a show room, but what will it feel like in a traffic jam on a hot day or on a long trip? The rear seat feels fine on one bounce, but what will it be like after half an hour? And how much do such things matter?

Generally, cars have been designed to fit the "average" man, who is about 5′ 10″ tall. This means that they don't fit the "average" woman, who is more like 5′3″ tall. In the old days, when domestic cars were all big, the "average" woman often had to put a pillow behind herself to be able to drive a domestic sedan, and a truly petite woman had to put one pillow behind her back and sit on another. Although I have made no scholarly study of the matter, my impression is that the hackneyed clichés about women drivers did not arise during the early days of motoring, the days when the Model T Ford gave you the visibility of a greenhouse and the maneuverability of a child's red wagon. As far as I can tell, these false truisms about women arose in the late 1930s and after, when women were forced to drive cars with extravagantly long hoods and idiotically small rear windows. To a degree, the advent of small cars did as much for women's liberation as anything else.

My private theory on women's liberation is that it started with the Volkswagen Beetle, the first car since coupes of the 1930s that the average woman could see out of. Also, young, single women could afford them, and the Beetle was so notoriously reliable that they felt secure in traveling alone. Although Detroit was extremely slow to catch on, the foreign car market came partly from women who simply wanted to drive without having to sit on a pillow and stretch to tiptoe to reach the gas pedal.

For reasons peculiar to the American auto market and to the American national psychology, domestic car manufacturers have long emphasized something they call "styling." Styling eventually overwhelmed ergonomics. Form did not follow function; indeed, form virtually ceased to bear any relationship to function. In the late 1950s, this aberrant design philosophy produced huge tailfins but, at the same time, the manufacturers were competing to see which could have the largest rear window, so visibility did not suffer. In the late 1960s and early '70s, this same philosophy produced excessively long overhangs—the body extended far, far beyond the front and rear wheels. Along with the overhangs came a hump just over the rear wheel and a high trunk line and, thus, an era of cars with virtually no rearward visibility, the Plymouth Duster and the Ford Maverick being particularly bad in this respect.

Public acceptance of such cars raises the question of whether people had the slightest interest in what was behind them or the slightest care about whether they bashed something when backing up. Although body styles have improved here of late, this design fault has by no means disappeared. The question to you as the buyer is: Do you care?

Once style, rather than use, begins to dictate design, the perversions get worse and worse. Open the door of a full-size (or even a mid-size) domestic car and measure how thick the door is. Then, measure a foreign car of comparable size. Generally, a domestic door is twice as thick and that extra thickness on each side is just so much more total width that you have to ease into parking spaces and past other cars on the road. Similarly, note the rear overhang, then open the trunk and see how much benefit you get from that overhang. Generally, the more exaggerated the overhang, the less the usable trunk space.

Several years ago, one of the so-called "consumer" magazines would "test" car trunks by filling them with Ping-Pong balls and then measuring the cubic footage the Ping-Pong balls would fill up. This method produced some very complimentary numbers for car trunks that would not actually accept a large suitcase. If the trunk is only a place to leave the spare tire until it is needed, of course, useful trunk space may not matter. What use do you anticipate for the trunk?

As another aspect of style, study cars from behind and note the distance from the center of the driver's head to the outer extremity of the body of the car. An examination of this sort reveals that big cars are rarely big on the inside and that style often interferes with the driver's actual ability to control the car. Of course, if the driver doesn't care, such styling doesn't hurt.

As noted at the beginning, you have your own sense of values. However, perhaps you had not thought about how a given car inculcates a sense of values. In fact, the car you choose does reflect your system of belief about the purposes a car serves. The car you will like, the car that will please you day after day, is one that is compatible with your own sense of values.

DEPRECIATION THOUGHTS

We cannot assert unarguably that a particular car is the best nor even assert that a particular one is absolutely the best for your purposes. We can, generally, say that foreign cars and the smaller domestics are more ergonomic, that function dictates their design.

Having thus betrayed a bias in favor of foreigners and compact domestics, we may as well pursue the issue into the arithmetic of *depreciation*, i.e., the loss of value a car suffers as it gets older.

Back to Elaine, the political scientist: in early 1977, she was quoted $3300 on a plain Chevette. She haggled around until she got the car for an even $3000, the Toyota and Datsun dealers being only a few blocks away from the Chevrolet dealer. In 1980, she went car shopping again and made a deal that gave her a $2600 trade-in on her Chevette. (At the time, used Chevettes equal to hers sold in Boston for $2900.)

So, in over three years, depreciation cost Elaine $400. If you figure on interest costs, the figure is slightly higher, but let's confine ourselves to the nominal $400. By simple arithmetic, Elaine got back 86 percent of what she spent on the car when she traded it in.

While Chevettes like Elaine's were selling for $2900 in Boston, larger three-year-old domestics that had cost $8000 when new were selling for around $3500. The owners had only 43 percent of their value left after three years. Two years later, when the 1977 models were five years old, the Chevette was still worth 50 percent or more of its original cost, while the bigger cars were worth only 35 percent.

If you study used car prices as a measure of depreciation, you find:

- The more expensive foreign cars, particularly Mercedes-Benz, but BMW often enough, are worth up to 80 percent of their original cost when five years old;
- foreign and domestic compacts are worth about 50 percent, as are the luxury domestics such as Cadillac and Lincoln Continental;
- and, ordinary full-size domestics are worth about 35 percent.

Depreciation patterns vary in response to the market. In early 1974, following the "fuel crisis" of 1973, a two-year-old Mercedes-Benz 240D diesel would sell in Chicago for *more* than the retail price of a new one (and the "wait list" for a new one was eight months long); by late 1974, the price had fallen to below that of the new one. Similar things happened with the Honda Civic and Volkswagen Rabbit in 1979–80. Thus, we cannot accurately predict rates of depreciation, but let us use the above rates, which have fair long-run validity, to play with some numbers.

We start with a BMW 320i two-door at $13,500 and a Buick Electra Park Avenue at the same price. Five years later, the BMW is worth up to $10,800 and the Buick is worth $6,750 to $4,725, depending on how we weight the depreciation dice. No matter how we load the dice, the difference is striking.

The BMW-Buick comparison doesn't really work, because the person who would buy the BMW would never look at the Buick (it's close to 50 inches longer), and vice versa. However, depreciation is clearly not to be overlooked when costing out a car deal. A low rate of depreciation may mean that you can afford to spend more than you thought. Certainly, the consequences of depreciation can make a car "best" for you when other factors won't settle the question.

When considering a deal, study the classified ads and note the high and low prices offered for similar cars that are three to five years old (we say "similar" to allow for model changes). Also, you can get the quasi-official word on depreciation from *Edmund's* or the "book" (which will be addressed in the chapter on used cars).

SAFETY

I**n** regard to the inherent safety of a car, people fall into two extreme camps: those who pay no attention at all to the question and those who are almost obsessed with it.

The industry itself has an inconsistent record. As early as 1941, the old Nash cars had crashworthy *unit-body* construction, though the fact was not emphasized in advertising until Nash and Hudson merged to form American Motors in 1954. However, American Motors concluded that references to safety were negative advertising, that prospective buyers didn't want to be reminded of the possibility of a wreck at all. Nonetheless, the industry did move toward (optional) padded dashboards and sun visors as safety items, Ford developed its "deep dish" steering wheel that offered protection from impalement, and the foreigners led the way with the collapsible steering column for similar protection.

While the industry did acknowledge the matter of safety long before it became a national issue, that acknowledgment came late and amounted to little. The truck driver in John Steinbeck's *The Grapes of Wrath*, published in 1939, describes a car wreck that left the driver impaled on the steering column, "a-wigglin' like a frog on a hook," and this was the normal consequence of a head-on collision in those days. People in big, 4000+-pound cars tended to survive in somewhat better shape than people in lighter cars, but given the marginal brakes and squishy suspension on the big cars, the passengers certainly needed all the help they could get. That is, the tarbrush of condemnation has no reason to spare any particular car of the pre-safety era.

The safety era began before 1960 (well before 1965, when Ralph Nader's *Unsafe at Any Speed* appeared), and for no apparent reason. Personally, I attribute it to the "cold war" and the high consciousness that people—especially younger people—had of tactical aircraft (fighter planes) and space vehicles. Suddenly, around 1960, younger people wanted seat belts and padded interiors to identify themselves with daring pilots and space pioneers. I saw this attitude among undergraduate students of 1960 but not, for example, among their parents. In any event, seat belts were virtually standard equipment by 1962, and American Motors had already gone to dual-circuit brake systems to preclude total loss of braking in the event of a broken hydraulic line. The concern for safety gained impetus, particularly under the "social consciousness" administration of President Lyndon B. Johnson, and it continued even under the generally (and properly) maligned Richard M. Nixon. By 1968, federal standards put seat belts in all cars, along with increased interior padding, side-impact protection, and more.

Alas, none of this seemed to make much difference to the automobile accident fatality rate. The fatality rate comes, first, from multiplying the number of cars in use by the average number of miles driven per year, thus to get a "vehicle miles" figure, then dividing vehicle miles by fatalities to get a rate of fatalities. Back in the 1920s, for example, the rate was about 19 per 100,000,000 vehicle miles. The rate fell consistently up to late 1977, then began to increase slightly. The rate for 1980 was 3.38 fatalities per 100,000,000 vehicle miles.

The crucial point here is that the fatality rate exhibited no significant decline following the imposition of safety standards for 1968 and later cars. The rate of fatalities continued to decline as it had been doing for years. The rate did, indeed, fall markedly for a couple of years after the 1973 "fuel crisis." Government officials claim the 55-mph speed limit caused the decline, but independent authorities ascribe the decline to reduced driving. After 1977, the fatality rate began to rise at the rate of about one percent per year, an increase that the 55-mph advocates either could not explain at all or explained by the dubious contention that everybody was ignoring the 55-mph speed limit. The rise continued through 1981, but in 1983, when the preliminary statistics for 1982 were reported, fatalities showed a 12 percent decrease (despite all those people exceeding 55 mph?). In reporting the decrease, the Department of Transportation pointed to its emphasis on safe driving, on more effective efforts to remove drunk drivers from the roads, and to reduced driving due to the economic recession. No doubt each of these factors had some influence, but taken together, what they really say is that nobody really knows what's causing the fluctuations in the fatality rate.

Whatever safety features may mean to the fatality rate, they are unquestionably good for the individual, the seat belt being the most useful of all the features. Unfortunately, most people do not use seat belts. While offensive to many, a law requiring use of seat belts would save many more lives than can be claimed as being saved due to the 55-mph speed limit. One of the most dreadful official crimes of our age is that we spend millions of dollars enforcing the 55-mph speed limit in the name of safety, and none in assuring the use of seat belts. (We will not digress here to dispel the public fallacies and official falsehoods that pertain to the 55-mph speed limit. For a hasty survey thereof see the Postscript.)

In any event, safety standards brought federal testing for crashworthiness, the testing brought ratings, and publication of the ratings brought protests from the manufacturers whose cars were given a "fail" rating. The protests had a sound basis. The tests, conducted by the National Highway Traffic Safety Administration (NHTSA), were "scored" on a 1000-point system wherein a car that scored 999 "passed," but one that scored 1001 "failed." Obviously, a two-point spread in a 1000-point system doesn't prove much—certainly not enough to call one car "safe" and another "unsafe."

The NHTSA tests are scientifically flawed in other ways, mostly because crashing a car into a wall does not replicate what happens when cars collide on the road. In sum, NHTSA tests never commanded respect from scientists and in 1981 NHTSA admitted the flaws by omitting "pass-fail" ratings from their evaluations.

For many people, the safety question reduces to whether a "big" car or a "little" car is the safer. Big-car advocates will say that a Cadillac Eldorado can certainly maul a Volkswagen Rabbit and come off less damaged. Small-car advocates reply that if the driver of the Rabbit is even half-awake, the car is so nimble and maneuverable that the Eldorado can never lay a glove on it. In the late 1960s, when Detroit-made cars averaged around 4000 pounds, the big-car theory dominated. Nowadays, when Detroit has been forced to make small cars, the small-and-nimble theory gets more attention.

General Motors has run a lot of splashy newspaper ads showing the results of surveys by the Insurance Institute for Highway Safety (IIHS, the insurance lobby in Washington, D.C.), surveys that purport to show that the bigger, fatter GM cars are "safer" because fewer injuries result when such cars are involved in wrecks. In fact, the IIHS surveys actually prove another point, provided you add the relevant demographics. For example, drivers in the 15–24 age group alone, in 1980, accounted for 23,000 of the total of 62,000 driver fatalities in the whole 15–70+ age group.

However, even those statistics don't tell the proper truth, for in the larger group of fatalities aged 15 to 34, men outnumber women about three to one. The numbers get even more interesting when you look at the blood-alcohol content (BAC) numbers: of drivers involved in fatalities who were tested for

blood-alcohol content (and only half or less get tested) 4277 men
in the 15–34 age group showed a BAC, and of those, 2773 had
a BAC in excess of .10—legally "drunk" in most states. By contrast, in the same age group, of all women tested, only 664 had
a BAC at all, and only 316 had a BAC in excess of .10. A close
study of the available data (which, unfortunately, are not perfect)
raises the question of whether general fatality statistics, male-
dominated as they are, can sensibly apply to women at all.

In any event, this same age group (15–34) also has more small
cars. Hence, IIHS charges the sins of the age group against the
cars they drive, which is neither honest nor scientific, and to
thus shift the emphasis to the driver corrects the fallacy that GM
and IIHS use as marketing propaganda for big cars with their
higher insurance premiums.

Thus, the third school of thought, which holds that safety is
a function of the driver. I believe this theory because I am still
alive despite some of the cars I have owned. Elaine, the political
scientist, corrupted Winston Churchill on my behalf to "Never
has anyone driven so much junk so far with so little trouble." I
have to agree. When my brakes were defective, I stayed well
behind other cars; when my steering and suspension were bad,
I limited myself to speeds at which I could control the vehicle.
The only time I wrecked a car, when I skidded on loose gravel
and overturned a Triumph TR-3, I was physically exhausted
and the official charge of "inattentive driving" seemed right and
proper.

(In my innocence of those days, I pled "guilty," paid the fine,
and suffered two "points" on my driver's license. A fellow I knew
had a virtually identical accident, crawled out of the wreck
screaming "Lawyer," and sued the county for inadequate road
maintenance. He got a new car out of it, and no "points" on his
driver's license. Some sort of lesson inheres in his experience.)

The point here is not to deny the importance of safety, but
to shift the emphasis from the car to the driver. No one really
knows how safe a particular car is: you can get hurt or killed in
any of them and to entertain the illusion of a "safe" car may be
no more than a cruel deception.

I will not try to make a case for one car's being significantly
safer than another; to do so would be intellectually dishonest,
for a collision involves far, far too many unpredictable elements.

Cars do not smash up in the same way every time and neither do people. Dummies that are firmly strapped in behave fairly predictably when the car they are in hits a barrier at 30 mph, but people are not dummies. They are rarely strapped in snugly, they sit sideways, move their legs and heads, etc., and the distribution of the mass of their bodies influences what happens when their car hits something. Indeed, the position of the seat, whether well back or half-reclined, also affects the behavior of a person in a car wreck.

While I will not take a position on whether one car is safer than another, we can make a distinction between cars with hard tops and those without, i.e., the CJ model Jeeps and their look-alikes and the convertibles that are coming back into vogue. We can say without doubt that soft-top cars are more dangerous in a collision.

Serious research into the effects of a collision began in the 1960s, and one of the first conclusions was that the primary cause of death in either a multi- or a one-car accident was passenger ejection. People were thrown out of the car and seriously injured or killed *after* being ejected. Hence, the first federal standards aimed at door locks, and later ones involved keeping the windshield from popping out when people smashed into it.

You don't have to be very smart to see that you can be thrown out of an open-top convertible or Jeep more readily than from an enclosed sedan.

Also, you can see easily that, if an open/soft-top vehicle turns over, you can be crushed underneath it. Quite frequently—more often than mortal sinners have a right to expect—people in a convertible wind up on the floorboards and are not crushed. However, they often smash their heads firmly against the pavement, too.

An open/soft-top car can be improved with the addition of a *roll bar*, a steel bar or pipe that forms a sort of arch behind the front seat. The shoulder belt attaches to the roll bar. Roll bars have long been required in racing and are common on Jeeps used for off-road, rugged-terrain use. If properly made and installed, a roll bar will keep an open/soft-top car from crushing its occupants, provided the car is not going too fast when it turns over.

Until you turn a car over, you will not appreciate how easily it can be done and, to be sure, modern cars have their weight—their center of gravity—close to the road and rarely turn over. Thirty years ago, a car that began to slide would often turn over; now, it more often slides until it wraps itself around a tree. Thus, the fear of turning over need not be exaggerated—except in the case of such short, high cars as the Jeeps and their look-alikes.

The car I turned over was a 1957 Triumph TR-3, a car particularly prone to skidding at the rear end. Gravel on the road caused my rear wheels to slither on a curve, washboarded pavement caused the skid to continue, and the sideways lurch caused me to pull the gear lever out of gear so I couldn't assert control by applying power (my hand was resting idly on the knob). To steer out of the skid meant heading directly into a stone culvert wall; the car hit the wall, bounced off, swapped ends, slammed rearward into the wall, and then rolled over so slowly and gently that I could watch the horizon switch places as the windshield collapsed in the most hypnotic series of spiderweb cracks and pinned my hand against the steering wheel. I was going 33 mph (2200 rpm in third gear) when the incident started; from the initial skid marks to where the car lay upside down was a distance of only 70 feet. Thus, the whole series of maneuvers took place in about two seconds.

I had been through the same curve many times at a tire-screaming 65 mph (6500 rpm) in second gear—and got caught the one time I was driving moderately. I have never been able to reconstruct the physics of the maneuvers the car made; however, I certainly learned how quickly things can go wrong when they do—and how hard your head hits when a car more-or-less picks you up and throws you down on the pavement.

Enjoy your convertible or your Jeep. Certainly, among the fresh-air faithful, few things are so pleasant as an open car on a summer day or a moonlit summer night—but don't get careless. Like many fun, exciting things, open cars can be dangerous.

AERODYNAMICS

When you have resisted blandishments about "styling" and have expressed skepticism about qualitative superiority, the car salesman may play the aerodynamics card on you. Aerodynamics involves the wind resistance a car experiences as it goes down the road. The less the wind resistance, the better the gas mileage, so aerodynamic styling is the most recent tactic in the race to improve fuel economy.

A car's score in the race is given as its *drag coefficient*, a concept that includes both the wind against the front of the car and the friction of the air passing over it and is usually represented as C_d or C_x, a low C_d value indicating low wind resistance and, thus, good fuel economy.

So, what does a low C_d get you? Well, it gets you the pleasure of participating in a fashionable masquerade, but that's about all.

A Volkswagen Rabbit has a C_d of .41 and gets 30 mpg in the city and 42 mpg on the highway, according to EPA estimates. The new Pontiac Firebird, the self-proclaimed winner in the aerodynamics race, has a C_d of .32. However, even with the smaller, four-cylinder engine, its EPA ratings are 23 mpg in the city and 35 mpg on the highway; with the V-8 engine, the figures fall to 17 mpg and 23 mpg.

So, what's that low C_d worth? If you're interested in fuel economy, you obviously gain nothing by buying the Firebird, despite its low C_d number. On the other hand, if you want the performance you get from the Firebird with the V-8 engine, you would still buy it even if its C_d were higher.

About all that the C_d figure means is that the manufacturer made an effort, an effort that often succeeds in the wrong direction. Get in and out of the Firebird a few times, or put a bag of groceries in the rear seat, then do the same with the Rabbit, and you will gain valuable insight into the comparative value of low C_d numbers.

Theoretically, a low C_d number should mean that a car will be more stable in gusty crosswinds and will be less buffeted about by passing trucks, but this generality fails if the car has a squishy suspension. The 1955 Ford sedan had a C_d of about .55, but its firm suspension made it quite stable on the highway. Similarly, a Triumph TR-3 roadster, with top down, has a C_d of about .75 but is much more stable than a modern, low-C_d full-size sedan when passing a truck (and, at 2200 pounds, will get 28 mpg at 70 mph).

You may be impressed with a low C_d number, but you should understand that the C_d changes if you turn on pop-up headlights, load the car enough to weight it down at the rear, or even crumple a fender slightly. In the absolute sense, aerodynamic styling is a good thing; hence, Saabs had a C_d of about .37 from the beginning and the Citroen DS19/21 models of twenty years ago had a C_d of similar value. Aerodynamic styling also helps keep dust and rainwater from collecting on rear windows and tail lights. However, a low C_d number in itself is no reason to choose one car over another.

EPA MILEAGE NUMBERS

As you already know, choosing a car means sorting through advertising chaff for kernels of relevant truth. The EPA mileage estimates you see in advertisements are a "relevant truth," but they are also a "relative truth," if this contradiction of terms be acceptable.

The EPA mileage estimates are relatively truthful in the respect that they err by a factor of 10 percent, plus or minus. The error arises from the fact that assembly-line products like cars will vary as much as 10 percent, and from the fact that the numbers come from laboratory tests and formulae, rather than from road tests. Road tests would be little better, unless the cars under test were driven by a robot whose driving style was entirely consistent. Furthermore, all tests would have to be conducted under identical weather and road conditions.

Once you allow for the error factor, the EPA numbers do a fair job of predicting the gas mileage a car will get—except for the one notable fallacy in the "highway" mileage number: that number comes from a simulation of driving at 50 mph, not even at the 55-mph speed limit that everybody respects so faithfully. Speed does consume fuel, so the EPA highway figure will apply (10 ± percent) only to people who drive 50 mph.

The manufacturers argued against the EPA mileage tests when they were first proposed, but once they had the numbers, they began using them in their advertisements. After a while, some manufacturers got tired of the sham and took the EPA numbers out of their advertisements and sales literature. Guess who did it first—Mercedes-Benz (who else?).

FAVORITES

About ten years ago, a friend named Kathy got her R.N. and began looking for a car wherewith to commute to her first professional job. She was facing the financial concerns of establishing a post-college existence and wanted a serviceable car that wouldn't give her trouble that she had neither time nor money to put up with.

She asked me, "What kind of car should I get?"

"You should," I told her, "look in the classified ads for the best 1962–64 Chevy II you can find."

A year or two later, Louie, a lawyer friend, terminally over-heated the engine in his Audi 100LS and asked me what sort of car he should get to replace it. "I drive twelve miles to work and twelve miles back home every weekday. That's all. Surely I don't need to spend the price of a new Audi just to do that."

"You should," I told him, "look in the classified ads for the best 1962–64 Chevy II you can find."

The original Chevy II, before it took on the "Nova" name and the lumpiness characteristic of all domestic cars in the late 1960s, was not a "great" car in the sense of the old Marmon or Due-senberg. Its greatness was more like that of the Model T Ford. It was an outstanding example of a sensibly designed, useful piece of machinery that did its job without fuss or frippery. It did not have an electrically controlled seat that would adjust in eight different directions, but few people ever complained about the way they fit into it. The engine would not burn the tires getting away from a traffic light; rather, it was a reliable mutation of the engine designed by Louis and Gaston Chevrolet back around 1910 and in the Chevy II form would easily run 100,000 miles with ordinary care.

The car was a handy size, would accommodate four people in as much comfort as many cars that were twice as big, and would make up to 25 mpg cruising in the 50–60-mph range. It was easy to see out of in every direction (except up or down, of course), and the ends were trimmed off bluntly enough that drivers weren't always knocking its fenders in parking lots. The front suspension did rather need its alignment set right more often than most cars, but the overall suspension was stiff enough to make the car manageable in a variety of road conditions. It had relatively small wheels, so the spare could be easily lifted from the trunk. In sum, as a form of personal transportation, it was one of the most space- and materials-efficient pieces of work Detroit ever put out.

Ford Falcon and Dodge Dart/Plymouth Valiant advocates will

now cry out their objections to this assessment of the Chevy II. Agreed, those were decent cars, too. Yet the Chevy II would run rings around both on a twisty, bumpy road and did not suffer that disturbing rear-end lightness that would stick a Falcon or a Dart/Valiant in mud or snow. The Chevy II had a more solid body than the other two, and the fact that its hydraulic valve lifters did not need periodic adjustments made it a more carefree car than the Dart/Valiant with its adjustable valve lifters.

For these and other reasons, I recommended the Chevy II to people of drastically different circumstances but of similar automotive needs. Kathy, the nurse, and Louie, the lawyer, both needed a means to run their errands and make their occasional trips, a way to haul the laundry and fetch the groceries, but they had no desire to carry around any more scrap iron and sheet metal than they could use.

The Chevy II appeared in the first era when Detroit tried to figure out how to deal with the foreign car challenge. By the late 1960s Detroit had decided that if they would ignore the foreign challenge, it would just go away. To Detroit, foreign cars were irrelevant because they were bought by granola-eating freaks, impoverished college students, and certified eccentrics rather than by the reliable suburbanites who preferred their products. In recent years, as foreign cars have become 30 percent of the market, Detroit has been in a mad scramble to switch from huge, overweight cars to small, fuel-efficient ones, and the logic of the Chevy II is back in many shapes and sizes.

To pick the current successor to the Chevy II logic, I will name the Ford Fairmont (and remind the reader that the Fairmont arose from a deliberate effort to copy a Mercedes-Benz). The Fairmont is straightforward, honest, ergonomic, and unburdened by stylish nonsense. The engine, a design that goes back to the Falcon of 1959, is capable and proven beyond question. I do not, personally, like the way I fit into the Fairmont seat, but most people have no trouble. Also, I find the car somewhat light in the rear when the roads are icy, but I find nothing about the car that offends me. By contrast, a Chevrolet Malibu is much too bulky outside and much too cramped inside. In the Citation, I am offended by the humps for the front wheels, since I think GM could have done much, much better about getting rid of them, and I see nothing but loss of cargo space in the angled line aft at the rear window. GM would say that that angled line improves the aerodynamics, but I suppose they would say the same thing about the abrupt drop at the rear window of the 1977 Cadillac Seville, that drop being a stylish throwback to the old Mark IX Jaguar and the Armstrong-Siddeley of the early 1950s (if not that, it was a throwback to the 1937 Chevrolet). All the Citation trunk line shows me is loss of visibility and a lot of hot sun on the passengers; of course, the line does save some sheet metal, so it either reduces cost or enhances profit. In any event, the Citation does not show me a high expression of the Chevy II logic.

Perhaps I make too much of the Chevy II logic. That the Chevy II was, or the Ford Fairmont is, a "good" car does not mean that other cars are not "good." A "good" car is one that does what you want it to do or, at least, doesn't interfere with what you want to do. Hence, my quarrel with excessive overhangs in the name of style: they interfere every time you parallel park, but do you no good at all the rest of the time.

As noted, the Chevy II logic dominates now (although numerous exceptions remain) even as it occurs in multiple forms; hence, the Volkswagen Rabbit, Ford's Escort/Lynx, the Dodge Omni/Plymouth Horizon, Honda Civic, Subaru, *et al.* However, these are boxy-looking cars and do not appeal to the person who prefers the traditional shape of the Fairmont. Of the boxes, I prefer the Rabbit, partly because of respect for Volkswagen quality and partly because the whole package—size, weight, engine, transmission—is so well-integrated and was so from the beginning. The first Escort/Lynx models had poorly rationalized gear ratios, which showed that the Ford Company didn't really believe in what they were doing.

Gear ratios aside, the Escort was the hottest-selling domestic car in 1982. The '83 models do have a proper gearbox. The Omni/Horizon, unlike the Rabbit, was not designed to be driven 100 mph on rough pavements and in crosswinds; hence, my preference for the Rabbit.

If I push my inquiry into larger domestic cars, I find myself unable to make distinctions. To me, they are all overdone in the interior but rarely have a glovebox that will hold a pair of gloves. As far as comfort goes, the seats in a 1948 Buick Roadmaster were equal to those in any modern full-size car, and seats in my

1955 Mercedes-Benz 220a were vastly superior. I see a lot of money being spent nowadays for exotic upholstery, and I am offended by the philosophy that spends the money under the seat of your pants rather than under the hood.

If I look for a car to suit full-size car needs, I wind up looking at a Peugeot 505, which has more front and rear head and leg room than almost any mid- or full-size domestic, and has the added benefits of European suspension philosophy, plus the virtue of convenient size for parking.

Traditionally, Americans have wanted cars with what has been called a "soft ride." I have decided, here of late, that they don't really want a "soft ride" at all. I think what they really want is reduced vibration. They sense vibration, either from the road or the machinery itself, and not knowing quite what they are feeling, try to capture the matter with the term *soft ride*.

The vibration business is real. After I drove a Triumph TR-3 from Pittsburgh to Chicago, a distance of 470 miles at a steady 70 mph, I needed a day to recuperate. On the same trip at the same speed with the Mercedes-Benz 190 SL, I arrived feeling good enough to turn around and go right back.

Generally, the heavier the car, the less the vibration; hence, that generation of domestic cars that weighed 5000 pounds or so. However, while the Americans cured vibration by burying it under weight, the Europeans cured it with sophisticated engineering—or, in the case of, e.g., the Triumph Herald or the Volkswagen Beetle, simply ignored it.

I freely acknowledge the success of the big domestics in solving the vibration problem, though I must point out that the 55-mph speed limit considerably eases the challenge. Nonetheless, even twenty years ago, the big cars were quiet as a prayer and as smooth as aged whiskey when running down a well-surfaced highway at 75 mph, and this virtue is just as true today. However, today, as twenty years ago, much of that quietness has been bought at the cost of a truly roadworthy suspension system. The big cars seem to presume slow speeds on city streets or cruising speeds on expressways and hardly recognize any other conditions. However, if these are the normal conditions of use, then the big cars do not need to be able to handle rough, narrow, winding roads.

Vibration relates to noise, for the two are aspects of the same thing, and one flaw of the current domestic mid- and full-size cars (and many smaller ones) is that you cannot drive them with a window partly open because of the noise. The defect arose in the late 1960s when air conditioning became common. With air conditioning, the windows were always closed, so the noise of an open window did not matter; indeed, the noise of an open window was given as a good reason for buying the air conditioner.

Generally, what I call a "slab-sided" vehicle is quieter than a bulbous-bodied vehicle when a window is "cracked" an inch or two. The Volkswagen van, International Travelall, Mercedes-Benz (which will not like being called "slab-sided"), Peugeot (which won't like it either), and many other relatively wall-sided vehicles can be driven at 70 mph with a window fully or partially open and without creating the noise of a rock crusher.

For reasons of style (which are now rationalized in the name of aerodynamics), Detroit created bodies with bulbous, curved sides in the late 1960s and early 1970s. On these cars, the upper curvature of the door extends into the roof; "crack" a window in a light rain and you get your shoulder wet; "crack" a window at speed, and you get the sound of canvas flapping in a gale. Either you buy air conditioning or you go deaf.

The more space- and materials-efficient cars hardly have this problem because they waste no extra metal in the bulbous body shape. Of course, people who don't like the slab-sided cars accept either the noise or the need for air conditioning. That is their privilege and, fortunately for variable tastes and individual choices, they can find cars that please them and for them such cars are "good" cars.

On this general subject, people often ask me, "What's the best car made?" I don't believe the question has an unqualified answer, not even if (or especially if) you establish a specific time frame, e.g., the 1920s, the 1950s, etc. I agree with the editorship of *Road & Track* of the early 1970s (not necessarily that of today) who called a Mercedes-Benz the world's "best-engineered car." Note, in this reference, that "engineering" takes in much more than just the body, the engine, or any one element of the car.

Privately, I have often said that the old Citroen DS19/21 models were the "world's most sophisticated cars," all things considered. However, I personally did not like the body shape, despite its virtues, and I found its engine gutless by my own standards of performance. I have no particular respect for a Rolls-Royce in its modern form. Years ago, R-R did some very respectable and sophisticated things with engines, but nowadays they are mostly leather and woodwork. In terms of mechanical quality, Detroit has equaled Rolls-Royce for twenty years and Mercedes-Benz has surpassed R-R for as long.

In the context of the "best car" question, an ordinary domestic sedan may well be the "world's best car for the money," especially if interest rates and maintenance costs enter the equation.

Just for fun of a sort, I like to turn the "best car" question around to: "What car would you have if you could have only one and had to keep it the rest of your life?"

For me, the answer is easy: a 1968 Mercedes-Benz 250 sedan. With an engine of right at 150 cubic inches that developed 150 hp, the car had all the acceleration (0–60 mph in about 15 seconds) and top speed (about 105 mph) that I would ever want or need. It would cruise expressways at 20 mpg in the 60–70-mph area and could handle rough roads and vicious crosswinds with comfort and security. It had ample room for passengers and luggage, and the trunk was one of the easiest to move stuff into and out of. The engine, except for its Zenith INAT carburetors, was immensely easy to work on. Nothing comparable even exists today, for Mercedes-Benz has loaded up its cars with unneccessary (to me) complications such as hydropneumatic suspension and little arms that stick out to hand you the seat belt. In a way, and Mercedes-Benz won't like this comparison, the 1968 M-B 250 sedan was the optimum expression of the same logic that produced the Chevy II: a sound, honest, reliable, strong, roadworthy, and civilized automobile.

As suggested, the Mercedes-Benz 250 sedan would serve virtually all purposes. However, as with any sedan, it would have its limitations: it would be not well-suited to towing heavy loads, going camping, or plowing through deep snow, although in this respect, its excellent weight distribution makes it much better than most cars. If the question gets changed to: "What if you could have two cars, what would they be?" The M-B 250 sedan becomes a 250 C coupe. It handles the daily routines and has a bit more verve when verve is appropriate. The second vehicle would be a 1970 International Travelall with the 258-cubic-inch, six-cylinder engine and a three-speed transmission with over-drive. The Travelall would serve as a mixture of car and freight wagon: big enough to carry six people or half a ton of cargo, long enough to sleep in, capable of towing its own weight of around 4200 pounds, yet civilized on the highway, and, with overdrive, capable of about 18 mpg. Alas, the Travelall went out of production in 1975.

"Very well," says my questioner. "Now, what if you could have three cars?"

The M-B 250C then becomes a M-B 280SL coupe, circa 1968, and the Travelall becomes a smaller Jeep Cherokee with a six-cylinder engine and four-wheel drive. The M-B serves for long trips and for going out in style, and the Jeep does the heavy work, including handling the snowdrifts: it would be the pre-ferred vehicle for making a trip in a snowstorm.

The third vehicle would be the general service vehicle and would be a tossup between a Saab 99 and a 1972 Toyota Corona. The Saab is noisier, but that matters little if it is not used for long trips. The Toyota is better in snow, but that matters little if the Cherokee takes care of that. The Saab, somehow, takes less effort to get around curves and is somewhat more stable on the highway because of its front-wheel drive, but in the absolute sense the Toyota corners as well and has one of the most precise steering systems anybody ever built. Both give easy ingress and egress, both have a decent trunk, both are easy to work on (bar-ring the inaccessible Toyota starter and the bucket tappets on the Saab). In short, a tossup, and a strange tossup because most people would not think of the two cars as being alike. Note, also, that both these cars are discontinued models. The current Saab 900 is a perversion of the 99 model, a totally unnecessary per-version that accomplished nothing; the current Toyota Crown fairly well replicates the honesty of the Corona of ten years ago, but only in a qualified way.

If allowed (or invited) to continue my list, my nostalgia begins to show: I would add a Triumph TR-3 because they are strong, durable, fun, and distinct. Also, an old Alfa-Romeo Giulia, be-cause they had such an excellent suspension; plus, a 1951 Stu-debaker Land Cruiser sedan, an M38A1 "Korean War" model Jeep, a 1937 Reo pickup, a 1948 Chrysler Town and Country coupe (unarguably one of the best, most attractive cars ever built in this country), and a 1937 Packard twin side-mount convertible (for those occasions when the M-B 280 SL would be pretentious and the Jeep unsuitable), not to mention a Mercedes-Benz 190 SL convertible.

The list could go on, but enough. Note that the list contains no exotica for its own sake—no Maserati or Bugatti, no Rolls-Royce or Armstrong-Siddeley, no Pierce-Arrow or Stutz Bearcat. All the cars in the list represent intelligent design responses to various needs and the design responses include a respect for efficiency and usefulness.

The list also contains no new cars. This is not because new cars are not good, but because new cars offer nothing that is not duplicated in older cars. Also, as admitted, the list slips from ergonomics into nostalgia.

"Okay," says the questioner, "do it again, only this time with new cars."

Very well, for a new car, a one-and-only to keep forever and ever, a Mercedes-Benz 300 TD diesel station wagon (at around $33,000). For two, replace the M-B 300 TD wagon with a Jeep Cherokee and add an M-B 380 SL convertible (at around $40,000) for the other errands.

And if I were to have three? Well, the two choices above, certainly, but what about the third? The Saab 900, as noted above, is a spoiled version of the Saab 99, so it's out. A Volkswagen Rabbit is too small, as are Toyota and Datsun, and domestic sedans are too squishy in the suspension, clunky when you shut the doors, and plain, damn silly in certain details. A BMW or Jaguar is just an ersatz Mercedes-Benz, so offers nothing to the list.

So, what's left as a good-mannered, capable, well-engineered car that will do everything you expect of a car? Well, a name that goes back to 1897, a name that won most of the Indianapolis 500 races before 1920, and a name I have sometimes called the "poor man's Mercedes-Benz": the Peugeot. In the context of "only three," I will prefer the gasoline-powered model 505 to the diesel, because I want the acceleration. Although Peugeot parts and service have been problems in the past, those difficulties have supposedly improved here lately, and the car exudes quality, has excellent engineering, and deserves much more attention than it usually gets.

Note that the selections given here, even the oldies, are cars that put a premium on roadworthiness, cars that presume an alert, discriminating driver. "Soft ride" and "style" are not particularly important to these cars, though they all have better styling than cars that make much of their "style." Among the world's artifacts, a sailing ship and a steam locomotive are always regarded as beautiful; yet, both are pure function, with virtually no embellishment at all. The cars in the foregoing list are like that: because they start out to serve a function well, they end up being more beautiful than cars that attempt to be beautiful at the expense of function.

Some people will object to the foreign domination of the list. I will agree to several things. First, mechanically, domestic cars are quite good. However, I just want a suspension system that communicates with the road and, thus, informs me of what the car is doing. Furthermore, I will agree that domestic cars are more intelligently designed now than they have been since about 1950; however, note that the most intelligently designed of them shamelessly copy foreign models. I will also agree that domestic cars are good bargains at the price in the full-size models (the smaller ones come off less well against such as the VW Rabbit or Honda Civic). In other words, my prejudice against domestics, while real, is not blind; it arises from genuine differences in roadworthiness and ergonomics, and these differences arise from different design philosophies here and abroad. As noted, domestic manufacturers are reverting (most reluctantly, grudgingly, and belatedly) to the good sense they showed 30 years ago, and as they practice good sense more, the better they will get at it. In other words, the domestics can be expected to improve in the future. In the meantime, many, many people like domestic cars just the way they are and have been for the past ten years. I am only pleased that the market offers enough variety to suit every taste.

MORE CASES, LISTED

Although the emotional exhaustion of the preceding discussion still has not produced a neat, simple formula to apply when choosing one car of many, we have, at least, established a few useful generalities:

- Smaller domestic cars and smaller foreign cars closely resemble each other in size, accommodation, handling, and price.
- Larger domestics sacrifice interior room to exterior bulk (in a misguided zeal for "style"), and sacrifice handling characteristics to a soft-sofa ride.
- Larger foreign cars tend to be more ergonomic; the Europeans have excellent road manners while the Japanese compromise somewhat in the direction of a "soft" ride; both the larger European and Japanese sedans cost more than domestics of equal interior dimensions.

These generalities provide some guidance, and we can improve on them by creating categories. For example, let's set up a class of Basic Two-Seaters of Minimal Size, a class that includes, e.g., Renault's Le Car, Ford's Escort, Honda's Civic, Toyota's Starlet, and various others of this type. If you go to a fully stocked car show, you'll find about 25 cars in this category, all costing about $6000 (at 1982–83 base prices).

Minimal Two-Seaters

	Base Price, No Extra Equipment
AMC Spirit	$ 6,000
Buick Skyhawk/Olds Firenza/Pontiac 2000	7,000
Chevrolet Chevette/Pontiac 1000	5,000
Chevrolet Cavalier/Pontiac 2000	5,900
Datsun/Nissan Pulsar	NA
Datsun/Nissan Sentra	5,000

Datsun/Nissan Stanza	7,000
Dodge Colt	5,500
Dodge Omni/Plymouth Horizon	5,900
Ford Escort/Mercury Lynx	5,600
Ford Mustang	7,100
Honda Accord coupe	7,500
Honda Civic 1300 cc	4,900
Honda Civic 1500 cc	6,000
Isuzu LS	5,900
Mazda GLC coupe	5,300
Mitsubishi Cordia	NA
Renault Alliance	5,600
Renault Le Car	5,300
Subaru DL	5,000
Toyota Corolla	5,400
Toyota Starlet	5,700
Toyota Tercel	5,000
Volkswagen Jetta	10,000
Volkswagen Rabbit	6,000

How to choose? Do you value Toyota's tight body and semi-plush interior, or do you prefer the VW Rabbit for its reputation? Do you prefer the boxiness of the VW, or the more cursive lines of the Toyota? Note how the differences of shape define what you can do with the car besides haul two people. On the other hand, do you prefer a domestic car because you feel service is more readily available, or, perhaps, because you simply prefer to "buy American"? You will find yourself choosing for reasons like these, or seeking the best financial deal, for the cars don't differ remarkably in what they will or will not do in ordinary use. In extraordinary use, the European cars have the advantage, but the Ford Escort was the hottest-selling car in 1982, so maybe ordinary use is what matters to most people.

*

Let's make another category—Pseudo-Sports and Sports Cars (no convertibles)—to include such as the Toyota Celica at $7200 and go on up to the Chevrolet Corvette at $18,500. Of these, the Audi and Renault are the most ergonomic, but the Corvette is the fastest in the absolute sense (a virtue that hardly matters in a traffic jam). However, if you line up the Audi, Renault, VW Quantum, Camaro, Toyota Supra, and Corvette in that order, you see at once that they break into two groups: Audi, Renault, and Quantum on the comfort and usefulness side, while those on the "stylish" end of the line-up are harder to get into and out of and have fewer uses. Okay, which do you want? At what price? Is the gingerbread and turbocharger on the Saab 900 Turbo worth the extra cost?

Pseudo-Sports and Sports Cars, Two-door Coupes

Audi	$12,370
Chevrolet Camaro/Pontiac Firebird	8,000
Chevrolet Camaro Z28	10,336
Chevrolet Corvette	18,500
Datsun 200SX	7,800
Datsun 280ZX	13,000
Dodge Challenger/Plymouth Sapporo	8,500
Mazda RX7	9,600
Renault Fuego	8,400
Saab 900	10,750
Saab 900 Turbo	16,500
Toyota Celica	7,200
Toyota Supra	14,000
Volkswagen Quantum	10,000

If reliability and ease (and economy) of service is your main concern, you'll prefer the domestics in this second category; if you want cachet, you'll want the distinctive Mazda; if you want maximum road handling under all conditions, plus good usability for many purposes, you'll want the Audi, or, for less money, the Quantum. On the other hand, if you value style, you can follow architect Louis Sullivan's dictum that "form follows function" with the Audi or Renault, or go for baroque with the Camaro or Corvette.

*

If you decide to go topless, the Convertibles category offers nine choices from Chrysler's $12,800 offerings up to Mercedes-Benz's $42,000 one. If you want maximum interior room, you'll prefer one of the Chrysler products or a Buick Riviera (that costs twice as much as a Chrysler and for no compelling reason). If fuel economy and nimbleness matter more than interior room, you choose between the Mustang and the Rabbit. If you need accommodation for only two, go for the Alfa-Romeo on one end of the price scale, or the Porsche, Jaguar XJ-S, or Mercedes at the other (don't let the price scare you off: after all, one Mercedes only equals four Rabbits).

Convertibles

Alfa-Romeo	ca. $13,000
Buick Riviera	25,000
Chrysler LeBaron	12,800
Dodge 400	12,800
Ford Mustang (convertible)	est. 12,900
Jaguar XJ-S	32,000
Mercedes-Benz 380 SL	42,000
Porsche 911SC	31,000
Volkswagen Rabbit	10,600

*

Proceeding from one type of specialty car to another brings us to four-wheel drive cars. These are immensely useful to people who drive a lot in winter storms, on unimproved roads, or off the road entirely.

Four-Wheel Drive

AMC Eagle, coupe	$ 7,600
AMC Eagle, 4-door sedan	9,200
AMC Eagle, wagon	9,900
Audi Quattro	35,000
Jeep, CJ-7	ca. 7,000
Jeep, Wagoneer	ca. 11,000
Subaru, sedan and wagon	7,000
Toyota Tercel, wagon	7,400

Of these, the Audi Quattro is easiest to eliminate: it's a 100+ mph European cruiser and hardly fits with the others at all. The Quattro is an anomaly anywhere: it can't exploit its 4WD on an interstate, and it can't use its speed in the places where it can employ its 4WD. It offers extremes that rarely ever coincide.

The AMC line is a sturdy trio, but the coupe is awkward—to get into, to see out of, and to move your feet in, and it's not significantly smaller than the wagon. The sedan and wagon are more convenient, but do not offer significantly more room than the Subaru or the Tercel, these latter two having the fuel mileage advantage.

The Jeeps, like the Audi, are a breed apart—bigger, heavier, and the best for slogging through knee-deep mud, towing a travel trailer off the beaten path, or dragging logs out of the woods. However, they have more capability than most people will ever be able to use. Their size does make them roomy, but also entails higher fuel consumption.

The real choices here are among the AMC, Subaru, and Toyota, for the Quattro and Jeeps are really specialty vehicles.

*

Our next list, Bread-and-Butter Sedans, is dominated by the "basic American" types from which most people choose a car, yet the cars (except for the foreigners) differ comparatively little. How, for example, do you distinguish between a Dodge Aries and a Chevrolet Celebrity? They are quite similar in size, usefulness, and handling, so the choice may be based on style—or on the deal you can make. The Mercury Marquis and the Peugeot 505 present a similar distinction of style. However, the Peugeot offers European-style road manners at no sacrifice to interior room (despite the greater bulk of the Marquis), but costs 50 percent more than the Marquis, so the value of its handling deserves serious scrutiny.

Bread-and-Butter Sedans

AMC Concord	$ 6,750
Audi 4000	9,800
BMW 318	13,000
Buick Century	9,000
Buick Regal/Oldsmobile Cutlass Supreme	9,300
Buick Skyhawk	7,700
Cadillac Cimarron/Chevrolet Cavalier/ Pontiac 2000	12,250

Chevrolet Celebrity/Oldsmobile Ciera/	8,000
Pontiac 6000	
Chevrolet Citation/Pontiac Phoenix/	7,000
Oldsmobile Omega	
Chevrolet Malibu/Pontiac Bonneville	8,000
Chrysler E-series/Dodge 600	9,400
Chrysler LeBaron/Dodge 400	8,700
Datsun Maxima	11,000
Dodge Aries/Plymouth Reliant	6,700
Ford Fairmont	6,500
Ford LTD	8,200
Honda Accord, 4-door	8,400
Mercury Marquis	7,800
Peugeot 505	12,000
Saab 900, 4-door	11,000
Toyota Cressida	13,000
Volkswagen Quantum	10,250

The Toyota Cressida has become a hot, $13,000 item since it appeared, apparently for its performance and for its long list of "standard" equipment (so maybe it's really a small "luxury" car). However, an equal list of optional gewgaws will bring a similar-size domestic right up there with the Cressida, so the Cressida is not that much different from a domestic and the choice is not so striking as the price suggests.

*

The Large Domestic Sedans are the most difficult to assess because this whole category has so little reason to exist at all. These cars are often billed as good for long trips, but unless they have "handling" or "touring" packages, their roadworthiness is dismal in the extreme. Almost any smaller car is more stable on a twisty road, equally stable on an interstate, and more manageable in crosswinds. The big domestics are also billed as "roomy," but in specific interior measurements, they are rarely as big on the inside as the outside would suggest.

Large Domestic Sedans

Buick Riviera	$15,300
Cadillac DeVille	16,000
Cadillac Eldorado	19,300
Cadillac Fleetwood	19,200

Cadillac Seville	21,500
Chevrolet Caprice	8,800
Chrysler Cordoba	9,600
Chrysler Imperial	21,850
Dodge Diplomat/Plymouth Grand Fury	8,200
Ford LTD Crown Victoria/Mercury Grand Marquis	11,000
Lincoln Continental Town car	17,000
Lincoln Continental & Mark VI	21,000
Oldsmobile 88	9,500
Oldsmobile 98	13,000
Oldsmobile Toronado	15,250

Despite this jaundiced view, the big cars have sold well right through the recent automotive sales slump and continue to do so, so they obviously please many people. Whether they please you will depend on a road test.

*

The foreign Luxury and GT (grand touring) Sedans are a different matter entirely. They are designed to run at 100 + mph on rough, undulating pavements and to be tractable while so doing. However, European road manners are not cheap.

Luxury and GT Sedans

Audi Quattro	$35,000
Audi 5000 Turbo	18,500
BMW 528e	23,000
BMW 733i	33,000
BMW 628Csi	36,000
Jaguar XJ6	30,000
Mercedes-Benz 240 D	22,000
Mercedes-Benz 300 D	30,000
Mercedes-Benz 300 SD	37,000
Mercedes-Benz 380 SEL	52,000
Peugeot 604 (diesel)	20,000

Of this group, the Mercedes-Benz 240 D and the Peugeot 604 are diesels of the leisurely acceleration type; the Mercedes 300 D with its larger five-cylinder engine is brisker, while the SD model, with its turbocharged diesel, will accelerate with most gasoline-powered cars. (We should note that Mercedes-Benz has never suffered the ignominy of a recall.) The Jaguar XJ-6 suffers an evil reputation for its malfeasances of several years ago, but these flies in the exotic ointment have been ironed out by the recent management reorganization (a shakeup for which Margaret Thatcher deserves the credit). The Audi Quattro, with full-time four-wheel drive, is an able car, but is often reckoned to be vastly overpriced; of course, some people would say that of the Mercedes 380 SEL, and some would say it of this whole group.

At bottom, you have only three reasons for looking at this list at all: You can justify the car by your driving style; you admire deep, below-the-surface quality engineering; and you want a status symbol that costs more than a Cadillac. The list allows you to buy at one of several levels.

*

Our last category, Station Wagons, includes the smallest and least-expensive and the largest and most-expensive, which makes it a difficult list to choose from. Perhaps price is the definitive element here.

The heyday of the station wagon was the late 1950s era of neat two- and four-child nuclear suburban families. In those days, a station wagon was judged by whether you could lay a 48″ × 96″ sheet of plywood flat on the cargo floor (the late fifties were also an era of do-it-yourself frenzy), and most station wagons would so accommodate a piece of plywood.

No more. Today, hardly any station wagon will accept an item that is 48″ wide, to illustrate which point we include the definitive width and useful height of several wagons on the list. The measurements do not indicate favoritism or preference; rather, they simply show what was available at the dealerships that were open on the Saturday afternoon that I went cruising with a tape measure (the '79 Ford LTD wagon, complete with owner and husband, was at a drive-in restaurant; the owner agreeably put aside her cheeseburger to let me measure). The height measurement is from the cargo floor to the headliner (upholstery on the underside of the roof) and indicates whether your dog can be a cocker spaniel or a Newfoundland.

The width measurement is the minimum, measured between the rear wheel humps. It makes no allowance, as a cubic footage measurement does, for extra width ahead of and behind the wheel humps. Also, because of manufacturing tolerances, the measurements can vary as much as half an inch from one wagon to another.

Station Wagons, All Types

	Width in Inches	Height in Inches	Price
AMC Jeep Cherokee	43½	37½	$10,000
Buick Electra			12,000
Buick Regal			10,000
Buick Skyhawk			8,000
Chevrolet Caprice			9,500
Chevrolet Cavalier			6,600
Chevrolet Malibu			8,200
Chrysler Town & Country			9,800
Datsun Maxima			12,000
Datsun Sentra			6,700
Dodge Aries	38½	32¼	7,600
Ford Escort/Mercury Lynx	35¼	36½	6,700
Ford Fairmont	36	32	8,500
Ford LTD/Mercury Marquis	36	33	8,500
Ford Crown Squire/Mercury Colony Park			10,250
Honda Civic 1500	44	29¼	6,300
Mercedes-Benz 300TD			33,000
Oldsmobile Cutlass Supreme			9,400
Oldsmobile Custom Cruiser			10,000
Oldsmobile Firenza			7,800
Peugeot 504 diesel			12,000
Pontiac Bonneville			9,200
Pontiac 2000			7,000
Renault 18i	34	31¼	8,600
Subaru	37¼	33½	6,500
Toyota Corolla			6,500
Toyota Cressida			13,000
Volkswagen Quantum	38½	29½	11,000
1979 Ford LTD	48	30	

The numbers reveal some of the illusions engendered by exterior dimensions. The Honda Civic is as wide as the Jeep Cherokee, and both are wider than the current Ford LTD/Mercury

Marquis. As noted, the *old* LTD, which is now the Ford Crown Squire/Mercury Colony Park, was 48″ wide inside. In comparing the Ford Fairmont and the Escort, you would expect more difference in the width, but you would hardly expect the Escort to have more height.

If cargo space matters, take a tape measure when you go shopping for a wagon. Don't expect the salesman to know the minimum width; rather, expect him to be half-insulted that you even ask. He will go rooting through the brochures for the answer, which won't be there. The brochure gives only adjectives and cubic feet, but not a minimum width.

Keep in mind, when considering a wagon, that with a wagon your cargo is always visible and, thus, tempting to thieves.

Our three generalities and eight categories did not produce a formula for choosing, but they do suggest how a system for choosing may regard several cars of similar type. This amounts to no more than saying that all the elements of the choice—use, preferred style, economy requirements, price—must be precisely honed to select one car out of the possibilities.

AUTOMOTIVE WRIT AND REFERENCE

If you don't know much about cars, it's hard to know where to start looking for the one that suits you. Obviously, you have some points of reference—previous cars you've owned, friends' cars, cars you rented or borrowed, etc. Still, these are a few of many and you must find out more before you go looking, lest you waste much of your time (and add to your confusion). The successful car search must focus the more exactly as you approach a purchase; hence, the need for guidance.

Public writ contains much such guidance: the "car" section of a newsstand will have numerous magazines and special-topic booklets (e.g., *Car Prices for 1983*) that offer some help. However, this help is not unqualified; many of these publications seem aimed at some special audience that does not include you and others report from narrow viewpoints that produce false or inapplicable judgments.

To note magazines, *Motor Trend, Road & Track,* and *Car and Driver* are the leading automotive consumer monthlies. However, *Mechanix Illustrated* and *Popular Mechanics* run a lot of car-related material amid the woodwork and plumbing, so they belong among the sources of information.

The beginner will, indeed, have to work a little to gain entry into the *lingua franca* of the car enthusiasts. Generally, *Motor Trend* is at the easy end of the scale, with *Road & Track* at the opposite end, and the others more or less in the middle.

I regard *Motor Trend* as the Standard American of the car magazines. The editorial tone replicates the quiet smugness of a middle-class suburb or a smallish city. The road tests, thus, are not particularly discriminating, the judgments not particularly strong, and the criticisms not particularly pointed. The attitude is basically optimistic, but not overstated; and the assumption is that all cars are pretty good and that anybody can find a suitable one. In sum, *Motor Trend* arises from and speaks to the democratic tastes of America in terms most people can understand. Its evaluations make the most sense to the most people. *Motor Trend*'s very good nature is its weakness: it simply doesn't have the passion to get excited about an outstanding car nor righteously indignant about a poor one. Nonetheless, for the beginner, for the person who wants a car only to use, *MT* is the first source of information.

Road & Track plays the role of The Bearded-But-Ever-So-Human-Savant. The editorship represents itself as clothed in robes of aloof wisdom, then throws in some pseudo-folksy stuff so you'll know they are really ordinary people like you and me despite their awesome credentials.

Road & Track road tests have the most and best technical information and test data. Unfortunately, the text portions rarely engage the significance of the test data and often exaggerate or dilute them with carefully selected adjectives. For example, the road tests note "lateral acceleration," or how much the car tries to go sideways when driven fast around a circle 200 feet in diameter. Having established the "lateral acceleration" for a given car and praised or faintly condemned it, *R&T* will (sometimes) acknowledge parenthetically that the same car might get a higher or lower score on a smaller or larger circle. The conclusion to be drawn from the "lateral acceleration" test, then, is not nearly so definitive as it is represented to be. The test data also make much of acceleration times and top speeds, but don't include the temperature, humidity, or atmospheric pressure prevailing during the test. Since engine output varies according to these conditions, a pretense to technical authority should acknowledge that fact.

Occasionally, the *R&T* editorship slips up and admits what all that technical stuff is worth; hence, the observation in regard to one car that its "...doors are *attention getting* [italics added] and therefore strong selling points for the car." So, we find out what really matters.

R&T does have one outstanding feature: its "owner survey," wherein owners report their experiences with a certain car over several years. The text portion of the survey reviews owners' experiences and impressions, both good and bad, and the tabular data give the percentage of owners who noted "problem areas," "best features," "worst features," etc. The *R&T* owner surveys, aside from their bias toward the car enthusiast, provide an excellent sense of "being there." Unfortunately, the magazine only runs a few surveys per year, so you won't find every car surveyed and, indeed, the current model may differ from the one surveyed.

Car and Driver you may safely ignore. It is the only car magazine that would be improved if it were written by the advertisers.

Mechanix Illustrated and *Popular Mechanics* belong to the Gee Whiz school of car testing. The editorial tone is that of a crew of high school boys at an automobile show and the judgments about as profound. If a car has a deficiency, it goes unnoticed in the excitement about the stereo system.

MI and *PM* have the genuine virtue of very down-to-cars question-and-answer columns (in contrast to the esoterica that dominate in *R&T*'s column). The questions asked by readers, in the sort of language you would use yourself, give you a notion of the types of problems that arise with cars and are highly educational in the respect that they indicate why mechanics often have a hard time figuring out what's wrong with a car.

If you read the road tests of any one magazine issue after issue—you will probably quit after a while. Once you learn the writers' systems of adjectives, you perceive a predictable pattern wherein the road tests say virtually the same thing about every car. True, the tests will offer such grave judgments as, "A Porsche 911 gets around curves faster than a Chevrolet pickup," but most people could have guessed that much. The other judgments, e.g., about how "pleasant" the car is to drive, are pure subjectivity—and what else could they say, anyway? Oh, yes, they will niggle about an awkward seat-belt latch to show their independent thinking, but a truly grievous fault gets coated under enough euphemisms to obscure it.

The absolute flaw of road tests comes from their inherent solipsism: Having measured one car in one set of circumstances, the testers assume they have tested all such cars in all conditions, and further assume that all drivers will drive as they did. Thus, the tests are dry-pavement, fair-weather events that don't predict what a car will do in other circumstances or suggest how a car will behave when loaded with several passengers or with luggage. Neither do the tests acknowledge how tenuous are their conclusions and numbers. So a certain car "stops well and in a straight line"; good, now what will it do when one tire is underinflated? So a certain car stops in 300 feet from 80 mph; right, but on what sort of road surface? Pavements are not uniform in their friction characteristics.

The test data are valid general indicators. Good lateral acceleration means cornering power and short stopping distances mean good brakes. However, for the data to hold up, you have to keep the car in the condition it was in when it was tested.

The road tests in magazines give you a few facts ("The car accelerates from 0 to 60 mph in 17.5 seconds") and many judgments ("The suspension is firm"). Study the road tests, but keep in mind they are written by people who are not as expert as they would have you believe and by people whose monthly paychecks ultimately depend on the goodwill of the advertisers.

Consumer Reports also assesses cars in its own perverse way as the Righteous Guardian. The magazine is published by Consumers Union, which was organized in 1936 as a sort of antiestablishment consumer league. The organization began with an ideological bias that persists to this day, and the effort to rise from ideology to objectivity produces some bad science. For example, *CR* takes safety ratings from the National Highway Traffic Safety Administration, openly admits that the ratings are faulty and misleading, and then proceeds to publish the NHTSA ratings as a guide to choosing a car. In a similar vein, the *CR* system for assembling data on repairs would disgust a competent statistician. *CR*'s one strength is its annual tabulation of external and internal dimensions. At a glance, you can compare the headroom or rear-seat knee room of one car to another.

Consumer Guide (which is often mistaken for *Consumer Reports*, to the satisfaction of the former and the annoyance of the latter) presents itself as Staid Authority. The "Auto Series" reports on new and used cars in clearly presented "thumbnail" sketches that are quite handy for quick reference, especially for sorting out models among makes. Their *Used Car Rating and Price Guide* notes the recalls on cars, which is useful, but the ratings on repairs and gas mileage bear little relationship to worldly experience and should be ignored.

These are the common newsstand sources of information and the bookstores have more, much of it flawed in the same way as the magazine reports: you get facts (e.g., "wheelbase is 95 inches") and adjectives ("car has a good repair record"), but little you can sink your teeth into. Perhaps the most useful are the *Edmund's* booklets on new and used car prices. The *Edmund's* books arose many years ago for the use of car dealers who did not subscribe to the National Auto Dealers Association (NADA) *Official Used Car Guide* (usually called the "book"). *Edmund's* gives the cost of a car to the dealer and the "suggested retail price"; these figures indicate the dealer's profit margin and the price room you have for maneuvering. *Edmund's* makes no assessments or evaluations but gives the facts in an efficient, small-type way. For "armchair shopping" before you go tire-kicking, *Edmund's* is the most thorough and easy-to-use reference.

The "book" that people speak of so often is an official publication of the NADA. Basically, it is a market report. If you're interested in a car, you look in the NADA "book" (or, as noted, in *Edmund's*). The "book" notes the original price, the average retail price, the average wholesale (auction) price, and the average loan value for cars up to five years old. The prices are simply the averages of many transactions reported by NADA members. The prices do not *dictate* the value of a car; they simply *report* the average price paid for a certain car in a certain geographical area during the past month or over several months.

Lending institutions use the loan value as a guide when making car loans and dealers use the wholesale values to assess what your car is worth as a trade-in. Since these items matter less to the individual buyer, *Edmund's* does not include them.

You can get *Edmund's* at virtually any bookstore or at the better-stocked newsstands. To look at the NADA "book," you have to visit a car dealer or a bank. Many car dealers willingly let you examine the "book" in their offices, but others seem to feel it contains secrets you shouldn't know and won't let you see their copy. However, banks usually have a copy in the loan department and they do not consider it sacred. They'll let you look at it any time and may even comment on exceptions to the "loan" value of a particular car; sometimes a car enjoys a higher, or suffers a lower, loan value than the NADA "book" indicates.

While the Sunday-paper car column is mostly a loss, the classified ads can be a lode. The cars for the next model year typically come out in October; thus the 1984 models appear in October of 1983, and a lot of people buy them at once. Around January or February of 1984, start reading the classifieds; if a certain new car appears in disproportionate numbers, then you know that some of those immediate buyers are disappointed and are prepared to "dump" their new cars. Call them up and ask why.

The reasons are not always bad news. For example, when the Chevrolet Citation came out, the first buyers thought they were getting a cheap, domestic version of the Saab 900. Since the handling and performance of the Citation bore no resemblance to that of the Saab 900, these early buyers were disappointed and many promptly dumped their Citations.

In fact, the Citation works well as a general purpose, domestic-style sedan. It is no European-style performer, but it is an excellent American-style work horse. Thus, in the case of the Citation, someone's disappointment became someone else's excellent bargain—at least until the bad news about the Citation brakes and the consequent recall, came out. By contrast, in the case of the first Jaguar XJ-6 and XJ-12 models of several years ago, successive owners simply sold their problems to new owners. (The latest Jaguar XJ-S models, since the company got a bit of a shakeup, have become honest cars again.)

We should note here that a Citation with a "handling package" will give a Saab 900 a very good run for its money and a Citation with a handling package and the HO (high-output) V-6 engine will give a Porsche a very good run for its money.

As our thumbnail reviews suggest, some car-related publications err because of the solipsism of those who write them, and others err by a dependence on bad science. The publication that proudly combines both errors is *The Car Book*, presently under the authorship of Jack Gillis and now published by E. P. Dutton.

The first edition of *The Car Book* was issued in 1980 (as the 1981 edition) by the NHTSA while it was under the direction of Joan Claybrook. Claybrook had been a functionary in Ralph Nader's enterprises, and accepted the Carter Administration's invitation to run NHTSA. Upon the departure of Carter and Co., she returned to the Nader fold.

The Car Book of 1980−81, then, arose from the same regulatory ideology, and the same bad science used to justify it, that characterized NHTSA under Claybrook's direction. The book contained a lot of dubious data about safety, maintenance costs, and such like in a series of graphs and tables that looked very convincing so long as you didn't ask any questions.

The matter of safety will illustrate the flaws of the original *The Car Book*. NHTSA crashed cars head-on into a wall at 35 mph, noted the damage sustained by dummies inside, then gave each car a "pass" or a "fail" rating. NHTSA did not make clear that very, very few cars run head-on into walls, and that such a crash gives only a highly qualified indication of what happens when cars collide corner-to-corner, as they more often do, when one car hits another in the side, or when a car skids off the road and wraps itself around a tree. The science of the other parts of the book was similarly flawed, and Claybrook's *The Car Book* earned the derision, if not outright contempt, of transportation scientists who were not on the NHTSA payroll. The criticism was so universal, and so pointed, that NHTSA ceased to issue the book.

However, since the original was public information and not

subject to copyright restrictions, a group of Claybrook's disciples slightly recast the material into a 1982–83 edition under the Tilden Press imprint—and charged $4.95 for it, a notable instance of how NHTSA's efforts benefit private citizens.

NHTSA distributed 1,500,000 copies of the original (1980) book as a "freebie," distribution being aided by the promotion Nader and his allies gave the book. Tilden Press didn't report 1982–83 sales at $4.95, but they must have been good enough to persuade the Dutton people to issue the current edition, which has all the faults of the prior two, plus additional nonsense that seeks to define the quality of used cars in somewhat the same misleading way that *Consumer Reports* does. In sum, *The Car Book* remains a product of science perverted to serve ideology and is no guide to conduct.

You should not—repeat: should not—end your research with published sources. Don't fail, as the old Packard advertisements said, to "Ask the man who owns one." This means friends, strangers, and members of marque clubs.

You know what your friends value and how they react to things, so you will communicate well. However, you may be surprised at how well you can communicate with strangers. So you're considering a Chrysler LeBaron and you see someone getting into one in a parking lot: hail the person and ask about the car. People who feel good about their choices will reply in about 5000 enthusiastic (if somewhat randomly chosen) words; people who think they have been victimized by a manufacturer, a dealer, or a car itself will reply in about 10,000 more carefully chosen (if more repetitive) words. Note that such people will be more like you than the automotive writers (who have the fundamental arrogance of the scribal class and who like to show off their wisdom by references to obscure technical details).

Marque club members are worth talking to, even if they are all slightly crazy (at least, crazier than thee and me). They join marque clubs because they are enthusiasts for a certain kind of car and can, and will, rave on at length about the virtues of their preferred marque. However, they are also martyrs who enjoy suffering for a cause (i.e., the marque) and if the car has built-in defects or some operational eccentricity they take great pleasure in telling you about it. They conceal nothing, for they believe their suffering demonstrates their love of the marque (which is true). If you want a full review of everything beautiful and beastly about a certain car, talk to a marque club member. Generally, local dealers will know of marque club chapters in your area and, if not, you can find an address in the classifieds of a car magazine or announcements of meetings in the Sunday papers.

Marque club members are worthwhile contacts because the club newsletter will have tips on how to deal with all manner of mechanical peculiarities. Generally, marque club members know more than dealership mechanics about how to keep the marque happy and well.

Since passage of the National Traffic and Motor Vehicle Safety Act in 1966, the National Highway Traffic Safety Administration has required automobile manufacturers to "recall" cars with safety-related defects. Dealers are supposed to maintain lists of all formal recalls, but if a dealer does not, you can get recall information from NHTSA, 400 7th Street, S. W., Washington, D.C. 20590. Indeed, you can call 24 hours a day, seven days a week on the toll-free (i.e., tax-paid) "hotline," area code 800-424-9393; people with impaired hearing call 800-424-9153.

Safety-related defects do not usually show up until after a car has been in production for a while, so recalls rarely apply to new cars. However, recall information is worth checking on used cars.

OPTIONS

After Ransom Edward Olds sold his interest in the Olds Motor Works (Oldsmobile) in 1903, he set up shop again to build cars under the "Reo" name. He must have had the industry guessing a bit in 1912, for the *Automobile Trade Journal* billed his Reo the Fifth model as a "farewell" car—and a fitting one, too, the *Journal* felt, for it offered three oil lamps, two acetylene gas lamps, an acetylene gas generator, a horn, and a complete tool and tire kit, all as standard equipment. For $100 added onto the $1055 base price, you could have a speedometer, an acetylene gas tank, side curtains, and—a windshield!

We have, indeed, come a long way from the time when the windshield was optional, extra-cost equipment, but the questions about options have not changed. The motorist of 1912 debated whether that windshield was worth its cost. After all, the Crescent Tire Company, which occupied the block between 57th and 58th Streets and Broadway in New York, offered excellent rubber-frame driving goggles for a dollar and pigskin-frame goggles with a silk lining for $1.50. Milady's goggles, at $2.00, were of kid, with velvet binding. Who needed a windshield? Why, if it got broken, a glazier might charge as much as $10 to replace it.

Motorists of seventy years ago would marvel at today's cars and would understand the uncertainty of the buyer confronted with today's options list. An electronic instrument cluster? A sun roof? Remote control "sport" mirrors? "Styled" wheel covers? What!

Whatever else it may be accused of, the automobile industry is in business to make a profit and it can only make money by inducing you and others to buy as many of their products as you are willing to go into debt for. Originally, you bought only the car. The windshield, as noted, might be extra. However, if you rejected the windshield and bought the Crescent goggles, the manufacturer lost the profit on the windshield. Car history buffs can argue about which car company first offered a windshield as standard equipment, but Hupmobile certainly did in 1912. You still paid for it and Hupmobile made a profit on it, but by calling it "standard" equipment, Hupmobile eliminated the question; you got the windshield whether you wanted it or not and you paid for it either way.

Eventually, the issue disappeared because all cars came with a windshield. However, a hand-operated wiper was optional; once it became standard, a powered wiper became optional, and when it became standard equipment, the optional two-speed wiper appeared, to be followed in turn by intermittent wipers.

The next mutation will be wipers that play "Singing in the Rain" when you turn them on.

At bottom, the options business is a marketing scheme operating in a context of competitive pressure. For years, the domestic industry had a cozy little thing going whereby practically everything but the engine and wheels was optional and, in general, the manufacturer's profit margins on options were better than those on the car. The $3000 for a basic car of around 1960 paid about 10 percent in profits, but the $1000 worth of options that could be put on it paid nearer to 50 percent. (These percentages are reasonably applicable today.) In the cozy days, nobody got greedy and no make of car had significantly more "standard" equipment than another.

Then the foreigners ruined the whole game just the way Hupmobile ruined the windshield option in 1912. They put much of the optional stuff on the car as standard equipment and included its cost (and profit) in the base cost.

"Sure," I heard people say around 1975, "a Toyota costs $1000 more than a Chevette—but look at all the options you get at no extra charge." In sum, people thought they were getting the options free. In any case, the domestic industry had to meet the competition, so cars are now priced with many "options at no extra cost" or as "price includes the following no-cost equipment." Nowadays, air conditioning and an automatic transmission are about the only remaining large-cost options, other than engine options; all the rest—rallye stripe, electric radio antenna, remote-control mirror, etc.—amount to trivia introduced into the constantly escalating options game for the purpose, like a carnival, of finding more diversions for people to spend money on.

Once many quondam options became standard equipment that was included in a base price that had to compete with the base prices of competitive cars, the profit level of extra features no doubt diminished. However, profit levels on true options— things you pay extra for—are still relatively high. This means that options are a good area for bargaining. Unfortunately, you may end up bargaining over things you didn't want in the first place.

A car dealer is simply a middleman between you and the manufacturer and he gets cars in only two ways: either he orders them to hold in stock, or he specifically orders a car at your behest.

If the dealer orders to fill his stock, he has to decide how many coupes, four-doors, station wagons, etc. to order and what accessories to order on each car. In this matter, he gets a great deal of help from the manufacturer; in fact, the manufacturer may all but dictate what he shall order.

"The marketing department believes pinstriping will be very popular this year," says the manufacturer at the dealers' meeting, "and we're going to advertise it heavily. We expect every dealer will want to order at least six cars with the pinstriping option." Although nobody says so, the dealers understand that if they fail to order their quota of pinstripes, they may find their relationship with the manufacturer somewhat strained. Years ago, before the federal government took a greater interest in the car business, dealers might be threatened with loss of a franchise if they didn't order various options. Nowadays, they are under less pressure, but they are not entirely free of it, either. So the dealer orders the pinstripes and then has the job of getting you to pay for them.

Your purpose in buying a car is not to solve the dealer's problems. If the manufacturer imposes on the dealer, that's the dealer's problem. If you don't want the pinstripes, don't pay for them. If that takes money out of the dealer's pocket—well, better his pocket than yours.

Alternatively, the dealer orders a car at your behest. Once you've picked the car you want, the dealer prepares a form that constitutes the formal order. The form has spaces or boxes wherein to note the desired options. Usually, the dealer fills in more boxes than you specify. If you object, the dealer says something like, "They don't like to ship a car with so little extra equipment."

Tell the dealer you don't care what "they" like; you are only interested in what you like. This may provoke some argument, which is fair enough: the dealer is in business to sell stuff; you can't blame him for trying to get you to buy it.

If you read the list of "no-cost options" on a price sticker, you will be surprised at how many items—e.g., glove box lock, interior light, day-and-night rearview mirror—hardly strike you as "extra" features; you have come to expect such things on a car. The list partly reflects escalation in the options war, but it is also a marketing ploy: the long list conveys the impression that you are being blessed with an unusually good deal.

Some of the options offered today would embarrass Louis XIV and others would embarrass a teen-age gadget freak. Cadillac offers a *power* recliner *passenger* seat, a *power* pull-down for the trunk lid, and a fuel filler door that locks when the *power* door locks are activated [italics added], and "accent striping." Chrysler offers a "sport" steering wheel, power radio antenna, an AM/FM radio with 40-channel citizen's band (CB) capability, 10-spoke aluminum wheels (they generously put four in the package), and three-speed wipers. Ford offers as many options, both useful and idiotic, as the other manufacturers do. Their 1982 sales brochures, however, didn't list the options. Rather, prospective buyers were advised to "Ask your Ford Dealer for the latest information on options, prices, and availability." In other words, you couldn't study the options on your own; you had to ask the dealer, and thus open yourself to a sales pitch. The strategy must not have worked, for the 1983 Ford brochures do list the optional equipment.

Be cautious of the options game. Caught up in the warm enthusiasm of the car deal, you readily accept the salesman's urgings. A floor mat for the trunk at $15? Why not. An electrically controlled outside mirror with a built-in thermometer at $40? Sure. Edge guards for all four doors at $30? Of course. An electrically operated sliding sun roof at $1200? You bet! Let's go all the way. When you add up the numbers, the options may well add up to 50 percent of the price of the car, which makes the dealer very happy. After all, you do want to make the dealer happy, don't you?

The options game also recalls Kafkaesque bureaucracy. The car you pick from the dealer's stock has air conditioning and aluminum wheels. You say you don't want them. The dealer says that he'll have to order a car without them, and therefore, you'll have to wait eight months for your new car; the dealer will look long-faced and sad about it, but allege a helplessness to do anything about it.

Of course, the dealer could offer to reduce the price of the options, if you don't want them, but he obviously doesn't like to do that. However, the point remains that you are paying for the car and you should dictate what you pay for. If a dealer can't arrange things at least 95 percent to your liking, you are quite at liberty to go to another dealer and you should not hesitate. When dealers see money walking out the door, their willingness to deal improves markedly.

However, if you are definitely set on a certain car, you have to put up with the situation. For example, a few years ago when the Honda Civic became a very hot item indeed, Honda dealers began selling them for prices above the suggested retail cost. Buyers complained and Honda headquarters made the dealers quit overcharging. The dealers responded to the reproof by ordering Civics with every item of optional equipment, which pushed the selling price and profit margins up to a level more to their liking. The car was so much in demand that if you wanted one at all you had to take the dealer's deal. In this instance, the dealer didn't care if money went out the door, because twice as much was waiting to come in. A similar thing occurred when the Honda Accord appeared, and also with the Volkswagen Rabbit in the 1979–80 "fuel crisis" era. In sum, you don't always get your way, even though you always pay the bill.

Generally, though, and especially with domestic cars, you don't have to be railroaded into buying options you don't want. To simply refuse will usually get you what you do want. Dealers will try every manipulation short of literally twisting your arm to get you to buy options. They will weep about the state of their business, berate you for your lack of social responsibility in not supporting the automotive industry, and tell you that the options in dispute are "very popular." Just keep your hand firmly on your pocketbook and don't give in. Remember, it's your money.

As noted in regard to the Honda Civic story, with foreign cars, you do have less room to maneuver because the dealer is several months or more away from the factory and special orders cannot be quickly arranged. Furthermore, the foreign manufacturers get around you by classifying many options as "standard equipment" and adding them in with the total cost. If the total cost is reasonable, you may as well take the options.

Optional equipment lists vary considerably, given that one engine may be "standard" on one car and "optional" on another, and given that smaller cars are more "stripped" than larger ones. To review some of the more useful and more dubious options.

Two-Door, Four-Door, or Wagon?

Although people don't think of the body type as an option, it's really your first choice. Is a two-door enough? If you've never enjoyed the convenience of getting the groceries out of the rear seat of a four-door, you should try one. However, you should also note that on most four-door cars, the front doors are somewhat shorter, fore and aft, than those on a two-door model. Hence, a large-bodied or infirm person may prefer a two-door for that reason. Similarly, a station wagon gives you four-door size, plus freight capacity; however, you can't put the freight out of sight in a locked-up trunk.

A good rule here is to have an open mind. Even if you feel you know exactly what you want, give the other body types a looking-over. You might be overlooking something.

Transmissions

On some cars an automatic transmission is standard and on others it is optional. Either way, the automatic may include an overdrive (OD) gear for economical cruising.

Whether a manual transmission is standard or optional, it is usually a four-speed; the three-speed of old does not suit smaller engines well (due to torque curves and gear ratios) and so has virtually disappeared. The manual shift option will be a five-speed wherein the fifth gear is an OD gear.

An automatic loses some energy in its torque converter and oil pump and the loss is the greater at low speeds; yet, an automatic may be preferred for a car that spends all its time in city traffic. However, because of the energy loss in an automatic, smaller cars should not have them and, indeed, the automatic transmission option for small cars has rather disappeared.

The energy loss of an automatic transmission causes many people to feel guilty about buying one. Such people take an unnecessarily sensitive view of the matter. An automatic has legitimate uses and serves legitimate purposes. That's why so many military and construction vehicles have automatic transmissions. Furthermore, a goodly number of people do not know how to drive a manual shift. People who grew up in cities ten or twenty or more years ago had a hard time even finding a manual shift to learn on, since most domestic cars were automatics, and driving schools, in those days, did not use many foreign or compact cars.

Have no qualms about the fuel consumption of your automatic. For perspective on the matter, keep in mind that to heat a decent-sized, three-bedroom house during the winter in one of the northern tier states will consume as much as 2000 gallons of fuel oil (effectively the same as diesel fuel), or enough to run an Oldsmobile diesel for five years at 10,000 miles per year, and enough to run a Volkswagen Rabbit diesel about eight years at the same annual mileage. The truly criminal wastage of energy in this country comes from those hideous city traffic jams and those repetitious, interminable lines at toll booths, especially on holidays. This wastage is the fault of those who administer the prevailing political dispensation, not the poor victims suffering the cars, both automatic and manual.

The five-speed manual transmission is good for people who like to shift a lot and for people who spend most of their time on the highway. Otherwise, the fifth gear becomes a sort of useless bother. Most four-speed transmissions are set up so that third gear serves for getting around in traffic. It usually pulls well from about 15 mph up to about 60 mph, so you gain little in traffic from the $150 cost of the five-speed option. Even when on the road in fifth gear, you often find you have to drop down to fourth every time you come to a hill or meet a stiff headwind. While it's a good idea, the five-speed option deserves thorough checking out before buying. Make sure it's what you want. In time, you won't have to choose; like the windshield, the five-speed is rapidly becoming standard on the smaller cars.

Radial Tires

Unless they are European radials, you aren't getting much. Tell the dealer you accept the tires, but not the price for them, and demand a price cut for the trouble you'll have to go through to get rid of the junky tires on the car.

As soon as you buy the car, go get decent radials and put the original tires in the closet. Three years later, when you sell the car, take off your now-bald tires and put the originals back on. Then you say to the prospective buyer: "See? Hardly any wear on the original tires at all!"

Air Conditioning

This is a personal matter, a raw question of whether you are willing to pay for it, originally or in use. However, if you spend most of your time in city traffic, you should have it.

Fundamentally, Americans are Puritans who think they are sinning if they indulge themselves, so they have a guilt complex about air conditioning. They feel sinful about using extra fuel for creature comfort. To allay these feelings, the automobile industry generated the falsehood that the wind drag from driving with open windows consumed more fuel than running an air conditioner. And, as might be expected, the automotive writers still tell people to roll up their windows and turn on the air conditioners to save gas in the summer.

Well, it's not true and never was, but nobody got around to investigating the matter even half-scientifically until fuel consumption and aerodynamics became important here of late. In any event, a pair of researchers did establish that using an air conditioner while cruising at 55 mph imposed about a .7 mpg to 1.6 mpg penalty, depending on the size of the car, while the fuel penalty for driving with open windows was "insignificant."

I was especially pleased at this report, presented at the Society of Automotive Engineers' conference in February 1982, because I have long driven in the summer with open windows and had never been able to convince myself that I was paying a fuel penalty. For example, my gas mileage, even at speeds up to 70 mph, would be the same during daytime, with windows open, that it was at night, with windows closed. Agreed, the results of the one study are not absolute, but the results are good enough. If you don't want air conditioning, don't be ramrodded into buying it on the basis of false claims.

Of course, you have to watch the consequences. Beginning several years ago, Detroit began making the windows in the rear doors of cars so they wouldn't open, on the claim that they were, thus, saving about 20 pounds of weight and, thus, giving car buyers a more economical car. To the car buyer's plea that the car was insufferably stuffy because you couldn't open the rear windows, the manufacturers replied, "Simple. Use air conditioning." Of course, the air conditioner added up to 100 pounds of weight and imposed a fuel penalty, but from Detroit's point of view, it brought in a much more handsome profit than the mechanism that rolls the windows up and down. In any event, if you buy a car that has rear windows that won't roll down, you either have to keep people out of the back seat or buy air conditioning.

Sun Roof

Air conditioning temporarily killed the convertible and the sun roof, but both are coming back. The sun roof has little to recommend it, certainly nothing to justify its cost of $300 to $1200, depending on the car. You can't use it in the winter, and in summer you can get a genuine sunstroke when driving with it open. (In a convertible with the top down, the air flow reduces the problem.) Worst of all, a sun roof may use up one to two inches of the headroom.

A sun roof is worthwhile only on warm summer nights. Try one out on a hot, sunny day before you invest in it.

Trim/Bumper Strips

One genuine nicety that came into vogue about ten years ago (about thirty years overdue) is the little rubberoid strip that runs along the side of the car to absorb the bumps from the door of the car parked next to you. These little strips prevent ugly chips in the paint and are worth the $40 to $50 they cost. The cost is outrageous, considering the material involved, but buying the factory version is better than putting on your own with auto store kits.

Wheel Covers

Wheel covers, or what people call "hubcaps" but which technically aren't hubcaps, are a purely esthetic detail, an esthetic enhancement that is minimal when compared to the cost—$75 for plain ones, and up $250 for a set of pseudo-wire-spoke ones. The fancy wheel cover serves no useful purpose at all. It does not notably improve the aerodynamics of the wheel. All it does is bounce off when you hit a pothole and, thus, require you to buy another to avoid having one naked wheel. The small cover that covers only the circle of lug bolts is quite good enough and much less likely to bounce off. Go simple.

Fancy Wheels

Human vanity being what it is, a lot of people have been persuaded to buy aluminum or chrome-plated wheels that are supposed to look like wire-spoke wheels, flying saucers, or cubistic abstractions. To date, these wheels provide no advantage whatsoever—certainly none commensurate with the $250 to $500 per set they cost. (The manufacturers admit that the energy cost to make a fancy aluminum wheel is about five times the cost of making a pressed-steel wheel.) Some effort has been made to claim that aluminum wheels give the brakes better cooling, but the claims are weak and brakes hardly need extra cooling in a land where 55 mph is the speed limit. Pressed-steel wheels have served well for fifty years. Ignore fancy stuff and don't be badgered into believing it's an improvement on anything but the dealer's profit margin.

If aluminum wheels are significantly lighter than pressed-steel wheels (and not all are), they do reduce the weight of the tire-and-wheel unit, and this reduces the burden on the springs when the wheel bounces up. This reduced "unsprung weight" matters to 1) people who drive fast on washboarded roads and 2) people who drive twisty roads at 90 mph (as they do in Europe). Otherwise, such wheels are just a way of transferring money from various parts of the country to Detroit.

Handling Packages

A handling package usually consists of stiffer springs, stiffer shock absorbers that have different responses to bumps, and stiffer *sway bars*. The purpose of the handling package is to give the car better manners at higher speeds and on rough, twisty roads; that is, to make it drive more like a foreign car.

By offering the package at all, Detroit admits that standard suspension systems aren't what they should be. Personally, I think the handling package should be the standard equipment; then, domestic cars would be as roadworthy as the ordinary European cars. Buy the handling package if it is available. The cost runs from about $90 to $150. The car will have a stiffer ride, but the steering will be less ambiguous and the brakes somewhat better.

Careful here, though; don't confuse the handling package

with a "sport package." A sport package is a lot of gewgawry for people who can't afford a Porsche. The Chevrolet Citation "sport package" costs around $1800 and the only useful part of it is the $100 handling package component.

Rear Sway Bar

The rear sway bar improves the way the car goes around corners. If the rear sway bar is an option, order it, but tell the dealer you expect to get it for dealer cost, not its retail price of about $40, on the contention that the car should have had it in the first place. The dealer will squawk, so you have an item for bargaining.

Power Steering

No car that weighs less than 2800 pounds needs power steering. Above 2800 pounds, power steering is a big help when parallel parking, and that's about its only benefit.

Power steering became the norm for the 5000 pound cars of the 1950s. Once the consumer ice was broken, Detroit began selling power steering for every possible car and so did the foreign manufacturers. Here again, power steering pays profits far out of proportion to its benefit to the driver, so the manufacturers have done their best to make people believe that it is necessary. You can disprove the notion by driving a 1948 Buick, which did not have power steering. Despite its fat, squishy tires and generally soft suspension, the 1948 Buick drove as nicely on the highway as any power-steering car of today. Agreed, being heavy, it was a pig to get in and out of a parallel parking space.

The bad thing about power steering is that it insulates the driver from the road. The system eliminates "road feel." Since people find this loss disconcerting, the system provides artificial "road feel" through hydraulic pressure in the system. The driver does not feel the road; the driver feels hydraulic pressure and takes it for the road.

The need to resort to such artificialities in itself betrays the worst feature of power steering: if powerful enough for parallel parking at idle speed, it is far too powerful at highway speed. Historically, Jaguar and Mercedes-Benz had the more sensitive power-steering systems, but to me, even they didn't have adequate road feel, compared to a car without power steering.

Some handling packages will include adjustments to the power steering to enhance the illusion of road feel. Here again, the existence of the adjustment demonstrates that the original system was designed with the wrong emphasis, to wit, ease rather than control.

In sum, buy power steering on full-size or oversize cars if you do most of your driving in a city. If a car weighs around 3000 ± pounds, testdrive both a power-steering and a manual-steering model before making a buying decision—provided you can find a manual-steering model to testdrive.

As with air conditioning, you may have trouble getting a car without power steering, but if you don't want it, you should get something off the roughly $200 it adds to the cost of the car—and it adds this cost even when it is listed as "standard equipment."

Limited-Slip/Positive-Traction Differential

A limited-slip differential (see page 353) assures equal power to both driving wheels even when traction at the drive wheels is unequal. Buy it. It will be worth twice its price (about $100) in wintry climes with snow and ice and on rough, gravelly roads because the equal traction at both wheels inhibits slithering and slipping.

Towing Package

Towing options may be limited to a wiring harness for trailer lights that costs around $30, and this is enough if you tow rarely or tow only a light load frequently. If you tow heavy loads a lot, go for the full $300–$500 package that consists of stiffer rear springs and shock absorbers, perhaps a factory-installed hitch of a capacity suitable for the vehicle, a plug-in for the trailer lights, an oversize radiator, and for cars with automatic transmissions, a transmission oil cooler.

Halogen Headlights

These are better. They cost about $20 more and are worth five times as much in visibility. Buy if available.

Fog Lights

The other optional lights (other than trunk light, etc.) are fog lights, which are immensely useful to people who drive in areas that have frequent fogs. Alas, fog lights are often buried in a "luxury group" or "touring group" so you can't get them without buying a lot of other stuff you may not want. Where available as an option by themselves, they cost about $100.

Undercoating

Undercoating is an asphalt ("tar")-based coating that is sprayed under the car, in fender wells, etc., presumably to protect the body from rust. Its primary value is that it deadens sound. It is no guarantee against rust. Indeed, when the undercoating ages, it begins peeling off and actually traps dirt and moisture in ways that accelerate rust. In most cases, you'll do better at a proprietary rust-proofing place (e.g., Ziebart, Rusty Jones, etc.). Ultimately, whether the car rusts is largely a matter of what you drive it through and whether you wash it often.

Carnival-Ride Front Seats

Some cars have front seats with power adjustments that go through assorted gyrations, presumably to give you the optimum seating position. Cadillacs even have a built-in memory system that allows the seat to go back to a preset position if somebody changes it. All this stuff is pretentious garbage, useful only for bragging about in the neighborhood bar or among people impressed by such things. Don't pay a cent for it—much less the $200 or so it costs (for one seat).

Rear-Window Defroster

Here again, another option that was thirty years overdue when it appeared and that should be standard equipment (note that a heater did not become standard equipment until about 1950). It should be much more effective than it is, too, but even its marginal effectiveness is better than nothing. In New York State, cars are required to have this option.

Rear-window defrosters that use forced air, as the basic heater does, work best. Unfortunately, most systems use a thin electric wire—that yellow grid in the rear window. With a car full of people on a cold, rainy day, the grid won't keep the rear window clear. Also, it won't melt snow, so you have to brush the window in the wintertime. In extremely cold weather, it may not even keep frost off the window. Despite its limitations, the rear defroster is worth its price of $100 or so.

Automatic Door Locks

A family car needs the system whereby shutting/locking the front doors automatically locks the rear doors. The system is virtually standard now, but if optional, it costs about $100. By contrast, the "security" systems that are supposed to deter car thieves may stop joy-riding delinquents, but they will hardly stop a competent car thief. While the $150 cost of a security system is dubious, it may get you a lower insurance premium, so check on that.

Sound Systems

Nowadays, you can get anything from a basic AM radio to an AM/FM with eight-track stereo and CB (citizen's band) capability. If not standard, an AM radio costs $30 to $50 and an AM/FM runs $75 to $125. The more elaborate radio systems cost $300 to $500, while a full "sound system" will cost over $1000.

Generally, if you only want a basic radio, you may as well take the factory offering, for a radio shop can rarely sell and install a radio for less than the optional-equipment price. However, if you are a hard-core sound freak, you should consult your sound-equipment supplier about the matter, and may prefer to order a car with no radio at all and tailor your own system. Some people spend as much as $2000 this way. In an effort to reclaim some of the money that has gone to this "aftermarket," General Motors now installs Bose sound systems as an option. If you like Bose equipment, you may as well take the option.

In any case, be forewarned that sound equipment is a favored item in the thieves' market, and the better your system, the more likelihood that someone will steal it and leave you with insurance-deductible broken windows and a half-wrecked dashboard. If you have a fancy sound system and park on the street of a large city, restrict the deductible factor of your theft insurance to the $50 or $100 minimum. Also, don't be misled into believing that a "security system" will save your sound system; all your "security system" gives you is something else to repair after the thief is gone.

Electronic Fripperies

Once the electronic industry applied solid-state electronics to pinball-type games, the automotive industry could not resist. Hence, a variety of lights and signals to calculate your gas mileage or to tell you that you left the trunk open. None of this stuff is worth its price. However, since it is standard on some cars, you have to buy it anyway.

One important qualification: Some of these electronic monitoring sytems specify such things as the oil change intervals, others indicate if the oil is low, and others indicate faults in the ignition or fuel system. These are good things. They probably aren't necessary—you can get by without them—but they do, at least, serve a useful purpose.

Cold-Weather Packages

Cold weather brings problems with dead batteries and engines that won't start, so some manufacturers offer an optional "cold-weather package." The "package" may include no more than a larger battery, but it may also include an electric engine heater.

If you live in an area that commonly has temperatures well below freezing, buy the package. If buying a diesel, get the biggest battery and highest-capacity engine heater available. You may not *need* these items, in the sense that you might get by without them. However, an oversize battery only has to save you from the aggravation and cost of one road-service truck to pay for itself.

You may not need the engine heater, either, but once you get in the habit of using it, you will come to love it. Plug it in when you arise (i.e., forsake the comfortable arms of Morpheus), then go about your breakfast, and when you go to leave the house, the engine will start promptly and the heater will be toasty warm.

Even if you have no garage and must park on the street, you can run an extension cord out to the heater on that sub-zero morning when the car won't start and, quite possibly, get it to start once you warm it up. In addition, consistent use of the engine heater in the winter could add as much as 30,000–50,000 miles to the life of an engine.

*

As noted, the dealer will try to sell you every option in the catalog and will claim that you will recover a handsome portion of the options' costs when you trade in several years later. This means that if you add $2000 worth of options to an $8000 car in 1984, the car will be worth $500 more as a trade-in in 1986 or 1987. That much is probably true, but it's hardly a sensible way to manage your money. You should not spend $2000 for options that you don't want for the doubtful pleasure of selling them three years later for $500. The money will be better off in a money-market fund during those three years—and better your fund than the dealer's.

ROAD TEST, NEW CAR

Having reflected at length on your sense of values, having made various lists of what you want in a car, and having shuffled the items on the lists into various hierarchies; and, having studied cars on the street, reviewed the car reviews in public writ, having talked to various people; and, having also consulted your pocketbook and looked into *Edmund's* to measure what you want against what you can afford, you now have a list of possibilities. You are ready to go car shopping.

As with an expedition up the Zambesi River or a visit to the dentist, car shopping involves considerable psychological preparation. Let us skip the preparation for now (saving it for our encounter with the car salesman) and jump ahead to the road test of the car while this matter of values is foremost in our minds.

Generally, the salesman will accompany you on the road test. The salesman does not come along because he's afraid you will steal the car; he comes along to keep some patter going so you won't have an opportunity to concentrate on the car. Hence, you must try to get rid of the salesman. If the salesman won't excuse himself, then bring along a friend to occupy the salesman in a discussion of Hegelian philosophy. This will keep the salesman from saying things like, "See how nice that seat feels?" or "Notice the elegant wood-grain effect on the dashboard—plastic, of course, but still elegant." With the salesman neutralized by a verbose companion, you can study the car without interference.

The road test seeks to answer several questions, each of which has its details. To proceed.

Do you fit?
Get in and out of the car several times. Have your companion get in and out and study the motions. Look for osteotraumatic gyrations and evaluate whether such contortions are tolerable.

Push the seat back until your left foot rests on the floorboard in the place where it will spend its idle time. Note how well the right foot can handle the gas pedal and brake and how easily your arms reach the steering wheel. If the steering wheel is adjustable, try it in several positions. If things don't feel right, move the seat until they do, then check on the left foot again. On some cars, things will never feel right.

Now, hook up the seat belt and shoulder restraint and assess whether the position is comfortable—or will be after half an hour or more. With the seat in the optimum position and the belt hooked up, reach for every control and, for smokers, the ashtray and lighter. Assess the degree of awkwardness or convenience and consider whether you are willing to live with it.

Can you see?
Swivel your head and look out the right rear quarter/door window, as if you had just passed a car and wanted to be sure you were clear before pulling back in front of it. Can you see? Do you care? Many people don't.

Continue the swivel and check the rear window. Do you see blue sky or the road? Can you see any of the car, e.g., the corners of the fenders? Again, do you care?

Swivel to the left and look out the left rear, as if you were pulling onto a freeway. Do you see the world outside or do you see car body? Do you care? Note how many people pull onto freeways without the slightest backward glance; if you're one of these, then visibility is of no concern and you needn't even check the rearview mirror. (You also shouldn't drive.)

Lay a piece of paper on the dashboard and note the reflection in the windshield. The more prominent the reflection, the more interference from all reflections, particularly at night.

Can you move?

Check the pedal motion: When the left foot comes up to get on the clutch, does the left knee hit the dashboard, parking brake release, or the steering wheel? Can the right foot move readily from the gas pedal to the brake, or does the right knee hit the dashboard on the way? How will this affect emergency braking? Do you care?

Can you live in here?

Look for places to put coffee cups, cigarette packs, toll or parking-meter change, a flashlight, notepad and pencil, purse, and other such things as you normally want around you. Consider what you will do about such things.

Evaluate the glovebox and try to avoid laughing: it hardly exists anymore and, consistent with trunk space, the bigger the car, the smaller the glovebox.

With the front seat in the optimum position for you, get in the back seat. Can you? Could a larger person? Once seated, do your feet fit? Obviously, if the rear seat serves only as a place to lay a coat, its usefulness for people does not matter, but a carpooler or the head of a family will want to put people back there. Will they fit?

You are now ready to start playing with the controls and will soon be in motion. When road testing a brand-new car, don't worry about clicks and grunts when it gets under way. They may be inherent in the car or may arise from mechanical faults. Either way, you can sort them out later. Do note the noises, though, and ask the salesman what they are.

Can you work the controls?

With an automatic transmission, note how well the gear-lever movement separates one gear from another. When you pull down from "Park" without looking, are you certain whether you are in "reverse" (first notch) or "neutral" (second notch); likewise, are the separations positive when moving up from "1" to "2" to "3" (or from "low" to "2" to "D")? Is the gear lever vulnerable to other motions? For example, does reaching for the radio knobs offer to bump it into another position?

Move the turn-signal lever. Do you need both hands, or will a fingertip move it, and which suits your style? Listen to the sound of the flasher: is it loud enough to remind you that you're signaling if you forget to watch the indicator light(s)?

Try the horn. Can you find it without thinking, or do you have to deliberately recall where it is and how to sound it?

Likewise, try the headlight dimmer. If foot actuated, can you handle it with the shoes you commonly wear, e.g., thick soles, high heels, etc.?

Try the ignition switch. How much manipulating do you have to go through to get the key out? To shut off buzzers and warning lights?

Hold the clutch down to relieve pressure on the gears and move the manual transmission lever through all gears. Don't worry if the motion is stiff and notchy, for the lever will loosen up as a new car gets some wear on it. Rather, note where your hand goes. Do you hit your own or the passenger's knee when going into reverse? Do you hit the dashboard when going into first or third?

Look for the parking brake. Could you really use it as an "emergency brake," or is its handle or pedal impossible to reach in a hurry?

Check the parking-brake release. Will you confuse it with the hood-latch release? Will it (or the hood release) snag pantyhose or the hem of a skirt?

Can you drive it?

Having surveyed the important controls (and adjusted the rearview mirror), you are ready to get under way. Before proceeding on the road test, first proceed to a service station with an air hose and increase air pressures by 10 percent or to the pressure recommended for highway driving. Manufacturers' recommended "normal" pressures are all too low. The salesman will object, saying you will spoil the "soft ride," so tell the salesman that you're buying the car and that you'll be driving it, not him.

Keep in mind, too, that the purpose of the test is to find out how you and the car get along. It is not a test of mechanical quality, for the mechanical quality of any modern car can be assumed to be good enough. (Performance quality, however, is a different matter.)

Drive the car normally and see if it exhibits any capriciousness. Does the suspension keep it going straight or does rough pavement cause it to wander? Turn some corners faster than you think you ought to: do you find yourself fighting with the steering wheel? Does the car lean and sway in an alarming manner? Go out on an interstate for several miles: does the steering wheel need lots of attention? How adeptly will the car make a sudden lane change? Is the passing acceleration good enough?

And how noisy is it? Does the wind sound like ripping canvas or like a baby's sigh? Can you talk to the passenger? Hear the radio at anything but maximum volume?

Check out the heater and ventilation system. On some cars, the aerodynamics are so bad that you have to run the blower at full speed to get fresh air into the car at highway speed. The Chevrolet Chevette sins badly in this respect, so hot weather entails the additional annoyance of having to listen to the blower.

Open a window, as you might when wanting some fresh air: does the air current flap your left ear and knock the passenger's hat off? Have the passenger open the window on that side: how do you react to those air currents?

Leave front windows closed: "crack" a rear window an inch or two, and study the air currents, for this arrangement usually gives the best ventilation on the highway.

Pass a tractor-trailer and note how the air currents buffet the car as you approach the end of the trailer and as you pass the front end of the tractor: is the car stable, or will you be afraid to pass a truck if you buy it?

Let the car wander off the right shoulder of the pavement— but keep both hands on the wheel: this could jerk. Note how drastically the suspension and steering react. Then, pull the car back onto the road: does it come easily? If you had to make such a maneuver to avoid a collision, how much confidence does the car give you?

Put the salesman and your companion in the rear seat and see how the car reacts to weight back there. Agreed, you may not intend to haul extra people, but you need to have some idea of how the car will behave if you do. Of course, if you car-pool, a full-load test is crucial.

You may ignore the brakes in this test. To test them properly, you need some way to measure the exact moment you apply them and the exact moment when the car stops, and even if you could do that, you might find as much as a 15 percent difference in stopping distance over several trials. In addition, your test wouldn't apply to hot weather when the brakes can't dissipate heat so fast but when the pavement may be sun-softened and sticky, nor indicate cold weather braking when the brakes can dissipate heat faster. In this matter, refer to the car magazine road tests, but view the stopping distances as comparative, not absolute, i.e., compare one car to another to get a relative notion of the quality of brakes.

If you go through several drills of this sort, you will find that no car is perfect; some, such as the Mercedes-Benz 380 SEC coupe, come close, but cost up to $50,000. Whatever you choose will be a compromise. However, you will be paying the bill and you will be driving the car, so you should choose the area(s) of compromise. In this reference, don't listen to the salesman. The salesman will say, "Well, yes, the seat does seem a little awkward—but you'll get used to it." The salesman does not have to live with the seat; you do. Or, the salesman says, "Yes, the glovebox doesn't amount to much, but you'd be surprised how much stuff you can put in your coat pockets, and your flashlight can go under the seat. You'll never miss a large glovebox." If you accept the tiny glovebox, do so for your reasons, not the salesman's. To be successful, the salesman doesn't have to be right; he only has to get your money, after which the problems are yours—after all, you paid a good price for them.

USED CAR

The ordeal of buying a car is much the same whether the car is new or used, so before we beard the dealer-lion in his lair, we should examine the used-car business.

The definitive word here is *used*. A used car is not a new car; that's why it doesn't cost as much. Since a used car is not new, you should not expect it to be in new car condition. If it is, good; if not, that simply means it lives up to its classification—"used."

The great fear when buying a used car, of course, is that it will suffer some grievous (and expensive) mechanical failure shortly after purchase. The validity of this fear is largely a matter of age and past history of the car. Obviously, the older a car, the more likely it is to have problems. Likewise, a car that has gone through multiple owners, all equally careless, has the odds against it, as does a one-owner car if the original owner dumped the car because of some impending disaster.

The problem of buying a used car is that of assessing its condition and predicting its future, and no one can do this with absolute certainty. I have driven cars with audibly "loose rods" for several months without having them come apart on me, although I had to drive slowly the while. This does not mean you should buy a car with a loose connecting rod; it means that even with a loose rod, you can't be sure whether the engine will last one more day or six more months.

Dealers do not want to mess around with cars that have serious, definable defects. They want to sell cars, not repair them, and they know full well that nobody wants a car that makes funny noises. Hence, while you should be suspicious, you can assume that the cars you find on used-car lots are presumably in sound condition.

People have an unreasonable fear of used cars because habits of fifty years ago hang around like a miasma over the used-car business. Back in the 1930s, used-car dealers put SAE 90 gear oil in engines to quieten loose rods and stuffed overripe bananas into differentials to dampen the whine of worn gears. At least, I am told such things were done. However, as acutely as I have watched and listened, I have never known of a dealer to do either of these things in the near-thirty years I have been studying cars. In fact, I suspect the practice was rare anytime, given that the civil law pertinent to fraud has been around longer than cars. Here of late, the law gets additional help from the consumer-protection business and while frauds do occasionally occur, most used-car dealers have no desire to spend any time in a courtroom. Be a narrow-eyed buyer, but don't be paranoid.

In this reference, note that cars that survive the first few difficult miles, with or without repairs, usually settle down to a fairly trouble-free existence until quite old. This means that a car with only 5000 miles on it is still in its vulnerable stage, while a car with 25,000 miles on it has lived through that stage: everything that is likely to go wrong has already gone wrong and has been repaired. The car has been immunized, so to speak. For this reason, disparaging reports about a car's "repair record" don't mean much. So a certain 1979 car has a high repair record: what does that mean in 1983? Answer: nothing, for all those repairs were made in the first year or two.

Now, while we don't anticipate major failure with a used car, we do anticipate normal wear and tear. Indeed, that's often why the previous owner traded in. Normal wear and tear is no reason to reject a *used* car; rather, plan to spend some money to replace/repair the common expendable items and then proceed in peace. These common items include the cooling system hoses, drive belts, the battery and its cables, brake linings, tires, universal joints, rubber bushings in the suspension, wiper blades, and light bulbs. When these items on a used car look (or sound) dubious, include the repair costs in your negotiations about the price. A car with no defects, of course, would be preferable, but such defects as these are no reason to reject an otherwise sound car. Fix the defect and go. Then you know that those parts aren't going to give trouble.

Of course, the more fixing, the more you should get off the price. And, of course, you can quickly reach a point of diminishing returns. This means the financial elements of a used-car deal are more complex.

To shop for a used car, first decide on two or three makes/ models that will serve your purpose, then study them closely on the street. For example, you will note that Datsuns and BMWs often have their front tires worn out on the inside; this is because a *MacPherson Strut* suspension tends to go spraddle-legged with age. It does not mean the cars are bad cars; it means the owners have not invested in timely adjustments.

However, it also means the used-car dealer will slap on a pair of cheap, new tires to hide the problem and it means that if you buy a Datsun, BMW, or other MacPherson Strut car with, e.g., more than 20,000 miles on it, you may have to have its front end aligned, maybe even have its struts rebuilt.

So check out cars on the street. Look at tire wear. Note patterns of rust. Look for windshields that are scratched because the windshield washer never works. Note the rust at the bottom of windshields and rear windows, for rust there means water leaks.

As noted in reference to burned valves in '73 model cars (see page 331), some cars have congenital defects that don't show up for a while. For example, in '75 and '76, Chevrolet put a good transmission in the Chevette. Then they found a corner to cut in the '77 transmission and, as a result, the reverse gear often went out on that year's model. Chevrolet did not recall the cars, since the defect was not safety-related, but they did issue a "Service Bulletin" to dealers declaring that the cars were to be repaired under warranty even if they were beyond warranty limits. A lot of cars have similar skeletons lurking in their closets. This does not mean such cars should be avoided, but only that such defects should be anticipated. The defect may be a bargaining counter in the purchase and, in any case, being forewarned is worthwhile.

So, go to a Brand X dealer and address the service manager thus: "I'm thinking of buying a Brand X car from my brother-in-law, who is a notorious liar. He says the car is perfect. I wonder if any 'Service Bulletins' were issued on the car; that is, what should I anticipate and can this shop fix it if it happens?"

The service manager may sniff some business and decide to be helpful. He may say, "Yes, the universal joints up to serial number thus-and-which tend to go bad, but we have them in stock and can replace them for so much money."

This being the case, the Brand X car need not be rejected for its bad U-joints; rather, let the repair cost figure into the whole transaction.

On the other hand, the service manager may not want to volunteer the information, lest it be an admission of fault in the marque. In this case, call the manufacturer's zone representative in your area. Zone representatives are charged with solving consumer complaints and they know about the Service Bulletins for their cars.

Recalls are a different matter, since they involve safety. However, a dealer should be able/willing to supply the recall list for a particular car. If not, reject that dealer and get the list from NHTSA.

Okay, time to go tire kicking.

When you approach a used car, your purpose is to identify its defects and determine whether additional defects will shortly appear. This means a thorough front-to-back-and-underneath inspection (which means wear old clothes). Take along a mechanically inclined friend if you have one; if not, and if enough money is involved, you might pay a mechanic to perform the inspection.

Your mechanically apt friend will ask no more than a drink at the corner bar after you're through shopping, but the mechanic will require a minimum of $15 and will require up to $50 for a truly thorough check that includes a compression test to assess piston rings and valves. You can spend a lot of money just having candidate cars looked over. You can try to escape the costs by asking the mechanic to "Drive it around the block once and see what you think." So the mechanic drives around the block, feels the car pull to the left when he puts on the brake, and declares, "The caliper on the right is stuck. Won't cost much to fix it." You buy the car and discover that the caliper is not the problem. Rather, the problem is leaking in the front half of the master cylinder, which means the car has long been running with only two-wheel brakes, and that means the brake linings are unevenly worn and you need a total overhaul of the whole braking system. So, did you spend your cursory $15 wisely, or just waste it? Would you be willing to spend $25 for a more thorough diagnosis, and then reject the car after spending your $25? How shall you deal with the matter?

The question has no easy answer. Perhaps the better policy is to talk to the mechanic first. Ask if the candidate car has a reputation for particular problems and whether a decent fee for evaluation will get you a discount on repairs if you buy the car. Nowadays, repair shops operate in a seller's market and they are under no pressure to grant concessions, but ask anyway.

In some cities you can find diagnostic centers that put a car on a machine and run a series of tests that presume to indicate the condition of wheels, drive shafts, axles, etc. I have no use for such systems because the diagnostic form with all its little boxes and numbers doesn't answer the question of, "So what?" The machine can detect an alignment fault, but can't separate a ball joint from an A-arm bushing from a wheel bearing from a bent strut, and the operator of the machine never looks beyond the machine. The diagnosis can measure rear axle end play, but can't specify its significance. Such a diagnosis calls for competent evaluation, but all the customer gets is a piece of paper with a bunch of disturbing remarks on it. Machines and standardized forms have their uses, but they are no substitute for intelligent inspection.

While numerical processes are tedious, they are organized. Hence, to proceed. (You will find explanations of technical terms in the Glossary.)

1. Look at the front tires, for uneven tread wear betrays front-suspension defects. However, used-car salesmen know this, too, and they know that people have been taught to look at the front tires, so they move the rear wheels to the front, since no one ever looks at the rear tires. So, look at the rear tires, too. If the front tires look good but the rears have an improper wear pattern, assume the rears were recently on the front and expect to give the car a proper front-end alignment.

2. Look at the steering wheel; if it is cocked when the wheels are straight ahead, then somebody once replaced tie-rod ends and didn't center the steering wheel properly. On worm-and-sector systems (page 362), this will create sloppiness in the steering wheel when the wheels are pointed straight ahead. On both worm-and-sector and rack-and-pinion systems, the cocked steering wheel will often cause the turn signal lever to cancel prematurely when you signal for the direction opposite to the way the wheel is cocked, and it may obscure the instruments.

The cocked steering wheel may also betray improper toe-in/ toe-out; chances are that the tires toe out, so study tread wear closely.

3. Resist the salesman's eagerness to get you into the car and to start it up. Ask to look under the hood first. The salesman will smile, for he knows the engine has been steam- or solvent-cleaned and will pass a white-glove test, that all the evil-looking oil leaks have been washed away.

As the hood goes up, look up at the underside just behind the latch. If you see a rusty, brown line, that's where the fan blades slung water, and that means the car overheated and boiled over sometime, perhaps several times (and the guy with the cleaning hose never thought to look up there and clean it off). If the radiator hoses look brand new, these signs confirm the suspected overheating.

The car thus becomes suspect: overheating takes the temper out of the piston rings and leads to excessive oil consumption. Indeed, overheating may have reduced lubrication and caused scoring in the cylinders.

Say something like, "I never understood which part is the 'head' and which part is the 'block.'" The salesman will eagerly show off his knowledge and point out which is which, so look carefully at the line where the two join: does the gasket look new? If so, the car probably overheated and blew its head gasket. However, the new gasket won't cure the bad rings or weakened bearings that might have accompanied the overheating. You'll want a credible explanation for that new head gasket before you buy the car.

4. Oil leakage from under the valve cover or from side covers is of no consequence, for those gaskets can easily be replaced. However, severe leakage could mean the oil once got so low that the bearings and rings were oil starved. Note the leakage, but reserve judgment.

More important, look for oil leaks at the rear of the engine, down low, behind the sump portion of the oil pan. This area will be virtually impossible to see, so look for oil on the body metal above the transmission, for this is where air flow carries oil from the rear of the engine.

Oil at the crankshaft may come from the rear crankshaft seal;

as the crankshaft bearings wear out, the looseness allows the crankshaft to wallow out the seal, so leakage suggests the bearings are close to terminal.

Be careful here, though; oil from the valve cover can create a false impression of a leaking rear seal, so try to trace the oil to its source. If the car appears otherwise sound, but seems to have a serious oil leak, have a mechanic inspect the leak specifically.

5. Pulling the dipstick in the engine proves nothing. Clean oil may mean a recent change, not a good engine; black oil, especially in a diesel, may mean no more than that the oil is doing its proper job of holding carbon particles in suspension so they don't form sludge inside the engine.

6. An automatic transmission dipstick is more indicative; the oil should have a healthy, reddish look (somewhat like a well-made Côtes du Rhône wine). A shift toward brown is a bad sign (as in wine), especially if the oil has an acrid, burned odor. An automatic transmission can have these signs and still work well, but the signs betray neglect (no oil changes over the years) or abuse (jackrabbit takeoffs, pulling a trailer). The suspicion may be reason enough to reject the car—nobody needs to buy a defective automatic transmission. However, if the transmission shifts smoothly, then assume an oil change and adjustments for it and don't reject it.

7. If convenient, remove the cap on the brake master cylinder and check the fluid: is it clear, or a dirty, blackish brown? If dirty, assume the brakes have never had attention, which means they are probably ready for it. Dirty fluid down in the cylinders may have formed sludge deposits, and to reline the brakes will push the pistons in the wheel cylinders into this sludge and make them leak. Don't reject the car outright, but make a question mark about the brakes. They may need a total overhaul—new linings and new cylinders.

On cars with vacuum-assisted brakes, the master cylinder will be bolted to the vacuum booster (which is itself bolted to the *firewall*). The booster, black and round, looks somewhat like two shallow bowls stuck together at their rims. The vacuum hose from the engine usually enters the booster on the forward side, above or below the master cylinder itself, which protrudes forward.

Check the hose connection to the booster and the joint where the two halves of the booster join (e.g., the "rims" of the "bowls"). Oiliness at either place indicates a leak whereby the engine can suck brake fluid out of the system, and that means a new booster.

8. Look for pollution-control hoses that have been disconnected and plugged with screws and such like. People who disconnect elements of the pollution-control system rarely know what they are doing and they upset the balance of the several elements. On pre-1972 cars, the upset is not serious and is less serious on smaller engines. The importance of balance increases after 1973, so regard loose, plugged hoses suspiciously. They suggest a car that may not idle well or may stall readily.

9. Look at the battery: an obviously old battery with its cable terminals covered with the green or white fuzz of corrosion is a good sign, for it shows that the car has been starting well for a long time and probably has no charging problems. A brand-new battery raises questions of "Why?" For example, did the car get hard to start and does this mean the starter was so frequently overheated that its demise is imminent? Or did the alternator have to work overtime, so that it, too, is near retirement? An ancient battery that hasn't been disturbed in years precludes these problems.

10. On many cars, the upper end of the shock absorber is visible from under the hood. New shocks are not necessarily a good sign, for they raise the question of why somebody put new shocks on a car and then traded it in.

11. Old, dry, cracked hoses for the radiator and heater are also good signs; they show that a hose never broke, that the cooling system has never given trouble, and the car has not overheated.

12. Old, cracked spark plug wires indicate neglect, but they are no reason to reject a car. A car that runs with bad wires will run better with new ones.

13. Look at the base of the carburetor for a reddish deposit. The reddish color comes from elements in gasoline that remain when gasoline evaporates. Heavy deposits indicate persistent flooding, even if of a mild type that never kept the car from running. However, heavy deposits imply an excess of gasoline in the oil over the years and, possibly, excessive wear from oil dilution. A little of this tinge is virtually unavoidable, but a lot of it is a negative detail.

14. On most cars, the steering box for worm-and-sector steering will be accessible on the left side under the hood. Because of the way the collapsible steering column is made, the steering-wheel shaft will be exposed. Grasp it and turn it back and forth just enough to take up the looseness in the steering box; then, twist more firmly while watching to see how much the tie rods move before the wheels react. If the steering shaft is not accessible or if the tie rods can't be seen, transfer this test to the steering wheel.

What you are trying to do is find the looseness in the steering system elements. If one part moves but the next one doesn't, then the joint between them is obviously loose.

Alternatively, stand beside the car with the door open and move the steering wheel to and fro enough to take up loose motion; note how far the steering wheel turns before the wheels respond. The looseness may mean only that the steering box needs adjustment. However, on a rack-and-pinion system, the adjustment is harder to make.

15. Some used-car buying guides say to grab the top of the front wheel and rock it back and forth to assess the ball joints. All you will get from this exercise is dirty hands. With the weight of the car on the wheel, you can't produce enough motion—or certainly can't produce motion with the necessary finesse—to tell anything.

However, do get down low and look at the rims; are they bent at the edge? Bends indicate forceful encounters with curbs and potholes and such encounters cause front-end faults.

16. Generally, reject any car that has aftermarket aluminum or pseudo-magnesium wheels. Likewise, reject a car that has those wheels that put the tires significantly farther out from the car. These are two of the favorite changes made by the loud-muffler *macho* element, and such cars have usually been used for egotistic expression. Rims that put the tires 'way out put improper loads on wheel bearings, axles, and suspension components and such cars drive badly.

17. Go to the tailpipe, stick your finger in it, and make a swipe on the inside surface (ugh!). Study the deposit: whitish to whitish-tan means a car running well; black and velvety means a car running fuel rich, which usually means one used in stop-and-go traffic. Neither condition is cause for concern.

Oiliness, however, is: if the deposits inside the tailpipe seem oily, the car is using lots of oil.

The reason could be as simple as a bad positive-crankcase-ventilation (PCV) valve, as complex as an imbalance in the vacuum hoses of the pollution-control system, or as extensive as bad rings and valves. Severe oiliness at the tailpipe means try another car.

18. Open the trunk. If recent rains have left it full of water, note the defect as a bargaining counter; likewise, if old rains have left it lined with rust.

Examine the spare wheel. If it is mangled, then it was on the ground once upon a time and the car suffered through whatever mangled the wheel.

If rust does not show on the outside of the car, look in the fender wells inside the trunk. A collection of dirt and debris, especially if damp, suggests that rust will shortly be coming through the fenders.

19. People are often told to push down hard on the fender of a car and see how much the car bounces. Lots of bouncing is supposed to reveal bad shocks.

This is a useless test; to do it properly requires two or three people to bounce the car hard enough and requires a refined knowledge of how much the car should bounce anyway. Some cars have shock absorbers that allow the car body to go down quickly (the "jounce"), but come up slowly (the "rebound"), and others are the opposite. Unless you know how the shocks are supposed to act, you can't prove much by heaving on the fenders. The only way to test shocks is to drive over a rough road. Generally, assume that shocks are good for 30,000 miles of moderately hard driving and for 50,000 miles of moderate driving, and expect to replace them accordingly. Note that driving on interstate highways at 60 mph constitutes easy driving where the suspension is concerned.

20. Okay, time to get inside. A car that gave good service to its previous owner will show wear on the seat and the floor mats; that is, wear at such places is normal and is nothing to be alarmed about.

However, one factor deserves close inspection: look where the right heel rests for evidence of rust. Snow and mud fall off shoes and collect there; if left, they grind away the floor mat and leave a damp lump of dirt that provokes rust. Evidence of this sort of thing suggests that the previous owner was a slob who didn't clean the car and an owner who was a slob inside the car may well have been a slob about maintenance, too.

21. Test the clutch pedal for free play; it should move about one-half inch to one inch before it takes up the slack in the linkage.

If the pedal goes a long way before it takes up the slack, the clutch needs adjustment.

If the pedal hardly moves at all before it takes up its slack, it has probably just been adjusted too far or the clutch disc is worn too thin and is ready for replacement.

22. On cars with power-assisted brakes, you can't tell much about the brakes until the engine is running.

23. Okay, time to crank up: give the gas pedal two full pushes to the floor, then take your foot completely away, and try the starter. If the car has electronic fuel injection, don't push the gas pedal.

On some used-car lots, someone goes around and cranks up every car every day. On others, cars go awhile between crank-ups, so don't be put off by a car that doesn't start right away.

Be acutely conscious of the noises the engine makes as it starts, and note how quickly the oil-pressure light goes off or the oil-pressure gauge registers pressure. Don't be quick to condemn if an oil-pressure gauge takes several seconds to respond, for some gauges are just slow to react. However, if clattering noises arise as the engine starts and diminish as the oil pressure rises, assume a worn, loose engine. That car will do for "around town," as a "take-me-to-the-train-station," and for trips at low speeds (40–50 mph), but a noticeably noisy engine is obviously undesirable for most purposes.

However, try to separate the clicking of loose valves or that of hydraulic lifters that have "run down"—had the oil leak out of them—from other noises, for valve train noises do not condemn a cold engine, especially one that has not been run for a while.

24. Drops of water from the exhaust pipe are condensation and are normal. A puff of black smoke at crank-up means you gave the car too much gas or that the automatic choke holds too tightly. A mere puff that goes away is of no consequence.

If black smoke continues, the engine is getting too much fuel; it is overrich. This implies some adjustment of the carburetor and suggests a close look at all the pollution-control elements.

Constant black smoke from a diesel means the same thing: too much fuel and a need for adjustments.

A puff of blue-gray smoke at crank-up that persists for a minute or two means oil consumption. If the smoke stops as soon as the engine warms up and the internal parts expand to fit each other, the blue-gray smoke is of little consequence.

During your road test, punch the gas pedal all the way to the floor while running at highway speed and watch in the mirror for a puff of smoke; then, watch for smoke again as you let off the gas pedal.

A modest puff of smoke—no more than a bagful—in this test suggests the engine will use about one quart of oil in about 1000 miles. That may be acceptable to you.

A constant outpouring of blue-gray smoke means rings or valve guides are gone; pay scrap-iron price for such a car (then buy a rebuilt engine from Sears or a used one from a wrecking yard, have a shop install it, and end up with a bargain).

25. After the engine has warmed enough to idle, run it at a brisk idle and see if the power steering works smoothly: bumpy motion means something wrong—maybe low pressure from the pump, maybe faults in the valve system, or stickiness in the hydraulic piston.

26. Try the brake pedal: if it goes a long way, assume new brake linings will be needed. If it feels rock hard, assume the wheel cylinders or calipers are rusted and stuck and assume the cylinders/calipers will have to be rebuilt or replaced.

27. With parking brake set, put an automatic in "D" and listen to the sounds. A mild grunt as the gears engage is okay. More important, listen for a pronounced "clunk" underneath and to the rear; in a front-wheel-drive (FWD) car, the clunk will be near the front wheels. Now, move the gear lever to "R" and listen to the clunk as the drive shaft turns the opposite way.

The clunk may be from normal slack in the differential gears. Or it may be from abnormal slack in the differential gears. It may be from worn universal/*constant-velocity* (CV) joints in the drive shaft or in the *half-shafts* of a front-wheel-drive car. With FWD, you can watch the shafts from under the hood and note whether they make a portion of a turn before they start to turn the wheels, but with front-engine, rear-drive cars, you have to lie flat on your back and look underneath to watch the drive shaft during the shift from "D" to "R."

The same test applies to manual shift cars too. Just ease up the clutch enough to take up the slack in the drive train in low gear, then again in reverse.

Bad universal joints in a drive shaft are no problem: just replace them. Bad constant-velocity joints in front-wheel-drive cars are a more expensive proposition and the price of the car should reflect the fact that repairs may be needed.

Pollution control has brought higher idle speeds and more impact on gears when a car goes into gear. As a result, differential gears usually have some slack. As much as one eighth of a drive-shaft turn is probably okay. Years ago, when I didn't know enough to be discriminating (I know now, but can't afford it), I would accept a vehicle with more than one-eighth of a drive-shaft turn of slack in its differential gears and I owned several with that much or more slack. I turned down invitations to drag race, engaged the clutch smoothly and gently, and drove such vehicles for a year or two before getting tired of them. I towed cars and heavy trailers short distances with them and towed light boat trailers longer distances, and never broke a differential gear—except the one that lost its oil. The repair manuals (properly) object to excess slack in the gears, but I have decided that, if you don't mind the "clunk" and are willing to avoid harsh shifts and brutal clutch action, a sloppy differential will go on forever. Of course, it shouldn't be asked to do heavy-duty towing and it should never lack for oil.

28. Okay, release the parking brake and take off. If the parking brake wouldn't hold the car, it may only need adjustment; or it may need new cables or the brakes may need new linings. You can't tell from the driver's seat.

29. Different cars locate the fulcrum for the clutch linkage in different places, and these differences, in turn, cause different responses at the pedal when the clutch disc wears thin. On most, a worn clutch allows the pedal to go farther before the clutch disengages; thus, if the clutch goes all the way to the floor, adjustment will usually fix things. However, if the clutch pedal rides high and does not engage the clutch until the pedal is all the way up, adjustment may not fix it, so assume a new clutch.

Hard shifting usually means the clutch is not separating totally, that the engine continues to turn the gears even after the clutch is depressed. Adjustment may fix it—or may not; the car may need a new clutch disc. The point here is that hard shifting rarely condemns the transmission itself.

As with the new car, stop at a service station and inflate the tires to 10 percent above the manufacturer's recommended pressure, then proceed to a road test. A plate near the door latch will give you the manufacturer's recommended pressures.

30. The test for a manual transmission has a brutal aspect, but you have to do it. Find a clear road or street, put the car in first, and speed up to about 15 mph. Then, as quickly as possible, punch the gas pedal to the floor and then completely release it. The car will surge forward under power, then slump forcibly when the power comes off. Before the car has fully recovered from the slump, punch the gas and get off again; then, do it again.

What you're trying to do is make the car jump out of gear; each successive time, let the car go faster before letting off the gas. However, don't continue the test beyond about 25 mph in first gear.

If this test "throws a rod" out of the engine, don't buy the car.

Repeat this test in each gear; start the test at about 15 mph in first, about 20 in second, and about 30 in third and fourth. Do reverse, too.

If the car jumps out of gear, either the thrust washers that hold the gears the right distance apart or the bearings the gears turn on are worn. A car that will tolerate a great deal of brutalizing before it pops out of gear will probably give no trouble in normal driving. However, it may pop out when climbing up a steep driveway. The quicker the car pops out of gear in the test, the quicker it will pop out of gear under severe load.

Don't assume you can hold a gear lever in gear by hand. I have bent gear levers or had them pull me out of the seat when the gear decided to pop out. In other words, don't try.

Besides the annoyance, as a gear pops out, it damages the gear teeth in the synchronizing clutches in the transmission. Soon, they don't exist anymore. Jumping out of reverse will shear off gear teeth on the reverse idler gear.

Summary: if the gears stay in under normal driving conditions, and pop out only under extreme provocation, the car will probably be good for thousands of miles of ordinary driving. If the gears pop out easily, the transmission needs new thrust washers, and maybe bearings, too.

A gear lever that vibrates mildly is no cause for concern, but a really active chattering indicates sloppy synchronizers or worn bearings. Such a transmission *can* go a long time before it starts jumping out of gear, but don't depend on that fact. Take the pessimistic view.

31. Assuming the transmission did not disassemble itself in its test, proceed to the roughest, most-washboarded pavement you can find and put the car over it briskly. If it offers to slither badly, it needs new shocks.

32. If the muffler falls off in this test, don't leave it lying in the road. If it stays on, the exhaust system is probably sound. Check more thoroughly by holding a gloved hand firmly over the end of the exhaust pipe and listening for leaks.

33. Test brakes carefully. The object is to find out if the car pulls to one side. Speed up to about 25 mph and put the brakes on firmly, with hands loosely on the wheel, ready to assert control. Increase test speeds and braking force.

If the car pulls, it obviously needs attention, but of what kind?

Say it pulls to the right: this means the left brake is not doing its share, but why? Because of a stuck cylinder/caliper, or because the left front-wheel bearing is looser than the right? On the other hand, the suspension system bushings on the right side may be battered out and the braking force may be cocking the right front wheel. Either way, something is not right. Either reject the car or subject it to fuller analysis.

34. With a front-engine, rear-drive car, put a block of wood in front of a front wheel and apply some power to force the wheel against the block, then put a second block behind the wheel. With the wheel thus "scotched" on both sides, apply slight power forward and in reverse, but not enough to roll over the blocks.

The object of this exercise is to see if the rear wheels will move the car body without moving the front wheels. Any such motion—the body moves but the front wheels don't—will usually be less than one inch, but even that one inch comes out of the suspension system bushings and will be quite enough to cause road walking and excessive tire wear.

This test works best on bigger cars; small cars, with smaller bushings, won't exhibit great differences. Also, don't misread upward motion of the body as fore-and-aft motion.

Sometimes this test will produce a "grunch" sound; that's usually a bad ball joint.

This test does not work with front-wheel-drive cars, though you can get a little of the same effect by scotching the rear wheels.

If the car passes all the above tests, it is better than 50 percent of the cars on the road. If it is still a candidate for purchase, the next step is to get underneath, and this really means a service station lift.

35. The object of the lift, besides a good look, is to get the weight off the front tires but still have the weight on the springs. Absent a lift, a floor jack under the suspension will do. With weight off a front wheel, move it in and out at top and bottom and see where the motion comes from. It will be at the wheel bearing (no problem; adjust) or at the ball joint (bad: costs money). Sometimes this test will reveal wear in A-frame and strut bushings, too.

36. Move the wheel to and fro as if steering and look for slack, usually at tie-rod ends or at the idler.

37. Look for engine mounts that are ready to give up (presuming they didn't give up during #30).

38. Note oil leaks.

39. Check slack in universal joints and in differential gears, i.e., see how much the drive shaft will move before the drive wheels react. On FWD cars, turn each half-shaft.

40. Check the fuel lines and brake lines for severe rust, which is bad.

41. Look for incipient rust in fender wells and other such cavities that collect mud, for example, above the headlights.

42. Jack up each rear wheel in turn, grasp each rear wheel, and push inward and outward; the motion will be the rear-axle "end play." The proper motion may be as little as .006″ for some cars and as much as .015″ for others, .015″ being about the thickness of a matchbook cover. Smaller cars exhibit less excess end play after many miles, but big cars may show as much as .125″, or one-eighth of an inch.

Excessive rear-axle end play does not indicate something is about to break. Cars can and do go very far with excessive end play. Unless someone has fixed them, any of the bigger General Motors cars from 1965 on up that have over 50,000 miles on them will have double or treble the end play they should and no one worries about it (since they don't know the end play is there).

Excessive rear-axle end play, however, does allow the rear tires to stay in one place while the car body slides from side to side. Even though the body may move sideways only, e.g., .025″ at the rear axle, when that .025″ is multiplied by the length of the car, it has more effect on the front wheels. In sum, the car will road walk mildly and for no apparent reason. A lot of useless front-end alignment jobs have been done to correct road walking that came from rear-axle end play.

On some cars, adjusting rear-axle end play is easy and on others it is a major operation. As noted, virtually any full-size car with 50,000 + miles will have excessive end play; yet nothing will break. The problem becomes one of tolerance, not necessity.

43. While under the car, check out the electrical wiring, if it is exposed. Wires may be ready to break and connectors may be so corroded that they will not carry electricity. Hence, the possibility that lights will quit on a rainy night.

44. Check out the parking-brake cable, especially where it goes into the wheels it acts on. If it has no shiny area that indicates motion, it may be rusted solid into its housing.

Notice that nothing has been said here about looking for wreck damage. That's because you hardly need to concern yourself about it. If the car was once wrecked, but drives and stops right, then it was properly repaired and the past wreck is of no consequence, unless the wreck takes something off the price. If the car does not drive right and the reason can't be seen in worn suspension parts, then the reason is of no consequence: even if not wrecked, you don't want the car.

Under current consumer protection laws, no one wants to bother trying to palm off a badly fixed wreck. Also, repair costs are so high that wreck damage that would make a car drive badly means the car is declared a "total." That's why you see so many sound-looking cars in junkyards. The cars don't look "that bad" and you wonder why they wound up in a junkyard. The answer is that they weren't worth fixing. On the other hand, if a wreck is a choice car, such as a Cadillac, that is worth fixing, it will get fixed properly and the fact that it was once wrecked matters little.

Up to the early 1950s, as the car market was still growing steadily and every car could find a buyer, body shops would go to extreme lengths to salvage a wrecked car. They would straighten bent frames (or try to) or cut two cars in half and join them to get one good car out of two wrecks. Such things are still done, and if done well, produce a perfectly sound car. However, if done with more attention to profit than to care, such repairs produce cars with the manners of an eccentric uncle at a lawn party.

People are often told to look for a freshly painted fender as proof of a wreck. Well, by all means look, but so what? Would you rather have the banged-up fender? Of course not. What you want is a car that drives well and a properly repaired wreck will do so.

45. The final details are to check out all the ancillaries/auxiliaries—lights, wipers, windows, glovebox lock, etc.

Now, the test is over. With impressions in mind and notes in hand, you can sit down and start bargaining.

DEALING WITH THE DEALER

Eventually, your search for the optimum choice of car must move from the living room to the show room. You have studied advertisements, read a few magazine articles, talked to several people, and picked up a few brochures. Now, you must go out and look at cars in their original habitat.

Before you set out, look around the living room of your house (or condominium). Whether you spent $25,000 for a bungalow or $250,000 for a chateau, you are looking at the one possession you probably spent the most money for.

The car is number two. Other than your home, it usually costs more than anything else you buy.

Before you bought the house, you studied the deal from every angle—where were the schools and the shopping center, how were taxes and municipal services, what did friends and family say? Also, you may have paid a surveyor to examine the house to check its foundation, look for termites, etc.

After all this care on your house purchase, you will go out and blithely spend $6000, $15,000, or even more for a car with no more than the salesman's advice for guidance.

Compare the price you expect to pay for a car to the cost of your house. If you rent, compare what you pay for rent during the life of the car—say, five years. Now, will you spend proportionally as much time choosing a car as you did choosing the place where you live? I know people who examined a dozen apartments (which seemed equally good to me) before choosing one, and then I have seen the same people buy a car during their lunch hour. Reflect on this a bit before you go car shopping.

As you set out, you need some notion of where you are going. In smaller towns and suburbs that have some sense of identity, you can ask people about a dealer's reputation. If a car has a sticker or license-plate frame that identifies the dealer, hail the driver of the car and ask. In smaller communities where dealers depend on repeat business, one buyer's opinion means something.

In a large city, dealers depend less on repeat business, so one transaction, whether good or ill, won't tell you much, and neither will the judgments of the Better Business Bureau or similar consumer-advocate agencies, private or public. Generally, an old, established dealership can be trusted, and a prominent, large-volume dealership obviously has some reason for its volume. Otherwise, you have little to go on except your impression of the place and the people in it.

When you go tire-kicking, you really should take someone with you, and your consort should understand his/her role. That role is to keep the salesman at bay as you study cars.

For example, as you enter the showroom, a pushy salesman runs over and starts badgering you about what sort of car you want and how much you want to spend, etc. When the salesman appears, your companion assumes the role of the prospective buyer, points to a car across the room, and says, "Well, can you tell me about that one?" This gets rid of the salesman. After you have looked your choice over alone, you can join them and bring up your own questions.

Your companion can be helpful as the source of additional impressions, but you must allow for his/her prejudices. For example, if you take my friend Jim Mortimer (of Natrona Heights, Pennsylvania), you will visit only Chevrolet dealerships. If you take my neighbor Raymond Cassidy, you will visit Ford dealerships. If you take me, you won't go into a domestic dealership at all.

Herein lies a sound principle: in fact, if you want a foreign car, take Jim Mortimer. He has little use for them and can find any number of reasons to reject them. If you want a Chevrolet, take Raymond Cassidy. If you want a domestic, take me, for I can curl my lip over a domestic the way Jim Mortimer can curl his over an import. A consort who plays the devil's advocate will point out objections to a car that you will never think of yourself.

Visit several dealerships, looking at cars in a casual way. When assessing, say, an Eclat Eight, ask the salesman why it is (putatively) better than the Sanguine Six in the dealership across the street. If the salesman categorically condemns everything about the Sanguine Six, you know you are dealing with a liar. However, if the salesman credits the Sanguine Six with its proper virtues, but suggests that Eclat warranty or service is better, you know you are dealing with a reasonably honest salesman. As you conclude your discussion, take the salesman's business card. On the back, note the car(s) you looked at and the price ranges.

Do not, at this point, bring up the matter of a trade-in on your old car. The trade-in is going to be a tricky part of the transaction, so keep things simple.

Some people prefer to pursue this initial, pre-buying business over the phone. You may find yourself getting talked into a deal, but you can always rethink the matter after you hang up. By contrast, if you get carried away in the showroom, you will be signing papers before you know it.

Personally, I dislike the phone approach, partly because what you are told over the phone may not be true when you get to the showroom; so be sure to get the salesman's name and review your notes of the telephone conversation before you go to the showroom.

"Very well, Mr. Goodeal," you say over the phone, "you're quoting me an Eclat Six two-door with air conditioning for $9500?"

"Yes, indeed," says Goodeal, "and we'll even throw in the vibrating seat back at no extra charge."

"Sounds good," you reply. "Do you have one like that in stock?"

"No," says Goodeal. "Everything we have is 'loaded'—nothing under $12,000 in stock—but if you come down, I'll take your order."

Now, when you go down later in the week or month with your telephone notes in hand, you can remind Goodeal of his promises. Otherwise, he may not remember the conversation and may tell you $10,500 is the bottom price.

My other objection to dealing over the phone is that the car purchase is a human transaction that can be influenced by the personality of the salesman. You may get down to the showroom and experience a severe distaste for Goodeal despite his phone voice. Yet, you will feel committed to deal with him, and your distaste will interfere with your dealing.

On the other hand, many people prefer to pre-shop by phone. If you're comfortable with it, by all means do so. People differ, and you should proceed in the way that suits you.

After several exploratory visits, you are ready to make a choice and start dickering, and here the matter gets messy because of your trade-in.

If you have no trade-in, you just haggle and buy and go home with a new car. If you do have a trade-in, though, you have to decide whether to introduce it early or late into the transaction and no general rule applies.

Suppose you go see Goodeal and, after vigorous haggling, make a deal on the Eclat Six for $9500. Then, you say, "Now, how much for my old car in trade?"

Goodeal will swear under his breath at this fresh complication, but will look your car over, perhaps consult the NADA "book," and offer $1500. So, you get the Eclat Six for your old car and $8000.

"But, 'book value' on my car is $2500," you say.

"True," says Goodeal, "but, if I give you full 'book' price on it, I have to charge full list for the new car, so I'll give you $2500 in trade on a list price of $10,500." You still have to shell out $8000.

Just as many people regard $9.98 as notably cheaper than $10.00, many will eagerly take the latter deal and boast to their neighbors that they got "full book price" for their old car. In other cases, the salesman will offer $3000 in trade on the $10,500 Eclat Six with $2000 worth of accessories, for a total price of $12,500. The buyer pays $9500, getting $500 off the list price of the accessories, most of which are useless and most of which weren't wanted in the first place. Yet, the deal looks too good to pass up—"Why, they gave me $500 above 'book' price!" Yes, and for that $500, they talked you into spending $1500 more, on which they made around $750.

You are no better off if you introduce your trade-in early in the dickering, the difference being that the trade-in creates a second area of bargaining—the value of your old car and the price of the new one. If you have reason to believe you know exactly what your car is worth (and you have no reason at all to believe that), you can handle the two-sided transaction, but you're better off not to try. You can get caught up in juggling too many numbers and that gives the salesman the opportunity to manipulate you in more directions.

So, in general, don't talk trade-in. If the salesman asks about your old car say, "No, I'm giving the old car to my kid brother (so he'll move to California)"; or, "No, we're going to keep it as a second car." Then, haggle like a fishmonger on the new car. Once you agree on a price, you know the "bottom line" on the new car and can then introduce the trade-in. This way, you deal with one question at a time and can more easily keep your eye on the main issue: how much money do you have to hand over?

At this point, a well-honed casuist might contend you have lied about your trade-in. In fact, of course, you simply changed your mind as you went over the deal and found out how much the new car cost. "By golly," you say, "I can't afford to keep the old car after all."

We will return to this trade-in later. For the moment, note the important point: make a fairly firm decision on what you want and how much you will spend, and don't give up on it readily.

The point here is that while you can't outsmart the salesman, you can defend yourself against manipulations by studying the matter fully before you start dealing.

The car salesman himself does not want to outsmart you. He wants your money. However, while he's not concerned to outsmart you, he has several ways of manipulating you into spending more money than you intended.

I daresay the standard salesman's tricks originated at the first camel bazaar of around 3000 B.C. They are standard ploys, reliable and durable, and I have been hearing about them for thirty years.

The most basic ploy is the standard *bait-and-switch*. Goodeal says over the phone that he's got your Eclat Six two-door in stock—"just come right on down," and you can have it for $9500. You hasten down and after greetings, etc., you and Goodeal step out behind the building where a punkish-looking employee is cleaning wheels on new cars.

"Hey, Leroy," yells Goodeal, "where's that green Six—the two-door?"

"The one with the vibrating seat back?" says Leroy. "It's gone."

"Gone!" moans Goodeal, in the tone of a *Titanic* survivor.

"Yep," says Leroy, "went out this morning."

"Oh, alas, alack," weeps Goodeal, "and nobody told me. Well, we'll just have to see what else we can do for you."

You get so caught up in comforting the distraught Goodeal that before you know it, he has led you to an Eclat Eight four-door with vicuña upholstery for a mere $16,500—and talked you into buying it!

When Goodeal cries, "Gone!" let him weep alone. When he dries up, ask, "How soon will you have another?"

This leads Goodeal to his next stratagem of, "*You can't get it.*"

"Oh, that was an unusual car," he says. "If we have to order one, we won't get another for six months."

The polite word for this sort of thing is "falsehood." The fact is, Goodeal's car store is connected via telephone/teletype lines to every dealership in the surrounding area and, ultimately, in the whole country. All he has to do is get "on the wire" and he can turn up the car you want, or one close to it. It may be a different color, may have more or fewer options, but he can find a car like the one you want if he will try.

You counter this you-can't-get-it ploy by saying, "Well, shucks, I guess I struck out here. Such a pity. I guess I'll just have to try another dealer."

Goodeal will change his tune and ask you to give him a day or two. You grant the delay and two days later he calls to say he has, by purest coincidence, located the car you want in a neighboring town and will have it for your inspection that afternoon. You go down, haggle the price, introduce your trade-in, haggle about it, and finally end up with your car valued at $2000 on a $10,000 list price.

With great satisfaction, Goodeal studies the unsigned sales agreement, and says, "Now, just excuse me a moment while I have the sales manager approve this." He disappears into a nearby office. Silence. Then you hear a mutter that rises to a roar: "For crying out loud, Goodeal, I've told you time and time again that we can't give these cars away"—the door opens, Goodeal retreats as the sales manager pursues him into the showroom—"I swear, I don't know how many times I have to tell you. You make some of the craziest deals I ever heard of, and you claim you went to Wharton, and—" The sales manager spies you, stops, gives Goodeal a withering look, and says, "I'm sorry, but I must apologize for Mr. Goodeal—he just can't seem to learn."

Goodeal hangs his head. Other salesmen give him scornful looks. The secretary snickers. Goodeal sniffles.

"There, there, you poor man," you say, "anybody can make a mistake. Let's go over that deal again." And sure enough, when Goodeal tacks on another $1000—"Just six-fifty a week over your three-year loan period"—the manager approves.

You have just been *lowballed*, as they say in the trade: Get the manager to play the villain and refuse the price as too low, then work the prospect up on the price, the manager's vehemence lending credibility to the ploy.

The response to this ploy is to say something like, "My, my, what a nasty man you work for, Mr. Goodeal. Why, I wouldn't buy a car in a place run by him at any price!" As you start to leave, Goodeal will regain his composure and offer to brave the ferocious manager again on your behalf—"Just don't leave yet," you and your money.

The variation on "lowball" comes when you introduce your trade-in. Goodeal assigns it a trade-in value of $2000 and goes to the sales manager for approval. The manager comes out, looking grim, and the three of you examine your car. The manager runs his finger over the scratch on the rear fender, opens and shuts the door in a disdainful manner, shakes his head at a cigarette burn in the carpet, then bursts out, "For crying out loud, Goodeal, we aren't running a junkyard here"—he makes the ignition switch catch in that tricky way it has—"I mean, what are we going to do with it?" He sticks his finger in the small cut in the upholstery—"We sure as hell can't put it on *our* lot!" He slams the door so that it fails to shut (you didn't notice Goodeal push the latch down so it couldn't shut)—"And we won't get $100 for it at auction." He throws up his hands. "You two are just going to have to look this whole deal over again." All the while, he hardly looks at you and if he does, his expression clearly indicates that he wonders what form of depravity would drive such a loathsome hulk as you have offered in trade. You hang your head and tremble in shame at your unworthy vehicle.

Highball: quote high on the trade-in, then let the villainous manager play the heavy, shame the customer, and cut down the trade-in allowance.

The response to this one is to stand stalwart beside your Old Faithful, and say, "Well, it brought me to this dealership and it will take me to another!" As you start to leave, Goodeal will act as your defender and say, "That's okay. The manager's just upset. Let me work on him a little."

Note here that you must offer to leave, and must be clearly willing to leave, to nullify these ploys. Vacillation will get you a higher price for the new car.

But this time you are angry, so you get in your car. "Leaving?" says Goodeal. You nod. "But where else can you go?" he says. "We have the best deals in town."

This conceit annoys you. "I think I'll stop in at Dzoh's Eclat Emporium," you say. "Dzoh's prices aren't so bad."

Before you are half a block away, Goodeal is on the phone to Dzoh. "Hey, Dzoh, we're sending one down. Yeah, a live one. We tried a highball but the boss overdid it. We quoted $2000 in trade on list. You quote $1800 on list and if you get the deal, we get our *baksheesh*. If she comes back here, you get yours. Right? Right."

Dzoh, of course, does not have to play the backscratching game with Goodeal. However, Dzoh also loses a lot of prospects, many of whom wind up talking to Goodeal. Both know this, and each would rather help the other get the deal than see you go to a third dealer. Dzoh realizes that Goodeal has "softened you up" and predisposed you to accept his own deal; if he gets the sale, he hands a commission of sorts to Goodeal. If you refuse Dzoh's deal and come back, Goodeal knows that Dzoh helped set you up to accept his deal, so he makes a gesture toward Dzoh.

For lack of a better term, I call this the *pincer*. It is not common, but it happens often enough when you attempt to play one dealer off against another. Usually, a pincer can occur only when both dealers handle the same make. However, in small towns, it can occur across brand-name lines. Thus, if you leave one dealership, don't specify which dealership you are going to next.

The foregoing ploys arise before you put down any money or

sign anything. Other ploys arise once you have signed and put down a deposit. In the trade, these latter ploys go by the name of "bushwhacking," or "bushing," and as the name implies, they involve enticing you into a trap.

The most obvious "bush" involves securing your agreement (and, perhaps, deposit) on a certain car, after which you are presented with a car that has more options than you specified. You are told that "All the cars are coming out that way" and are led to believe that protest is futile, so you accept the options and their price.

Here again, to refuse will usually get you what you want. However, in a "bush" wrought by a maestro, you will be made to feel like a perverse malcontent; you will be handed a "guilt trip" about how you are inconveniencing the poor salesman and will succumb to the "bush."

Keep in mind that you are not responsible for the salesman's feelings and you need not care what the salesman appears to think of you. Remember that what the salesman really cares about is how much money he can separate you from.

Bushing occurs most easily when you order a car. You can watch it happen. You say you want the Eclat Six two-door with air conditioning. That's all. Goodeal takes an order form (Dzoh only offered you $1800 in trade, so you went back), fills in the relevant data, then begins checking off various options. You see him check "power steering," "rallye stripe," and "power antenna." When he finishes, he adds up the numbers: $11,400. With $2000 for your old car, you pay $9400—well above the $8000. When you protest, you get the "They're-all-coming-out-like-this" routine.

One way to deal with this "bush" is to let the salesman fill out the form and add up the numbers. Then, take the form and cross out the things you don't like, hand it back, and say, "Now, add the numbers again." That's all. "The bottom line, please," and no arguments about it. If the salesman balks, leave.

Other people, who enjoy the combative elements of the transaction, object as soon as Goodeal puts "power steering" on the form, and object each successive time he enters something else they don't want.

This second approach is good for the people it is good for. However, it does not work for everybody. For example, the salesman enters an extra-fancy $50 outside mirror on the form. You object strenuously. The salesman argues. You bat the matter back and forth until the salesman gives in. Good, except that now you feel guilty about being so argumentative and, further- more, since you won on the mirror, you feel you owe the sales- man one—one such as the $300 set of silly wheels that comes next, and that's why the salesman marked that cheap mirror first.

You should know your competence and limitations. If you are good at argument and don't find it distasteful, proceed, as Shake- speare's Hotspur said, to "cavil on the ninth part of a hair." Keep in mind, though, that the truism among salesmen of all types is that the most-argumentative customers are the ones who can usually be talked into the best deal—for the salesman. Alter- natively, you can be stern and impassive. Say nothing until the order is complete, change it to your liking, and say, "The bottom line, please."

Without being patronizing or sexist, I recommend this latter course. Admitting the legitimate complaints of the women's movement does not alter the fact that women are less likely to argue over a car deal than men. Women have been taught to accept the word and will of men and, thus, are at a disadvantage in an argument with a car salesman. As a result, buying a car is often more unpleasant for a woman than a man and they are especially vulnerable to "bushing." To simply refuse to argue, to mark out unwanted items and say, "The bottom line, please," minimizes the exposure to manipulation.

"Bushing" gets nastier once you put down a deposit, usually a nonrefundable deposit. Such deposits have a legitimate pur- pose. You like the $9200 Eclat coupe in the showroom. "Hold it for me," you say, "until I see if I can get the money." Goodeal says he needs a $100 deposit to hold the car, so you give him $100. As soon as you leave, someone else comes in and offers to buy the car. "Can't sell it," says Goodeal. "We took a deposit on it." The second customer then goes across the street and buys a Sanguine Six. You come back and say, "Well, I can borrow $8000, so I'll pay that much for it." Goodeal points out the $9200 list price (which he just turned down). "Sorry," you say, "$8000 is the best I can do." When Goodeal won't sell for that price, you demand your deposit back.

We can make a case for the notion that you really owe Goodeal the $100, for he did, indeed, take a loss on your behalf. Similarly, suppose you order a car with a peculiar set of options that few other people would want, then back out of the deal when the car arrives. This leaves Goodeal with an oddball car to sell and for his trouble, he has, perhaps, a fair claim to your deposit.

Most people will say, "Lose no tears over the salesman's plight." I do not like to so totally disregard the salesman. However, I must note that the nonrefundable deposit more often gets used as a psychological and financial bludgeon on you.

Suppose you go in to buy an $8000 car. The salesman baits, switches, and "lowballs" you into a $10,000 deal. You put down $100 earnest money and intend to come back the next day for the car. That night, you think better of that $10,000, so when you come back, you say you've changed your mind: you want the $8000 car you asked for in the first place.

"Well, we can change the deal," says the salesman, "but you'll lose your deposit." So, to save your $100 deposit, you spend $2000 that you didn't originally intend to spend. In fact, you would be better off to give up the deposit and thus save $1900, but your attitude toward the deposit will almost always cause you to buy the more-expensive car—and that's one reason car dealers across the country have persuaded state legislatures to give them nonrefundable deposit laws.

Ethically, if you're still in the same dealership, the $100 deposit ought to be just as good on the $8000 car that you really want, rather than be restricted to the $10,000 one you got "talked into buying," but many dealerships will refuse to look at it that way.

Moral: don't put down deposits at all, unless the dealer actually has to order your car from the factory. Make no deposits on cars in stock. True, a certain car may get sold out from under you, but you can always find another.

Once you start signing papers and giving deposits, the transaction moves to a higher level of seriousness, so don't do either until you are ready. You may be invited to sign assorted pieces of paper that, presumably, do no more than reserve a certain car for your salesman or authorize him to commit the car to dealer preparation. Then, when you decide you don't want the car, you are told that you signed a sales agreement.

Such pieces of paper rarely have legal force, in the respect that the dealer is hardly going to sue to force you to follow through with the purchase. No car dealer wants to expose his business methods to courtroom inquiry. The pieces of paper mostly serve to scare you into going through with the deal on the presumed threat of a suit, or to make you feel like a welsher if you don't go through with it.

If you do sign something and find yourself being backed into a legal corner (a remote possibility), the escape maneuver is to charge "misrepresentation." Misrepresentation has long been the standard legal ploy for escaping an inconvenient contract: you charge that the terms or the goods were "misrepresented" by the other party. Here of late, consumer-protection laws to insulate the gullible from agents for encyclopedias and aluminum siding have made the misrepresentation strategy even more effective.

However, if you actually make a deposit, you may have to sue (or threaten to) to recover the deposit if you get "bushed," and the odds are that you will not win in court. So-called "consumer-protection" laws mostly apply *after* you own the car; in the "deposit" stage, the dealer holds the legal cards. State legislatures, generally, have been very good to the dealers in this matter.

Summary: don't give deposits or sign papers until you are completely through looking and dickering and have made a deal that gives you great satisfaction when you think of it.

The recognizable ploys that involve the car and its price are not all. Since you are human, you are vulnerable to psychological ploys. Some people buy more than they want because the salesman shames them by implying they are welfare cases. "No, no," the salesman says, "the Eclat Eight with the zebra-skin roof and gold-anodized wheels is not for you—you (obviously) can't afford it."

On the other hand, the agent flatters: "Didn't I see you on the six o'clock news the other night? And which trust company do you direct?"

According to an apocryphal story, Carroll Shelby, who once built sports cars based on Ford components and is now doing a similar thing with Chrysler products, guaranteed sales of his Cobra sports cars by giving prospective buyers a sidelong look and asking solicitously, "Are you really sure you can handle this car?"

Whether we admit it or not, we are susceptible to such suggestions. A friend we trust, one who can snicker discreetly at such nonsense, will help us keep our head in order, and that's another reason for having company along.

For most people, the car-buying transaction is a psychological encounter wherein they start out one-down and simply hope to come out no worse off than that. The dealer's show room feels as alien as old Aunt Minnie's parlor, where you couldn't move without fear of breaking a knickknack and could hardly speak for fear of sacrilege. The salesman speaks so assuredly, the other customers seem so confident, that you feel that to be disagreeable would be a faux pas of the worst order. This is why you should visit several showrooms—to dispel the mystique. In fact, a car dealership should be thought of as a "car store," just as you think of other places as the grocery store or second-hand store.

And, while in the car store, every time the salesman pauses in his spiel for dramatic effect, just say to yourself:"It's my money." The agent, who can give a dozen persuasive reasons why you should have the more-expensive model and the longer list of options, can argue away your resistance on those points if you give him a chance. However, when you remind yourself that money is involved and that "It's my money," the salesman can't manipulate you.

YOUR OLD CAR: TRADE-IN OR SELL?

If you were paying close attention, you noticed the chicken-and-egg principle back there in regard to your old car as a trade-in. We say, "Know what you want and how much you intend to spend." Yet, unless you know how much your old car is worth as a trade-in, you won't know how much money you have to come up with to get the new car you want.

People generally fall into two camps: those who undervalue their trade-ins and those who overvalue them. The first group gets suckered because they get "highballed" on the trade-in; the second group gets suckered because they will buy three times as much car as they want, so long as they get "above book value" in trade-in. You need some outside advice to determine which camp you are in and to help you establish the value of your car.

One way is to go around to those used-car lots that have a sign saying, "Cars bought." You can generally assume such lots will offer you 50 to 60 percent of what they think they can sell your car for (unless your car is in some way unusual, which may earn it a better price).

Alternatively, go around to used-car lots and look at cars like your own. However, a "lot price" of $5400 does not mean a purchase price of $5400. The purchase price may be $4500 if you bargain vigorously on the car.

In addition, study used-car ads. You will find, for example, that in early 1983 a 1978 Pontiac Firebird sold for a range from $3000 to $4000. Now, where in this range would your '78 Firebird belong?

Also, how good are those classified ad prices? Clearly, the $3000 price—the low end—is probably firm, but does $4000 mean $4000 or does it mean you can bargain the seller to $3000?

Thus, the classifieds don't really give you firm guidance about what your old car is worth.

Edmund's and the NADA "book" help, but they can be three to six months behind a quick change in the market. During the price instability of the 1973–74 "fuel crisis," big cars fell to worthlessness in December of 1973 but bounced back to full value by August of 1974, and the "book" couldn't keep up with the fluctuations. In sum, you cannot find out "exactly" what your car is worth. Ultimately, your car is worth what somebody will pay for it and you won't know that until you advertise it widely and find a buyer.

In the car-buying transaction, the salesman—the specialist— is much better qualified than you to guess what your car is worth and the salesman is, obviously, not going to give up an advantage by telling you.

This leaves you in a sort of limbo: your car has *some* value and that value influences how much you will spend on the new car— yet you can't tie that value down to closer than 10 percent, if even that. If you undervalue your car, you may be left feeling uncomfortable after the trade; if you overvalue the car, you may pass up a number of sound deals because you took a pigheaded attitude about an inflated evaluation of your car.

About the best you can do is accept that plus-or-minus 10 percent on your old car. Actually, if you, as the amateur car trader, can come to a good 10± percent figure, you're doing fairly well. The salesman won't do much better.

To review: used-car ads, used-car lots, *Edmund's*, and the NADA "book" are the credible guides to what your car is worth.

Unfortunately, besides being unresponsive to sudden market changes (as noted earlier), *Edmund's* and the "book" can't indicate the influence of "turnover" on the value of your car as a trade- in. For example, a Peugeot is an excellent car, but it is not a popular one. A dealer who takes a Peugeot in trade may even- tually sell it for "book" value, but the Peugeot may sit on his lot for several weeks before he does.

As with rooms in a hotel, every space on the dealer's lot must produce income regularly. So Goodeal holds your old Peugeot for a month and sells it for $3000, making a profit of $300. In the same time, he might have sold four Fords for the same $3000 each and made $1200 in profit. Thus, he effectively lost $900 on the space your old Peugeot occupied for that month.

Goodeal knows this (or he would have gone broke long ago) and will not be moved to give you "book" value on a car that he cannot sell right away. Yet, when Goodeal finally does sell the Peugeot for $3000 and reports the transaction to the NADA for inclusion in the "book" averages, his $900 loss will not be recorded.

In sum, while basic, *Edmund's* and the "book" do not apply perfectly, and they apply less perfectly to cars *hoi polloi* regard as "offbreed."

You have to be objective about your car. If it's full of rust holes, you have to admit they are there. If the brakes are gone, you have to admit that. On the other hand, if the car has been scrupulously cared for and looks new despite being five years old, you should enjoy the benefits of its quality.

You should observe a few simple, common-sense rules about presenting your car as a trade-in. First, wash it and vacuum out the dirt. Wipe stains. If the engine is filthy, have it cleaned before you go a-trading. Generally, have little things like broken tail lights or loose mirrors repaired. The dealer will have to fix these things before he can sell the car, and in a large dealership the paperwork will cost more than the repairs, so the dealer will look most critically at such small failings.

You should not replace tires to trade a car in, simply because the dealer can make a better deal on tires than you can. If you have to pay $100 apiece for new tires, the dealer can probably get them for $60 each. Thus, bald tires are not so serious a defect as the dealer might suggest. If a dealer protests about your worn tires, say, "Okay, I'll go get four $30 recaps, but I want $250 more for the car—for that's what you'll do with it."

Last, when the dealer wants to look over your car, don't go with him. Give him the keys and say, "I'll just wait here for you."

If you go with the dealer, he will note where your ring has scratched the paint above the door handle and sort of linger over it. He will note a crimp in the chrome molding strip and run his finger over it while looking very grave. He will open the door in a way that makes you feel ashamed of your car. Once he has subjected you to this psychological put-down treatment, you will be more inclined to deal on his terms. That's why he looks so jaundiced as he wiggles the key in the lock and that is why he mutters under his breath as he studies the cigarette burn on the dashboard: to make you ill at ease and a more tractable subject for his own sales pitch.

To avoid all this, don't go.

The dealer may return from his inspection and say, "Well, your car has bad shocks, the muffler is falling off, and the universal joints are going."

Don't let this bother you. Bring the dealer back to the bottom line: "How much for the new car with mine in trade?" In other words, don't go on the defensive about your car. If the dealer points out flaws in it, say, "Look, Mr. Goodeal, if the car were perfect, I wouldn't be buying a new one, would I?" Keep the dealer's attention on the issue: how much money? If the figure isn't right, don't agree to it. Shop some more. If lots of shopping establishes that you overvalue your car, don't be ashamed to go back to the first dealer and make the deal.

You may decide to sell the car yourself rather than take what seems to be a beating on its trade-in value. However, the problem remains the same: you still don't know what to ask for it. If the first person who answers your advertisement pays your price, you probably didn't ask enough for the car, for a car priced properly will virtually always provoke some waffling and dickering. However, if half a dozen people come and look but do not buy, you don't know whether you priced the car too high or if they simply were not seriously interested in the first place.

In the several instances wherein I sold a car through classified ads, I found that of a dozen people who will call, three or four will come to look, and one will buy—a 12:1 ratio, but I was selling vehicles with narrow, particular appeal. If a vehicle lacks distinction, the ratio will go up, and after you've answered phone calls for a week, you will be so disgusted that you'll cut the price in half just to rid yourself of the hassle. In sum, selling a car is not as simple a matter as it is often represented.

By now, one thing should be clear: to make the best car deal possible, you have to work at it, although all of your work will not tie the matter down to absolute predictability. You must assess what you can get for how much money, come to some judgment about what your old car is worth, and decide whether you are better off to trade it in or sell it yourself. No matter what you do, uncertainties will remain even as you walk into the showroom. However, the more you have studied the matter, the fewer the uncertainties.

We should note, as epilogue here, that the same uncertainties, the same need for homework, apply whether buying a new or used car.

WARRANTY

The car-buying business took a quantum leap in 1955 when Oldsmobile announced a 50,000-mile warranty on their engines: if you had to add oil to the engine during the first 50,000 miles, Oldsmobile would replace/repair it.

Before crediting Oldsmobile for this leap, we must note that as much or more credit must go to the much-maligned oil industry, for Oldsmobile could not have offered the warranty without the improved oils that appeared at the same time.

In fact, the warranty was so hedged with qualifications that it did not mean much, but it did set off a "warranty war" in the industry. By the early 1960s, warranties had come to mean something and were transferable to successive owners. However, as the industry entered what must stand as its sloppiest era for quality, the late '60s and early '70s, warranties became burdensome so Detroit began dropping them like passé celebrities.

However, the public had become spoiled; they wanted warranties, and so arranged for them through the Magnuson-Moss Act of 1975. At least, they thought they did; in fact, Magnuson-Moss was Detroit's way of defusing the whole warranty issue. Magnuson-Moss does not require manufacturers to issue a warranty at all; it only specifies the terms of a warranty when a warranty is issued, but the Act is sufficiently ambiguous to be useless to the consumer. Since few people are aware of the limitations of the law, they enjoy a false feeling of security about what a warranty means. Meanwhile, Detroit pursues "business as usual," so everybody is happy (by this measure, Magnuson-Moss is an excellent law).

In any case, warranties now do provide for repairs to the engine, transmission, differential, and suspension, usually for one year or 12,000 miles, whichever comes first. The manufacturer promises to replace defective parts or to correct defective workmanship; however, these corrections are not always free. Furthermore, you may go through considerable travail to get a defect corrected. For example, certain Chevrolet/GMC light trucks of 1979 had poorly machined differential housings that ruined the gears. GM replaced only the gears (through dealers), but not the housings, so if you bought one of those unhappy vehicles, you got a new set of gears every three or four months until you went out of warranty, then you bought new gears *and housing* at your own expense and had no further trouble. No point in suing GM: you got what the warranty specified. Similarly, after building the excellent Chevrolet/GMC six-cylinder engine for fifty years, GM turned out a bunch in 1979–80 with bad camshafts. Some failed early and were replaced; others managed to last until 12,001 miles, so were not within the warranty.

You will get a warranty on a new car whether you ask for it or not. However, the warranty may be worthless, once you figure in the aggravation of trying to get a problem corrected under warranty.

To benefit from the warranty, you must return a car to a dealer as soon as the slightest problem appears and make sure the work order specifies the problem and the fact that it is a warranty matter. In the unhappy event that the problem remains after the warranty has run out, then you are stuck with a "lemon." If you accept the situation, then enjoy your "lemon." If you don't accept it, then you will probably have to sue to correct the situation. A wholesome lawsuit arranged by a lawyer with a vicious streak will usually get you a decent out-of-court settlement (which will not make the headlines, so you don't know how much of this sort of thing goes on). Agreed, this method is troublesome to pursue, but it beats the alternatives, i.e., you pay for a car that won't work.

Every manufacturer claims the best warranty. Being uncertain, you ask the dealer why you should have any faith in the warranty. Now, the dealer is on the spot: if he tells you how many warranty claims he satisfies with repairs, he effectively admits his cars are trouble-prone. Accordingly, he waffles and tells you nothing. You are still uncertain.

This uncertainty has no resolution. That which comes from the fallible, human hand is subject to failure. You cannot escape the risk. The warranty is some protection, but it is no guarantee of perfection.

The owner's manual will describe the warranty and procedure for obtaining warranty service. Two problems commonly arise: 1) you and the dealer disagree about whether a certain fault is covered by the warranty, and 2) you disagree about whether the problem has been corrected. In either case, you should take the problem to the manufacturer's zone representative, whose address will be in the owner's manual or will be available from the dealer. The zone representative will try to sort out the matter, but if you are not satisfied with her solution, you can go an echelon higher, to the manufacturer's Customer Relations or similar office.

On the way up with your complaint, you may get diverted into various informal programs that have been set up under Federal Trade Commission prodding. In these informal systems, the manufacturer and the customer refer the problem to the mediation of a third party, usually some agency operating as a consumer advocate. In most instances, the agency is the Better Business Bureau or its competitor, the Automotive Consumer Action Panel. Everybody involved—the manufacturer, BBB, or AUTOCAP—makes much of the fact that the mediation service is free, though you may wonder why anybody would expect you to pay for mediation of a warranty problem when a new car is defective. The BBB and AUTOCAP involvement is fairly new, so their track records are ambiguous. Both agencies claim they achieve satisfactory results, but we may reserve judgment until we hear from the car owners involved.

Generally, the most effective way to neutralize a hostile element is to make it a member of the institution toward which it is hostile. Thus, large corporations silenced radicals in the late 1960s by appointing them to advisory positions on the boards of directors. To me, the rapprochement of the industry with the BBB and AUTOCAP agencies smacks of the same sort of thing; in other words, give the mediation service a try, but be suspicious and don't get into a corner where you must accept a resolution that you don't like.

If not satisfied with the formal or informal systems, you can appeal to state or federal consumer-protection groups. Generally, this approach is useless to people who want prompt action; it involves so much paperwork, so many forms passing back and forth, that a resolution can be delayed interminably. Thus, rather than pursue the official agencies when the formal and informal systems have failed to satisfy you, you should consult a lawyer well-versed in consumer law and let the lawyer take over your dealings in the formal/informal systems. Even here, you have to be careful, for the lawyer can sell you out cheap for the sake of his own fast buck.

In sum, if the warranty game turns nasty, it can become nasty, indeed. Do not be misled by newspaper headlines about someone who got a huge settlement on a warranty matter: those incidents make the headlines because they are as rare as a man biting a dog.

All that is the bad news. The good news is that nineteen states now have "lemon laws." Basically, lemon laws say that if your new car is inoperable for a total of thirty days (not necessarily consecutive) or if the dealer can't make it run satisfactorily after four repair efforts, you get another car or you get your money back. These laws may be the best thing for car owners since hydraulic brakes. They are now in effect in California, Connecticut, Delaware, Florida, Illinois, Maine, Massachusetts, Minnesota, Montana, Nebraska, Nevada, New Hampshire, New Jersey, New York, Oregon, Texas, Washington, Wyoming, and Wisconsin.

Modern cars have fewer problems than those of thirty years ago. However, the consumer consciousness of recent years has created a fearful impression that new cars constantly fail. Detroit recognizes this fear and uses it as a marketing ploy by offering the "extended service warranty." Basically, this warranty says that, if you let the dealer do all maintenance on your car for 50,000 miles, any failure will be covered by warranty. Some manufacturers, somewhat more honest, call the program a "maintenance" program. These programs resemble the service contracts that offices get for their typewriters and copying machines. At bottom, they are the manufacturer's admission that the product is not reliable. To the consumer, the contract is a gamble on the probability of the need for repairs and their cost versus the cost of the contract. Either way, the program is a gimmick to scare you into using dealer service, a way to dissuade you from going to independent garages after your car goes out of warranty.

When I look at the overall performance record of the 8,000,000 domestic cars produced, say, in model year 1978, and consider that each of those cars travels an average of 10,000 miles per year, I see no evidence that such service contracts are necessary. True, they are immensely helpful to the one or two percent of buyers who have serious trouble, but other people get nothing for their money except the pleasure of paying dealership labor rates and parts costs for regular maintenance. I see much benefit to the dealers in such programs, but very little for the consumer. At bottom, I ask, "Why do we need these contracts now, when we got along without them for so long? And why should we need them just when the manufacturers are telling us that cars are better than ever?" In sum, if you want double protection, perhaps you will want the service contract, but most people will get nothing for it except high-priced service.

FIXING UP AN OLD FAITHFUL

Often enough, the questions come up of, "Why buy a new car at all? Why not just fix up the old one?"

Why not, indeed? Well, partly because America has so long been a use-and-discard society that the notion of reconditioning is not a part of our consciousness. Also, partly because we get tired of what we have driven for several years and want something new. And, finally, because while banks will readily loan money to buy a new car, hardly any will loan money to recondition an old one. A car over five years old and not listed in the NADA "book" effectively has no loan value.

This latter is the crucial factor in a desire to keep an old car. If you have the money and like your old car, you can spend one-third the cost of a new car and drive your old one another five to ten years. The major qualification here is rust: to truly repair rust so that it does not come back in a year or two can run the cost of reconditioning beyond sensible limits.

Assume a reasonably rust-free car five to ten years old, and assume all costs at shop labor rates: the overhaul bill will run approximately thus:

	Low	High
overhaul engine	$1200	$2000
overhaul transmission	400	600
overhaul brakes (linings and cylinders)	200	400
overhaul front suspension	400	600
replace tires	400	800
repaint	75	300
odds and ends	100	100
	$2775	$4800

The low-range figures here will apply to most ordinary domestic sedans, while the high range applies to semiluxury domestics and the ordinary-run foreign cars; estimates for, e.g., BMW, Mercedes-Benz, and Jaguar will be about double the high-range estimates. Also, the figures make no allowance for rust, since rust damage is less amenable to repair estimates.

If you spend around $2500 to recondition, say a 1972 Plymouth Valiant, or $5000 to completely redo a 1965 Mercedes-Benz 230, you virtually start over with a new car that should last as long as the original. As noted, no one is going to loan you money for the project; with good credit, you can do it as a "signature" loan, but otherwise you just have to do it out of your pocket. However, for a car you truly love, reconditioning is well worthwhile.

The car many people "truly love" is not always the one they

drive. Often, it is a favorite car bequeathed by a parent or relative, an older car with sentimental value from childhood, a car they want to preserve but without going to the extravagant restorations done by the antique car freaks. Such people ask the local repair shop whether the car is "worth fixing up" and generally get told, "Naw, you're wasting your money. Nobody'll give you anything for it when you get it done."

The logic is patently false: such people aren't fixing the car to sell, but to keep, so sale value is irrelevant. Yet, being uncertain, they accept the shop's advice. Rather than fix the car they continue to drive it occasionally on warm Sunday afternoons and watch it decay in the meantime.

If you feel strongly inclined to recondition an old car, you should not be dissuaded by the irrelevant factor of sale value. However, if you are inclined toward such a project, you should seek out a shop that is sympathetic to your wishes. The shop will be suspicious, so show that you can afford what you propose; that way, the shop doesn't have to worry about how it's going to get its money out of an old car if you can't pay. Prove you can pay beforehand.

However, don't let the shop treat the project as a "back burner" job; since you don't need the car to go to work, the shop will tend to give it a low priority when other owners demand attention for their cars. The more the shop gives your car a low priority, the more it tends to lower the priority over time and your project, which should take a month, ends up taking a year. Hence, the need to find a sympathetic shop, which generally means a smaller, low-volume place.

You can go to restoration specialists. They are worth talking to, but are so often involved with 1939 La Salles or 1951 Bentleys that your paltry 1965 Ford Fairlane hardly bears notice. Also, the price at a restoration shop will be double that of the general service shop, but you will get excellent upholstery and body repairs for your money. Check it out.

Major point: the desire to recondition/restore an old car is not a mark of insanity. To do so often makes economic sense and even if it only makes sentimental sense, you may as well spend your $3000 fixing up your 1955 Willys Aero as making a trip to Greece.

LEASING

The question, "Why buy a new car?" can be modified to "Why buy a car at all? Why not lease?"

At present, leased cars amount to about 15 percent of new car sales. Many, of course, are "company" cars, but a great many are leased by individuals—and for the same reasons companies lease: to avoid tying money up in a car, to leave money free for other purposes.

Most car leases are made through large organizations, such as the airport rental car people, but many leases are made through dealers. Either way, a leased car makes sense to a private individual only if the car is primarily used for business purposes (or can be credibly represented as such). To use a car for business entails assorted deductions from taxable income and the extent of such deductions can tip the economic scales in favor of a lease. As a pure alternative to personal ownership, leasing offers no benefit.

If leasing has some appeal, check the "Automobile—Renting and Leasing" heading in the Yellow Pages. You may find that your particular financial circumstances make a lease worthwhile.

PART II

Maintenance and Repair

MAINTENANCE
PROGRAM

When 'arf of your bullets fly wide in the ditch,
Don't call your Martini a cross-eyed old bitch;
She's human as you are—you treat her as sich,
    An' she'll fight for the young British soldier.
    —Rudyard Kipling, "The Young British Soldier"

The "Martini" Kipling refers to was the British military rifle back in the days of the Boer War, the Khyber Pass, and all that. Kipling knew a poorly maintained rifle with maladjusted sights would send its bullets "wide in the ditch" and he also knew a machine can assume human qualities of caprice and loyalty. "She's human as you" applies to a car as well as to a rifle; indeed, even more since the car does more things. When the car regularly fires up on cold mornings when others grunt their batteries to death; when the family huddles inside as the faithful vehicle brings them home through lashing sleet and storm; when the car breezes serenely to the peak of some scenic tor, passing steaming casualties on the way up—then, the owner develops a special affection for it, and the more so if the owner has taken an interest in its health.

If you studied widely and wisely chose a car that fits your needs and pocketbook, living with the car should be easy; indeed, it may be a supreme pleasure. On the other side of the coin, taking care of the car should be no great problem either; a modern car is remarkably fail-safe, considering the number of parts it has and the number of things that can go wrong but usually don't.

As recently as twenty years ago, cars were supposed to have an oil change and a "grease job" every 2000 miles. The grease job consisted of squirting grease into as many as 25 little fittings, most of them in the steering and suspension systems. By contrast, modern cars rarely have grease fittings at all and the manufacturers recommend oil changes at intervals of as long as 7500 miles.

Likewise, as recently as ten years ago, cars needed an annual (and semiannual was better) "tune-up," which consisted of replacing most of the ignition system—distributor points, rotor, cap, and spark plugs—and adjusting the ignition timing and carburetor, plus replacing the air filter and adjusting adjustable valves, where applicable.

Nowadays, the manufacturer's recommended tune-up interval may be as much as 25,000 miles and when the tune-up comes, the only parts replaced are the spark plugs and air filter.

To pursue the question of the annual tune-up for the moment, the spark plugs are the weakest link in the under-the-hood stuff, and this is not because spark plugs are themselves weak, but because of the composition of fuels, and the composition of fuels is a matter of combustion characteristics. General Motors and Standard Oil, through their joint venture, the Ethyl Corporation, began adding tetraethyl lead to gasoline in 1924; to skip over the technicalities of "charge stratification" and "flame-front propagation," just note that lead in gasoline gives it combustion characteristics—the "octane rating"—that allow engine designers to come up with engines that are small, powerful, and very efficient.

Ultimately, the lead in gasoline had an unwholesome effect on the atmosphere, so the oil refiners began cutting back on the lead even before unleaded gasoline became required. Instead of lead, the refiners now use bromine and chlorine compounds to achieve the desired combustion characteristics. Bromine and chlorine work well enough, but they leave deposits on spark plugs, particularly if a car is used mostly in stop-and-go driving, especially in the winter time. Once these deposits accumulate on the plugs, they will not burn off (as carbon deposits will) and the plugs must be replaced. Even at as much as $2.50 each (at shop prices), a new set of plugs every year doesn't amount to much, especially when compared to the tune-up demands of ten years ago.

Nowadays, a proper tune-up may involve the pollution-control system more than the engine itself. The components of the system are guaranteed for 50,000 miles, but they may need attention in the meantime; for example, positive-crankcase-ventilation

(PCV) valves may need cleaning at intervals (they gum up with sludgy oil) and the system that keeps fuel vapors from going into the outside air may need checking. In general, though, a modern car needs comparatively little attention.

Older cars will *seem* to need more attention. For example, people complain that "something always needs fixing." In fact, the unhappy maintenance record of an older car is mostly the product of neglect and where it is *not* the product of neglect, it is often the product of thievery or incompetence among mechanics.

For example, an acquaintance bought a car that had 50,000 miles on it and, apparently, its original battery. When the alternator charge indicator light began flickering on at low speed, a shop sold her a new alternator for $125. The alternator did not solve the problem, so the shop next sold her a new battery for $80. Although I did not see the car before the work was done, I am sure her problem involved no more than dirty battery connections, that being reasonable to expect after 50,000 miles. The lady did not have trouble with the car so much as she had trouble with the mechanics. Of course, she had no way of knowing that.

If you spend the money to put an older car in good condition, it will need little attention to stay that way (review the used-car section to note what sort of defects older cars may have). To be sure, older cars that do not have electronic ignition do need semiannual tune-ups, and if they have grease fittings, do need grease now and again.

With an older car—one bought second-hand, for example— you probably won't have an owner's manual, which leaves you looking for an organized maintenance program. Those given in workshop manuals, such as you find in the automotive section of a bookstore, will do. You may object to spending $10 for a manual just to get the maintenance schedule; however, the manual has other uses, too, and is worth its price. For example, suppose you seek out a shop for a tune-up and the mechanic says, "I'd like to help, but we don't see many cars like yours, so I don't have the tune-up specifications." If you have the manual, the mechanic can get the specifications from it. Similarly, if you have trouble on the road and the handiest mechanic is unfamiliar with your car, you can say, "Here's the manual. Will it help?"

When a mechanic must deal with a strange car, the manual is a big help, indeed.

Against this background that minimizes maintenance needs, let us look at particulars.

First, on a brand-new car that is under warranty, follow the manufacturer's maintenance program scrupulously. Look at the maintenance chart in the owner's manual and compare it to the shop bill: Were spark plugs replaced, if they were supposed to be? Were drive belts checked for proper tension? Was the differential oil checked? And so forth, straight from the owner's manual. During the warranty period you must insist that all "inspect" and "check" items be done adequately, for you are protecting your warranty if something goes wrong. If you follow the manufacturer's recommendations, you cannot be blamed if something goes wrong during the warranty period and you may even have a justifiable claim for service beyond warranty. Suppose a brake self-adjuster goes bad at 12,500 miles—just beyond the 12,000-mile warranty: were the brakes truly inspected at 10,000 miles, and, if so, why wasn't the developing defect noted?

Once the car goes out of warranty, dealership service is good for people who can afford it. You take the car to the dealer's shop and say, "Give it what it's supposed to have." Most dealers take this as a blank check and will do everything they can find an excuse to do; for example, they'll charge $5 to smear some grease on the hood latch. However, as the car gets older, dealer shops get bored or lazy. They look at the fan belt because it's easy to see, but don't stoop to look underneath at battered-out suspension strut washings. They grease door latches, but don't look at the parking brake cables to see that they are rusting solid into their housings, much less oil them to loosen them up. They don't give the steering wheel a wiggle to see if the steering box needs adjustment. They don't notice corrosion accumulating on battery cables and clean the terminals. Indeed, many of the manufacturers' maintenance schedules don't list these items.

The upshot is that as a car gets older, you may have to dictate the maintenance program yourself.

The situation becomes more critical at independent, nondealer shops that, typically, work in an *ad hoc* way. A car comes in with clunking universal joints, so the mechanic replaces the U-joints, but pays no attention to the metallic dust on the inside of a wheel that shows a brake disc is being ground away by a worn-out brake pad. Or, the car comes in for new brake pads, but the mechanic doesn't bother to grease and adjust the wheel bearings (where applicable); after all, it wasn't on the work order. If he tries to sell you on the idea, you'll think he's just trying to make more money out of you, and if he does it without authorization, you'll squawk and refuse to pay, so he does what you ask and stops. If your brakes are no better after the new pads because loose bearings make the front wheels stand spraddled, is that the mechanic's fault?

I would say it was his fault, for he is the specialist upon whom you depend. However, I also understand why, so often, the mechanic does nothing extra. In any case, you end up having to define the maintenance program yourself. So, therefore, we must engage the program head-on.

Our maintenance philosophy may be summarized as, "If some is good, more is better, and too much is just right." We will endorse excess (despite the classical Greek philosophers). On some items, we will reject the manufacturers' maintenance intervals as too long. The manufacturers will squawk that I am slandering their products, but let them squawk. You have the car and the manufacturer has the money, so whose interests and comfort shall we serve? More maintenance will never hurt you, though it will cost more money, but less can hurt you and end up costing even more money.

The Engine

Obviously, you want the engine to run well, to start promptly on cold mornings, and not to stall in rush-hour traffic jams. Hence, maintenance begins with the engine.

You don't have to do much for the engine except keep the cooling system topped up with a 50-50 mix of antifreeze and water, keep the crankcase topped up with quality oil, and put the proper gasoline in the tank.

Engine oils are classified by the American Petroleum Institute and the Society of Automotive Engineers (SAE). A car with a gasoline engine should have oil labeled as suitable for "API service class SE/SF," and diesels should have oil of the API service class recommended by the manufacturer, either API service class

CC or CD. Multiviscosity oils, which will be labeled as "SAE 10–30/40," are good because they don't get so thick when cold. A *W*, as in 10W-40, indicates an oil designed for winter use. Such oils have extra additives to handle the condensed water and fuel that gets into the oil in the winter and are preferred (but not necessary) in the cold season. In any case, use only the oil recommended by the manufacturer during the warranty period.

The big flap nowadays about oil involves so-called "synthetic" oils. Some such oils are purely synthetic and some are merely worked-over petroleum-base oils. In any case, they cost about $5 per quart but flow readily in cold weather and claim an ability to go 25,000 miles between changes.

The question, of course, is whether synthetics are suitable for use in an engine. Be guided by the API: if the synthetic has an API rating, accept the rating as good; if not, pass. Also, if synthetic oil leaks out or if an engine seems to burn it (when it doesn't burn conventional oil), blame the oil before the engine and don't be bashful about switching back to conventional oils.

Although experience is still a-gathering, you might sensibly use a synthetic during the winter for easy starting and go back to conventional oils in the summer. On the other hand, if the synthetic works, i.e., you get no leaks or excessive oil consumption, feel secure in using it. However, as a double check, have a shop add an oil-pressure gauge to your instruments to monitor the behavior of the oil. If a synthetic won't sustain oil pressure, compared to a conventional oil, don't use it.

Feed the engine its proper diet of *leaded* or *unleaded* gasoline. Lead additives in gasoline give it desirable combustion characteristics and provide a form of lubrication for the valves. Cars that use unleaded gasoline have valves of a metallurgical composition that can tolerate heat without the lubricating benefits of lead.

You can use unleaded gasoline in a car that calls for leaded gasoline (e.g., if unleaded is the only gasoline you can find), provided you don't overdo it. For example, use a 50-50 ratio, and don't use unleaded fuel when towing a trailer through Kansas in August.

However, while leaded gasoline will burn in all cars, if you put leaded gasoline into a car that calls for unleaded fuel, the lead will promptly kill the catalytic action of the catalytic converter and your car will spew pollutants. A new catalytic converter will cost up to $150.

The "octane rating" you see on service station pumps pertains to the combustion characteristics of the gasoline, not to its energy value. Gasoline rated at 87 octane for cars has the same energy content as 100-octane aviation gasoline. However, the higher the octane, the more resistance to that "pinging" you often hear when accelerating hard. If you use gasoline of too low an octane rating, you may get this pinging.

Tune-up

The tune-up, done annually or every 10,000 miles, whichever comes first, applies mostly to the ancillaries on the engine. In the tune-up, you should get new spark plugs, have the ignition timing set, get the air filter replaced, and have all carburetor linkages oiled or checked to assure free, easy motion. All pollution-control and cooling-system hoses should be examined for potential failure, and drive belts should be checked for tension. In addition, the tune-up interval may as well serve as a time to change the oil and oil filter.

The tune-up procedure has been vastly improved upon here of late by built-in diagnostic systems. Many cars have a plug under the hood that is wired into the ignition system and carburetor, plus much of the pollution-control system. The mechanic plugs a diagnostic machine into the car plug and reads engine performance on gauges, on a cathode-ray tube (CRT, as in a television set), or on a computer printout. These systems simplify the process and guide the mechanic in making adjustments.

As noted, an older car that does not have electronic ignition calls for more new parts in the tune-up.

Note here that we call for new plugs every 10,000 miles despite the fact that the manufacturer may only call for a new set every 15,000 to 25,000 miles. In fact, if you drive slowly all the time, e.g., from home to the store to the post office, etc., you may find that you need new plugs as often as every 3000 to 5000 miles. If so, change them. Don't be pigheaded about either my 10,000-mile or the manufacturer's 25,000-mile interval. If your driving style fouls plugs in short order, just accept your driving style as your own (which you have a right to), but give your engine new plugs if it needs them.

Now, *do not neglect*—repeat: DO NOT NEGLECT!!—valve adjustment if your car has adjustable valves. The valve-opening and valve-closing system must have a certain amount of looseness in it; you can sometimes hear this looseness as a satisfied ticking under the hood. As the parts of the system wear, the looseness diminishes. If it diminishes enough, the valves won't close fully and will "burn," which entails an expensive removal of the cylinder head to replace burned valves. Once a year or every 10,000 miles is good enough for most cars, but a car driven hard and fast deserves a valve adjustment every six months, or at least, a check on the free-space clearances.

An annual tune-up is also a good time to check on some of the other things listed below.

Oil and Oil-filter Changes

In general, take the manufacturer's recommended intervals and cut them approximately in half. If the manufacturer specifies a 6000-mile interval, change oil at 3000 miles; if 7500 miles, go to 4000 miles. With an interval as long as 4000 miles and if convenient to do so (such as your being a do-it-yourselfer), get oil filters and oil from the discount stores—about $3 for the filter and $1.50 for a quart of oil—and change the filter even more often, say every two months. Yes, this seems excessive, but it is actually a form of insurance: it insures that your engine stays its best as long as possible.

The reason for changing the oil at all is to replace oil that has degraded to the point that its ability to provide lubrication and cooling has been compromised. The oil degrades, first, from heat; and, second, from contamination.

The heat, of course, arises from the normal operation of the engine. Obviously, the engine, overall, will run hotter in the summer than in the winter and will develop more heat when towing. Furthermore, during its lifetime, an engine may overheat—frequently or rarely, grossly or mildly—due to some flaw in the cooling system. All car engines, then, do not experience the same amount of heat.

The contaminants that degrade oil are moisture that condenses from the air, and unburned fuel that escapes past the piston rings. Short-run driving in cold weather, when the engine never fully warms up, produces both of these contaminants, and a mechanical failure such as a defective spark plug, sticking choke, or faulty fuel injector produces unburned fuel.

The manufacturers do a lot of testing to establish suitable oil change intervals for their engines, but their tests presume "average" use that does not include nonaverage circumstances. Thus, the manufacturers' intervals tend to be overly optimistic.

The manufacturers defend their optimistically long oil change intervals by saying that the long intervals save people money. This is "penny-wise, pound-foolish" logic, especially since oil is so cheap when compared to the total cost of a car.

To simplify the arithmetic by omitting labor costs, let's assume two do-it-yourselfers: Nancy Normal, who changes her oil and filter every 6000 miles, or twice a year, and Zoë Zealous, who does so every 3000 miles, or four times per year. If both buy one filter and five quarts of oil for each change at the discount store, Nancy's annual bill for oil and filter changes will be $21 and Zoë's will be $42. In five years, Nancy will spend $105 and Zoë $210.

If Nancy and Zoë own the same kind of small-engine car and drive much the same way, Nancy's car will be wearing out in five years, while Zoë will get a sixth year from her car. Now, is that sixth year worth the extra $105? Of course it is; in fact, it's a fantastic bargain. Obviously, if the oil and filter changes are done at a shop, the respective bills will be about double, but the sixth year of use is still cheap at the price.

I can't prove that more-frequent oil changes will guarantee that sixth year, but no one can prove that it won't.

A car with a bigger engine will also benefit from more-frequent oil changes, but since big engines easily go 100,000 miles, the benefit is harder to predict. If 100,000 miles represent ten years of use, most people won't care what the engine is like after ten years: they'll be ready for a new car no matter how good the engine is.

Also, a car that spends most of its time at highway speed, rather than in traffic, benefits less from extra oil changes. The car that needs extra changes is the one that never gets fully warmed up, e.g., the car that goes only from the house to a commuter parking lot or only to and from the store, to and from the school, to and from the train station, etc.

Automatic Transmission

Manufacturers specify an interval wherein the oil (automatic transmission fluid, or ATF) in an automatic transmission should be changed and, where applicable, the oil filter/screen should be replaced or cleaned. In many years, I have met only one person who follows this recommendation (others may exist, but I've not met them) and that is my neighbor Raymond Cassidy. Ray would leave his 1978 Ford Fairmont at a dealership twice each year and say, "Give it what it needs," and one thing he got was fresh ATF at least once a year. After 120,000 miles, the only serious repair was one relining of the brakes at 90,000 miles and a radiator leak (caused by a stone) at 103,000 miles. Later, Ray had to get a new alternator, but he felt that 123,000 miles from the original alternator meant he got his money's worth the first time. Ray's car is a good example of how long a car can be trouble-free if you spend some money on maintenance.

Ray bought the Fairmont when the rust on his previous car, a 1972 Pinto, offered to drop him through the floor onto the pavement. The Pinto had 140,000 miles on it and had never experienced a mechanical failure. Ray's experience underscores an important point: the driver has much to do with how long a car lasts.

Back to the automatic transmission: Give it an oil change once a year. If it has a replaceable filter, as certain Chrysler products do, change the filter too. If it has only a screen, you probably needn't replace it, for I have never seen a filter screen clog up in normal use; usually, the screen clogs up only after the clutch discs inside the transmission have shed some of their linings for some other reason. If the shop is equipped to do so, have the bands and control pressure (if adjustable) adjusted, too.

Manual Transmission/Differential

Manufacturers also specify an oil-change interval for a manual transmission and for the differential and here again, nobody ever does it. It is worth doing at least every 25,000 to 30,000 miles (two to three years). You can get by without it in most cases, but to do it is insurance of longevity. Also, an alert mechanic will note any suspicious metal chips in the oil and be able to apprise you if trouble is brewing. If you tow a lot, change transmission and differential oil annually.

Clutch

As the clutch disc associated with a manual transmission wears thinner, the clutch pedal must travel farther before it can disengage the clutch, whereupon the clutch linkage must be adjusted. The time interval depends on your clutching style. At the very least, the clutch needs adjustment once a year.

Personally, I prefer to see clutches adjusted more often so that the clutch linkage is always operating in the most precise way. Unfortunately, the clutches on many smaller cars are simply incapable of precise adjustment. As you let your foot off the pedal, the linkage comes to rest in a slightly different position each time, which means the adjustment differs each time, too. The linkage is simply too unstable to allow precise adjustment, so mechanics leave things "loose" (by my standards).

The issue may be irrelevant if the "loose" adjustment works well. However, you must be sensitive to how the gear lever feels; if the gear lever begins to get hard to shift, have the clutch adjustment checked. Be especially critical during the warranty phase with a new car (and be even more critical when testdriving a new car before you buy), for the warranty period gives you a right to frequent clutch adjustments and those frequent adjustments will establish the norm for clutch action; that is, you will learn how far you must push the pedal and how easily the gear lever moves when things are in good order.

Cooling System (Radiator)

A new car comes with "permanent" antifreeze (that usually looks blue or green). All you have to do with the cooling system of a new car is check the coolant level. It should change only slightly and you should not need to add much over a year. However, do not add plain water: add a 50-50 mix of water and antifreeze, for the antifreeze contains rust inhibitors and anticorrosion additives that keep rust from forming.

After a year or two, you will find you have to add more coolant and, perhaps, add it more often, and may even find discoloration in the coolant. At this point, have the system flushed to get rid of rust and corrosion and refill it with fresh coolant. The change should get you another two trouble-free years, after which the coolant will degrade again.

An older car that has a lot of rust in its radiator and engine block needs a thorough flush, the "back-flushing" method with water under pressure being best. After a good flush, use the 50-50 mix.

Steering

Like automatic-transmission oil changes, steering system adjustments never get done. People drive on, year after year, with the steering wheel getting sloppier and sloppier, and their mechanic never bothers to check the matter or make timely adjustments.

On big cars, the steering box part of worm-and-sector steering needs adjustment at least once a year. On smaller cars, worm-and-sector steering boxes need adjustment less often, but once a year is easy to remember. If an annual check shows no need for adjustment, good, but better to check it than to neglect it. A rack-and-pinion system does not have a steering box, and the equivalent adjustment needs adjustment less often and the adjustment is more difficult, but it should be done if the steering wheel gets sloppy.

Tie-rod ends and steering-linkage idlers will get sloppy over a period of time, too. Say you have 1½ inches of free play in the steering wheel. You go to a shop and seek a remedy. The mechanic replaces two tie-rod ends (which perhaps were not really that bad) and thus reduces the free play to ¾ of an inch. This still leaves ¾ of an inch of slop that comes from the steering box, and most mechanics will leave it there. Your only hope here is to find a mechanic who is ideologically committed to well-adjusted steering boxes (I've never met one) or learn how to wiggle the steering shaft yourself to determine if adjustment is correct, then make a point of demanding a timely adjustment. To learn to wiggle, review the used-car survey, item 14.

Wheel Alignment

If you look closely when the car is parked on level ground, you will see that the front tires point slightly inward in the front; that is, they are pigeon-toed. This is a *toe-in*.

If you look again, you will see that they lean outward at the top; that is, they stand sort of bow-legged. This is *camber*.

You can't see it by looking, but they also have a *caster angle*; that is, the degree to which they carry the load ahead of or behind the center of the wheel.

Proper positioning of toe-in, camber, and caster is what is meant by "front-end alignment." Toe-in and camber affect the way the tires wear, and all three factors affect how stable the car is on the highway and how well it corners.

The alignment can be upset by bumps, but it also changes slightly over a period of time as suspension parts wear and as the metal in the car "stretches," so the alignment should be checked on a proper machine anytime the tires show uneven wear across the tread.

Most alignment faults can be corrected by toe-in adjustments, which is most fortunate, since you can hardly persuade a shop to check on camber and caster, much less adjust them. Indeed, many don't know how, and others aren't willing to work that hard.

The difficulty here is that evidence of alignment faults largely comes from analysis of tire wear, and if you can't perform that analysis yourself, you won't know the front end is out of alignment. The run-of-the-mill "front-end specialist" will check the toe-in and stop there. Alignment faults are usually too subtle for you to notice, and the shameful part of the matter is that they steal the roadworthiness of your car without your knowing it.

A *capable* front-end shop is easy to find, but one *willing* to do a full alignment is almost impossible to find. A dealership shop, or a dealer's recommendation, is about the best solution if you suspect alignment faults or simply want everything—toe-in, camber, and caster—set right.

Tire Rotation

As you go around a curve, the car leans in the direction opposite to the curve; that is, on a curve to the right, the car leans to the left, and vice versa.

I typically take curves to the right faster than curves to the left because, as the car leans to the left, the tires on the left side run near to the center line and the center line provides orientation that helps me know what the car is doing. On a curve to the left and with the car leaning to the right, I have less sensitivity about what the tires on the right side are doing.

In consequence of the way I take curves, I scrub off the sides of my left tires sooner than those on the right. You probably have some habits of this sort, and even if you don't, your car has peculiarities of its own that will cause minor differences in the wear of each tire. To even out these differences, you *rotate the tires*, i.e., shift them to different locations on the car, say, twice a year—more often if you drive as I do and on roads with many curves. The owner's manual will specify the recommended interval and pattern—e.g., right-rear to left-front, left-front to right-front, etc.—for your car.

In the absence of a recommended pattern of tire rotation, I always do an X. That is, left-front and right-rear trade places, as do right-front and left-rear; then, the next time, I go front-to-back, i.e., left-front goes to left-rear and vice versa; the next time, I go back to the X. Thus, the pattern is corner-to-corner, front-to-back, and corner-to-corner again. This means that each tire occupies each position on the car for a while.

Some authorities, though, don't like to rotate radial tires in this pattern. Presumably, radial tires get "accustomed," so to speak, to rotating in only one direction. If you put them on the opposite side of the car, they rotate in the opposite direction, and this opposite rotation is thought to upset the way the tire has "broken in," causing it to shed its tread.

In summary, you may find that the manufacturer's recommendations conflict with these other authorities to whom I refer. I would say that if you have foreign radials, don't worry about it. If you have domestic radials, ask the tire dealer. If the dealer says you may, indeed, lose your treads if you rotate from one side to the other, confine yourself to the front-to-back rotation pattern.

Brakes

You can't do much with brakes, since they are all self-adjusting now. However, if you are a moderate driver, you should get at least 30,000 miles or so from a set of brake linings. An annual check is worth the cost, though, to monitor wear and to make sure that one side of a disc brake caliper does not stick and cause the opposing pad to wear out prematurely.

If the parking brake works through the normal road, or "service," brakes, you can monitor brake-lining wear by how far you have to move the parking-brake lever to hold the car from rolling. However, this monitoring doesn't work on cars that have one set of linings for the service brakes and a different set for the parking brake; ask a dealership mechanic what system you have.

The extreme brake-maintenance gesture (which no one but me ever does) is to change the brake fluid every 10,000 to 20,000 miles. The fluid undergoes chemical changes in use and picks up microscopic particles of rubber and metal; these particles, along with the products of chemical change, settle out as a corrosive sludge that etches pits in the bores of the brake wheel cylinders. This sludge can cause the brakes to stick and will abrade the rubber pistons so that they leak.

Years ago, mechanics used to flush brakes, but they hate doing it now because modern dual-brake systems are hard to flush and refill. The problem is in evacuating the air that enters the system during the flushing. As a result, mechanics will try to talk you out of a brake flushing, saying, "You don't need it—after all, nobody ever does it." This leaves you with the fear that the mechanic will do a sloppy job of it if you do insist, since he doesn't believe in what he's doing, and that fear may justify seeking a more sympathetic shop.

Exhaust System

If your muffler isn't rattling around or absolutely dragging the ground, you will have little notion of how well it's holding up. The quick, easy check is to hold a gloved hand over the end of the exhaust pipe while the engine is running: You should be able to build up a substantial pressure and should be able to hear a sputtering of sorts from any leaks throughout the system.

If you do not build up a substantial pressure and if you do hear assorted sputterings, the system deserves a thorough under-the-car checkup.

Many cars have a catalytic converter in the exhaust system to reduce pollution. The catalytic material in the converter eventually gets used up, usually at 50,000 miles or so. The manufacturers specify a certain interval at which the converter should be replaced, but the manufacturer's recommendation is often ignored because of the exorbitant cost—up to $150—of a new catalytic converter. Rather than replace the converter, people eliminate it from the system; and they are encouraged to do so because so many people claim to have improved the way their cars run or have markedly improved gas mileage by taking the catalytic converter out of the system. This is not supposed to be the case; the converter, whether still doing its job or not, isn't supposed to affect the way the car runs. Unfortunately for normative science, on many cars the converter does seem to have negative effects. In any case, the converter is supposed to be replaced at 30,000- to 50,000-mile intervals and, of course, all socially responsible, right-thinking people who believe in the EPA will eagerly and willingly do so.

Windshield Wiper and Washer

En passant, we will note that the windshield wiper was patented in 1903 by Mary Anderson and was first used on streetcars. It was not standard equipment on automobiles—at least in the powered form—until 1923.

Windshield-wiper blades degrade from ozone and from the ultraviolet part of sunlight and so lose their ability to wipe well; the degradation is hastened in cities with high levels of air pollution, particularly sulfur compounds. Annual replacement is the barest minimum, and every six months is better. In any case, don't go into the winter without new wiper blades. The blades cost about $3 in discount stores and anyone can change them.

When you replace your wiper blades, don't use those that mount the rubber wiper in a plastic blade if you live in a cold climate. The plastic blade gets so stiff from the cold that it can't conform to the curve of the windshield.

Without exception, windshield-wiper blades are longer than

they need to be. The car manufacturers create excessive glass areas, mostly for reasons of style, then set up the wipers to wipe the whole area. This foolishness works well enough until you get into a fierce winter blizzard and your defroster will not clear the whole windshield. You have a clear spot in the middle that is surrounded by slushy snow, and as your wiper blades move up, they drag slush with them. When they reach the end of their stroke, they encounter the cold wind rushing over the car and the slush freezes solid. Then, on the next swipe, they pick up more slush and so on until the whole wiper blade is a lump of ice and you can't see anything through the windshield. When I see cars askew and aslither in the ditch in a snowstorm, I often wonder how many of them wound up there because the driver couldn't see through a lump of slush.

You can vastly reduce this problem at no significant cost to vision by using wiper blades that are shorter than the standard size for your car. If your car has wiper blades 16 inches long, 13- or 14-inch blades will do as well; you will lose a portion of the top arc and some of the bottom arc, but that's not where you look: you look through the middle.

The windshield washer, like a tail light on each side at the rear, is such an excellent idea that I wonder why it took so long to become standard equipment. If the automobile industry has been criminally negligent in any way, they were certainly negligent in waiting till the 1950s to offer windshield washers widely.

Unfortunately, people who drive cars are equally negligent and don't keep the washers working. Keep the canister filled and give the washers a brief squirt every day or two so they don't clog up.

Over the years, domestic manufacturers have endorsed and promoted the notion that the driver is the least-important element of the driver-car relationship.

One expression of this philosophy is in the windshield wiper/washer systems that assume drivers are too lazy or too stupid to wash first and wipe next, i.e., the wiper switch that won't allow you to wash without wiping. For example, on my Saab, I can squirt washing fluid until I get the smashed bugs or dirt softened, then apply the wiper. By contrast, turning on the washer in the Chevrolet Suburban set the wipers going even before the washing fluid got to the windshield.

The net effect of Detroit's way is a lot of scratched windshields because you end up running wipers across a dry windshield covered with abrasive dust.

Battery

The battery can be represented as being like bucket with a faucet (see page 372). All you have to do to it is keep its faucet from clogging, such "clogging" being evident when fuzzy accretions form on the battery posts and cable terminals. The symptoms of "clogging" will be those of a dead battery, and a shop will happily sell you a new one. To take the old battery out and put in a new one somewhat dislodges the corrosion on the terminals, so things work for a while. Then, the battery goes dead again, and this time the shop sells you an alternator. The third time, you'll get the new battery cables that you really needed in the first place.

Sometimes a shop will cut an old, corroded terminal off a battery cable and install a bolt-on replacement. This works until corrosion gets going in the clamp part of the bolt-on terminal, then the trouble starts again. So, don't accept the bolt-on solution unless you are a do-it-yourselfer who is willing to clean the cable thoroughly and fully solder the bolt-on clamp to it. You probably won't be able to get a shop to do that, so insist on a totally new cable.

Under the Car

When your car goes up on a service station lift for an oil change, have the mechanic check the universal joints for looseness and look for worn bushings in the suspension, plus exhaust-system clamps/hangers that are about to break; if the muffler itself seems soft and squishy from rust, replace it before it falls off (as it will just as you drive up to a ritzy restaurant for valet parking). Check, also, on parking-brake cables, fuel lines, and brake lines, to see if they are getting rusty; replace or repair, as needed.

Last, have the mechanic look for oil leaks from either end of the engine, from the end of the transmission, and from the differential. A modest, greasy moistness is no cause for concern, but serious dripping calls for assessment and correction. For example, if your automatic transmission leaks one quart per month, you can have the service station add oil regularly and you can live with the fault. However, replacing the transmission seal (and bushing, to ensure the new seal) will eliminate the possibility of ruining your transmission if the leakage suddenly gets more severe; for example, if you make a long trip in hilly country, you will leak more oil going uphill than you do driving around town (that is, with a front-engine, rear-drive car).

As noted, the cars of twenty years ago had as many as 25 grease fittings in the suspension and steering, and another dozen elsewhere. A "grease job" really meant it. Now, cars have hardly any grease fittings (because of the use of rubber bushings, sealed bearings, etc.). If a garage makes a hefty charge for "chassis lubrication," find out what they are charging you for.

A long-time European habit that has recently crossed the Atlantic is the practice of spraying oil on the underside of a car. When doing an oil change, the mechanic takes the old oil and sprays it all over underneath the car, up in the fender wells, etc. Done often, this practice is the best guarantee against rust that is available (except rust that proceeds from the inside out, e.g., from inside the trunk). If your car is in good shape, find a shop that will oil spray it regularly and that will keep it that way.

Otherwise, when driving a lot on roads that have been salted during the winter, run the car through a fast-wash place frequently. At a wash-it-yourself place, be scrupulous about spraying under the fenders. Look for places where mud and slush collect and clean them well.

MAINTENANCE SCHEDULE: GOING BY NUMBERS

The prior discussion has emphasized—indeed, belabored—the fact that different cars get used in different ways. By logical extension, then, different cars have different maintenance needs. Yet, when we set up a schedule for routine maintenance, we declare that a single maintenance schedule will suit all cars, even though we know our declaration is not true.

Our maintenance schedule, then, generalizes about matters that may differ drastically. However, it will work well enough for most cars, especially since it is biased in favor of the "more is better" approach. Like most maintenance schedules found in owners' manuals and workshop manuals, our schedule is systematic and cumulative: you do a number of minor things frequently, a number of more important things less often, and truly major things rarely. The minor things seem trifling, but they provide monitoring for the larger things. When the time comes to check a major item, the numerous minor things may have already provided for it.

For example, we specify an oil change at 3000–4000-mile intervals and a check on the manual transmission oil every 6000 miles. Now, suppose you buy a used car and immediately give it an oil change and check its transmission. After 3000 miles, you change engine oil again; while the car is on the lift, the mechanic takes a quick look at the outside of the transmission and sees no evidence of leaking oil. After 3000 more miles, he still sees no signs of leaking. He may say that the absence of drips means he need not remove the filler plug in the transmission and stick a finger in to literally check the oil level; rather, the oil level has been adequately checked by inferences based on external inspection.

On the other hand, if he found dripping after the first 3000 miles, he would check the transmission oil anyway, even though it is not on the 3000-mile list.

Qualifications like these remind you that your maintenance program will be more successful if it is done by the same shop. The shop will love you if you follow the schedule given here, because they will make about twice as much money off you as they do other people. Furthermore, they will make relatively easy money: the mechanic would much rather get paid to inspect your brakes at 24,000-mile intervals, and perhaps reline them a little early, than have you ignore them until your calipers are frozen beyond redemption, your discs scored beyond salvaging. The inspection is a much easier and cleaner job than a total brake overhaul, and one new disc alone will cost as much as several inspections.

Given a good relationship with a shop you trust, you can let the mechanic modify the maintenance schedule. For example, he may say, "You don't really need to replace these V-belts after 24,000 miles." The answer to that one is, "Go ahead and change them, but leave the old ones in the trunk for spares." Thus, 24,000 miles later, you can indeed forgo new belts because you have spares readily available, and you will be looking at the belts every time you check the oil anyway.

Remember, though, that when in doubt, chose to err on the side of excess.

Don't ask a dealership mechanic to follow the maintenance schedule here on a new car that is still under warranty. The warranty is closely tied to the manufacturer's maintenance schedule and you could, in theory, invalidate your warranty by changing oil more often than the manufacturer recommends. This is an absurdity, of course, but is an absurdity such as the world runs on. Once the car goes out of warranty, of course, you can change its oil as often as you like.

For about thirty years, various organizations that study such things have reported that the "average" American car gets driven about 10,000 miles per year. Thus, 10,000 miles may be considered one year in the life of a car. However, because I don't totally trust that 10,000-mile-per-year figure, and because a 12,000-

mile base allows more convenient multiples, i.e., 1000 miles per month, our schedule assumes a year of 12,000 miles. That means it will reasonably fit cars that run from 8000 to 15,000 miles per year. That is, you think in terms of once per month, every three or four months, every six months, once a year, and every two years, rather than in terms of rigid numbers. However, a warning: our mileage intervals mean, "Don't let the car go beyond this mileage without checking on this item." The intervals are maximum limits, subject to the qualifications about differences and the advice of the mechanic.

In our schedule, the word *inspect* means "look at," while *check* entails doing something with your hands. You take off the radiator cap to "check" the coolant level (item 10a on the schedule) and look at—"inspect"—the battery cables (item 12) while you're at it. Obviously, if the cables are covered with greenish-whitish corrosion, you resolve to do something about it.

Similarly, when the car goes up on the lift for an oil change, the mechanic gives each wheel a wiggle to assess its bearings and tie-rod ends, a spin to see if a brake is dragging, and a quick survey of the exhaust system. He can do these things during the five minutes that the old oil is draining from the engine. The mechanic may think you're fussy to want so many things checked on, but tell him that you are, indeed, quite fussy—you paid too much for the car to be casual. In any event, the words *check* and *inspect* do not entail complex operations. The "check," "set," "adjust," and "replace" items, of course, do entail some work.

An owner's manual will list periodic checks on the components of the pollution-control system. Most of the officially recommended checks are useless: you can't tell that an exhaust-gas-recirculation (EGR) valve is defective by looking at the outside of it. However, a defective EGR valve will show up in the exhaust-gas values (16c), so we cover the whole pollution-control system in item 16, which requires us, at least once per year, to find a shop that has an exhaust-gas analyzer. The owner's manual will also include checks on such things as the inertia locks on the seat-belt reels and the seat-belt warning lights. You may ignore such things: to test the inertia lock, you have to bash the car into something, and as a sapient human being, you don't need the warning lights at all: you fasten your seat belt as a matter of habit.

Maintenance Schedule

Item	Service	Interval, miles
1. oil	check level	1,000
	change	3,000–4,000
2. oil filter	replace	3,000–4,000
3. air filter	replace	12,000
4. PCV valve	inspect	12,000
5. spark plugs		
a. conventional ignition	replace	6,000
b. electronic ignition	replace	12,000–15,000
6. distributor		
a. cap		
b. rotor	inspect	6,000
c. points	replace	12,000
7. spark-plug wires	replace	24,000
8. fuel filter	replace	12,000
9. V-belts		
a. fan		
b. air conditioner	inspect	1,000
c. power steering	replace	24,000
10. Cooling system		
a. coolant	check level	1,000
b. radiator	replace	24,000
	flush	24,000
11. cooling system hoses	inspect	1,000
12. battery	inspect	1,000
13. exhaust system		
a. pipes		
b. mufflers	inspect	6,000
c. clamps and supports		
14. valve clearances		
a. moderate driving	check, adjust	12,000
b. hard driving	check, adjust	6,000
15. ignition timing		
a. conventional ignition	check, set	6,000
b. electronic ignition	check, set	12,000
16. fuel system (carburetor, fuel injection)		
a. idle mixture	check, adjust	12,000
b. idle speed		
c. exhaust gas values		

Item	Service	Interval, miles
17. clutch		
linkage	adjust	6,000
a. hydraulic fluid	check level	1,000
	replace	24,000
18. manual transmission		
a. oil	check level	6,000
	replace	24,000
b. shift linkage	inspect	12,000
19. automatic transmission		
a. fluid (ATF)	check level	1,000
	replace	24,000
b. filter	replace	24,000
c. bands	adjust	24,000
d. control pressure	check, adjust	24,000
20. drive shaft, universal joints	inspect, lubricate	6,000
21. differential oil	check level	6,000
	replace	24,000
22. wheel bearings, front and rear	check, lubricate, adjust	6,000
23. brakes		
a. fluid	check level	1,000
	replace	24,000
b. linings, disc and drum	inspect	24,000
c. parking brake	adjust	12,000
24. steering and suspension		
a. steering box	check oil level, adjust	12,000
b. power steering fluid	check level	1,000
	replace	24,000
c. tie-rod ends and ball joints	inspect	6,000
d. strut bushings	inspect	6,000
e. shock absorbers	inspect	6,000
25. wheel alignment	check	If tire wear is uneven, or following a severe impact (e.g. jumping a curb at speed).
26. tires	check pressure, inspect outside inspect inside	1,000 6,000
27. latches: hood, doors, trunk	lubricate	6,000
28. windshield-wiper blades	replace	12,000

Item	Service	Interval, miles
29. body rust	inspect cavities, clean, apply oil	3,000 (winter)
30. air conditioner		
a. hoses	inspect	1,000
b. refrigerant	check supply	12,000
c. heat exchanger	remove debris	12,000

Maintenance Lists

1,000 miles
   check oil
   check coolant
   inspect V-belts
   inspect hoses
   check hydraulic fluids (brake, clutch)
   check power-steering fluid
   check automatic-transmission fluid
   inspect battery
   check tire pressure

3,000–4,000 miles
   change oil
   replace oil filter

6,000 miles
   replace spark plugs (conventional ignition)
   check ignition timing (conventional ignition)
   adjust valve clearances (hard driving)
   inspect exhaust system
   adjust clutch linkage
   check manual-transmission oil
   check differential oil
   inspect universal joints
   inspect suspension-system components
   inspect tires, inside
   lubricate latches

12,000 miles

inspect PCV valve
replace air filter
replace spark plugs (electronic ignition)
replace distributor cap, rotor, points (conventional ignition)
replace fuel filter
adjust valve clearances
check ignition timing

24,000 miles

replace spark-plug wires
replace V-belts
flush radiator, replace coolant
replace power-steering fluid
replace hydraulic, brake, and clutch fluids (where applicable)
inspect brake linings
replace manual-transmission oil
replace automatic-transmission fluid
replace automatic-transmission fluid filter (where applicable)
adjust automatic-transmission bands and control pressure
replace differential oil

CHOOSING A SHOP

Having worked out a maintenance program, you have to find a shop to execute it. As noted, a new car under warranty should be serviced at a dealership to protect the warranty. Once out of warranty, you may prefer to have the work done elsewhere.

My experience as a mechanic began at home with the traditional junker under a tree (hence, "shade-tree mechanic") with its engine dangling from a block-and-tackle swung from a limb, progressed into wheatfields and trucks, diverted into foreign cars, broadened to include experience at two shops under others' management, and concluded with my own three-car shop, the relevant factor here being the progression from disorder to order and what you learn from it, a lesson I heard well stated by Eric Hoffer when he appeared on CBS-TV in 1968. When asked what would interest him if he visited a Russian factory, Hoffer replied, "I would say, 'Bring me the records of maintenance,' and if I found one special nail where the broom always hung, I would say, 'This is the nail of immortality.'"

I have been impressed with Hoffer's answer ever since I heard it, and I fully believe it. In one tiny detail, Hoffer found the proper sign of the competence of any productive organization: to wit, a respect for order. When you go into a garage—or any business—look for the broom, for what you see will tell you what sort of enterprise it is. If the broom is in the corner with the dustpan and looks as if that is its place, the shop is probably good. If the broom looks as though it was dropped right where it was last used, the shop is second rate, for the care of the broom indicates larger patterns of thought and work.

Don't be put off by a shop that looks messy in the middle of a workday—an old muffler lying beside a car, empty oil cans near another, spark-plug packages strewn about—for those are the normal consequences of getting something done. Look for the broom: if the broom is obviously a respected implement, the shop probably knows what it's doing.

Besides the broom, note any music that may be playing in the shop. Automatically reject a shop that plays so-called "rock" music. If the mechanics are paying attention to it—snapping their fingers and jerking their heads to the rhythm—they obviously aren't paying attention to their work. If they aren't responding to it, if they seem indifferent to it, then they are obviously thick-headed louts who lack the alert sensitivity required to do a good job. That is, if they can ignore rock music, they can ignore what their other senses and their instruments tell them; if they can tolerate such an auditory perversion in their work environment, they can also tolerate mechanical aberrations in a car.

If you're concerned about engine work, look around the shop for electronic analyzing equipment. These units are often painted red and have some sort of cathode-ray tube (CRT, or "TV tube") display. A shop dealing with post-1975 cars with electronic ignition requires such equipment, particularly when tuning cars with complex emission controls. Obviously, a shop that specializes in mufflers, brakes, or radiators hardly needs an electronic engine analyzer, but shops doing engine work do.

Exceptions to this rule can be found in general repair shops that have several mechanics, each of whom is a sort of specialist on certain cars, e.g., one mechanic is the General Motors specialist and another the Chrysler product specialist. In such cases, each mechanic usually has a special affection for certain cars and learns their habits by experience and study. Such a mechanic will know what sort of defect in which one of a dozen pollution-control devices makes a Ford engine act up in a certain way, and such mechanics have less need of electronic instruments. As a rule, though, the presence of an electronic analyzer is a healthy sign—unless it's dusty.

Note how each mechanic keeps his own specific work area. A naked-lady poster is a suspicious sign, though not categorically negative. Still, prefer the mechanic who decorates his work area with an epigram from Lao Tzu. A quotation from Francis Bacon or John Locke—rare anywhere nowadays—would be the best sign of all.

Next, note the toolboxes: those plastered with decals for assorted automotive products are suspicious, though a few casual stickers are acceptable. Most of all, look for the brand name on the toolbox.

Snap-On tools are the aristocrat of tools. They are refined designs and cost a lot of money. Mechanics who buy them must be able to see their quality, must be willing to pay for it, and must be good enough to afford it. Possession of Snap-On tools is not a guarantee, but it is a good sign.

Proto tools are almost as good a sign, and mechanics who use Proto tools would say they are a better sign than Snap-On tools; but to me, Snap-On is still the aristocrat.

Other brand names on the toolboxes are negative signs, though not categorically so. They betray a sort of "bargain" mentality that goes with bargain-quality work. However, they may indicate a mechanic with a large family, so don't judge hastily.

Although maintenance and order indicate a good shop, be suspicious of a shop that looks like a demonstration for cleaning products. A shop that looks too neat and too perfect is one where little work gets done, which means the shop pays its overhead by charging exorbitant prices for the work it does do. Likewise with fancy waiting rooms: somebody has to pay for all that Danish modern furniture; specifically, the customers.

Due to brand-name loyalty, many people will prefer dealership shops. However, as a general rule, people who drive used cars, especially older cars, should avoid dealership shops because they charge such high prices for parts—about 50 to 100 percent more than independent garages. Dealership shops tend to regard service customers as a sort of captive "audience" and seek to make the most out of them.

However, if you buy a new car from a dealer, that dealer has already made some money off you and hopes to sell you another new car in a few more years. If you get hit with a severe repair bill, you can tell the dealer you were sold a lemon and prove disagreeable, or you can buy your next car somewhere else. Dealers want repeat business from new-car buyers and work harder to keep them happy, but they have less regard for business that comes in off the street. By contrast, the independent shop regards every new customer as potential repeat business. They assume their customers can and will go elsewhere if not satisfied and prefer to keep them. Since they don't have the franchise advantage, they make up for it with price breaks or better service.

When a well-used car comes into a dealer shop, the dealer is inclined to try to sell the owner a new car—perhaps by scaring the owner with high estimates/costs for repairs. The independent shop, though, has nothing to sell but its service and will try to keep the car running so, in time, it can sell the owner more mufflers, brakes, oil changes, etc.

Thus, independent shops are probably better for people who drive used cars. Exceptions, of course, do arise: for example, independent shops may not have the repair manuals for new cars (indeed, the dealers do not always have them), so a second-hand car, if only about a year old, perhaps should go back to a dealer shop—but check with the independents first. Also, fairly new foreign cars may need to go to a dealer shop, particularly if they are the more expensive ones; the independents don't see such cars often enough to be experienced with them.

Note the "perhaps" and "may" here; these are not absolute rules, and many independent shops can do better work than dealership shops, even on exotic foreign cars, sometimes because the independents are under less pressure to "move" cars briskly through the shop.

Service station shops are a mixed bag and too often follow the low-volume syndrome; that is, a two-bay station can't handle many cars, so must make as much as possible off every one.

In the old days, service stations did tune-ups, exhaust systems, clutch adjustments, and such like along with oil changes and grease jobs. The grease job has all but disappeared and oil change intervals have become much longer, so station shops have had to expand their repair service to make up. Unfortunately, being small, they can't always afford the diagnostic equipment new cars require and since the mechanics often must pump gas and check oil, too, station mechanics are often of apprentice quality. This does not mean stations should be totally avoided; it means they call for an acute evaluation.

One generality: a station habituated by punkish louts with noisy, overdone cars should be avoided. The mechanic(s) may be capable on the cars they like, but they have little respect for cars unlike their own and tend to be indifferent about them.

When assessing a shop, note the cars already there: a collection of junks implies versatile mechanics who know how to patch and make-do to keep old stuff running, mechanics who know just how far a part can go before it fails and who know which wrecking yard will have a second-hand part. Such shops usually have skilled, intelligent mechanics because the mechanics are often back-yard car freaks gone professional, people who really enjoy cars. However, as the cars in the shop indicate, they are often behind the times—no one ever brings a new car in, so the mechanics are not practiced on new cars—but if you drive a junker, these are the shops for you.

A shop full of new cars implies money: the mechanics assume the owners have money and will replace a part if the paint on it is scratched. Also, while the mechanics are competent, their work is often "just a job." The consequence of this attitude is not poor work, but a lack of enthusiasm about getting it done. Hence, high labor costs. Also, new cars imply impatience with irregular problems: Suppose the alternator charging light goes on and off erratically, but the battery is always charged and the fan belt has already been tightened. The mechanics in a shop full of new cars will not be interested in the subtleties of the problem; they will replace the alternator and regulator (and perhaps never test the old one while it is still on the car). If new parts don't cure the problem, then the fancy-shop mechanics will bestir themselves to look for the subtlety and finally find the loose wire under the dashboard that caused the charging light to flicker.

The junk-car-shop mechanics will be attracted to the subtlety at once, and will rather enjoy solving a puzzle. However, they'll probably smear the steering wheel with greasy hands while they're at it.

The middle-ground shop with a mixture of clunkers and new cars is probably a good shop. Such shops treat clunkers like new cars, so the owner of a rusted-out hulk worth $200 gets the same $400 brake overhaul that the owner of the car worth several thousand does. You can object to the economics here of spending more for repairs than a car is worth, but you must respect the underlying logic that believes in making things right.

Shops to avoid are those that have a large collection of cars awaiting work and that can't move them. In some instances, such shops are waiting for owners to get paychecks so work can proceed, but to allow the cars to collect betrays sloppy management, so you should regard such shops with suspicion.

Shops that never have work waiting on the street or in the back lot are making their money on low volume, which implies high costs, but also implies lots of attention to any one car; check these out.

As noted, dealerships are for new cars, preferably bought at that dealership, for traveling people who have no time to look for another shop while on a trip, and for owners of the more-exotic foreign cars.

When seeking a shop, shamelessly exercise every resource. Ask your friends. Ask people you meet at self-serve service stations. So you just bought an old Peugeot and wonder who can deal with the Gallic logic of its electrical system? Ask the driver of another Peugeot. Don't hesitate to accost the person in the car next to you at a traffic light.

The marque club people—the ones you consulted before buying a new car—are one of the best sources. They will know the best mechanics at the dealerships by first name and will know of any back-alley, hole-in-the-wall shop that has some wizard who can diagnose a car's ailments by the mere laying on of hands and who can execute any repair blindfolded. The club membership usually includes several who have a decently equipped shop at home and whose evangelical zeal for the marque will induce them to make occasional repairs to other people's cars.

Most people are eager to talk, are eager to praise a good shop, and twice as eager to condemn one they don't like. (Note the implicit qualification here: a shop that someone doesn't like is not necessarily a bad shop, for some people can't be satisfied even with perfection.)

I do not recommend consultation with the Better Business Bureau or similar agencies, for I think that most people who report businesses to the BBB *et al.* are chronic malcontents or just plain paranoid psychotics. People do not realize the extent to which the BBB and similar agencies have discredited themselves by assuming that an aggrieved customer is always right and for failing to discern how often an aggrieved customer is a liar or a thief. I do not believe I have met a single tradesman— mechanic, carpenter, plumber, etc.—who has any respect for the BBB. Many say that BBB complaints usually arrive after they try to collect from a delinquent customer; that is, the customer drives the car happily for three months and, when pressed to pay the overdue repair bill, suddenly finds assorted reasons to protest about the quality of the work or the size of the bill. While listening to bill-collection proceedings in small claims court, I have noted how often a delinquent sought to intimidate his way out of an overdue bill by soliciting the offices of the BBB. In sum, if you're looking for a good shop, BBB reports won't help.

Here of late, the National Institute for Automotive Service Excellence has got a lot of favorable attention (most of it generated by NIASE press releases) as an agency that certifies the competence of mechanics. I am suspicious of NIASE because of its address (1825 K Street, NW, Washington, D.C., 20006), for the address suggests some sort of lobbying organization that is devoted to seeking favorable legislation for some particular interest. I don't know what that interest may be, but I doubt that it is disinterested compassion for car owners. In any case, NIASE administers multiple-choice tests from Educational Testing Service (ETS, the SAT people) and confers the right to wear an NIASE shoulder patch on mechanics who pass the test.

If you believe in multiple-choice tests, you may take comfort from a shop displaying an NIASE sticker. Comfort may be all you'll get, for you certainly get no guarantee of competence from a mechanic who learned how to work on a car by making marks on a multiple-choice answer sheet.

The placards you see on shop walls that indicate that a mechanic completed a factory training program don't mean much either. They show that the mechanic learned how to go through the motions of replacing parts, but they prove nothing about analytical ability or conscientiousness of performance.

In sorry sum, in choosing a repair shop as in choosing a car dealer, you are terribly alone. Generally, look for signs of care (the broom) and quality (tools, equipment, clientele).

You should ask about a warranty on repair work, but be forewarned that a warranty on repairs rarely does more than assure that parts are "free from defects." It may apply to workmanship, but "workmanship" usually means no more than "parts properly installed." That is, a repair warranty does not guarantee that the car will run.

If you can get the service manager to spend a few minutes with you, tell him pointblank your fears about incompetent workmanship and rip-off prices. Let the service manager's answers help you decide about the shop. If the service manager claims a perfect record and gets defensive about your questions, eliminate that shop. If he says something like "Look, we're just trying to make a living here and we have to know what we're doing. On the other hand, we're human and we make mistakes, but we try to make good on them"—an answer along those lines—you know you're dealing with an honest man. His honesty does not mean your relationship will always be untroubled, but it's a good place to start.

DEALING WITH
THE SHOP

A job that should take an hour will consume a day, for it takes about eight hours to find out what needs to be done and how to do it. In many cases when one part is duly fixed something else is thrown out of adjustment, and then comes a puzzling search, sometimes taking several days... The owner just sits down and trembles until the job is finished.

—"Horseless Age," August 21, 1901, cited by James J. Flink, in *America Adopts the Automobile, 1895–1910* (1970)

$\mathbf{A}$s with choosing a car, once you choose a shop, you have to get along with it; your car depends on you to do so. You have to grant the shop several things. First, it is in business to make money, to make a living for its managers and mechanics. Second, the prices it charges may seem outrageous, but the prices are rational in the respect that they are, ultimately, a product of supply and demand. The prices for parts are somewhat different, since the parts business replicates the economic model of oligopoly (few suppliers, many buyers), but the independent shop itself has little control over the parts situation and the dealership shop has even less. Third, you must recognize that cars are not always beautifully simple; sometimes, they deliver themselves of ailments that are not in either the mechanic's experience or his workshop manuals, and solutions can be elusive. Fourth, you have to make allowances for the nature of the business: a garage cannot run like an assembly line and delays will occur.

Most people are willing to grant all this. They just want the car to run reliably; indeed, most people are willing to feel cheated on the bill, so long as the car runs well. What drives people to despair and to lawyers is to pay the bill and have the car stall a block from the shop (or, worse yet, refuse to start at home the next morning).

Under normal circumstances, the way you minimize the probability of faulty workmanship is 1) to define the problem clearly for the mechanic, and 2) to review the repair procedure as you pay the bill and thus certify that all symptoms are accounted for. A clear definition of the problem, obviously, helps the mechanic aim toward the solution; a review of the repair procedure not only allows the mechanic to review his own logic, but gives you a better notion of what the repair involved.

As you review the repairs with the mechanic, bring out the workshop manual—the one you bought for the maintenance program—and say something like "I don't really understand this book, but can you sort of show me what you did to the car?"

Mechanics, as much as everybody else, like to show off how smart they are, so the mechanic will flip to the relevant section and point at the fuzzy photographs as you nod in complete noncomprehension. You probably won't learn much, but sharing the manual brings you and the mechanic closer. The mechanic will appreciate your honesty in admitting your ignorance and will admire your willingness to buy the manual and ask questions.

The review also gives you an approach for understanding the situation if repairs turn sour, plus a basis for complaining about it: You go over the symptoms and the mechanic explains how they were disposed of. When the same symptoms reappear when you get a block away from the shop, you can promptly return to the shop and say, "You said you did this and that, but the car still does thus and so." The mechanic will have to pinpoint new problems or acknowledge the inadequacy of the repairs. The post-repair review of symptoms will not guarantee the performance of the mechanic, but it will help certify the legitimacy of your complaints if the repairs did not correct the problems.

For an example of a car owner who did not clearly define the symptoms or the problem, note the following dialogue:

Distraught '76 Saab Owner: My clutch has gone out. I can't shift into gear.
Mechanic: How did it happen?
Owner: I don't know. I just can't get into gear.
Mechanic: Even with the engine not running?
Owner: I didn't try that.
Mechanic: Well, if you can't get it into gear now, that must be a change. Surely, you could get it into gear at some time or other.

Owner: Oh, sure, but I can't now.

Mechanic: Okay, now what events or circumstances arose between the time you could get it into gear, and the time now when you can't?

Owner: I don't know. When I got it back, I couldn't shift.

Mechanic: "Back" from where?

Owner: Oh, some friends borrowed it and when they brought it back, it wouldn't shift.

Mechanic: And it always worked perfectly before they borrowed it?

Owner: Well, no, it was getting harder and harder to shift and then they borrowed it for a few days and when they brought it back, it didn't work at all.

Mechanic: How could they bring it back if the clutch wouldn't work?

Owner: Well, if you put it in gear and push the clutch down you can start it, and then you can sort of shift after you're moving.

Mechanic: So, it will go into gear with the engine not running, and the clutch does work a little.

Owner: Well, yes, I guess, but it was replaced three months ago and shouldn't be worn out already.

Mechanic: Agreed, so it probably just needs adjustment.

Owner: But they [previous mechanics] said you couldn't adjust the clutch.

Mechanic: Yes, they were right; the '76 Saab has the self-adjusting clutch, so the symptoms suggest hydraulic trouble—the clutch master cylinder or the *slave cylinder* isn't doing its job, or the hydraulic fluid lines are leaking.

Owner: Oh, yes, they said something like that, that I needed a new master cylinder, but I couldn't afford it.

Mechanic: So what did they tell you would happen?

Owner: Well, they said I would have to add fluid.

Mechanic: So, did you?

Owner: No.

Mechanic: Why not?

Owner: Well, I forgot.

Mechanic: So, they told you that your master cylinder was leaking, and told you to add fluid if it got low, and you've ignored it for three months?

Owner: Well, uh, yes.

Mechanic: Okay, before we condemn your clutch, let's check the fluid in the master cylinder.

The foregoing dialogue fairly well represents a conversation I had with a car owner. The relevant point here is to note how much digging was required to ferret out the facts that applied to the situation. In this particular instance, the owner failed to pay attention to what the previous mechanic had told him about adding fluid and had, as a result, worked himself into great alarm when all he needed to do was to top up the clutch master cylinder. If he had given a coherent, orderly review of the history of the clutch, I could have made a sound diagnosis at once, without all the circumlocutory interrogation. Indeed, if the owner had made a list of symptoms when the clutch was replaced three months before, had reviewed the matter with the mechanic, and had made a written note about the leaking master cylinder, he probably would have remembered the master cylinder business.

Note, also, that an unscrupulous mechanic, or one who took the customer's word literally, would have sold the fellow a new clutch. A goodly number of repairs arise in just that way: The mechanic, from larceny or stupidity, sells work that isn't needed. The owner says, "My car won't start, so I guess I need a new battery," so the shop obligingly sells a new battery, and never looks for another problem. A lot of new starters get sold because of dead batteries (or because of corroded battery connections), and new carburetors get sold because a piece of the automatic choke linkage falls out of place. Unfortunately, unless you are well-studied in such matters, you cannot protect yourself from thievery/stupidity of this sort.

To return to the point, when the car begins acting up, study its symptoms closely. Note the constant or variable circumstances when they come up. Have your spouse and scions who use the car contribute to the list and write the symptoms down.

For example, consider a stereotypical (or hypothetical) domestic situation: You drive very moderately, your son drives like a teen-ager, and your husband has a sensitive nose. At the dinner table, you say, "Something's wrong with the car. The brake pedal starts out hard but gets spongy after a mile or two."

Your son says, "Yeah, and it's awfully sluggish, too. Won't get away from a light like it ought to."

Your husband says, "Yes, and I smell something funny by the time I get to the train station."

You record these remarks and present them to the mechanic. "Clearly," he says, "your brakes are dragging. Thus, your loss of acceleration. As you drive, the brakes get hot and half-boil the brake fluid, so the pedal gets spongy, and the brake drums make a smell like a dry skillet left on a stove burner." Agreed, he doesn't know why they are dragging, but he does know a lot more than if you had simply said, "My brakes don't work so good," or had said, as many people do, "It's sluggish too, so I probably need a tune-up, too." In most shops, a remark like that will get you a tune-up even if you had one only a week ago.

In collecting symptoms, you must try to be complete, but must be able to omit irrelevant matters. "I hear this 'clunk' every time I step on the gas," you say, "and the radio fades out when I drive between tall buildings." The radio, obviously, has no connection with the "clunk" and need not be mentioned. However, if in doubt, tell more rather than less, for the connections between parts can be strange. "The engine sputters and shakes when I put on the brakes," you say. These events would not seem related, but I recognize an air leak in the brake vacuum booster that is letting too much air into the engine (and making the air-fuel mixture too lean).

Very well, when the car starts acting up, note the symptoms closely, particularly how or whether they occur with other events. For example, your list may read:

- Car races when started up (in the morning) and won't slow down even after driving awhile.
- After a while, car stalls and is very hard to start again; "backfires" a lot when being started; puts out black smoke when it does start.
- If it starts and gets up some speed, it seems to run all right, but stalls when it slows down.

You leave the car, the mechanic goes to work on it, and when you come back, his (properly itemized) labor bill reads:

- automatic choke stove, R & R (remove and replace)
- choke unloader, R & R
- adjust idle mixture

"So what's this stuff?" you say.

"Well," he will tell you, "the automatic choke 'stove' has a little spring that pulls your choke on when the engine is cold and lets it off when the engine is warm. Your stove spring was rusted into a lump and wouldn't let the choke off. That's why the engine ran fast all the time and that's why it would stall after it warmed up. It was being choked to death."

"Okay," you say, "but why would it work if I drove fast enough?"
"This 'choke unloader' pulls the choke off if you apply power, but yours wasn't going to work soon enough. It should have pulled the choke off—'unloaded' it—a lot sooner."
"And this 'adjust idle,'" you say, "does that have to do with the black smoke?"
"No, the black smoke was from having too much gas in the engine because the choke was sticking."
"What about all the backfiring?"
"Same thing," he says, "a product of the flooding from the sticking choke."
"So what's this 'adjust idle'?"
"The merest twitch on a screw to refine the carburetion, the maestro's touch, but not significant to the rest of the situation." (Actually, this overstates the case; the true maestro would have entered the exhaust gas carbon monoxide values on the bill.)

Note the procedure: You list every symptom when you bring the car in and account for every symptom when the repair is complete. In addition, you ask about the relevance of any other operations (e.g., "adjust idle") shown on the bill.

This foregoing example is a bit false, in the respect that it fits a pre-1973 car with few pollution controls. Also, it points to only one type of automatic choke; two other types are commonly found—one with a different kind of stove and one that is fully electric. On more modern cars, problems like those given in the example can arise from elements in the pollution-control system. Also, the symptoms of an electronic fuel-injection system (or even an old-style mechanical one) would not be the same as those for a carbureted system, and the symptoms could vary according to the specific type of fuel-injection system. Given the complexity of the pollution-control devices that influence fuel and ignition systems on new cars, problems require electronic diagnostic machines. Suppose you say to the mechanic, "My car won't run right; what might the problem be?" If the mechanic says, "How the hell should I know?" he's not joking. In many cases, he has to ask a machine to tell him.

People who consider themselves prudent will go over every item on a $20 restaurant bill to make sure the charges agree with the menu and that the total is right. Yet, the same people will hardly question a $200 repair bill for their car. The difference is that people universally esteem themselves expert on grilled-cheese sandwiches and *tournedos périgueux*, not to mention Napa Valley or Côtes d'Or wines, and so are prepared to quarrel over a restaurant bill. By contrast, they fear that if they inquire about a shop bill, they betray their ignorance (and vulnerability) to a grease-stained serf to whom they wish to feel superior.

Generally, you can harass a waiter without fear, but you have to be careful with the mechanic. Quarrel with the mechanic, and he may come back with, "Look, lady, don't blame me because your altitude compensator gave out and messed up your enrichment valve." Hearing this, you lack a *mot juste* as rejoinder and fear that to rejoin at all will just get you in deeper, so you shut up and pay, despite the blow to dignity and pocketbook.

Things need not be this way. Your relationship with your mechanic need not be an adversary one. Grant the mechanic his ability, admit you don't comprehend the depths of his wisdom, and invite him to share some of that wisdom with you. Go over the bill and ask, "Now, why did you do this operation and replace this part?" However, don't sound offensive; let your manner invite a dialogue among equals who respect each other (if you don't respect your mechanic, you have the wrong mechanic).

The weakness in this recommendation is the time constraint; the mechanic or the shop foreman hardly has time to talk to you, for a competent, well-run shop always has more work than it can get done. Your psychiatrist bills you for time spent talking, but the mechanic bills you for time spent accomplishing results (this being a primary distinction between psychiatrists and mechanics). The time the mechanic spends talking to you is time taken away from the next job.

In addition to the time constraint, large dealership shops put you in a waiting room with piped-in music and cut off your access to the mechanic; they encourage you to feel that sensitive, civilized people are above concern with their own greasy, misfeasant cars (just as civilized people are above cleaning septic tanks). If you try to breach the barrier, to gain access to the work area and to those who labor there, you are regarded as if you had proposed some grave social error. Indeed, the shop's insurance policy or state labor laws may bar you from the work area. If you do bluster your way into a conference with the mechanic, the mechanic may be conscious of an irregular situation and try to get rid of you quickly to avoid the disapproval of his own boss(es).

Well, don't let any of that stuff bother you. You're paying the bill, and you have the right to know what's going on. Let the ability and willingness of the shop to deal with you personally, rather than exclusively with your car, be a factor in your choice of a garage.

In summary:

- Carefully note and itemize symptoms when the car acts up, and present the list of symptoms to the mechanic.
- When repairs are complete, ask how each symptom was relieved and how each item on the bill relates to the relief.

If you make an effort on the first item, odds are that the mechanic will be willing to join you for the second.

ESTIMATES

For reasons that do not relate entirely to the quality of cars or mechanics, a lot of grief is going around now about how mechanics take advantage of people, and numerous self-proclaimed guardians of the public weal rave about the value of estimates as a means of self-defense against unreasonable charges. Indeed, in some states, laws require shops to give written estimates before making repairs, and shops are not allowed to assess charges significantly above the estimate.

Note, in passing, that such laws do not, in fact, require a shop to give an estimate; they only require an estimate as a condition of contract between the car owner and the shop. The shop makes an estimate, the customer agrees and signs a work order, and the work proceeds. If the shop doesn't want to deal with you, and no work contract is anticipated, you have no right to demand an estimate.

When I reflect on written-estimate laws, I am the more persuaded that the mechanics in those states have the legislatures right in their toolboxes. In most states, thieving mechanics have to be at least a little clever; in states with written-estimate laws, they need only be able to write an estimate.

Where mutual respect exists between shop and customer, estimates will be verbal and casual. You say, "What's it going to cost?" and the shop says, "Oh, probably around $200." You automatically add $50 and the final bill comes to $265. You express astonishment, plead poverty, the shop knocks the bill back to $230, and you leave happy. Alternatively, the shop may say, "We can't estimate closely because we may run into this problem or that." If you trust the shop, you will accept that statement in good faith.

Everett Vight runs a garage in Conway, Massachusetts, just down the road a piece from where I live in Ashfield. One day, a customer brought in a '72 Saab 99 that was making a horrible noise (I hate to bring in another Saab 99, but it's such a perfect example here). Vight didn't know what was making the noise, but he did know he would have to take off the cylinder head to find out. What he also didn't know was that a '69–'72 Saab 99 cylinder head is about the world's most impossible to get off if it has been on for 50,000 miles or so because the steel stud bolts corrode to the aluminum cylinder head. Thus, Everett spent almost all day getting the cylinder head off (in one piece, that is; after he had spent several hours on it, I advised a cutting torch and a sledgehammer).

Now, what would Everett Vight have done if he had been legally required to provide a written estimate before pulling that cylinder head? He would have told the owner, "I'm not familiar with these cars, so you'll have to take it elsewhere," and the car would have wound up at a (very high-priced) Saab dealership. The dealership would not, under written-estimate laws, contract to pull the head as an exploratory gesture because they would know all too well how hard the head is to get off. Rather than explore far enough to find the broken piston ring and one ruined piston that Vight found, they would declare that the whole engine was ruined and would cheerfully estimate and contract for a new engine at around $5000. The customer would refuse to spend the money on a car ten years old, so the car would go to the junkyard. Thus, one consequence of written-estimate laws is to help new car sales, and that's one reason we have such laws.

Another reason is to persuade people to stand still as their pockets are picked, for written-estimate laws create a false sense of psychological security; that is, people agree to absurdly high estimates because the legal standing of the estimate invests it with credibility. "The shop is legally required to give me this estimate," the customer thinks, "therefore, the estimate must be sound."

You have looseness in your steering: should the mechanic estimate a steering-box adjustment and risk your squawking if he finds a loose tie rod and that is not in the estimate? No way. He will estimate you two new tie-rod ends and an idler, and perhaps a set of ball joints, too, and since his estimate has legal standing, you will assume he is telling you the best he knows, so you will agree. If you do not agree because the price is too high, you can go to another shop, but under written-estimate laws, all the shops will be protecting themselves in the same way, so you won't do any better. Once you have agreed, he'll sell you all you agreed to whether you need it or not. The steering-box adjustment would take ten minutes, and he could charge you the shop minimum of, say, $15. By contrast, the shop will buy two tie-rod ends for $10 each and charge you $25 each for them ($30 profit), buy the idler for $15 and charge you $30 for it (a total of $45 profit on parts), and charge $30 for labor (total bill, $110)—and you may have needed only one tie-rod end, or even none at all. Thus, written-estimate laws are an immensely effective marketing scheme for new parts and that's another reason we have them. However, they create an illusion of security in a gullible public, so the public willingly participates in being robbed all the while believing they are being saved from the very thieving mechanics into whose grasping hands they have been delivered by their state legislatures.

Even where written estimates are not required by law, public writ is heavily burdened by savants advising car owners to "demand an estimate" before authorizing work. The same logic applies here: an estimate mainly protects you from shock at the bill and not always then.

Try this: You hear the right rear brake dragging and bring in the car. The mechanic concludes that one self-adjuster has been acting ahead of the others and that he can reset the adjuster and put things in good order.

Accordingly, he estimates the adjustment on one wheel. When he takes off the brake drum, he sees that the problem arises from a rusty parking-brake cable that has stuck and that the brake linings on that wheel are well worn. What does he do? If he fixes the parking-brake cable and thus goes beyond the estimate, you will squawk. If he doesn't fix the parking brake, the problem will still exist and you will squawk.

Alternatively, suppose he goes ahead and relines the brakes on the one wheel. The "book" and the mechanic's experience tell him not to replace the brake linings on only one wheel, but to reline wheels as a pair, front or rear. Also, brake linings come in sets; to get enough for one wheel, he has to buy enough for two. If he tells you this, you will assume he is lying just to make more money off you.

In any case, he relines the rear wheels, takes the car for a test drive, and finds that the front brakes are lousy, too. If he does nothing except tell you about it, he is admittedly returning you to the road in a dangerous car and could be legally liable if you run into something. But if he relines the front brakes, you will squawk and refuse to pay on the basis that the front brakes were not part of the estimate.

The obvious solution, of course, is to call you at work. He does. You are in an "important meeting." What does he do then? Pack up his tools and begin work on another car, knowing he may have to go back to your car shortly? Have we anything in the estimate to pay for the time lost in switching projects and then going back? In any case, your meeting ends and you call back. He crawls from under the other car he has begun working on to speak to you. You review the situation. After several minutes of uncertainty, you say you want to see the car before authorizing more repairs and will come down after work. Where does that leave him? First of all, he doesn't get to leave his job at five o'clock as you do, because he has to wait on you to come make a decision that you are not qualified to make and that he has already come to. Furthermore, as soon as you hang up, a car blowing steam appears at the shop door; the owner needs a new water pump right away, but your car is blocking the work space. Does he put your wheels back on and push your car aside (the front wheels are off so you can see your worn brake pads when you arrive), or does he change the next customer's water pump outside, where he must do more running to and fro for tools, etc., and in whatever weather fate delivered that day?

So, what would you do?

My personal solution is to refuse to deal with only one wheel. I would tell you that I will overhaul your whole braking system—take it or leave it. That way, I can cover all possibilities and when I get through, all you have to squawk about is the price.

This is the major consequence of those rigid estimates so loved by the consumer-conscious writers: try to box the mechanic in with a tight estimate, and the mechanic just makes the box big enough to hold everything.

Obviously, not all repairs present such problems. For example, the parts and labor costs to replace a leaking water pump can be accurately estimated. However, suppose you do not tell the mechanic that the water pump has been leaking for two weeks and the car has been boiling like a moonshine still all that time, so when he removes the water pump, he finds the cooling system full of oil from a blown head gasket. What does he do? If he replaces the water pump, the car is no better off; it will still overheat. Yet, he doesn't have a head gasket in the estimate.

Note where all this points: You will be satisfied with estimates of any sort only if you fully trust a shop, and if you do, you will not feel compelled to hem the shop in with tight estimates. If you know and trust your mechanic, you become partners with a mutual interest in saving your car, rather than hostile elements on opposing sides of a financial transaction.

In general, then, regard an estimate as *only* an estimate. If you do not trust the shop, then go ahead and define the job very narrowly, e.g., "replace the water pump," and accept the wasted effort if the problem turns out to be a blown head gasket. Or, if you define the task as "diagnose and correct overheating," then you just have to accept the fact that all the shop can do is offer a hierarchy of estimates, the top one of which covers the most-expensive possibilities. Obviously, if you authorize repairs under such an estimate, you are handing the shop a sort of blank check; on the other hand, if you don't dare authorize such open-ended repairs, you may spend money for a new water pump or radiator cleaning and still be stuck with an overheating car.

Note, in all this, that the troublesome estimates apply to problems (e.g., overheating, sticky brake) that may have several causes. Obviously, a routine tune-up and oil change can be estimated down to a penny. However, the public indignation over repairs that cost more than an estimate indicates does not arise over tune-ups; it arises from problems that do not have a single, obvious solution, and the more you insist on a rigid estimate, the more you will get the maximum solution. After all, what would you do if you were the mechanic?

You can, of course, try to beat the system by shopping around. Say your automatic transmission is slipping badly, so you run from one shop to another seeking the most credible estimate; halfway between two shops (and estimates), the transmission quits completely. Now, you are no longer seeking estimates on a slipping transmission, but estimates on one that doesn't work at all, and you've got a tow-truck bill in the cost schedule, too.

You may begin to feel that you are pretty helpless: you can't tie the shop to a rigid estimate, but you don't dare give the shop a blank check, and while you dawdle, a serious problem degenerates into catastrophe. You are right; you are close to helpless. That's why you should seek a shop you have confidence in and develop a relationship of trust. That will not guarantee that the shop never takes advantage, but unless you spend the time to learn as much about the car as the shop knows, you cannot be absolutely safe.

In sum: An estimate alone will not fix your ailing car; it will only give you a rough notion of costs, but it can anticipate all possible costs only by going to extremes. Thus, put your faith and energy into cultivating the shop rather than in demanding iron-clad estimates. A mechanic will be fairly honest if you treat him and his competence with respect; try to tie him down with rigid estimates, and he'll estimate in enough stuff to assuage the injury to his dignity when you show distrust by insisting on a tight estimate.

No matter who fixes your car or what it costs, you will be appalled at the cost of parts. How about $90 for the front (roller) bearing in a transmission? Or $10 for a front crankshaft seal that you can cover with your palm, or even $2.50 for a spark plug barely bigger than your thumb? You can do little about the cost of parts except complain—that may get you a break, but don't count on it.

The cost of parts reflects overall economic circumstances and if indexed to, say, 1960, parts actually cost less nowadays. Still, the costs are outrageous, partly because parts go through several middlemen between the manufacturer of the parts and the retail outlet, and each middleman marks them up 50 to 100 percent. Dealers charge the most for parts and try to excuse the practice by saying, "The manufacturer requires us to sell it at this price." They lie, of course—the manufacturer doesn't care if the dealer gives parts away, so long as he pays the manufacturer the manufacturer's price for them.

Independent shops get parts from independent auto-parts stores and add their own markup. They buy spark plugs for about 75 cents to $1.25 each, and sell them (to you) for as much as $2.50. Thus, they both make a profit and get paid for their time in going after the parts. In general, the cost of parts at an independent shop will be only 50 to 75 percent of the cost at a dealer's shop.

THE FLAT-RATE MANUAL

The estimating game, obviously, includes a factor for the amount of time required to perform a certain repair. Although any one given mechanic could estimate his own time for a particular job, the trade needs some way to even out differences among mechanics. Some mechanics are more dexterous and, thus, faster than their brethren. Some have particular aptitudes, e.g., will be fast on tune-ups but slow on brakes. Most will be fast on their favorite cars but slower on ones they esteem less. Also, if a mechanic loses one hand in an accident, he needn't give up his trade, but he's certainly going to be slower than a mechanic with two hands.

The trade seeks to even out these differences with *flat-rate* manuals, the two popular ones being published by Chilton and Motor (Hearst). The flat-rate manuals list virtually every operation that can be performed on a car and specify the time required to perform the operation. Mechanics consult the manual when undertaking an unfamiliar operation, and the shop foreman consults it to get the labor factor for an estimate. Say the manual rates a certain job at two hours: if one mechanic does the job in one and a half hours and another does it in two and a half hours, the shop makes the same labor charge. The manual also helps establish the labor charge when a mechanic has to leave one job to estimate a brake job or to hold one end of an exhaust pipe for another mechanic—in other words, when he does a job in several discrete operations. The foreman knows that the time involved may be less or more than the allowance in the flat-rate manual, but he also knows that since the manual is used by everyone in the trade across the whole country (and around the world), he's giving you the most credible estimate he can.

Note here that the flat-rate manual deals in *time*, not money, so the total labor bill, obviously, depends on the hourly rate— as low as $12 per hour at small, rural shops and as high as $30 per hour in urban dealerships.

The flat-rate manual has long been a target for crusading consumer-conscious writers who view it as the mechanics' license to steal. For reasons never specified, the writers whereof I speak have decided that the time allowances given in the flat-rate manuals are too generous. These writers contend, again without apparent reason, that *all* mechanics or *any* mechanic can significantly beat the flat-rate time *all the time* and, such being the case (by their own declaration, if no one else's), the writers in question urge the abolition of flat-rate manuals. One has even called for a federal law against them. Others have urged car owners to reject flat-rate time allowances out of hand and to quarrel over labor charges based on the flat-rate manual, or to demand, before authorizing repairs, that labor estimates not be derived from flat-rate manuals.

None of the writers involved here ever submit experience as

a mechanic as evidence that they know what they are talking about. I have seen many, many excessive labor charges on repair bills, and in every case the labor on the bill far exceeded the flat-rate allowance. The customer was not robbed because the flat-rate manual *was* followed, but because it was *not*.

The flat-rate manual does have one egregious fault: it presumes a new car, not one with rusted bolts and with its engine buried under an accumulation of loathsome oil spillings. Thus, its time allowances will not apply properly on older cars. For example, the manual may allow 30 minutes to replace the gasket where the exhaust pipe joins the exhaust manifold, but the manual assumes a new, rust-free bolt. It certainly does not allow for the rust-weakened bolt that twists off, leaving a stub in the exhaust manifold that the mechanic has to drill out and replace.

Despite the attractive simplicity of the notion, you should not try to out-maneuver a shop by objecting to its use of the flat-rate manual.

Try this scenario: You have a Chrysler-made car with a V-8 or "slant six" engine and an automatic transmission. The transmission begins to hesitate between gears, then one day it stops completely; the engine races, but the car goes nowhere. You call a tow truck. When the truck arrives, you tell the driver what happened and say, "Let's see what it does now." Behold, it goes— for three blocks, and then stops again, so you give up trying and the truck tows you to a shop. You give the mechanic an orderly, coherent review of the symptoms, then ask him to fix it.

If you stop there, you're safe. Since it is a Chrysler transmission (not a Ford or General Motors), he recognizes an exact pattern of symptoms and tells you that your filter is clogged, that he'll change the filter, gasket, and oil, and adjust the bands while he's at it, and have you functional for little money and less time.

But suppose you're full of some critic's view of the flat-rate manual, so you say, "Now, I expect you to fix this, but I want no 'flat-rate' nonsense—see here? I've read magazine articles about how you guys are all thieves and the flat-rate manual is your main burglar's tool, and I'll have none of that."

If you tell him that, he may tell you to take the car to the person who wrote what you read and let him fix it. On the other hand, since he sees that you believe in false doctrines, he decides you deserve what you get, so he says, "Yes, ma'am—customer's always right, ma'am. Now, I reckon you've burned up your bands and clutches, so we'll just have to rebuild your transmission. But we'll take 10 percent off the flat-rate time. Right?"

You've heard about "bands" and "clutches," so this sounds reasonable to you. You figure you've really pulled off a clever stroke. "Just goes to show what happens if you stick up for your rights," you proudly tell your co-worker at the office. Meanwhile, he sells you a transmission rebuild you don't need and, being practiced at the Chrysler transmission, he beats the flat-rate manual time by 25 percent, partly because he doesn't bother to change some of the small sealing rings that come in the parts kit, so he's ahead of you by 15 percent. Also, he buys a parts kit for $50 to $75 and charges you $125 to $175 for it, so he's ahead even more.

This is what you invite when you try to tell someone his business as a mechanic, especially if you quote magazine articles written by people who have never worked on cars or tried to equal—much less beat—the flat-rate time on changing the timing gears on an early small-block Chevrolet V-8 (a nasty, nasty job that can hardly ever be done within the flat-rate time).

The flat-rate manual is no absolute for anyone (and does not pretend to be). You may well ask a mechanic why a job took longer than the flat-rate allowance and you may flatter him by asking how much, on the average, he can beat flat-rate time, but don't tell him you expect him to follow the flat-rate manual rigidly. He may take you at your word.

None of this is intended to excuse ignorance or thievery among mechanics. Rather, the point is that you won't protect yourself with magazine articles written in ignorance of what is involved in repairing a car or in ignorance of the more subtle forms of thievery mechanics can practice.

FAULTY FIXINGS

Alas, into every life a little rain must fall, for the best of shops does a bad piece of work now and then (poor shops, of course, do so regularly). Then, you find yourself in the unpleasant business of having to take the car back and complain.

Obviously, if your relationship with the shop has been good in the past, you will be able to straighten out a problem. The shop can correct its error without loss of dignity, you can reasonably pay any reasonable charges involved, and your good relationship continues.

On the other hand, if you're effectively a stranger at the shop, problems can develop. The problems take several common forms: You take the car in for repairs and it runs no better despite the repairs (and the bill). Or you feel the extent of the repairs (and their cost) is unreasonable. Or you get charged for repairs or parts that were not necessary or that weren't provided at all.

If the car doesn't run properly following repairs, you have to *take it right back.* At once. If you do not take it right back—if you wait a few days—an unscrupulous shop can say that the problems are totally new and unrelated to the repairs they made. If the shop is honest, to delay bringing the car back may cause additional problems to develop—and will these be the shop's fault, or yours?

A good shop will try to correct matters as soon as you return with your car sputtering or dangling astern of a tow truck. To readmit your car to the shop, obviously, dislocates the other work going on and the shop foreman may say, "Leave it and we'll get to it first thing tomorrow." You must insist as strongly as *noblesse* allows that the car be re-examined at once, in the operating mode wherein the trouble arises. For example, carburetion and ignition system faults may occur only when the car is warmed up; automatic transmission or brake faults may occur only in stop-

and-go driving. Unfortunately, if the shop refuses to take the car back right away, you can't do much about it. Even if you seek out another shop, you will find it full, too.

In any case, make your list of symptoms again. If the symptoms are the same as those on your original list, you may presume that either the shop did not do all it claimed when you reviewed the bill, or they overlooked something in making repairs. You may even suspect that what they did do was useless work, but don't push this conjecture too far. It's tempting, but weak. If your new list consists of new symptoms, you may assume the shop did not do enough; or that to correct one set of symptoms they simply made others noticeable; or that they did things wrong and caused new symptoms, but don't push this conjecture too far, either.

If you just spent $100 for a tune-up and the car won't run properly, you obviously want the shop to fix the car. You are more interested, for example, in having the car run right than in getting your money back. However, if the shop tries to put you off, tries to delay taking the car back into the shop, you may wonder if they even know how to make it run properly. If you have doubts of this sort, you may prefer to lose your $100 and start over at another shop.

On the other hand, if you spent more money—perhaps $500 for automatic transmission repairs—the stakes are such that you virtually must give the shop a second chance. Of course, this creates the possibility that they will charge another $500 but do no better the second time. You won't get the car back without a legal hassle unless you pay the second $500, and you will certainly have to go through a legal hassle to get a refund of any kind on the first $500.

If the shop takes the car back and returns it shortly in good order, you have no reason to feel seriously abused. Anyone can make a mistake or overlook something. However, life becomes, as Hobbes said, "nasty" and "brutish" if the shop fails to correct the problem. The easiest solution, if we can call it that, is to look for another shop. That leaves you having wasted time and money, but you may count yourself fortunate to have got the measure of the first shop before you commissioned more complex repairs. On the other hand, having spent money in the first shop, you justifiably feel the shop should make good (and not charge you a second time), so you take the car back. If the shop fixes it, fine. If not, you have to choose between repeatedly taking the car back or giving up and going to another shop.

In most cases, the shop gets things fixed the second time around. Suppose the car sputters badly, so the shop attacks the carburetor side of the engine and pollution-control system. The immediate results seem good enough, so the shop does no more and, being pressured by other customers, does not road test the car. When you drive away, putting the engine under load, it still sputters, so you come back and the shop finds more faults in the exhaust side of the system, faults that wouldn't show up until the car was driven. Okay, you get a second set of repairs, but they are legitimate. You aren't being cheated.

Note, in passing, that in big cities a proper road test is a virtual impossibility by late afternoon; to spend half an hour idling in a traffic jam hardly constitutes a road test, so big city shops will not routinely do a road test. In fact, a road test is not routine anywhere; in most instances, it's not needed anyway.

In any event, you bring the car back once, twice, thrice; you berate the mechanic, harangue the shop foreman, and argue with the cashier; finally, the car works again. By this time, you and the shop are sick of each other and neither wants to see the other again. However, your experience need not condemn the shop; if the shop foreman winced at your reappearance, but said, "Bring it in"; if the mechanic swore under his breath, but delved under the hood with fresh energy each time; then the shop didn't give up, didn't try to escape their responsibilities, and they deserve your respect for that.

Your serious problems begin when the shop claims the car runs well when it doesn't. With a new car that is under warranty, you call in the zone representative in cases of this sort. With an older, out-of-warranty car, you find another shop.

In sorry sum, if a shop doesn't make the car right after several attempts, you have to go elsewhere. If you can be nasty enough, you might browbeat the shop into making a refund, but don't count on it. To get a refund, odds are you'll need a lawyer.

Unfortunately, inadequate repairs don't always show up as soon as you leave the shop. Suppose you bring a car into Shop A on a hot day and complain of overheating; the shop flushes out your radiator, but finds no serious accumulation of rust.

Shop A does not know how severe the overheating is and may not be able to find out unless they spend a lot of time driving the car around town as you do, so Shop A reckons the radiator flushing is enough. The next day, when you pick up the car, is rainy. The wet, rainy air does a better job of cooling the radiator, so you experience no overheating. On the third day, with the August sun out again, you take off on a trip and get 50 miles away when your radiator starts steaming like a clam kettle. You lurch your way to Shop B and, after a thorough diagnosis (that takes full account of your well-flushed radiator), Shop B reports that you have a blown head gasket that is allowing the fires in the cylinders to blow right into the coolant.

Now, is the blown gasket the *cause* of the original overheating, or an *effect* of it? If the former, is Shop A responsible for your car's being in a shop 50 miles from home because they did not find it? If it is an effect, is Shop A still responsible because they did not solve the original overheating problem? How will you argue when you get back to Shop A? How will anyone know whether the blown gasket is cause or effect?

What you have a right to demand of Shop A comes to turn on the issue of whether Shop A failed to find the cause of the overheating, due to either haste or incompetence; or whether Shop A's performance was reasonable and adequate under the circumstances presented to them. For example, the fact that you had no problem on the rainy day would indicate to Shop A that they had done as well as could be expected. Only the engine knows the answer in this case and, of course, it's not talking.

You and Shop A can argue interminably about responsibility here and Shop B can contribute its uncertain assessments about how long the head gasket had been leaking, but none of you can be sure about the cause-effect relationship. All you know is 1) that Shop A did take reasonable corrective measures and 2) that you have a blown head gasket. Those, at least, are positive facts, though they don't prove much—certainly not enough for you to insist that Shop A is responsible for your blown head gasket.

The difficulties arising from repairs that didn't work are, at least, definable: the car runs or it doesn't, it conforms to the manufacturer's specifications or it doesn't, its exhaust gas values are proper or they aren't. Whether you got sold something you didn't need is more difficult to tell. Mechanics tend to follow paths of least effort, and these paths coincide with the shop's path of maximum profit. Given a dead battery and badly corroded terminals, the mechanic could make many complex motions to clean the terminals, but to replace the whole battery is physically simpler and requires no brains at all; furthermore, the shop makes a handsome profit on the battery. Thus, over the past thirty years, the mechanic's trade has shifted from being labor-intensive to being capital-intensive, and this shift is the main reason people get sold things they don't really need.

Where this all leads, unfortunately, is back to its starting point: unless you are a specialist, you aren't going to outsmart a specialist who is trying to outsmart you on his own turf. At bottom, your best defense remains in making a good choice of a shop and cultivating a good relationship with it.

LAWSUITS GET YOU NOWHERE

According to various sources, complaints about car repairs are the most common complaints made to private and official consumer-protection agencies. The number of complaints, however, does not accurately measure the quality of repair service. For one thing, state and federal agencies actively solicit complaints about cars (but not, e.g., about the educational system) and to express a strong demand for anything will eventually bring a generous supply into being. In addition, American society has become particularly litigious here of late, at the same time that the automobile industry has just come through its cut-and-try development of pollution-control systems. Curiously, as cars have come to last longer than ever before—100,000 miles being routine—and as maintenance demands have become the least—only two oil changes per year required—complaints seem to be rising.

Also, people neglect cars. They allow minor problems to degenerate into major ones, then try to shift the responsibility elsewhere via a complaint. People who have regular maintenance programs rarely get unpleasant surprises.

Few people understand their cars and even fewer can stand nearby and watch the mechanics fix it. The mechanic probably wouldn't mind, as long as the customer didn't offer any advice, but insurance provisions and state labor regulations usually won't allow customers into a work area. By contrast, the appliance repairman replaces the faulty valve in the washer as you watch. When the job is done, you understand what was broken and how it was repaired. People nowadays have no similar experience with cars. Shops that save worn parts, show them to the customer, and explain the fault—e.g., a disc brake pad with the lining worn down to the metal or a water pump with evident leakage around the shaft—have few complaints, but not all parts lend themselves to such neat demonstrations. An ignition coil is simply a black cylinder, a carburetor a lumpy mass of metal, and a squealing clutch throw-out bearing may look healthy enough when removed. Thus, the owner has less comprehension of what goes wrong with the car than what goes wrong with a dripping faucet.

More people own cars than work on them and, as with any majority, car owners think of themselves as innocent, honest folk exploited by thieving mechanics. In fact, if thieves and liars are evenly distributed throughout the population, they will be more numerous among car owners than among mechanics, since car owners are more numerous, and many complaints come from car owners who are liars and thieves and who resort to consumer complaints to secure an advantage over the garage.

For example, on the early Fiat 124 coupes, the owner's manual specified that the timing-belt idler must be replaced at 30,000 miles. In a shop where I worked, we tuned a Fiat 124 with 27,000 miles on it and suggested that the idler be replaced. The owner refused. At 33,000 miles, the idler bearing gave out, so the timing belt went slack and did not turn the overhead camshaft, and the pistons smashed into the valves, destroying the pistons, valves, cylinder head, and camshaft.

The owner claimed we dropped a bolt down the carburetor when we tuned the car 6000 miles earlier and that the bolt caused the damage. We pointed to our note about the idler on the previous bill and to the worn bearing in the idler, and refused to replace the engine at our expense. The owner then reported us to the Better Business Bureau. The BBB sent us a copy of the owner's complaint, wherein the owner made no mention of the idler or our note on the bill. We responded to the BBB by phone and the person we spoke to expressed no interest in our side of the story, but told us to replace the man's engine or our "reputation" would be injured. We hung up on the guy, figuring our time was better spent getting work done.

Another incident involved a Volkswagen Beetle. The owner asked us to adjust the brakes. We discovered that we could not turn the adjusters because they were corroded solid. From experience, we knew that if we removed a wheel, we would find brake linings that needed replacing. Indeed, the worn linings were visible through the brake-adjustment hole. We also knew the new linings would push the wheel cylinder pistons inward over deposits and pitting and make the cylinders leak. We knew, too, that if we rebuilt the cylinders, the rusted bleeder screws would twist off and we wouldn't be able to bleed the air from the system. In addition, we knew that if we replaced the cylinders, the brake fluid lines would be so rusted to the fittings that they would twist off when we tried to unscrew them from the wheel cylinders. In sum, correcting the problem—a product of consistent, long-term neglect—would entail a total overhaul of the whole braking system.

The owner rejected this approach, accused us of trying to rob him, then reported us to the BBB for leaving his life at hazard by refusing to adjust his brakes. We threw this BBB complaint into the waste basket and did not respond to it. Eventually, we came to treat all BBB complaints that way.

My presumption is that a goodly portion of consumer complaints, if examined carefully, would be as misguided as these examples. However, let me now put the shoe on the other foot: I have seen repairs that were criminal in their ineptitude. I have pointed to things on cars and told the owners that "The mechanic who did that deserves to be horsewhipped!" I once found loose front-wheel bearings that were dry of grease, needing both adjustment and grease. "Oh, yes," the owner said, "my mechanic said my wheel bearings were worn and would soon need replacement." Fact is, adjustable wheel bearings will never need replacement if they are kept adjusted and greased; yet rather than spend five minutes on each front wheel, her mechanic was prepared to destroy a set of bearings for the sake of a more lucrative job later on and leave her with bad steering and ruin a pair of tires in the meantime.

I have seen a loose rear-wheel bearing ruin new brake linings because the mechanic was not smart enough to recognize the loose bearing nor did he understand its consequences.

I have seen new shock absorbers that did not get their bolts tightened and which came loose, got hung up in the suspension, and were ruined.

I have seen hastily installed distributor points that were so badly aligned that the car ran only a few miles.

As amply noted hitherto, I enjoy a fondness for the Saab 99. When Christine Cassidy, my neighbor's daughter, was looking for a cheap car, she came across a 1970 Saab 99 in the classifieds that was listed as having a "cracked head." Chris asked me if I thought the car could be salvaged.

"Something is not right here," I told her. "The Saab has an aluminum cylinder head and aluminum heads hardly ever 'crack.' Warp, yes — but not crack. Call and ask if they mean a 'cracked block.'"

She called and spoke to the owner, a woman. "No," the owner said, "the shop most definitely said a 'cracked head.' They said you could see it."

"Let's go look," I said to Chris.

We went and looked. We could find no crack in the cylinder head or in the block. The owner told of overheating the car to the point that it made horrible sounds and leaving the car at a service station. The station mechanics said they would have to pull the cylinder head to assess the damage. Having done so, they called to report the "cracked head" and said they could get one from a junkyard for $250. Since the car was eleven years old and too, too rusty, she decided against spending money for the repair.

As I turned the head over and over looking for the alleged crack and studied the cylinder bores looking for some other reason for the mechanics' remarks, I noted that the timing-chain sprocket gear was off the bracket that holds it when you remove the head, and the timing chain was looped over the bracket for the sprocket.

Now, on the Saab 99, if you inadvertently release the timing chain when you remove the sprocket, and thus allow the chain to go slack, the chain tensioner down inside the engine jumps out of place and you have to pull the whole engine out of the car and take off a cover to put the tensioner back where it belongs. That's a full day's work.

So things were clear: The mechanics accidently loosened the timing chain and were faced with pulling the engine to repair their own error. But who was to pay for this labor? By telling the owner she needed a $250 cylinder head that she did not need, they could, in effect, get her to pay them for correcting their own mistake.

As I looked over the situation, I wondered how many other people had been victimized in similar ways by inept mechanics.

So, Chris bought the car and I put it together and things worked well until the excessive rust caused the front suspension to collapse. We got another "junk" Saab 99, this time a '73 model, and I went through the cylinder-head and timing-chain drill with it, too (but for different reasons), after which Chris took the car to Boston.

When Chris returned home to attend a wedding, the clutch began giving trouble. She had to push the pedal farther and farther to get any clutch action and finally reached a point where she could hardly shift at all. When she sought help at a service station, she was told her clutch was worn out and she must have a new one.

Having an intimate acquaintance with that clutch, I knew very well the car did not need a new clutch. Upon examination, I found the locknut that secures the clutch-adjusting rod had loosened and the rod had worked its way out, thus nullifying the action of the clutch pedal. A simple adjustment that took five minutes solved the problem.

Now, maybe I didn't tighten the locknut enough when I put the car together. If so, then I caused the problem. On the other hand, maybe the threads where the rod passes through the clutch housing were worn a bit and the rod loosened by itself. Either way, the clutch had nothing wrong with it.

So, I wonder: Was the mechanic she spoke to simply stupid? Or merely a thief who thought he had a victim at hand? Or some combination of both? And, in any case, how many million times has an incident of this sort been repeated across the country? Many, many times, I am sure.

How can you protect yourself? First, by having a notion of how the car works. This book is by no means a workshop manual and its mechanical survey (Part IV) is drawn quite broadly. However, that survey provides sufficient reference for you to understand what system or what part of a system may be at fault; it provides the reference from which you may ask the mechanic, "Why does the car misbehave? How is it different from the way it should be, and how did it get that way? And what do you propose to do about it?"

Obviously, these questions are useless if the mechanic won't talk to you, and that's part of choosing a shop: try to find a mechanic who will talk to you. I have said you should be prepared to respect the mechanic, but you should—indeed, must—demand equal respect from the shop. Your car is an object, but you are not. You are no mechanic, but you are not stupid and a mechanic has no reason to refuse to talk to you about the car. Unfortunately, mechanics are not always articulate and can rarely tell you what they know in clear terms. Still, they should be able and willing to answer questions like the three above.

You will not, when repairs go sour, do yourself much good by going to public consumer-protection offices. A formal complaint through such channels may take several months of paper shuffling and processing. Furthermore, the bureaucrat who handles the matter will probably not know anything about cars, but he will have a profound sense of bureaucratic self-preservation, the first rule of which is, "Don't embarrass the bureau." If the bureaucrat calls on the shop, he will see that he is out of his element, that he is incompetent to argue with the mechanic about your car, with only your complaint to go on. Unless the mechanic pulled some incredibly stupid blunder that is so clear that it admits of no argument at all, the bureaucrat will back off and go chase people selling swamp lots in Florida.

You won't do noticeably better going to court. A few car-repair cases have made the newspapers over the past ten years, but they made the papers because they were exceptional and the fact that shops have, at rare intervals, been penalized for shoddy work or thievery does not assure a similar result in every case.

Try this scenario: Your car needs a tune-up and it also overheats. You ask a shop to do the tune-up and to correct the overheating. When you pick up the car, you are billed only for a tune-up. You ask about the overheating and the shop says they found no problem.

Odds are that the shop only gave the cooling system a cursory check or forgot the overheating completely. In any case, you drive away, get stuck in a traffic jam, and the car promptly overheats and blows a head gasket. You come back to the shop and demand that the shop fix the car for free, your point being that their failure to correct the overheating caused the blown head gasket.

The shop refuses, so you sue. In court, the shop's lawyer represents you as responsible because you didn't get the car out of traffic and turn off the engine at the first sign of overheating; or the mechanic lies smoothly by claiming that the shop, not you, brought up the problem of overheating, and claims that you said you didn't have time to let them fix it. Could you *prove* otherwise?

Keep in mind that courts do not operate on truth or falsity but on what can be convincingly proved according to rules of evidence. Also, remember that being under oath does not make people truthful; it only makes them cautious, particularly where their self-interest is concerned.

An impartial judge has no way of knowing who is the liar and may assume you are, since you have more to gain. Judges see a lot of self-serving chicanery from allegedly honest consumers and don't, therefore, always assume the customer is more truthful than the shop.

A claim against a shop for work not done or work improperly done requires proving. For example, in this case, you should have had the mechanic write a note on the bill about the overheating, e.g., what was done, how the shop concluded no problem existed, etc. Note how this pertains to a system of recording symptoms and reviewing the bill.

Work done badly is obviously harder to prove than work not done. A shop leaves your car running badly; you return it, but it comes out again as bad as ever. You take it to another shop, get it properly fixed, then try to get your money back from the first shop. Well, you destroyed the evidence for your complaint when you got the car fixed.

So, you ask the second shop to fully diagnose the problems, note them on the bill, and itemize what they did to correct things. Now you have documentation, but be careful: the list of things may not prove anything against the other shop.

However, you are confident. You have documentation, so you sue. Now, the case becomes a test of lawyers and the first shop's lawyer makes mincemeat of the second mechanic who finally did fix the car, so your proud list proves useless.

Or you get your case ready, then tell the second mechanic you need him as a witness against the first. The second mechanic knows that he, too, may make a mistake one day, knows that he could find himself on the defending end of a similar case, so he's not eager to testify. Either he proves unavailable or his testimony is so watered-down that it does not prove your case. Like doctors, mechanics tend to cover for each other, because they know their turn may come next.

Despite the optimistic representations of consumer advocates, the car owner is pretty helpless when trying to attack a shop legally and such cases are not lucrative enough to attract lawyers who are expert mechanics. Lawyers involved in medical or engineering matters often study some medicine or engineering, but no lawyer will become a mechanic for the sake of "nickel-and-dime" suits against repair shops.

Now, some qualifications: None of this applies to purchases of new or used cars; those are different matters and pertain to a product (car) rather than a service (repair).

Also, this foregoing applies less to dealership shops than to independents. If you take a Pontiac to a Pontiac dealer and get poor or ineffective repairs, you can carry your complaint up through several echelons of corporate bureaucracy to the president of General Motors. However, you must have your complaint in order and should not expect results for a month or two unless the problem involves a new car under warranty.

As a lesser qualification, the foregoing applies less to repairs that were, in your judgment, too expensive. Suppose you burn a valve and ask the shop to do a "valve job." The shop gives you a nonbinding estimate on "grinding the valves." When you pick up the car, you find the bill much higher than expected because instead of a grinding you got several new valves, plus new valve guides and valve seats. You sue to reduce the bill to the original estimate.

The shop says (in court) that if they had only ground the valves, the valves would have burned again promptly and you would have been back complaining they did poor work, so they installed the new parts to assure the longevity of the repair. The shop also points out that they had no way of knowing the condition of the valves and seats until they got the car apart.

If you were the judge, what would you do?

The judge might point out that the shop could have warned you of the possibility of extra parts. The shop might rejoin that you told them the car had been acting up only "a few days" and so they had no reason to assume the valves were so bad.

Odds are, in a case of this sort, that the judge will suggest the shop sell you the new parts at cost and give you a discount on the labor—in effect, split the disputed amount. Since your lawyer will cost you three times what you will regain, a lawsuit is hardly worthwhile. Indeed, we could argue here that you have no valid complaint at all, since you did get a thorough, honest valve job.

The logical place for a suit over a repair bill is small-claims court. However, you should visit the court as a spectator before filing a suit, and you may not like what you see. According to the "underground" press in Boston, the Suffolk County (Massachusetts) small-claims court is biased against the car owner. By contrast, the small-claims court in Franklin County, currently presided over by Judge Harvey Kramer, is a model of equity and justice (I know; I was there several times, but not over cars).

Generally, you don't need a lawyer in small-claims court, but be wary; if the shop does have a lawyer, you may wish you had one, too. A lawyer will usually discuss your problem for nothing (or for a token $15–$25 fee), so if your case has some tricky elements, you should ask a lawyer whether your case requires assistance.

Fortunately, the car-repair business does not offer rewards adequate for truly devoted thieves (who gravitate toward law and politics), so the dangers of being victimized in the ways described above are remote, but the fact remains that the car owner is pretty helpless when attacking a shop (unless the shop is run by utter amateurs).

HIGHWAY ROBBERY

To have car problems of any kind is annoying enough, but as long as you are close to home base, you can handle the situation. However, if your car breaks down on a trip, the difficulties are obviously greater.

Where you take the car depends on the overall situation. You may prefer dealership shops on the assumption—not always valid—that they should be able to resolve a problem most expeditiously, though you will probably pay more money. Also, if dealership repairs prove ineffective, you have a sort of recourse via complaints to the manufacturer. On the other hand, if the problem is a simple one—a leaking water pump, a dangling muffler—that any shop can handle, you can go to the nearest place. If you must be towed, the tow truck may be associated with a shop; or the driver will be able to recommend one.

If you have followed prudent vacation policy—that is, you took half the clothes and twice the money you thought you would need—you can pay for repairs and proceed. Otherwise, you're limited to shops that accept credit cards, which largely means service stations and dealerships. If you have neither cash nor credit cards, you virtually must go to a dealership. A dealership is usually a well-financed operation that has some sense of kinship with other dealerships, such as the one where you bought the car and have had it serviced before. Therefore, if you anticipate trouble paying the bill, the dealership can financially tolerate a delay and can, if willing, call the dealership where you bought the car and verify your good reputation or the quality of your personal check. You cannot assume a dealership will make any such arrangement, but a dealership can certainly do it more easily than an independent garage.

You get the estimate from the shop foreman, then consult the general manager. "Look," you say, "I've just ruined my differential and we haven't even got to Grandma's yet, much less to the seashore, so we're going to have to go right back home unless we can work out something on the bill. Perhaps you could call Mr. Goodeal, where I bought the car, and ask his recommendation." Goodeal wants no bad taste in your mouth about the car since he wants to sell you another one someday, and he'll be glad to say, "Yes, the lady's all right. She'll be good for the money and I'll stand behind the bill." Since Goodeal and the other dealer drink together at dealers' meetings, they can probably work something out. Otherwise, you may, indeed, have to cancel the trip.

You may get robbed at either a dealership or an independent shop, in terms of paying outrageous prices or getting sold more repairs than you need. However, those shops are "honest" thieves; they may steal in the process, but they do try to solve problems. On the other hand, you must be on guard against the "dishonest" thieves you can meet in service stations in the back woods or on those desolate stretches of highway out west. These shops operate like the brigands of old who used to raid camel caravans. Your out-of-state license plate marks you as a victim, a person in no position to quarrel about repairs, and one who can be depended on not to come back, so the station estimates how much robbery you can afford and still drive away, and sets about separating you from your money.

The most loathsome brigandage occurs when your car is running fine, you pull in for fuel, and the attendant creates a problem while you aren't looking. For example, the attendant runs an icepick through the sidewall of a radial tire while checking its pressure and then "discovers" a slow leak, or sloshes some coolant under the hood while checking the oil and "discovers" a leaking radiator. The possibilities are endless; indeed, the attendant can point out the oil drip at the rear of the transmission, the drip you've had for the past 50,000 miles, and make a convincing case that you need a transmission overhaul.

The probability of encountering such a shop is hard to predict. About ten years ago, they were common along the routes connecting Los Angeles and Las Vegas and they have been reported in other states. However, consumer-protection laws now hold the major oil companies responsible for frauds perpetrated by their franchise holders, and such laws impose severe penalties on shops that damage a traveler's car for the sake of selling repairs, so their practices seem less common nowadays. Nonetheless, be suspicious.

Suppose your alternator light flashes on as you are driving along. You do not overheat, which means the problem is not a loose or broken fan belt. You proceed to the next service station, a rickety edifice served by an apparent refugee from a 1930s Western movie or from a rock musical. Now, how do you determine if the place contains "honest" or "dishonest" thieves?

Approach the situation thus: Ask for a telephone, ostensibly to call a dealership in the next town. If the attendant points out the phone, offers to make change, and only mildly demurs from your stated intention, you are probably in friendly territory, and if the attendant suggests that he can correct the problem himself, you may allow him to proceed. However, if the attendant acts hostile about your desire to call a dealership, you may suspect he sees a "mark" escaping and escape may be the best thing.

Similarly, you may propose to call the state police to ask where a good shop can be found. If the attendant demurs strongly, says you needn't call the state police at all, that an excellent shop may be found a few miles farther along, and otherwise tries to get rid of you, you may suspect the station has an unsavory reputation that is known to the state police (and the station knows its reputation is known), so you should leave. Given a flashing alternator light, you may require a battery charge to do so and if so, watch as the attendant hooks up the charger, for he could hook up the cables backward, throw a heavy charge jolt to your battery, and explode it; the odds are against this, but it is possible, so watch to see that the red cable goes to the " + " post on the battery and black to the " − " (see "Jump Starting," on page 306).

Even if you are not suspicious, demand an explanation of what the mechanic proposes to do and why before you allow him to start taking the car apart (which will truly leave you at his mercy). If you are too inquisitive, the dishonest shop will not push its luck (thieves do prefer "easy" marks) and will either minimize what it does or will urge you on to the next town. The honest shop will find your questions a bit tedious, perhaps, but stations along major highways see a lot of eccentrics, so they will put up with you.

If the car is ailing when you pull into the station, you obviously have little room to maneuver. You can't be sure whether the car will get you to the next town and you must exercise caution while under stress—that is, when you are less able to be totally rational and when you are psychologically the most vulnerable. You have to make judgments about the kind of person you are dealing with, knowing full well that a truly clever thief can entice you with solicitude or browbeat you with false urgency. Still, you have to do the best you can.

Don't be quick to condemn the car that just hauled you over a thousand miles of mountain and desert. If it showed no symptoms before you pulled into the shop, it probably has no faults— at least, no faults of major proportion. If the attendant condemns your transmission, ask "Why hasn't it acted up?" Also, with an automatic, check the oil level, and watch to make sure the attendant pushes the dipstick all the way in. He could hold it partway out and cause the dipstick to show a low oil level. Or if the attendant squirts brake fluid behind a wheel and then says your brakes are going out, try the pedal: if it feels normal, don't take his word for it too soon. Also, check the brake-fluid level in the master cylinder; if it is full, you do not have a leak (see "Under the Hood," on page 226).

The other line of defense is to watch as the attendant checks over the car. Literally go with him as he looks under the hood and stoops at the tires. If you wish to visit the rest room, wait until the attendant is through, then move the car away from the gas pumps. The short move will demonstrate that the car is in order; if the attendant points to some fault when you return, then you can say you know who did it.

If you have a passenger, take turns going to the rest room. Children about twelve years old are excellent car-watchers because they notice so much and are so curious about what people are doing.

That such care and suspicion are justified is a sad commentary on the level of virtue that obtains in the land, but you'd better be suspicious where suspicion seems merited.

AUTOMOTIVE CACOPHONIES AND OTHER SENSORY IMPOSITIONS

As a defective muffler reminds us, cars make a lot of noise. Likewise, when we take an ailing car to a shop, the mechanic usually opens the hood and says, "Let's see what it sounds like." Sound, a normal product of the car, provides one primary means of monitoring its health and, if closely attended to, is often the first warning of trouble. However, sounds must be related to what you can see, smell, and feel. From such signals, even the driver who lacks mechanical sense can get some notion of what's going wrong with a car.

To catalog the distinctive sounds requires putting sounds into words. This is not easy. For example, does your dog say "Bow-wow" or "Woof-woof"? Does a slipping fan belt make a "squeal" or a "shriek"? Since the sounds can't be faithfully represented in words, you have to pay close attention to the circumstances wherein they occur to tell what they mean.

Squeal/shriek: the fan belt
Start with the fan belt; if it's too loose, the belt will slip when the engine speeds up, as when pulling away from a traffic light. When it slips, the belt produces a mixed squeal and shriek that dies out when the fan and alternator accelerate enough to catch up to engine speed.

Note the relevant circumstance: a) a marked increase or decrease, mostly increase, in engine speed accompanied by b) a squeal-cum-shriek of short duration.

If the sound occurs when the air conditioner is turned on, then it means the AC drive belt is loose. If it occurs when the steering wheel is turned to the extreme right or left, it points to the power-steering pump belt; thus, the sound commonly heard when people are wiggling out of a parallel parking space. However, in this case, the sound may originate within the power-steering pump, rather than come from the belt. Whether from the fan or air-conditioner belt, these squeaks and shrieks mean the belt needs to be tightened. As noted, a squeal from the power steering may come from the pump, but do check on the belt.

Clicking
Clicking under the hood may come from valves that need adjustment, from a dislodged spark-plug wire, or from a fan belt that is frayed, the most common source being valves. Valve noise is clear, metallic, and pronounced at idle speed and may seem to diminish as the engine speeds up. Such noises point to defective hydraulic valve lifters or to excessive clearances in the valve adjustment. Have adjustments made or hydraulic lifters replaced.

If a spark-plug wire comes loose from the plug, the spark will jump to "ground" by whatever path it can find. As it does, it makes a very clear, crisp "snap" or "click"; the sound lacks the metallic component of the valve sound and occurs in direct relation to engine speed.

If the end of the loose wire is close enough to the end of the spark plug, the spark will go to the plug, the plug will fire, and the engine will run normally. However, if the wire flops away from the plug, the spark will go elsewhere and the plug will not fire, so the engine will run roughly; the fewer cylinders it has, the rougher it runs, e.g., a four-minus-one cylinder engine will be rougher than a V-8-minus-one engine.

So: a snap/click, directly responsive to engine speed, and possibly accompanied by roughness in the engine—look for a loose spark-plug wire. Stick the wire back on the plug. If it fits too loosely to stay on, crimp the end slightly with pliers.

Drive belts are a composite material of cord and rubber, the cords being on the outer side. If the belt frays, cords may come loose and whip against some other part of the car. The loose cord will whip every time the belt makes a circuit, so the sound will follow engine speed.

The sound resembles the noise you make if you whip a solid object with a piece of cord.

Of the three sounds in this under-hood-clicks category, this one demands the most prompt attention, for it means the belt is going to pieces and you are in danger of losing water-pump and/or alternator function. Don't drive into a traffic jam, onto a long bridge, or through a tunnel with this sound going on. Stop and put on the spare fan belt you have with you, or let the remnants of the old one get you to the closest shop.

And how will you know whether the sound is from valves, a spark-plug wire, or the belt? If you're acute (and astute) enough, you can tell from sound and circumstance. If not, you just have to pull over and look under the hood to see what the wires and fan belt are doing; the valves you won't be able to see.

Timing chain: General Motors V-8
On many older General Motors V-8 engines, the metal timing gears have a layer of nylon over the teeth to quiet them. As the engine gets old, the nylon often cracks and comes off the teeth. This makes the gear smaller and that makes the timing chain loose, and the loose chain may smack the timing gear cover. The sound is distinctly metallic and may range from a "clack" to a "knock"; however, it may be erratic—several sounds in a row, then a skip or two.

The sound is also the sound of falling coins, for replacing a GM V-8 timing chain is a messy job. Fortunately, the problem rarely occurs before about 60,000 miles.

Loud looseness
Engines can produce other sounds when parts wear excessively. Pistons "slap" (which is really a "knock"), connecting rods "knock," main bearings "thud," piston pins "clank," and broken piston rings go "clickety-click." These sounds require more skill to distinguish; however, they matter less to the average driver. If not accompanied by loss of oil pressure or severe overheating, they do not presage imminent disaster. If a knocking rod is loose enough to stop the car, for example, the sound will be accompanied by low oil pressure. As long as the engine has some oil

pressure, a loose rod will get the car off the road at low speed. If the oil pressure goes to zero or the red indicator light goes on, stop before you destroy the engine.

A knocking rod means an engine rebuild; only one rod may need attention, but the motions to repair are those of a total overhaul. However, if you stop, you have something left to rebuild; if you keep going, you will "throw a rod," i.e., the connecting rod will come loose from the crankshaft and punch a hole right through the engine block.

Back in the 1930s and '40s, when many cars had bonded (nonseparate) connecting-rod bearings and oils weren't so good, a "knocking rod" was a common experience. Nowadays, few people have ever heard the sound.

Combustion knock
The "knock" that does persist today is the sound that ranges from a knock to a clatter to a pinging and comes from aberrant combustion within the cylinder. Instead of burning at the proper rate as the piston moves down, the fuel-air explodes all at once and delivers a hammer blow to the piston. In the old days, such a "knock" could shatter a piston. The reason we began putting lead in gasoline was to inhibit such explosions. However, faulty timing or air leaks into the intake manifold will also cause "knock."

Good old-fashioned "knock," then, is a bad thing. Usually, you will hear it when you push the gas pedal all the way to the floor as you leave a traffic light or climb a steep hill. Either way, ease off the gas until the knock ceases. Make sure you have the proper gasoline for your car, and have the timing and the hoses to the intake manifold checked.

Now, for the qualification: newer cars with pollution control run with quite lean air-fuel mixtures, so newer cars often (almost normally) produce a limited form of "knock" that is audible as a pinging-clicking when accelerating hard or when climbing a steep hill. You often hear this sound from a car that is passing you. This modern "pinging" is a much less pronounced combustion event than old-fashioned "knock" and is not reckoned to be harmful in small doses. If you drive moderately, you will not produce it, but if you do hear it, it won't damage a newer car if it is not sustained. For example, you may produce it long enough to pass another car and do so repeatedly without harm.

Cooling system (radiator):
squeal, shriek, groan, whine, spew, sigh

When a liquid-cooled car overheats, its coolant turns to steam at fairly high pressure and the steam tries to get out wherever it can, usually through the radiator cap. The sound it makes is that of a gas escaping from confinement; however, the note produced will vary from a vibrato moan to a falsetto whistle.

Whatever the sound, it will be accompanied by a high reading on the temperature gauge/warning light and by a cloud of vapor issuing from under the hood. Sometimes, you can hear the boiling water gurgling in the block and radiator. The sounds may also be accompanied by a steamy odor; if the cooling system has antifreeze, the odor will have a sickly sweetish component.

These sounds/circumstances mean *stop*. You may have damaged your engine already; if not, stop while you still have something left to save. The next stop is to get the car to a shop for diagnosis and repair.

Noises at crank-up

After an engine sits for a while, all the oil drains off its parts. When the engine cranks up the next time, the parts have no oil "padding" so they make a lot of clanking, clattering noise. The noise usually just indicates an old, worn engine. However, it may point to specific defects, such as a defective oil pump or a clogged oil-pump strainer (both possibilities being unusual and unlikely). Or, on some cars, such as the Toyota Corona four-cylinder of the early 1970s or on Mercedes-Benz products, excessive noise at crank-up may point to excess slack in the timing-chain tensioning device. Determine whether your tensioner depends on oil pressure; ask a mechanic, and have him check the tension of the chain when the engine is cold. This may require the removal of the valve cover, but that's better than having the chain jump and allow the valves and pistons to smash each other.

Misfire, backfire

Technically, a car "backfires" when the fire in the cylinder starts before the intake valve closes and the fire travels "back" up the intake manifold and comes out the carburetor with a loud blast. The force of the blast may wreck the air cleaner and the fire may set the carburetor ablaze, though these latter events rarely happen.

Alternatively, if the fire in the cylinder is still burning briskly when the exhaust valve opens, the fire goes out the exhaust pipe and the pressure may split the muffler. In any case, the misfire makes a loud noise when it leaves the exhaust pipe; it sounds like a rifle shot, but without the whine of the bullet.

On older cars with little pollution-control equipment and with conventional (nonelectronic) ignition systems, such misfirings are normal when decelerating rapidly and may be common when starting up if the engine is cold.

Persistent misfiring of this sort, though, betokens something wrong on any car. The problems can arise from such fuel-system faults as a clogged fuel line, producing ultra-lean mixtures. However, they more commonly arise from ignition timing faults, either from the distributor or from the vacuum controls that advance or retard ignition timing according to engine speed.

As a sort of anomaly, misfiring on my Chevrolet Suburban arose from snow that got up on the distributor and melted, so the water provided paths for the sparks to go to the wrong plugs. Some cars are particularly susceptible to this sort of thing when running in deep snow or heavy rain.

Either way, fuel or ignition system, misfiring can damage the air cleaner, carburetor, or exhaust system and calls for a visit to the shop. However, if misfiring develops on a trip, you don't have to stop right beside the road. Try to find the gas pedal position that produces the least misfiring and continue on to an exit.

Wheel sounds: grind, growl, scrape
Generally, if you hear anything from your wheels, it is only the hum of the tires as they run along the pavement. If you hear anything else, you'd better check on it.

Sounds from wheels will almost always come from the brakes, except for the very few instances when they come from bearings.

On some cars—for example, the GM family—the disc-brake pads are designed to make a mild but constant squeak when they wear down; the squeak goes away when you apply the brakes firmly. If you have these symptoms, get new brake pads.

A growling, scraping, grinding that may be faint as you drive along but that grows louder as you put on the brakes means the brake linings are worn down to the metal backing and the metal backing is grinding away on the brake disc/drum. Get to a shop at once, before you ruin the disc/drum beyond further use.

A grinding that increases with speed but that is not responsive to the brake pedal points to wheel bearings. Failure may be imminent, so proceed slowly to a repair facility.

One qualification: since the brakes will somewhat stabilize a loose wheel, the noise from a loose wheel bearing may be responsive to the brake pedal. The sound will moderate when you put on the brakes.

Clunking underneath

A "clunk" when an automatic transmission goes into gear or when a manual transmission gets under way points to looseness in the differential gears or in the universal joints.

Worn differential gears can go on forever if not abused. By contrast, worn U-joints may allow the drive shaft to come loose. If it comes loose at the differential end, it will flail around and tear up parking-brake cables, brake lines, *et al.*, plus bend the body metal on the underside.

If it comes loose at the transmission end, it may dig into the pavement and literally pole vault the car up in the air—with no way of predicting how it will come down.

Therefore, don't ignore a "clunk"; have a mechanic find out where it's coming from. The best way is to put the car on a service station lift so you can see things clearly. (See the "Used Car" section, item number 27, page 89.)

However, newer cars idle fast because of pollution control. Therefore, they normally make a pronounced "clunk" when an automatic transmission goes into gear. Still, check on a "clunk" to determine whether the noise is normal or arises from looseness.

Grunchy cornering

Another critical noise is a sort of "grunch" that usually occurs when you straighten the steering wheel after turning a corner. The noise indicates a loose, badly worn ball joint. The ball joint may make a lesser version of the sound just as you turn into the corner, too, and the sound may be audible when you stop. The ball joint could come loose completely when the car goes over a bump, so have a shop check it out.

Tires and suspension

Suppose you hear a pronounced "whap-whap" at one corner of the car as you motor along; the noise may have a "thump" or "thud" quality and will be the more pronounced if at either of the two wheels that support the engine. Along with the sound, you feel an up-and-down jiggling or a low-frequency vibration in the steering wheel.

These symptoms point to an out-of-balance tire. That is, the tire has a heavy spot somewhere on its perimeter and the heavy spot first tries to lift the wheel by centrifugal force (the jiggling) and then smacks heavily downward on the pavement (the noise). If severe enough, tire imbalance can shake the whole car.

An out-of-balance tire wears at an accelerated rate and batters the suspension system, so have a tire shop balance the tire.

However, you must make a refined distinction between whether the jiggling accompanying the noise is bouncing the car up and down or is pulling it first to one side and then to the other. A cyclic side-to-side pulling suggests a defective tire that doesn't have its tread on straight; thus, the tire is making an elongated snakelike track and is also wearing out rapidly. Wear or no wear, replace the tire.

However, side-to-side motion also points to looseness in the steering system, specifically the tie-rod ends, the tie-rod idler, or the steering box; and the symptoms will include excess free play in the steering wheel.

These are the noises that occur when the car is moving and that require some sort of immediate response. However, as the chapter on buying a used car indicates, cars make other sounds, too. Also, as noted, sounds are not the only symptom of problems: some problems produce distinctive smells; for example, the hot, steamy odor of a boiling radiator.

Hot oil

An overheated engine has both a steamy odor and a hot-oil smell. In familiar existence, about the nearest thing to the hot-oil smell is the smell a wax candle leaves when it is snuffed.

A hot-oil smell by itself suggests a leaking gasket, usually one that allows oil to drop on the exhaust manifold; that is, on the part of the engine that conducts hot exhaust gasses to the exhaust pipe. Such leaks often develop if a car sits for a long while, such as in storage or on a used-car lot, because the gasket dries out and shrinks. They also develop because gaskets get old and lose resiliency. Either way, a trifling leak does not stop the car; just check the oil frequently, don't let it run low, and have the gasket replaced as soon as possible.

However, do not neglect to investigate the smell, for it may indicate a serious leak, say from the oil filter. The oil filter looks like a fat tin can; it is usually painted in a color to contrast with the engine and will be a prominent protrusion low down on the engine. If the oil filter is leaking, you will see fresh oil dropping from where its base meets the engine. A leak from the filter is under pressure from the oil pump and could empty the crankcase in a few minutes, so don't ignore a hot-oil smell, especially if it develops suddenly. If it is accompanied by wisps (or clouds) of smoke, the leak is greater and its cause more serious, for the smoke indicates that large quantities of oil are falling on the exhaust pipe. However, the smoke does not presage a fire.

Hot brakes

Remember the time you put the cast iron skillet on the hot stove burner just as the phone rang, and when you finally hung up, you found a very hot, dry skillet? Remember the smell? Well, a smell like that in a car indicates a dragging brake. Usually, you will notice it when you come to a stop, when the wind no longer dissipates the smell; and sometimes the smell will be accompanied by a spongy brake pedal or by the car's pulling toward the side that has the stuck brake.

Once stopped, you can tell which wheels are involved by putting your hand near (or on) the wheels themselves. You will feel the heat. The brake may be sticking for one of several reasons—stuck cylinder piston, faulty self-adjuster, stuck parking-brake cable, broken brake-shoe return spring, clogged return port in the master cylinder, severely worn/out-of-adjustment wheel bearing, etc. In any case, you must consult the specialist at the shop.

Hot clutch

A hot, dry odor with an acrid component that stings like needles in your nose points to a slipping, overheated clutch. Even if you don't recognize the smell, you will know the clutch is slipping because the engine will speed up out of proportion to road speed, or the car may not climb a hill, i.e., the engine will race, but the car will slow down.

The clutch may need only an adjustment, but don't count on it. Once a clutch seriously overheats, the clutch-disc friction facings get brittle and crack. If you get the clutch adjusted promptly and it suffers only one or two instances of mild overheating, it will probably survive, but prolonged overheating puts the clutch disc on the terminal list.

Burning wiring
Since few people burn old tires in their back yard anymore, people have forgotten the smell of burning rubber and few recognize the more modern smell of burning plastics. The smell is hard to describe—a sort of penetrating acridity—and it occurs in a car when a severe short circuit melts the insulation on the wiring. If behind the dashboard, the hot wires may produce smoke (they may produce smoke under the hood, too, but you're less likely to notice it).

Usually, as the insulation melts, the wires short circuit among each other and the car stops, along with all its electrical devices. However, short circuits can cause fires. You can eliminate the danger of fire by cutting off the source of power to the wiring; that is, by disconnecting the battery. Of course, you won't have a tool to do this and if you had the tool, you might not be able to disconnect the battery before the hot wiring sets off a serious blaze simply because the battery connections are not always accessible. The proper responses, done simultaneously, are a) to go for the fire extinguisher (which should be under the front seat so you don't lose time fetching it from the trunk), and b) to get your passengers out of the car and upwind—you want no one downwind of the fuel tank if it decides to participate in the fire.

If a fire starts under the dash and you have no fire extinguisher, attack it with well-shaken canned soda or beer, both of which contain carbon dioxide. Beer is only about 4 percent alcohol, so the alcohol in it won't add to the fire. Any other noncombustible liquid will help, too, and will not bring the danger of fatal or injurious shock that liquid does with household electrical fires.

Attack an electrical fire under the hood in the same way or throw dirt on it. However, look at the large, thick round object more or less in the middle of the stuff under the hood (or, a black shoebox-looking thing on one side): that's the air cleaner, and the carburetor or fuel-injection system is right underneath or beside it. That means liquid gasoline will be spewing as soon as a fuel line burns in two. If you see fire there, give up: you can't fight a gasoline fire without a proper fire extinguisher, so get the passengers away and upwind, pull the hood down to contain the fire (and any fuel explosions), and get away from the car. *Don't lock the hood*, for firemen will need ready access to the engine. You will have time, if you move promptly, to remove valuables from inside—camera, overcoat, etc.—and, in fact, the fire may burn out without spreading to the rest of the car. However, don't press your luck: once the fire gets to the fuel system and starts feeding on gasoline, forget the car and protect yourself.

Obviously, cars can produce other sounds, such as the vibrating of a loose window (stick a book of matches between the glass and the door) or the rattle of gravel in a wheel cover. However, those described are the common ones that involve the security and safety of the car. Take good care of your car, and you'll never hear any of them.

CARBON MONOXIDE

Your car can make one other mixture of sound and smell, the sound of the Grim Reaper claiming his harvest, which comes along with the foul smell of death. These you get from a leaking exhaust system.

The exhaust gasses of the car are primarily carbon monoxide (CO), which, as you learned in high school chemistry, wants to become carbon dioxide (CO_2), so it grabs the available oxygen in your blood when you breathe it. Eventually, it asphyxiates you as stealthily as a cat stalks a mouse.

Technically, carbon monoxide is odorless. However, while you can't smell CO, you can certainly smell the unburned hydrocarbons (HC) and nitrous oxides (NO_x) in the exhaust, and you needn't trouble yourself about the technicality: if you smell exhaust stuff in your car, you're being executed.

If you haven't been exposed to "mono" when you knew it, you may not recognize the smell. Twice I ran a car in a closed garage (because of cold weather outside); I knew I shouldn't, but I reckoned I could monitor myself and clear out in good time. I learned that "mono" is as seductive as a single peanut—you take in a lot more than you think a lot quicker than you realize. I finally staggered out when I felt my knees getting rubbery even as my feet became leaden. Since then, I have not mistaken the harsh, edged acridity that dries your nose and mouth, the irritation that leads to weeping eyes, the lightheadedness accompanied by a mild headache. If you don't know the smell/sensations, just sit down behind your car and sniff its exhaust pipe while it's running—but don't stay long!

Generally, the wind you set up while driving carries exhaust gasses away. Also, if your car has no rust holes in its floorboards or trunk, you usually won't get exhaust inside. However, neither generality is sound enough to bet your life on, so don't tolerate a leaking exhaust. If you have exhaust leaks and rust holes, you're just asking for it. The full-size General Motors sedans of the late 1960s were prone to rust under the rear seat, and once a rust hole developed, it provided a path for carbon monoxide to enter the car. Similarly, the Ford Mustangs of the same era would rust out in the trunk, and the gas came in through the trunk. The aerodynamics of the early Mustangs were peculiar in the respect that the driver never noticed the carbon monoxide, but a rear-seat passenger got literally gassed.

When a misfire from wet wiring split the muffler on the Chevrolet Suburban, I got carbon monoxide through a rust hole in the floorboard that is several feet forward of the muffler. That is, the air currents flowing around the vehicle did not carry the carbon monoxide away; rather, peculiar air currents brought it into the vehicle, right past my face, and out the driver-side window. Note well: in this case, opening the window a little did not help. I had to open the window completely and stick my head almost all the way out to avoid the smell. However, when I turned a corner and put the vehicle in a stiff crosswind, the smell disappeared completely.

As noted, the symptoms include dryness in the throat, mild headache, and perhaps a sort of stinging in the eyes. People usually get irritable and start snapping at each other.

People who don't smoke will notice carbon monoxide before smokers do. If you smoke and your passenger does not, and if the passenger sniffs something awry, don't discount it: check out the exhaust system and replace it if it is full of holes. Put your hand firmly over the end of the exhaust pipe while the engine is running and listen for spewing, sputtering sounds. If you don't hear these sounds but you still have a suspicious odor, have a shop check the exhaust manifold for cracks or its gaskets for leaks.

Don't tolerate the sound of a defective exhaust system. Say the car has a noisy, leaking exhaust system; you only hear it, but the kids in the back seat get cranky, irritable, sick to their stomachs, rub their eyes, and are flushed in the face. Well, get them out of there: they're being killed! More than one unfortunate couple have come home from a trip, gone to take the baby from the back seat—and found the baby no longer with them. Put the kids up front and run the heater blower full blast to get fresh air into the car. Experiment to determine whether the "heat" or "defrost" position produces the most fresh air. In the Suburban, for example, the "defrost" position proved better.

TIRES

When you think about buying new tires, you go to the newspaper advertisements. There, you see *bias-ply*, or *conventional*, tires advertised along with *bias-belted* and *radial* tires, plus tires called "*recaps*." In larger sizes for larger cars, tire prices will range from about $30 for recaps up to $300 each for the best new tire.

So, what does all this mean?

Tire Types

Bias-ply, bias-belted, and radial refer to the way the tire is constructed, specifically to the pattern of reinforcing cord or wire that is molded in with the rubber. If you could strip the rubber off a tire and look at the reinforcing material underneath, a bias-*ply* tire would show you layers of cord running from side to side and crossing each other at angles of about 45°. A bias-*belted* tire would show you layers crossing each other at a similar angle, and then a belt of cords running around the diameter of the tire; layers of cord in the belt might lie at an angle to each other or they might lie parallel to each other and in the direction of travel. A radial would show you layers running exactly crossways; that is, at 90° to the direction of travel, and a belt of cords running parallel to the direction of travel (though some radials have crossplies on the belt).

Originally, Michelin (France) made radial tires with belts of steel wire, while Pirelli (Italy) and Semperit (Austria) offered radials with belts of synthetic cord or steel. Some cord-belted radials had a slight advantage in traction, were less noisy, and gave a marginally softer ride. However, they also transmitted less "road feel"; whereas they were, in fact, as secure as steel-belted radials, they did not feel that way, so people came to prefer steel-belted radials, and that's about all you see nowadays.

Bias-belted tires have been made with both cord and steel belts, but cord is more commonly used.

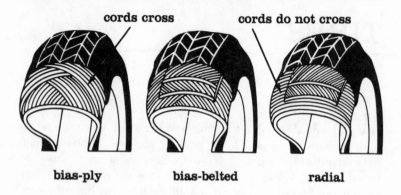

cords cross · cords do not cross

bias-ply · bias-belted · radial

Types of tire construction

A tire belongs to a particular type according to the lay of its cords and whether it has a belt around it.

Up to around 1950, America had a constantly growing car market and a constantly expanding network of good highways. National conditions, therefore, dictated the cheap, easily mass-produced bias-ply tire.

In Europe before 1950, a car was the toy of the wealthy more than transportation for the masses, and European cars ran on roads that had been paved by the Romans. Hence, the premium was always on speed (due to social class) and handling (due to the roads). Thus, radial tires were developed by Michelin and came on the market in 1951. Semperit shortly followed with radials, as did Pirelli. The sports car freaks of the 1950s adopted radials because of the advantage they conferred in racing. The word spread among foreign car owners, radials became common on foreign cars, and by the late 1960s, the domestic industry reluctantly faced up to the necessity of making radial tires.

Technically, a radial tire is best because it is lighter and more flexible, so it builds up less heat in the first place and can dissipate heat faster in the second place. Because it is flexible, it can keep a flat "footprint" on the pavement over bumps and when cornering, an advantage especially important at high speed. Being lighter and more flexible, it has less resistance to rolling and so it gives a car slightly better gas mileage.

However, watch that last item. The gas mileage improvement can be reliably predicted to average about 3 percent, but will hardly ever exceed 5 percent. Do the arithmetic: this means that at the best a 14-mpg car will go up to 14.7 mpg and a 30-mpg car will go up to 31.5 mpg. If a change to radial tires makes more difference than that, something else was wrong before— probably inflation pressure was too low.

Now, suppose you can buy four bias-ply tires for a total of $200 or four radials for $400. With a 20-mpg car, a 3 percent increase in mpg, and fuel at $1.25 per gallon, you will have to drive about 100,000 miles to save $200 worth of gasoline to pay the higher cost of radials. You can find lots of reasons for buying radial tires, but fuel economy is about the last one.

Radials do have one notable limitation. Their flexible sidewalls are inherently weak. "Weak" does not mean radials are not good. "Weak" means radial sidewalls have little tolerance for being gouged, poked with sharp objects, or scrubbed against curbs. Also, the weak sidewall means that radials do not tolerate over-loading well; overload a radial, and you'll cause the belt to sep-arate from the casing. Likewise with improperly high pressure: inflate a radial much beyond its maximum pressure, and the belt will separate from the rest of the tire. By contrast, bias-ply tires can be overloaded, overinflated, and scrubbed up against rocks without being hurt much. This does not mean you should treat them that way; it just means they will take more of this kind of abuse than radials.

Matter of Quality

Okay, that's the generality. Unfortunately, you can't depend on it because, as with anything else, the good idea of a radial tire can be executed in a shoddy manner, and much of this sort of thing has been done in America. In fact, it's about all America has done with the radial concept. Hence, only the most-expensive domestic radials are even worthy of the name and many of the cheaper ones are not as good as a well-made bias-ply tire.

The question becomes one of distinguishing the good stuff from the junk. However, the question also becomes one of what you need from your tires.

For example, suppose you drive 10,000 miles per year in a

city that doesn't have potholes; you go only to work and to the grocery store, and never exceed 30 miles per hour. If so, the cheapest tires you can find will give you complete security and they will probably last you 40,000 miles if you keep them inflated properly.

If you contend with numerous potholes and do a fair amount of highway cruising, you need better tires. However, if you can avoid the potholes, even the junkiest tires of today will tolerate the minimal demands of cruising at 55 mph.

On the other hand, suppose you want more. Maybe you just want to have the best. You want the best in stopping ability, the best in cornering ability, the most resistance to skidding, etc. In this case, you should buy quality radials.

Now, to provoke a scream from the domestic tire industry: The only American brand-name radial tire I have any faith in is the Sears radial (which is manufactured by Michelin). Otherwise, if you want the best and have the money, buy European radials, preferably Michelin, Semperit, or Pirelli. Radials from Japan are about as good as domestic radials.

Yes, yes, I know American radials have run up a fair record in the past few years, but I also know that at current legal speeds tires hardly get a serious workout. In fact, I believe the 55-mph speed limit saved the American tire companies from total collapse in the face of competition from European radials. I suspect that if people still drove 70 mph the casualty rate among American radials would be noticeably higher and the superiority of European radials would be more visible.

To further anticipate a rebuttal from the domestic tire industry, a tale about government science: In 1979, the National Highway Traffic Safety Administration (NHTSA) imposed its Tire Grading System (TGS) wherein tires were rated according to treadwear, traction when braking on a wet pavement, and resistance to heat, this last item being the one most closely related to the ability of a tire to tolerate high speed.

The treadwear ratings were a patent absurdity from the beginning. Since every tire could not be tested in 40,000+ miles of driving, the federal ratings depended on estimates, estimates that could not account for variations in driving style. Although domestic radials generally rated above foreign radials in treadwear, the domestic manufacturers protested the factitious character of the ratings, and in July 1982, NHTSA rescinded the treadwear ratings.

The heat-resistance ratings remained in force, though, and the only radials to earn "A" ratings were certain Michelin and Pirelli models. Michelin's XWX, Sears' Roadhandler Radial, and Pirelli's P3 earned "B" ratings, as did the Japanese Bridgestone. The only domestic radial to earn a "B" was the Goodrich Lifesaver; all others got "C" ratings for heat resistance. (Semperit, Metzeler, and several other low-volume manufacturers in Europe were not represented in the ratings.)

By contrast, among conventional bias-ply tires, Armstrong's Tru-Trac 60 and Uniroyal's Fastrak earned "B" ratings for heat resistance, the others getting a "C." All bias-belted tires got "C" ratings.

The heat-resistance ratings, developed by laboratory testing, enjoy general respect, and they confirm my assessment of domestic radials. While I am on the subject, the Europeans have a few ratings of their own, which are sometimes applied to domestic tires. The rating "HR," in Europe, designates a tire capable of sustained speeds up to 130 mph, and "VR" designates one capable of speeds up to 150 mph.

Among those screams of protest, I hear some noise about the "rugged" radials on the "off-road" vehicles. You know—those big, fat knobby tires with the white letters you see on the Jeep look-alikes. So, you have a 4WD Chevrolet Blazer that weighs about 3500 pounds—and it has these huge, "rugged" tires that are about 10 inches wide. Well, those big tires will probably support about 2500 pounds apiece. In other words, they aren't being loaded at all on the "off-road" vehicles, and since they are rated for around three times as much weight as they actually carry, they certainly ought to hold up. However, the fact that they do hold up under minimal load proves nothing about tires for an ordinary sedan.

Now, to shift the emphasis: I don't believe any other country can make conventional tires better than the American ones. Although my '71 Saab 99 has four Michelins (because I could not find a handy Semperit dealer; I wanted the Semperit "all-weather" tire), when I bought the most unbelievably rusted-out hulk of a 1974 Chevrolet Suburban for a temporary vehicle, I put conventional tires on it. Its front suspension was warped and slopped out enough to limit it to a 60-mph cruising speed and I did not take corners in it as fast as I do in the Saab, so it did not need radials.

Similarly, I couldn't afford radials for the Mercedes-Benz 190 SL I drove in Chicago in 1972, so I put on a set of Sears bias-belted tires. Bias-belted tires are a sort of middle ground between bias-ply and radial tires and if made well, as the Americans do them, are a very good middle ground, indeed, for the marginal superiority of a radial over a good bias-belted tire is a very narrow margin. I normally drove the turnpikes between Chicago and Pittsburgh on those tires at a steady 70 mph and 85 mph when feeling frisky, and I did so in complete security. Here again, bias-belted tires are suitable for many people's driving habits.

Advertisements often show a car screaming through curves to suggest that only Brand X tires will get around a corner like that. Well, if you don't take corners that way, then you clearly don't need Brand X tires. Fact is, how fast you get around a corner is largely a matter of how hard you want to work at it and how well you know your car—plus the suspension system, too. With a given car, an ordinary racing driver can take a set of conventional tires and beat a good amateur driver with radials in virtually any cornering situation.

Differences in the stopping ability of tires matter more than cornering ability. However, advertised differences and the differences reported in the "tests" in the car magazines don't always mean much. For example, the most important factor in tire performance is proper inflation. If you don't have your tires properly inflated, you aren't going to stop as fast. Similarly, if you have your car loaded funny, i.e., lots of weight in the trunk, your car won't stop the way cars do in the ads and tests.

The list of factors that affect stopping distances could go on and on. In final fact, the driver is the most important factor of all. *You should drive on the assumption that your brakes are not good.* That is, always leave yourself lots of room to stop, slow down when you see a kid on a bicycle two blocks away, and prepare to respond if he darts out in front of you, watch traffic carefully, etc., etc. Agreed, better tires will give you an advantage, but you may not be able to exercise the advantage. Therefore, don't program the advantage into your expectations.

Mix or Match?

While on the subject of radials, we'd better take note of the "mix-or-match" question. Radials stop better than conventional tires. Also, the tires that support the engine have better traction than the other two. Thus, if you can afford only two radials, the rule is to put them on the rear. If you put them on the front, they will stop better than the rear and that will cause the rear end to skid around and the car will swap ends in a panic stop. However, if you put two radials on the rear, the rear end will stop better than the front; the effect is as if a giant grabbed your rear bumper, and it helps keep the car straight.

This general rule has effectively been elevated to the status of law, and like much well-intentioned law, its foundation in experience is weak.

Do not misunderstand me here. I agree with the theory and I endorse the idea that if two of the four tires are radials, the radials should go on the rear. What bothers me is to see people afraid to drive if they can't organize a car that way.

For example, suppose you already have four radial tires with normal tread. Winter comes and you want snow tires, but either you can't afford radial snow tires or you can't find them in your tire size. According to the popular assumption, you can't put two conventional, bias-ply snow tires on the rear and must go through the winter on your radials with normal tread.

Or suppose you have a front-wheel-drive car with bias-ply tires. When winter comes, you find a nice pair of radial snow tires, but the conventional wisdom says you can't put them on the front, so you don't get them and spin through the slush all winter. Or you commit the silliness of putting snow tires on the rear wheels of a front-wheel-drive car.

The preference for radials at the rear, as noted, arises from sound logic, and having arisen, has assumed a legal quality. Many tire dealers will not put radials on the front of a car unless they can also put them on the rear because they fear being sued if the driver smashes up the car and blames the crash on the mismatched tires. Of course, in the long run, the legal element helps them sell more radials.

Front tires normally wear faster than rear tires, so if you have two worn tires, they will more likely be on the front. So, you want to buy two radials and enjoy the benefits of stability and precise steering, and add two more radials at the rear later? Well, you may not be allowed to do it. It may be illegal.

In practice, the difference in the fore and aft behavior of radials has been exaggerated. I know dozens of people who drive all kinds of cars and who go through the winter with bias-ply snow tires on the rear and radials at the front, and I have never known any of them to suffer any problems as a result. To be sure, these people keep their brakes, steering, and suspension in good order, so the car has no mechanical bias to exacerbate the difference in traction of the two types. Also, these people drive intelligently: they don't get drunk, go hurtling through curves, and expect their tires to save them from their stupidity. If you're like these people, you can mix your tires. I endorse the idea only in the short run—e.g., you bought one bias-ply tire to get home from a trip, or you mix because your snow tires are not like your others. In other words, you can break the rules if you do it with your eyes open and take care as you do so.

Studs—Ugh!

Since the subject of winter driving came up, a word about studded tires.

I disapprove of studded tires on several grounds, mostly because of the way they chew up a smooth pavement and wear ruts in it. Also, I drove with studs for a total of five winters in Chicago and Pittsburgh, and I believe that they make a car unstable at cruising speed on a dry pavement. In effect, the car begins to ride on the points of the studs instead of on the rubber tread. Last, I found studs to be helpful only in an extremely narrow range of conditions; specifically, on packed snow or hard ice. Otherwise, I find them no better than ordinary snow tires.

If you must drive daily in wintry climates, I suppose you can justify studs. However, in the interest of preserving the pavements and in the interest of stability, you should cut your highway speed down to about 45 mph. Yes, yes, I know you will say, "But my car feels fine with studded tires at 60 mph." Agreed, but what your car feels like and what its tires are doing are not necessarily the same, especially on domestic cars, which do their best to insulate you from the road. Try a panic stop at speed on dry pavement with studs and you may well go cartwheeling down the road like an ice skater.

Recaps

A woman I know owns a new Mustang with one of those funny-looking spare tires that is intended only as a get-you-to-the-service-station spare. Detroit began using these a few years ago, presumably to save weight and space but actually to save money. The car manufacturers were not totally venal; experience showed that tire failures are so rare that most people never use the spare tire, so Detroit reasonably sought to save a few bucks. Anyway, she fit herself and four other people into her Mustang, drove 30 miles, and then had a flat. She put on the spare, but noted that her owner's manual warned that the tire should not be loaded heavily. Accordingly, she left two of the passengers at a roadside rest, took two home, and then went back for the other two—two trips, because she wasn't sure what "heavily loaded" meant.

I have not tested the Mustang spare or any other similar temporary tire, but I am certain she could have hauled the whole carload home in one trip—provided she drove slowly, say at 35 mph rather than 50 mph. Heat, which is the worst enemy of a tire, arises from the way the tire flexes as it meets the pavement. To slow down spreads the same amount of flexing (i.e., distance traveled) over a longer time span and allows better heat dissipation.

She got everybody home, but since she didn't want to confront the same problem again, she decided to replace the temporary spare tire with a normal tire. She then encountered the question of whether a *recap* or a used, second-hand tire would do as a spare.

A recap is made from a tire that wore most of its tread off. The recapper buffs off the remnants of the old tread, wraps a new tread around it, and glues or vulcanizes (heat bonds) the new tread to the old tire (somewhat like putting new soles on old shoes). Recapping used to be quite common, and its very popularity led to a lot of shoddy recaps. Now, recappers are fewer and quality is much better.

I would rather have a quality recap than a shoddy brand-new

tire. Twenty years ago, I drove on recaps much of the time. In fact, I put four recaps on the '54 Ford that I drove to Alaska in 1961. The car was weighted down with various personal effects (mostly books) and 1200 of the 4500 miles to Fairbanks were on a gravel road (the Alaska Highway). The tires survived the trip better than the car (the overdrive unit went out and I also broke the right rear *U-bolts*). As new tire prices declined, recaps lost some of their advantage, but in recent years tire prices have climbed and recaps are in demand again.

Here again, a little ordinary sense must prevail: I would not put recaps on a car, load it down with vacation gear and children, and go blasting down a hot pavement in August. I would keep the weight down and would make sure my inflation pressure was proper, but for "around town" and for legal cruising speeds without a heavy load, recaps are quite good enough.

Used Tires

Technically, a recapped tire was used once, but "used" here refers to those odd tires you see heaped around tire shops and service stations. The shops/stations get them in trade and if the tires have a fair amount of tread left, the shop/station keeps them rather than sells them to a recapper. People on marginal incomes buy them, as do people who need a "get home" tire when on a trip.

My barber chose a used tire, for which she paid $10. The tire had no gouges on the outside nor cuts or cord separations on the inside, and had a good third of its tread left. The tread did have uneven wear that showed it had been on a car with an improperly aligned suspension, and that explained the tire: the previous owner got a front-end alignment and decided to start over with new tires up front.

Western Massachusetts has many "casual" people who drive beat-up pickups and who spend their money on anything else but tires. Many of these people drive all the time on second-hand tires and their vehicles never have two tires that match. They seem quite happy spending $5 to $15 apiece for used tires, discarding them after a few months and buying more.

I sympathize with this approach to the tire question because I followed it during the first few years I owned cars, and for the same reason: I couldn't afford anything else. My experience is that a decent used tire, if not visibly damaged, often has much life left in it—as a spare, as a tire to get home on, or for a car that ambles around close to home all the time.

Often enough, some well-heeled car owner ruins one tire of a matched set and buys four new tires at once; the three good tires that come off the car are the next person's bargain and good at the price.

CHANGING A FLAT TIRE

As we have noted (to our dismay), most of the things that go wrong with a car will be beyond your ability to fix. The one thing you can, and must, fix is a flat tire. Everybody, even the aged and infirm, who drives a car should be able to change a flat tire: help may not be available.

Many people join car service clubs such as Allstate or the American Automobile Association (AAA) in an effort to avoid the unpleasantness of changing a tire. Invariably, they have a flat on the very day the service club trucks are towing stalled cars out of rain puddles or jump-starting them on the first cold day of the winter. Car club dues give you membership, but you will never change a flat tire by waving a membership card at it. Like it or not, you may have to change the flat.

Given a single-bit axe and a tall tree, I can fell the tree, cut it into lengths, fashion the lengths into wedges, and drive the wedges under a car to raise it off the ground. However, I much prefer to raise the car with a jack. With the same axe and a cold chisel,

I can remove lug bolts, though I much prefer a wrench. Thus, the right tools make any job easier.

The proper tools for changing a tire consist of the appropriate *jacks* to lift and support the car, *chocks*/blocks for a wheel so the car doesn't roll, a long *screwdriver* or short wrecking bar to remove the wheel cover ("hubcap"), a *six-point, deep-socket wrench* to turn the lug nuts (the actual "lug bolt" stays on the car), a long *flex handle* (also called a "breakover" handle) for the socket wrench; and a length of pipe to slide over the flex handle to extend it, thus to increase your leverage when turning the lug nuts.

Jacks come in several types, the familiar one being the *bumper jack* that hooks under the bumper and has long been standard equipment on the larger domestic cars. As the bumper jack raises the car body, the springs on the car extend, so you have to lift the body high enough to take all the stretch out of the spring

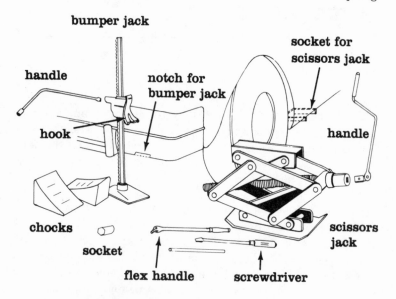

Tire-changing tools

Here's what you need to change a tire. Note the notch for the bumper jack. A car intended for use with a scissors jack will have a socket of some sort to receive the top of the jack.

before the wheel will come off the ground. That puts the car high up on one corner, which makes it inherently unstable—ready to fall if slightly encouraged.

To help stabilize a car supported by a bumper jack, use the other common jack, a *scissors jack*, so named because its action replicates two pairs of scissors, joined at the blade tips, and opening up together. As you turn the handle, a long screw opens the scissors "blades" and lifts the car. If a scissors jack is part of the standard equipment for a car, the car will have special sockets for the jack just behind the front wheels and just ahead of the rear wheels.

The third familiar jack, a *tripod* or *bipod* jack, is not standard with any car, so you have to get one from an auto store. It consists of two or three legs that form a base and a long screw, turned by a crank handle, that lifts on the bumper of the car. The wide base and the finesse of the screw action make these jacks more stable than bumper jacks. If your larger domestic car no longer has its original-equipment bumper jack (or if the jack is rusted beyond use), get one of these jacks. For that matter, if you simply want a jack more secure than the standard bumper jack, use a bipod/tripod jack. Cost: about $20.

The normal assumption is that you need only one jack to change a tire; and indeed, the normal assumption is true in the ideal circumstances of, say, changing a tire on a smooth, flat, hard surface. However, you rarely have a flat in ideal circumstances: the shoulder of a road is soft or sloping and even the flat, hard shoulder of an interstate highway exposes a car on a jack to severe buffeting from passing cars that can cause the car to fall off the jack. If the car falls, the jack usually ends up wedged under the car in such a way that you can't get it out—which leaves you waiting for a road service truck that may charge as much as $50 to remedy the situation.

Generally, if a car is designed for lifting with a scissors jack, and if its jack is in good order, a scissors jack is all you need. However, with a car designed for a bumper jack, you should trust the bumper jack about as much as you trust a snake-oil peddler. True, bumper jacks will work, but they involve more luck than you should have to depend on.

The upshot is that if your car is equipped with a bumper jack as standard equipment, you should add a scissors jack to your tool kit. The jack will cost about $15 at the auto parts store and will have a long handle that allows you to slide the jack under the car without having to flop on your back. You use the scissors jack in conjunction with the bumper jack to ensure the stability of the car as you change the wheel.

If you know where you will place the auxiliary scissors jack, and if the place does not require a long jack handle—i.e., if you can reach it easily from beside the car—you may choose to get a scissors jack from a wrecking yard, for the ones for a Saab or a Toyota are particularly handy.

The old Volkswagen Beetle, and the Porsche and Mercedes-Benz cars of the same era, used a screw-type jack that fit into a socket on the side of the car. These jacks are also prone to slipping—the car can roll forward or backward—so use an auxiliary scissors jack with these cars, too.

Your problem will be in deciding where to place the scissors jack, and cars vary so much in detail that we can't offer a description here that will lead you directly to the best place. At the rear you should try to get under the rear axle about where the spring attaches. You will have to do some stooping here; better yet, check out the car at home one day when it's sitting conveniently in the driveway.

If the car has *coil springs* at the rear, you will see these coiled springs—one per side—stuck between the body and the axle (or, more properly, the axle housing). Try to put the scissors jack immediately under the place that the lower end of the coil spring rests on.

If the car has *leaf springs*, you will see several strips of metal—about ¼ inch thick and about 2 inches wide—running lengthwise. They pass under the rear axle and are held to it by *U-bolts*. Try to get the jack under the axle and just inside the leaf spring; you could go immediately under the leaf spring itself, but the tips of the U-bolts may interfere.

If you can't get under the rear axle itself, go forward from it and look for a solid, reinforced place on the body.

At the front, don't put the jack under the spring. Put it inside the front wheel where you see suspension attachments on the frame or at a solid-looking place just behind the front wheel. "Solid-looking" places will have some sort of additional metal attached to the basic sheet-metal floorboard of the car.

Note the underlying presumption here: a car supported by a jack is inherently unstable. When changing a tire, you must assure the stability of the car, must make certain that it doesn't fall off the jack.

Similarly, in the tire-changing process that follows, the sequence of steps is arranged to minimize the amount of time that the car is supported by only the jack and nothing else. If the car falls off the jack before you get the flat tire off, it will fall right back on the flat and you can recover the situation; if it falls when the wheel is off the car, you may wind up with the jack under the car. So, the process minimizes the time when only the jack, alone, supports the car.

The screwdriver you need should be at least 15 inches long, and around 18 inches is better. It will be so big that it will look absurd. You use it to remove the wheel cover and as a pry bar to lift the wheel, if need be. I prefer a big screwdriver to a small wrecking bar, but if you prefer the wrecking bar look at the small 12- to 18-inch wrecking bars in the hardware store. Make sure the end of the bar is thin enough to slip under the lip of the wheel cover.

The proper wrench, as noted, is a socket wrench, so named because a nut fits into it as into a socket. The standard socket is short and has twelve "teeth," or points, inside, but you want a deep socket that is longer, and you want it with only six points, for the six-point socket will be less likely to slip. However, if you can't find a six-point, deep socket, use a twelve-point. A good one—and you must have a good one that fits snugly on the lug nut—will cost about $6. The clerk at the auto store will help you "pop" off one of your wheel covers to determine the size you need for your lug nuts.

The socket wrench fits over the lug nut at one end and has a square hole in the other end. You stick the end of the flex handle into this square hole to turn the socket. The size of the square hole defines the "drive" of the socket and you need a half-inch drive; less will not do.

The flex handle, which will cost about $15, should be 15 to 18 inches long, the longer the better, to give you maximum leverage when you go to turn the lug nuts. To extend the leverage, slide your piece of pipe over the end of the handle. The pipe, from a hardware or plumbing goods store, should fit snugly over the handle and should be the same length, so you can store them together. If you can't turn the lug nuts with the handle alone, you slide the pipe over the handle, say, 6 to 8 inches, then exert your leverage on the pipe. If you start out with an 18-inch handle and add 12 inches more with your pipe, this gives you a 30-inch lever. A 100-pounder standing on the end of such a pipe exerts roughly a 250-pound/twist (torque) on the lug nut. If standing doesn't do it, a slight jump on the end of a 30-inch lever will give a 300-pound impact on the lug nut and a hard jump will give up to a 500-pound one. This will loosen virtually all lug nuts, even those that have been vastly overtightened by those inept gorillas in tire shops and service stations who wield their compressed air "impact wrenches" with the finesse of a boar pig in rut.

The chocks are triangle-shaped blocks that you stick behind (or ahead) of one wheel, on the opposite end from the flat, to keep the car from rolling. They cost about $8 a pair at an auto store.

These are the necessary tools. As a refinement, add a spray can of water-displacing penetrating oil—e.g., WD-40, CRC, LPS, etc.—to your kit. Spray the perimeter of the wheel cover to help ease it off (and back on), and spray the lug bolts to ease the job of removing them. Give your jack a shot, too, to keep it from rusting.

You will not want your tools rattling around loose, so get a discount store suitcase or suchlike to contain them. A soft type works very well. Don't get a metal toolbox: it's awkward, slides around, and gouges everything it gets close to. A small, cheapie "overniter" will fit into more places—even in cars or station wagons that do not have a trunk—and with a shoulder strap will be easy to carry when you loan the kit to the neighbor across the street.

While in the discount store, get a pair of cheap hand towels and a small bottle of Johnson's Baby Oil. Soak one towel in baby oil and seal it in a plastic bag: after changing the tire, use the oily towel to clean your hands and the other to wipe them dry, and your manicure will be as nice as when you left the house.

Beyond tools, the next crucial element of tire-changing is the worksite. You would not bathe a Newfoundland in the kitchen sink, and neither should you try to change a tire in an unsuitable location.

When a tire goes flat, you don't have to stop right where you are. If you must, drive on the flat about as slowly as the car will go—say, 5 mph, with flashers on—until you get to a good place to change the tire. If you must go far, you may ruin the tire but that will be better than having the car fall off the jack and hurt you or puncture the tire you're trying to put on. Also, don't let your flat tire be trapped by the curb; either pull a good foot or two away from the curb or drive to a curbless area. A vacant driveway is a good place; if a driveway has a car sitting in it, ask permission at the house to block the drive long enough to put on your spare.

Since a car on a jack is inherently unstable, every effort must be made to prevent the car from moving as the jack lifts and supports it. Ideally, this means a level place, but level places rarely occur in the same places where tires go flat. Either the shoulder of the road slopes to one side or the car winds up pointing uphill or downhill. Either way, the jack will tend to ease the car in the downhill direction—forward, backward, or sideways—often enough to cause it to fall off the jack.

As a bumper jack lifts a car, one end of the bumper goes higher than the other. That is, the jack remains perpendicular to the ground (assuming a level surface) but engages the bumper at an angle that increases as the corner of the car goes higher, and the forces at work can cause a bumper jack to slip along the edge of the bumper. The tendency becomes much worse if the bumper starts out at an angle, e.g., if the car is on the sloping shoulder of the road. To be sure, most cars have a special notch on the bumper where the jack fits, and this notch is supposed to keep the bumper jack from slipping—but it doesn't always.

On a big car, the lower edge of the bumper will be about six inches off the ground when a tire is flat. When it is high enough to get the tire off the ground, the same bumper will be close to 30 inches from the ground. This extreme elevation at one end causes the car to roll toward the end that is not elevated. Thus, when using a bumper jack—or any jack, really—you have to counter the fore-and-aft and athwartship forces that arise from the terrain and from the angles generated by lifting the car. This requires you to study the disposition of the car, to analyze which way—right or left, forward or backward—the car will try to move as you raise the affected corner. For example, with a flat on the left-front and on a shoulder sloping down to the right,

I have put my auxiliary scissors jack on the right side to counteract the tendency of the car to slide to the right as I lifted the left side. Usually, though, the exercise will present few subtleties, and they will be still fewer as your location is flatter and firmer.

A word about that "firm" business: Add an 8-inch square piece of ¾-inch-thick plywood—a lumberyard scrap—to your kit as an enlarged base for your jack. You will need it if you wind up on soft ground.

Okay, now go through the whole drill: You feel the car pulling to one side, hear a rear tire flopping, and pull over onto a fairly steep, grassy shoulder just as the right-rear tire gasps its last. Note that we are setting up "worst case" elements here: As you raise the right-rear corner of the car, the left-rear tire will offer to slide to the right on the grass and the jack will tip over. To complicate things, assume the car is pointed uphill. You set the parking brake, of course, but to raise the right-rear corner will take some weight off the left-rear tire, too, so it may threaten to slide backward even though locked by the parking brake. If the parking brake works on the front wheels, the same problem arises with a flat on the front.

Besides dealing with the problem of stabilizing the car, you have to do something with the people in it. If you don't mind lifting their additional weight, you can leave them in the car. A single passenger should sit on the side you are lifting, to avoid weighting the other side down and, thus, increasing the athwartships angle as you jack up one side. Two passengers should sit in the opposite end from the one you are lifting—in the front if the flat is on the rear, and vice versa—and should sit on opposite sides for balance. If the seat will hold three passengers, put them all there; if not, put the third one in the other seat, on the side *with* the flat.

The passengers have only to sit still—not so catatonic as a meditating Trappist monk, but simply at ease. However, children must not be permitted to romp back and forth across the seats, lest they jiggle the car off the jack.

Where road and weather conditions permit, passengers can alight and gather flowers as you change the tire. Even beside a busy interstate, they can go well off the shoulder, for they have no good reason to stand right beside the car, being buffeted by gusts from passing trucks and exposed to danger from ill-con trolled vehicles. With a guardrail on the passenger side of the car, they should scramble over the guardrail.

All this sounds good, but it rarely applies because you always have a flat in the midst of a driving rain or in a blizzard, when the passengers must stay in the car. They certainly should in bad weather, but they must relax as they do. They may, of course, roll down a window occasionally to offer encouragement or well-meaning advice as you change the tire.

Okay, right-rear tire is flat on an awkward worksite; now, note the steps carefully. *Note, especially, that we do not go for the jack first.*

1. Get the block(s) or chock(s) from the trunk and put it *behind* the front wheel if the car points *uphill*; if the car points downhill or is on the level, put the chock in front of the wheel. Put the car in neutral and let it roll against the block; if need be, put the car in gear and apply slight power against the block. You do this to get the front tire firmly against the block and to set the block firmly in/on the ground. Once the block is set, set the parking brake and put an automatic transmission in "Park" and a manual shift in reverse. Obviously, with a flat on the front, put the chock at the rear.

2. Fetch out the prying instrument, e.g., the long screwdriver, and remove the wheel cover. On most domestic cars with full-wheel covers, you begin at the extreme edge. However, the full-wheel covers on many foreign cars (e.g., some Mercedes-Benz models) are in two parts, so you attack only the smaller, center portion.

Push the tip of the screwdriver between the wheel cover and the rim (the wheel itself). If it won't go, look for a special notch. If you don't find one, tap the end of the screwdriver with the socket wrench handle and drive it between the wheel cover and rim. Pry inward and outward to see which way produces the best results. After the edge of the wheel cover comes outward a little, work your way around as when you pry the top out of the cocoa box. Set the wheel cover aside where it won't be in the way and lay the screwdriver in it.

3. Examine the lug nuts as you spray them with oil. Virtually all turn counterclockwise (or leftward when facing the wheel) to loosen. However, if you see an "L" mark on the end of the lug bolt, that means "left-hand (to tighten) thread," so with "L" bolts, go clockwise or rightward to loosen.

Slide the socket over the lug nut. Since we so wisely chose a deep socket, the other end of the socket sticks out far enough that the wheel (rim) itself gives no interference as we stick the flex handle into the square hole.

We want our flex handle as nearly horizontal as possible; let it point slightly upward rather than downward.

Give the handle a downward push. Shucks, the lug nut won't turn. Okay, assuming you're "right-footed," stand facing the car, brace yourself against the car with your hands, put your right foot on the handle, and put your weight on it.

Still won't go? Okay, add the pipe and try again. Won't go? Okay, give a little jump on your right foot. If that doesn't work, give a hard jump.

If this still doesn't loosen the lug nut, you are close to stymied. But keep trying. First, slide the pipe out as far as possible to create the maximum leverage; or stick the factory lug wrench or your screwdriver into the end of the pipe to increase the leverage. If that doesn't work, you're out of options. You have to call a road service truck.

Odds are, though, the nut will loosen. When it does, the handle/pipe will aim toward the ground and you will slide off, so be ready to keep your balance.

Repeat this procedure with all lug nuts. Once they have all been loosened a couple of turns, completely remove every other one. On a six-lug wheel, that means three; on a five-lug wheel, remove two. On a four-lug wheel, remove the two that lie most nearly on a horizontal line. With some lug nuts removed, you have fewer motions to make once the wheel is completely off the ground. Put the lug nuts in the wheel cover.

4. Remove the spare tire and roll it to the side of the car. For small people who drive big cars, getting a large heavy spare tire out of (or into) a "stylish" trunk will be the hardest part of the exercise. However, since we haven't touched the jack yet, at least the car is slightly lower and we need not lift so far.

If you are right-handed you'll be inclined to remove the flat and thrust it to the right; therefore, put the spare on your left so you'll be bringing it from left to right to put in place.

5. Now (where applicable) set up the bumper jack. You will have a flattish base piece with a sort of socket in it. You also have a vertical piece that has notches on one side and has another piece that moves up and down; this latter piece has a hole for the jack handle, i.e., the factory lug wrench, and a little lever that goes into an "up" or a "down" position. Stick the vertical piece into the base with the notches facing you, i.e., not toward the car.

The sliding piece may have an additional piece that hooks onto it to catch the bumper, and somewhere along the bottom edge of the bumper will be a notch or indentation where the hook affair catches. The locating notch may be a hole that fits over an upward dimple on the hook section.

Put the "up-down" lever in the proper position and work the handle up and down until the hook will catch the bumper; notice how you can feel the notches as you work the lever.

If you are on a flat surface or if the surface has only a slight slope, you should place the bumper jack so that it is perpendicular to the ground. It will not, therefore, be perpendicular to the bumper once the car is elevated, but that notch on the bumper should keep it from slipping.

However, we have set up a "worst case" situation and have a severe slope to the right and our flat tire on the right. If we set the jack perpendicular to this severe slope, it will literally push the car sideways as it comes up. To get out of this problem, we apply our screwdriver as a pick and the base of the jack as a shovel and create a flat spot for the base of the jack to rest on. We place the jack on this flat spot so that it points straight up and thus minimizes the tendency of the car to go sideways.

On soft, muddy ground, put the piece of plywood under the base of the jack; in snow, dig down until you come to a firm surface.

6. Start jacking. Use slow deliberate strokes and listen for the positive "click" on the downstroke that tells you the jack has caught in a notch and is ready for the next upstroke.

As soon as you have room under the car, put the scissors jack in the place you chose for it and raise it until it is in firm contact with the car.

Make several strokes with the bumper jack and then several

with the scissors jack so that the load is always divided. Watch very carefully for any tendency of either jack to slip. Be sure that the scissors jack carries a goodly share of the load.

If the car has a scissors jack as standard equipment, you obviously began with it. As you raise the car, be sure it does not offer to roll and tip the scissors jack at an angle. A scissors jack, by virtue of being placed more under the middle of the weight it is lifting than a bumper jack, is inherently more stable, so you should have no problem.

7. As the flat tire comes off the ground, assess whether you can get it out from under the fender and whether you can slide the spare in under the fender. Jack high enough to do so. If the wheel will come off, remove the remaining lug nuts and remove the wheel by wiggling it outward from the bottom. Do not—repeat: DO NOT—jerk and heave on it, for you could tip the car off the jack if the jack has only a tenuous purchase.

Another warning: please—PLEASE!—do not sit down, stick your feet under the car, and heave on the tire in that position, for the car could fall off the jack and break your legs at the least or cut them off at the worst.

8. Often, the wheel won't slide off readily because it catches on the threads of the lug bolts. So, stick the screwdriver underneath and pry upwards as you wiggle the tire out.

9. As the wheel comes off, move it to your right, lay it flat, and shove it under the car. If the jack should fail at this point, the car will land on the wheel and you won't wind up with the jack wedged under the car.

10. Slide the spare in at the top. Put the screwdriver underneath again to manipulate the tire up and down. If it goes on easily, fine. If not, just as soon as it will go on far enough to start a couple of lug nuts, start them. The point is to have the weight on the wheel if the jack should fail at this point.

11. With one or two lugs started, jack up enough to start the others. With the wrench, run up every other one to mild firmness—not tight—then bring up the others, and tighten all to a moderate firmness.

12. Lower the jacks, heave the flat into the trunk, then tighten the lugs more. With a five-lug wheel, tighten in the sequence 1–

3−5−2−4; on a six-lug wheel, tighten three lugs in a triangle, then the other three, then make a pass on all six.

Push downward when tightening, so you use your weight rather than your back, and just lean your full weight on the end of the socket handle. That will tighten the lugs amply. If you are anorectic, emphysematous, or unusually frail, add the pipe and stand on it. However, most people will be able to tighten lug bolts well enough. *The important detail is to have all lug nuts equally tight.* If in doubt, have someone at a service station retighten the lug nuts.

When a wheel stays on a car for a long time without being removed, rust forms between the rim and the surface it is bolted to, e.g., the outer face of a brake drum. After you change a wheel and drive off, this rust grinds away and leaves the lugs loose. If you find rust there, you must retighten the lugs after five or ten miles. When you get the flat repaired at the service station, ask the attendant to scrape the rust off the mating surfaces before putting the wheel back on.

13. Remove the block and put it and the tools into the trunk. You can bump the wheel cover into place with the heel of your hand; however, be sure to put the tire valve stem (the short black, rubber tube) through its little hole in the wheel cover.

A flat on the front of a big car will require more strenuous effort on the jack handle, since you have to raise the weight of the engine, but the procedure is the same except that the chock/block goes at the rear wheel.

The foregoing procedure applies to a smaller car with a scissors jack, the important reminder being that the jack must be perpendicular to the ground. Also, since these jacks usually have a small base, you should use the block of wood under them.

Review the several crucial elements here: You *do not* apply force to the lug wrench while the car is supported by the jack— only when the wheel is on the ground, the car must be kept from moving during the tire-changing process, and the car is supported by the jack alone for the shortest time possible.

Whatever the type, any jack will work much better if it is kept oiled. However, don't put oil on the teeth of a bumper jack.

UNDER THE HOOD: SIMPLE CHECKS

The vast majority of car owners do not want to become do-it-yourself mechanics. The car doesn't interest them that much, or it is so alien that they don't believe they will ever understand it, so they ignore it.

Life with a car will be happier, however, the more you can dilute your sense of the car as a malign object. Therefore, for every car owner, I recommend some minimal under-the-hood checks, plus tire checks. The object is to get you under the hood often enough to overcome your fear of what's there. As you get used to looking, you will notice more things, and, over the years, you will be the first to know if anything starts going wrong.

The basic checks are on oils, coolant, battery connections, brake fluid, and drive belts. With a new car, you can locate these things via reference to the owner's manual; with an older car, you may have to buy a workshop manual, such as *Chilton's, Clymer's,* or *Haynes*—about $10 each. The manual will show you where things are, and if you are inclined to become a do-it-yourself mechanic, the manual will give you some introduction to the business.

Once you get under the hood a time or two, it won't seem so fearsome anymore, and you may want to start topping up the liquids contained there. This means oil for the engine, automatic transmission, and power steering, plus coolant, brake fluid, and even windshield-washer fluid. You can get all these at a discount store, a mass merchandiser (Sears, Penney's, etc.), or an auto parts store. These vital fluids are packaged in pints, quarts, or gallons for convenient use, and people who change their own oil can get a handy five-quart jug of oil sufficient for a single change.

You can use the same jug to dispose of the oil you drain out.

Use a funnel to avoid spilling, fill the jug, and take it to a service station or to a recycling depot that accepts oil. Often, the local Boy Scout troop will have such a depot.

Do not—please—commit the environmental atrocity of pouring used oil down a storm drain in the street. Oil contaminates sewage treatment plants and any waterways it finds its way into.

The pictures in the manuals are not always clear, so when you raise the hood, you may not know what you are looking at or where to start.

Okay, let's try it: raise the hood and prop it open. What do we see? Well, start with the battery. It looks like a plastic box. In the old days, it was always black. Nowadays, the bottom part of the box is usually white plastic and the "lid" some other color. It has two large—about as big as a man's finger—electric cables going to its posts, one usually red and the other black. The cables have a circular terminal that surrounds the battery posts, which are on opposite ends of the battery. As an exception, General Motors cars' cables connect on one side and are held by small bolts. Note that the battery has two posts, or terminals, one marked " + " or "pos," the other marked " − " or "neg." The "pos" cable connects to the starter solenoid, whether the solenoid be remote-mounted, as on some Ford and American Motors products, or is integral with the starter, the way everybody else does it.

If the terminals are covered in fuzzy greenish or whitish corrosion products, replace the cables (see Maintenance Program, pages 123–141).

Now, look at the engine. Usually, it mounts on the fore-and-aft line, but in the smaller front-wheel-drive cars, it may mount *transversely,* or athwartships. With an in-line engine, you can readily tell whether what you are looking at is placed lengthwise or crosswise. V-type engines will be mounted lengthwise, as will flat, or opposed, engines.

To check the oil, we must find the dipstick. It is either a piece of small rod or a narrow, flat strip with a loop on the end for your finger. It is usually (but not always) on the side of the engine opposite the exhaust pipe, so you don't burn your hand checking the oil in a hot engine.

Okay, so how do we know which is the exhaust pipe? Look for a pipe about 1½ to 2 inches in diameter that has heat-blistered paint on it and that disappears under the car. Often enough, the exhaust manifold and exhaust pipe are on the same side as the intake manifold and carburetor.

So? And how do we find the carburetor?

Well, it's under the air cleaner, the air cleaner being a big, flattish, round thing. On some cars, the air cleaner will be a black plastic box, about the size of a shoe box, mounted on the side of the engine. The air cleaner usually has a decal that either gives the model of the engine or says "Service every 10,000 miles" or some such.

On a car with a cross-flow cylinder head, such as a BMW 320i, the intake manifold will be on one side and the exhaust on the other (hence, "cross-flow"), so look for the dipstick on the intake side, under the air cleaner.

Once you find the dipstick, pull it out, wipe it with a tissue, paper towel, or cloth (or a pants cuff, as farmer folk do); reinsert it, withdraw it again, and note the oil level in relation to the marks. The top mark means, "Don't let the oil get above this mark." The lower mark means, "Don't let the oil get below this

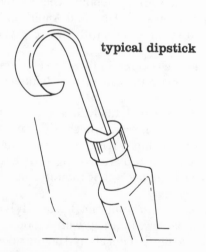

typical dipstick

Typical dipstick

The dipstick for checking the oil in the engine is typically a narrow, flat piece of metal, or a large wire, with a loop on the end.

mark." The marks usually represent a difference of one quart.

If the oil gets low, you may have enough to maintain oil pressure but you will not have enough oil to carry away heat, and excessive heat inside the engine will cause premature wear on all parts. So, to protect the engine, add oil if the level falls to that lower mark.

If, for some reason, you add too much oil and go above the top mark, the crankcase will not "breathe" properly, and pressure inside the engine will force the oil out and make a mess under the hood. In fact, you have about a one-quart margin, so if you overfill by a quart, don't go through the hassle of trying to drain one quart of oil. If you overfill drastically, the easiest way to get rid of an extra quart of oil is to change the oil filter, since a new filter will soak up about one quart.

If the car has an automatic transmission, you may as well check it while you're there. The transmission dipstick resembles the engine dipstick; however, it goes into a longish tube about as big around as a thumb that rises up from the transmission into the engine area. On most cars, you will find it back near the firewall

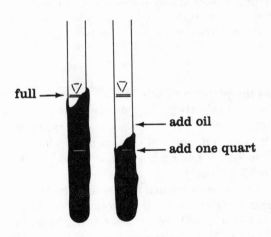

full →

add oil

add one quart

End of the dipstick
The end of the dipstick that goes into the engine has one mark to indicate "full" and another, lower down, to indicate "add one quart."

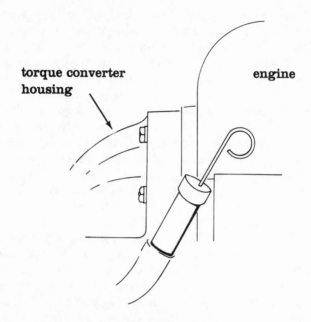

torque converter housing

engine

Automatic transmission dipstick

Since an automatic transmission depends on oil to function, it has a dipstick, too. If the engine mounts fore-and-aft, the automatic transmission dipstick is usually on the passenger's side of the engine compartment, near the rear of the engine.

on the passenger's side of the engine, but exceptions occur: in front-wheel-drive cars, you may find the dipstick at the front, or at the side if the car has a transverse engine. When you pull the stick out, you will find an inscription on the end that says "check with engine hot at idle speed," or it may only indicate "hot" and "cold" levels.

The owner's manual will say to warm the engine up, move the gear lever through all its positions to fill all the transmission cavities with oil, then check the oil, or automatic transmission fluid (ATF), with the gear lever in "Park" or "Neutral" and with the engine idling.

Do what the book says, and note carefully where the oil level comes on the dipstick. Later that day or the next morning, check the oil level with the engine cold, before you start it. After a check or two like this, you will know where the oil level should be when the engine is cold and you won't need to go through the warm-up-and-through-the-gears routine.

As with the engine, if the oil level in an automatic transmission gets low, the transmission will overheat and the clutches will shed their linings. If the oil level gets extremely low, the clutches will slip and shed their linings even faster. So, don't let an automatic transmission get low on oil.

The symptoms of low oil will be a delayed reaction when shifting into gear and hesitation between shifts.

In some cars, the ATF circulates through a portion of the radiator for cooling (and an additional oil cooler can be added for towing). Ford products usually don't cool the ATF, so Ford cars require a more heat-resistant ATF than other cars. Ford products, and cars with similar automatic transmissions derived from Borg-Warner designs, use ATF "Type F." All other cars use "Dexron"-type ATF. Type F will work where Dexron is specified (I've done it many times), but Dexron may not tolerate the heat in a transmission that is supposed to have Type F (I've never tried it). So, don't substitute Dexron if Type F is specified except as an emergency, "get home" measure, then drain the Dexron and refill with Type F.

The latest models of Ford-made cars call for transmission fluids with even more alphabetical designations; that is, Type F does not universally apply to the latest Ford products and other types may be specified. Here again, use what is specified unless you can't get it, then prefer Type F as a "get home" measure, and use Dexron if you must. Once home and with the leak repaired, refill with the type that is specified.

Since the power-steering system uses ATF, too, we may as well have a look at it. Look at the end of the engine that has various drive belts: on most cars, this will be the forward end, though it may be the right or left side on transverse engines or the rearward end on some front-wheel-drive cars. You will see drive belts running around pulleys on several round, lumpy-looking things.

The round object with wires going to it is the alternator; every car has one. The one with hoses or tubes running from it into the exhaust manifold is the *air-injection pump* for pollution control, though this pump is rare now that the catalytic converter has taken over its job, so you may not find one. The round device with thumb-size aluminum tubing running from it is the air-conditioner compressor; if the car does not have air conditioning, you obviously won't find a compressor.

The last round, bumpy-looking thing, therefore, must be the power-steering pump. It generally looks oily, has two metal or rubber tubes connected to it, and has a filler cap. The dipstick is under the cap. The power steering calls for ATF. If Type F

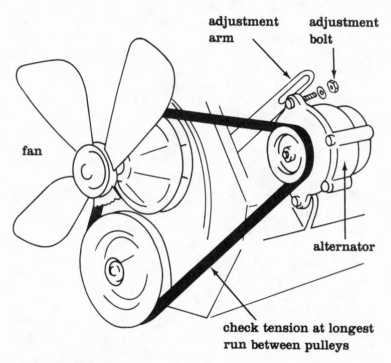

adjustment arm   **adjustment bolt**

fan

alternator

check tension at longest run between pulleys

Drive belt tension

Loose drive belts slip, which means they don't do their job. Slipping belts also overheat and come apart. When looking under the hood, give each drive belt a pluck to check its tension. To tighten the belt, loosen the adjustment bolt, which goes through the slot in the adjustment arm, and move the accessory (i.e., alternator) outward.

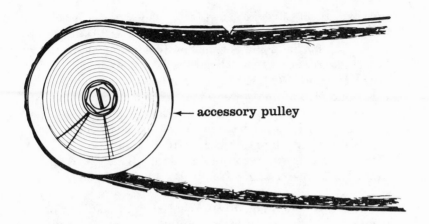

←— accessory pulley

Damaged drive belt

When poking around under the hood, inspect the drive belts for the
alternator, water pump, air conditioner compressor, etc. for nicks, cracks,
fraying, etc.

is specified, use Type F; if Dexron is specified, use it, but you
can use Type F in a pinch, as I said earlier.

Having found all those belts, give each one a pluck with your
fingertip. They should all feel tight, so arrange to have any loose
ones tightened. Look for signs of fraying or cracking, and also
for signs of oil on the belts; if you find oiliness, try to find the
source and have a shop correct the problem (probably a leaking
gasket somewhere).

Now we have to locate the fluid reservoirs for the master
cylinders for the brakes and the clutch (where applicable). They
will be on the driver's side, about in line with the pedals. The
brake master cylinder may be made of cast iron with a metal cap
over the reservoir, or it may have a clear plastic reservoir with
a black cap. Either way, two metal tubes about the size of a pencil
run from the end or side of the master cylinder.

The fluid level in the brake master cylinder falls as the brake
linings/pads wear, and the lowering of the clutch fluid level provides some monitoring of clutch wear. Top up the reservoir
regularly, and if the level changes drastically from one check to

the next, assume some excessive wear that deserves checking on. Top up only with brake fluid rated as "DOT III/3," for it has the highest boiling point. Fortunately, that's about all the stores bother to carry, so you have little worry about getting the inferior "DOT I/1" and "DOT II/2" types that boil more readily.

Recently, brake fluids even more resistant to heat have appeared, and the ratings now go up to "DOT V/5." Also, so-called silicone brake fluids have become widely available. Some newer cars may require the more heat resistant fluids, so check the owner's manual. And read the label: brake fluids based on hydrocarbons can be mixed with each other, *but not with the inorganic silicones.*

The next relevant liquid is the coolant in the radiator or its overflow tank. To avoid losing antifreeze, some cars have an overflow tank—a plastic bottle—connected to the radiator; the expelled coolant goes into the bottle, then goes back to the radiator when the engine cools off.

The radiator is at the front, except on certain peculiar cars like the MG 1100 of twenty years ago or the rear-engine Renaults and Fiats of that same era. You can identify the radiator because it has big, fat rubber hoses running to it, either one at the top and one at the bottom (vertical flow) or one at each upper corner (horizontal flow).

The coolant is checked either at the radiator or at the overflow tank. The cap usually has a warning that says, "Do not open when the engine is hot." *Respect this warning*: If you loosen the cap when the engine is hot, hot coolant will boil out and scald your wrist. If you are compelled to loosen the cap when the engine is hot—for example, you want to add coolant to an overheated engine—cover the cap and the top of the radiator/ overflow tank with a thick cloth, such as a towel.

The overflow tank will have marks to indicate where the coolant level should be. If everything is in good order, the coolant level will stay at the same place relative to the marks.

When you take off a radiator cap, you will see either the little tubes that the coolant runs through or else a flat metal plate about an inch below the top of the radiator. The coolant level should be about one inch above the ends of the tubes or should be even with the metal plate. Don't fill the radiator to the brim, for the excess coolant above the tubes or above the little plate will just be forced out as the coolant expands. That's what that overflow tank is for.

As long as the coolant level stays the same, everything is fine, but if the level falls and you find you must add coolant frequently, look for a cause. First, try a new cap; the old one may not be holding its pressure. Next, look for leaks at hose connections, at the lower corners of the radiator (where rust most often develops), and at the water pump.

The water pump is normally in the midst of all those belts. It bolts directly into the engine, has a pulley to turn it, and a large, fat hose that leads to the radiator. On cars that *do not* have an

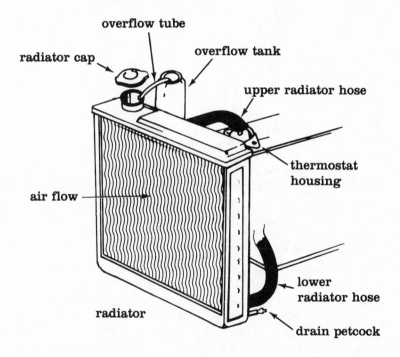

Radiator and related elements

The radiator and cooling system (along with the oil in the crankcase) protect the engine from self-destruction and so deserve careful maintenance. Check coolant level at the overflow tank, examine the radiator hoses, and keep debris out of the radiator itself.

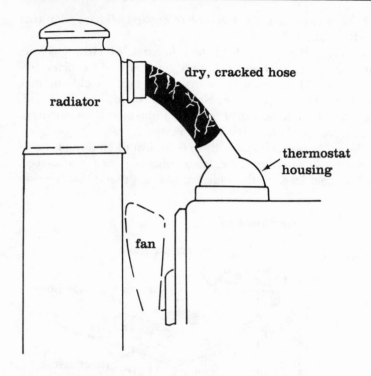

radiator

dry, cracked hose

thermostat housing

fan

Bad radiator hose

Once a radiator hose begins to show cracks on its outer surface, it should be replaced.

electric fan, the fan is on the water pump. As the unavoidable exceptions, the Saab 99 and 900 and the Triumph TR-7 have a gear-driven water pump.

Last, look for a white plastic container attached in one corner of the engine cavity. It will have hoses or wires, or both, going in at the top or bottom and will be full of a bluish liquid. This is the reservoir for your windshield washer. You fill it with a mixture of alcohol and water (which you buy pre-mixed); the alcohol helps dissolve road film and keeps the fluid from freezing. Use this pre-mixed washer fluid rather than your own soap-and-water mix, for soap will clog the washer nozzles. If your nozzles clog, clean them with a straight pin.

The windshield washer has nothing to do with your engine; however, it can save your life. No one knows how many wrecks have happened because of a dirty windshield, but I suspect many, many.

Having made these checks, you may close the hood with great satisfaction, knowing that all is well; or, if not, that you have discovered the fact before it developed into trouble. So far, though, you have only been an inspector. Now, you are ready to take the next step and become the doer and user of tools— the checker of tire pressure.

A change of such magnitude calls for some ceremony. Members of the "granola culture" customarily fast for three days before taking a tire pressure gauge in hand for the first time, and others gravely intone "Ommm" as they perform the ceremony. For most people, kneeling obsequiously at each tire is quite enough.

You may well wonder why you are bothering to check tires at all. Why not go to a service station? First, because you're doing well nowadays if you can find a station with an air hose. Self-serve stations rarely have them, and in big cities the air hose has usually been vandalized.

Second, because no two service station pressure gauges are alike. I've found differences of 10 pounds between one station and another across the street, and I presume a 5-pound difference between any two stations chosen at random.

We make a big issue of tire pressure on pages 74 and 90. If that advice is to be useful, you need a consistent standard for tire pressure. Hence, your own gauge. Your own gauge may err by 5 to 10 percent, but that matters less than the fact that it will be consistent. If convenient, crosscheck your gauge with another. However, if you buy a quality gauge—a bicycle shop is one good source and an auto store another—its error will not likely be more than 2 percent. I recommend the dial-type gauge over the type that has a little graduated bar that jumps out when you check the tire. Be willing to spend up to $10 for a good dial-type gauge. For a car, the gauge need not read more than 50 pounds, but if you use the same gauge for a bicycle, you'll want one that reads up to 100 pounds.

You check the air at that short rubber-covered tube that sticks out from the inside of the perimeter of the wheel. This is the *valve stem* and it should have a *valve cap* on it to keep water out of the *valve core* in the stem.

To contain pressure as you take the reading, the pressure gauge must necessarily fit quite precisely on the valve stem. Most people find the process a little tricky the first time or two, but practice will make it easier. Remove the cap, place the gauge squarely and firmly on the end of the stem, and press down. When you do it properly, you will get only a mild "pfft" as you push the gauge onto the valve stem and another "pfft" as you remove the gauge. You should not hear air escaping as you take the reading. If you release a lot of air, you aren't sealing off the air with the gauge. You may be inept, or the gauge may be one that requires unusual precision in use. Practice on the spare tire, lest you flatten a tire while you're just trying to check it.

Once you have the routine down to the first "pfft" going on and the second "pfft" coming off, take several readings to see if your gauge is consistent. That is, readings done immediately after each other should not vary. If they do, the gauge is unreliable, so junk it and spend more money for a better one.

Tires are slightly porous, some more than others, for reasons not well understood, so you may find that your tires leak some air over a week or a month. To lose, say, only one pound of pressure per week is a nuisance but hardly merits concern, though you should keep the pressure up to assure even wear on the tires and to get the best performance from the car. A faster leak, say five pounds or more per week, indicates a leak, rather than loss through porosity. Such a leak may be from a puncture or may be from a poor seal at the rim. Have a tire shop check it out.

On a car with small tires, e.g., wheels 12 or 13 inches in diameter, you can easily "top-up" tires with a hand pump. You can top-up bigger tires with a hand pump, too, but to do so will require twenty minutes of pumping. Alternatively, use an electric pump that plugs into the cigarette lighter. These pumps, available at auto and discount stores for about $25, will inflate a small tire in five to ten minutes and a large tire in ten to twenty minutes, even if the tires are totally flat.

As noted elsewhere, a car will usually handle better if the tires are inflated about 10 percent above the manufacturer's "normal" pressure. For example, if the manufacturer's normal pressure

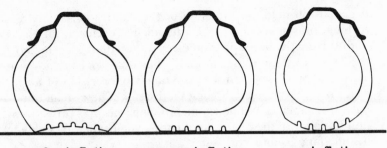

under inflation   proper inflation   over inflation

Tire inflation

If a tire does not have enough air, the middle of the tread collapses inward and the tire runs on the edges of the tread. With too much air, the middle of the tread bulges outward so that less rubber makes contact with the road. Either condition makes a car handle poorly, invites skidding, and wears tires prematurely.

When properly inflated, all the surface of the tread makes contact with the road.

is 24 pounds, go to 26 or 27 pounds. Some manufacturers specify a "normal" and a "highway" pressure. For normal use, inflate to halfway between the manufacturer's two recommendations, but follow the "highway" specification on long trips.

In any case, *do not* inflate a tire beyond the maximum inflation pressure—usually about 35 pounds—stamped on the side of the tire.

*

These three—lubricants, coolant, and tires—monitor the basic symptoms of car health. Any sudden or marked change in them alerts you that something has changed and needs attention or, at least, needs watching. Also, as you are poking around under the hood, you will note anything amiss—a fresh oil leak, coolant spattered about, wires touching the exhaust manifold and getting their insulation burned off, fuzzy corrosion products accumulating on the battery posts, rust eating out the bottom of the battery holder, strings whipping off the fan belt, a clamp cutting through a radiator hose, etc. Also, as you kneel at each tire, you will note the condition of the tread, will see any disturbing abrasions or cuts in the sidewall, may even note an excess of dust from the brake pads on the rim. You don't have to know the "why" of these things to know they don't look right. Once alerted, though, you can seek the timely intercession of a specialist before a problem becomes a disaster. These small things have the larger consequence of bringing you into closer communication with the car—and of letting you be the first to know if something is not right.

BMW—1982 320i

Here are two cars of similar size, similar weight, and even similar shape (and both now out of production). The BMW cost about $13,000 when new, while the Ford Fairmont cost only about $7000. Is what you get for that extra $5000 really worth it? For many people with many uses, the answer is "No." *Photographs courtesy of BMW North America, Inc., and the Ford Division.*

Ford—1981 Fairmont

Saab—1979 model 99

One of the most successful car designs of recent years (I drive a reconstructed '71 model), the Saab 99 had no genuine design flaws (barring the fact that a tall driver can't find a good place for the left foot). Saab built it for ten years, from '69 to '79, and it became somewhat of a cult car; its marque club is one of the most active, and Saab 99 drivers typically flash headlights when meeting. Saab turned away from its own cult of loyalists and went pandering after the pseudo-macho set with the successor model, the 900. The 900 has virtually the same mechanical elements, but its body lines lack the sweet, flowing originality of the 99. If choosing "only three" among older cars, I'd have to flip a coin to decide between a Saab 99 or a Toyota Corona Mark II of the early 1970s for the last of the three. *Photograph courtesy of Saab-Scania of America, Inc.*

Mercedes-Benz—1954 190 SL

In time past, I resurrected two of these — a '58 and a '59 — from scrapheaps, rebuilt their engines, patched up their rust, and drove them a year or two. Like a number of other fools who did the same thing, I sold them to buy something else, but I am resolved to have another one day. This was not a hell-for-leather sports car in the manner of the old XK 120 Jaguar; rather, it was a mini–grand tourer and very good, indeed, at so being. *Photograph courtesy of Mercedes-Benz of North America, Inc.*

Peugeot—1983 505 sedan

The Peugeot has long been a car that even Mercedes-Benz would not
have been ashamed to produce, and the 505 sedan has more interior
room for legs and arms than many full-size domestic sedans, plus the
benefits of European-style suspension. The third of "only three" among
current cars. *Photograph courtesy of Liaison Agency, Inc.*

OPPOSITE

Mercedes—1983 380 SL roadster (above)

This is the current mutation of the earlier 280 SL (which, in turn, was
a mutation of the 190 SL) and is distinguished by its more aerodynamic
"wedge" shape. Aerodynamic or not, it certainly doesn't look any better
than a 280 SL, but if I had to choose "only three" of current cars, I
would choose it in spite of its wedge shape. *Photograph courtesy of Mercedes-
Benz of North America, Inc.*

American Motors—1983 Jeep Cherokee (below)

American Motors Jeep Cherokee, a sensible, tractable, space-and-
materials-efficient vehicle for rough use and hauling freight, yet a car
civilized enough for valet parking. One of "only three" choices among
both current and older cars. *Photograph courtesy of American Motors.*

Mercedes—1983 300 TD wagon

For a "one and only to keep forever" among current cars, I'd take this: Mercedes-Benz quality (and price), road manners, and performance, yet with freight and towing capacity. *Photograph courtesy of Mercedes-Benz of North America, Inc.*

Mercedes—1968 250 S sedan

If I could have only one (among older cars) and had to keep it the rest of my life, this would be it — compact, sensible, roadworthy, fast, economical, and rugged beyond the ken of most people. Mercedes-Benz has since changed from this model, but I don't believe they improved upon it by much. *Photograph courtesy of Mercedes-Benz of North America, Inc.*

International Harvester— 1971 1010 series Travelall

Gone, but not forgotten: the International Travelall was a truck-like station wagon that had the guts of a dump truck but, given its stiff suspension, had better road manners than most large domestic sedans and wagons of its era. Its clean lines kept its bulk from looking ugly, and you didn't have to be ashamed to turn it over to the most martinetish valet parking flunky. It was damned by its own strength, for with its heavy weight and its V-8 engine designed for use in a truck, it got relatively poor mileage (14–17 mpg). Alas, Harvester discontinued the Travelall in 1975, partly because they needed the engines for trucks and partly because they didn't want the problem of certifying the vehicle for the EPA. Still, if I were to have only two of the older cars, this would be number two. *Photograph courtesy of International Harvester Archives.*

Chevrolet—1962 Chevy II sedan

As far as I know, no automotive writer has sung adjectival praises to the Chevy II, and no magazine ever gave it a prize of any sort. Yet, it was one of the most intelligent designs ever produced in this country. It was compact without being cramped (as was, say, a Volkswagen Beetle or Rabbit), would handle a variety of road surfaces well, got good gas mileage, and was built with typical American strength for longevity. Note how the shape of the body replicates what Mercedes-Benz and BMW have been doing for the past thirty years (and what Detroit is belatedly returning to). *Photograph courtesy of Chevrolet Motor Division.*

PART III

Driving

MODERATION

First get your car, then learn how to use it. This homely phrase...sums up in a few words the matter of learning to drive a car. After the car has been duly purchased, the glib salesman will show [you] in about four minutes how to drive [it]. Yet after all this assistance, it will take almost any man of fair intelligence a whole week or more to learn to run the car alone and with confidence, while he will continue to learn additional points as long as he continues to drive.

—"Automobile Driving," in *Cyclopedia of Automobile Engineering* (1916)

The classical Greek philosophers knew what they were talking about when they preached moderation, for they knew that moderation in habits would allow habits to be practiced longer. Just so with cars: to make a car last a long time, drive it moderately.

Moderately does not mean "slowly." Indeed, on a decent highway, 70 mph is moderate for a car that will run 110 mph. Neither does *moderately* mean you have to "baby" a car; you don't. A car simply has absolute limits of performance—limits of how fast it will go, how fast it will stop, how fast it will make a corner, etc.; and *moderately* simply means operating at a comfortable (for the car) level below those limits.

A car driven at its limits all the time may break anytime. By contrast, a car driven moderately will be strong enough to go to its extremes when you need it to.

Back before Richard Nixon imposed the 55-mph speed limit, I always drove 70 mph on interstate highways, a speed where both my car and I were comfortable (and a speed that most drivers had chosen for and by themselves). Since 70 mph did not tax the car severely, I felt confident in its strength on those occasions when I felt frisky and decided to drive 85 or 90 mph across the top of Indiana on the Toll Road. Similarly, I used to drive north from Pittsburgh to daysail on Lake Arthur, an impoundment in Moraine State Park, the first 40 miles of the trip being on the excellent surface of Route 8, the last 20 miles being on incredibly rough secondary roads. Because I usually drove moderately over the rough part, I was not afraid to drive hard and fast on it occasionally. Because I rarely ran the engine (in a Mercedes-Benz 190 SL) up to its 5750-rpm redline, I was not afraid to crank it up well beyond to 6500 rpm now and again.

In sum, moderation *most* of the time buys you the ability to drive at extremes *some* of the time. However, to drive at extremes most or all of the time means something in the suspension or drive train (transmission, drive shaft, etc.) is always ready to give trouble and means the engine will wear out by the time it's well "broken in."

Moderate means the avoidance of unnecessary strains.

It means slowing down for potholes (or dodging them completely).

It means moderate acceleration, rather than drag racing away from every traffic light.

It means modest rates of acceleration and modest speed until the car has warmed up a bit.

It means giving air conditioners a few minutes to get organized before being asked to cool off a hot car, i.e., don't turn the AC up to "high" until it has run for a few minutes.

It means closing doors gently rather than brutal slamming.

It means watching traffic and avoiding severe braking.

It means rounding curves below the limits of the tires, rather than at the rubber-screeching extremes.

Generally, you shouldn't run your engine at a sustained speed that makes your pistons (see page 323) go through their up-and-down motions at a rate faster than 2500 feet per minute. To exceed a piston speed of 2500 fpm causes accelerated wear on the pistons, piston rings, and cylinders. On the Saab 99, the pistons move three inches downward and three inches upward as the crankshaft makes one revolution, so the pistons make 2500 fpm at an engine speed of 5000 rpm. Incidentally, after calculating through the gear ratios and the circumference of the tires, 5000 rpm gives 85.5 mph in third gear of the automatic transmission. The big domestic V-8 engines achieve a piston speed of 2500 fpm around 3200–3500 rpm, which gives you a suitable sustained cruising speed of around 65–70 mph.

As another way to establish the proper cruising speed, the engine should be run at 70–75 percent of the rpm "redline" (see page 347) where the manufacturer obtains the maximum horsepower rating for the engine. The Saab 99 is rated at 88 hp at 5000 rpm; 70 percent is 3500 rpm, or 59.8 mph, and 75 percent is 3750 rpm and 64.1 mph, so I cruise it at 60–65 mph.

Since I had rebuilt the engine in the M-B 190 SL myself and trusted it, I ran it at 4000 rpm on the highway, or about 75 mph, and drove the TR-3 at 3500 rpm, or 70 mph, both speeds being 70 percent of the respective "redlines."

In sum, *moderation* means regarding the car as a person, and asking yourself, "How would I like to be treated?" Would you like to be kicked out of bed on a cold morning and be required to hit the floor running? No, and the car doesn't like it either. Would you like to run full speed up a steep hill on a hot day? No, and neither does the car.

Suppose you drive in a city and parallel park a lot: Do you turn the steering wheel to the absolute extreme and set the power-steering pump to squealing? Do you slam the tire into the curb and send a shock through the whole suspension system? Do you shove the gear lever into "Park" while the car is still rolling? If so, you are a bad person and should be required to walk.

On the other hand, do you dodge potholes? Slow down for "washboard" strips of pavement? Do you apply the brakes gently, well before you get to the red light? Do you dodge rain puddles, to keep your brakes from rusting? If you do these things (and others), you are a good person and will probably get a lot of use out of your car.

Most people think of moderation in regard to a new car. Like the new baby, they think they have to be very delicate with it, and they are encouraged in this attitude by notions of a "break-in" period.

The "break-in" period, another relic of the old days, is no longer necessary. Before about 1950, the limits of assembly-line production technique meant that only about 50 percent of the surface of the moving parts of a new car fit together; the other 50 percent had to wear in. Hence, the break-in period, usually 1000 miles, during which the car was driven slowly.

Nowadays, cars come off the assembly line with 90 percent or more of their bearing surfaces well-mated, so the break-in period no longer applies. However, a remnant of the break-in period does remain: Don't drive a new car at any one sustained speed for long periods of time until it has about 1000 miles on it. Traffic will impose this rule on you in town; on the highway, though, don't hold a steady 50 or 60 mph for hours. Rather, speed the car up or slow it down at intervals.

This rule pertains mostly to the differential gears, not the engine. To hold a constant, steady speed with a new car may cause the differential gears to whine after the car gets a few thousand miles on it.

GAS MILEAGE

Besides being the way to automotive longevity, a consistently moderate driving style is also the secret to good gas mileage, a subject that provokes a lot of cute little newspaper articles about how to improve your gas mileage. These articles say things such as, "Keep your car well-tuned, and you will improve your gas mileage by 25 percent," the underlying presumption being that your car is always in need of a tune-up (which is probably not true).

Suppose you had the car tuned three months ago and you get 20 mpg, but an extra 5 mpg sounds good, so you get a fresh tune-up. Your gas mileage is still 20 mpg. Why? Because a decent tune-up will be effective for a year on post-1975 cars with electronic ignition and should be good for six months on older cars. Thus, the advice is true and good—it just hardly ever applies. People who don't give cars regular tune-ups, of course, could benefit from the good advice, but they are the very people who pay little attention to gas mileage or advice on how to get good mileage.

A lot of the gas mileage advice is like that; yes, you will save gas if you don't let the car warm up a couple of minutes on a cold morning, but the saving amounts to spoonfuls and is far outweighed by the happiness of a warmed-up engine.

And, yes, you will save gas if you shut off the engine when stuck in stop-and-go traffic and must idle in one spot for over 30 seconds, but what if you "vapor lock" in hot weather while you're sitting there saving gas? What if you run your battery down by frequently cranking the car? Will the paltry amount of gas you save this way pay for the tow truck that will have to come rescue you?

The other popular advice is to "slow down," a notion now enforced by some of the more dubiously rationalized law the country has seen since the Salem witch trials. Given the national patterns of driving—so much urban, so much rural, and so much on interstate highways—the 55-mph speed limit may save as much as one-half of one percent of the fuel that would otherwise be used. In other words, to clear out the traffic jams in Manhattan for one day would probably save more fuel than the 55-mph speed limit does on the same day.

Most of the things I do that save gas, I do for other reasons.

I time myself to get through traffic lights because I don't like to stop.

I stay well behind the next car, whenever possible, because I don't want the car ahead dictating my own driving. If I see its brake lights go on, I let off the gas at once because I don't want the additional bother of moving my foot to the brake pedal if I can avoid it.

I keep a steady foot on the gas pedal because an erratic rate of speed serves no purpose for me.

I keep my tires firmly inflated because the car handles better that way.

I keep the car properly tuned because it starts easier that way.

I do not use an air conditioner on the open road because I would rather feel fresh air through open windows.

I keep my brakes in order, so they don't drag, because I want them to work when I need them, and they won't work well if they are overheated from dragging.

I keep the front wheels properly aligned because the car drives nicer that way and the tires don't wear out so fast.

I use European radial tires because I want the security of good tires and the gratification to my snobbish vanity of having them. I use 10W–40 oil. The thicker end of the range, the "40-weight" end, means I use extra fuel to pump thicker oil, but I'm willing to spend, say, a cupful of gasoline out of 10 gallons for the guarantee of good lubrication.

I use 80W–90 oil in the differential because I pull a boat trailer and I want the thicker 90 end of the range to protect my gears when towing. The higher viscosity of the 90 end costs me extra fuel, too—spoonfuls out of a tankful—but I make it up in the winter with the lighter-viscosity 80W end.

I have an automatic transmission because that's the way the car was when I got it. An automatic imposes a fuel penalty but is better in winter traction conditions and more convenient when launching and retrieving the boat, so I accept the extra fuel cost. I'm not sure what that cost may be, though, since the car gets over 25 mpg at 60 mph (and 23 mpg when towing the boat).

I often take two 40-pound dogs with me. Their combined weight might cost me one tenth of a mile per gallon, but they keep vandals out of the car and their service is cheap at the price.

Once you choose a certain car and develop consistent driving habits, you are not going to change your fuel mileage much, assuming the car is in proper order, e.g., properly tuned, tires properly inflated, brakes not dragging, etc. By avoiding unnecessary braking, by a steady foot on the gas pedal, and by keeping the car in good order, you might improve mileage by one or two mpg; to increase it by more than that just shows that you were a sloppy driver before—or the car had something wrong with it.

The real significance of fuel mileage is a noticeable change and what it indicates. Suppose you usually get 20 mpg and head west on a windy day; if the wind is strong enough, it can cut your fuel mileage by 50 percent. However, in this case, you know why.

In the absence of an obvious reason, a notable change in fuel economy tells you to look for something wrong. Consult your mechanic, have him fix things, and your mileage will go up again.

Gas mileage, of course, does relate to the cost of driving. My 1970 International Travelall with V-8 engine and automatic transmission got 17 mpg on the highway. However, when cranked up on a cold winter morning and driven five or six miles in hilly

country at low speed—the worst conditions for economy, especially with an automatic—it averaged 10 mpg. I could have
improved the mileage by swapping the engine for a smaller one
and the transmission for a manual. For example, the six-cylinder
Chevrolet Suburban with a manual transmission weighs about
the same as the Travelall but gets almost 19 mpg on the highway
and nearer to 15 mpg in the cold weather, short-run situation.
My response to the fuel consumption of the 8-cylinder, 4200-
pound Travelall was a four-cylinder, 2600-pound Saab 99, which
gives me over 25 mpg on the highway and about 22 mpg in the
cold weather, short-run use. In one year, I paid for the Saab
(second-hand) with the money it saved on fuel. In a case like
that, fuel economy becomes quite important. However, the change
was feasible only because I no longer needed the freight capacity
of the Travelall (the Chevy Suburban was a temporary vehicle
for use while the Saab had a blown head gasket—but that's
another story).

The point here is that fuel economy is just one element in the
use of a car; it may be primary or may be inconsequential. In
any case, take a rational attitude toward fuel economy and don't
expect too much of the magic spells offered in the newspaper
columns.

As a footnote for thought, back in 1939, the Shell Oil Company
Research Laboratory organized a competition among the em-
ployees to see who could drive a car farthest on a measured
quantity of gasoline. The affair grew into the Shell Mileage Marathon wherein cars have gone over 375 miles on a gallon of
gasoline. However, the cars are so modified that they hardly
constitute "cars" in the usual sense and are driven in a style that
involves low-speed, full-throttle acceleration in top gear, followed by a coasting period during which the engine is turned
off.

In the Sportsman Division of the marathon, where the cars
and conditions more closely resemble daily driving, the results
are still impressive, e.g., a 2400-pound Volkswagen Beetle getting 49.9 mpg, a 3990-pound '68 Chevrolet Chevelle with automatic transmission getting 25.8 mpg, and a 5320-pound '66
Buick with automatic transmission getting 18.7. Figures like these
demonstrate, once again, the relationship of weight and fuel
consumption.

CAVEAT DRIVER

Natalie, the marketing consultant, had a problem with her Chevrolet and chose to leave it in New York with the mechanic she knew, rather than take it back to Philadelphia, where she did not know a good shop. I brushed the dog hair off my passenger seat and offered her a ride back to Philadelphia. This was before I rebuilt the engine in the Saab, and its worn crankshaft was rattling, so I drove in the "slow" lane, i.e., the right side, of the New Jersey Turnpike. In that lane, of course, I was constantly slowing down to let a car on an entrance ramp get in ahead, or speeding up against the protests of the crankshaft to get ahead of one entering.

"Why don't you just get in the middle lane?" Natalie asked.

"Because," I answered, "the middle lane doesn't give me any escape routes." In the right or left lanes of a three- or four-lane divided highway, I can more-or-less move to either side if I need to. In the middle, I'm hemmed in on both sides. If I need to avoid something ahead or something coming from the side, I have no place to go.

This is my first rule of safe driving, anywhere and everywhere: Monitor conditions and have some notion of what I'm going to do and where I'm going to go if my position on the road becomes untenable.

In the wintertime, I note the snowbanks I expect to head into if I meet someone skidding broadside. In city traffic, I note empty parking spaces at the curb and estimate how much damage I will do to the suspension if I have to dodge in and jump the curb to avoid joining a pileup ahead of me. In New York City, of course, no parking spaces are ever vacant, so I consider which car I will choose to hit if I must dodge something else (prefer a Mercedes-Benz or BMW: you meet a better class of people that way). In sum, I organize driving around the anticipation of problems and the selection of "escape routes."

The threat does not always come from another car. In "falling rock" areas, it can be rocks. Once, on I-95 in Rhode Island, it was a huge tire that fell off the back of a truck. In New York City, Boston, or Pittsburgh, it may be a pothole deep enough to drag the muffler off the car. Out west, it may be cattle sleeping on a warm pavement. Anywhere, it may be a child or a bicyclist.

Obviously, you can't apply the rule unless you actively monitor traffic. When you look ahead, you should see not only the car in front; you must look through its windshield and monitor the behavior of the next several cars ahead, and the ones in the other lanes, too.

You must monitor what's coming up from behind, too, and that brings up rearview mirrors. Rearview mirrors should not be set simply to show you the lane behind. Rather, the mirror should cover "danger" areas, or "blind spots." For example, the corners of your rear fenders are relatively blind. However, you can control where you put your right-rear fender and if you drive in the right lane of multilane highways, no one can readily attack you on that corner. By contrast, your left-rear fender is vulnerable to every drunk who wants to pass, which means you need to monitor the left-rear fender more than the right. So, don't set the inside mirror to see straight back; cock it just a little so you have a better view of the left rear. On the Saab, I adjust the mirror until I can just see my right ear, then move it back the other way until the ear disappears. Thus, the image in the mirror is oriented toward the left rear, but loses nothing from what is straight behind.

When we look in a rearview mirror, we like to see something that gives us orientation in space. If we see nothing, we are disconcerted. Hence, most people set the outside mirror so that it shows the same thing the inside mirror does, and by so doing they *nullify the value of that mirror*. The important distinction here is that the inside mirror should show you what is *behind* the car, while the outside mirror should show what is *beside* the car.

To illustrate, consider thus: You come up behind a car. You look through its rear window and you see the driver's face. Since you can see a face, you know the same face can see you. So far, so good.

Now, you move into the left lane to pass. You look ahead at the outside mirror on the car ahead, and once again, you see the driver's face, so you know the face can see you.

Okay, keep passing, but continue to watch his outside mirror. About the time your front bumper comes alongside the rear wheel of the other car, the driver's face will disappear from his mirror and that means you have become invisible to him. Likewise, if your own outside mirror is set the same way as your inside mirror, and if a car has just come up to your rear wheels, you will not see it in your own mirror. Similarly, if you change lanes to pass, the mirror will not show what's behind you in the passing lane.

So, set the outside mirror to cover the blind spot at the left-rear fender. For example, I see nothing in my outside mirror until a passing car is right at my bumper. As the car continues to pass, it eventually disappears from the mirror. However, it disappears just as its hood gets alongside my door and enters my peripheral vision.

An outside mirror on the right can be set the same way, though I turn my head and look before I pull back in front of a car I have passed. Since I have less need of the right-side outside mirror when moving to the right, I set it so that if I stretch my neck, I can barely see the right-rear tire; thus, it helps immensely in close-quarter maneuvers, such as when parallel parking.

Obviously, you will get no benefit from an inside rearview mirror if you use the shelf behind the rear seat as a mixture of storage space and garbage dump.

The '53 Ford two-door I drove briefly while an undergraduate had unusually good brakes (for a Ford of its era). Once, when leaving the campus, I had occasion to jam on the brakes at about 45 mph. Instantly, I got a helluva rabbit punch from Volume II of Blair, Hornberger, and Stewart, *Literature of the United States*, a 10-pound compendium encompassing everybody from John Greenleaf Whittier to Robert Penn Warren. The book flew from the rear shelf, hit me hard enough to stun me momentarily, and drove my chin against the steering wheel hard enough to loosen several teeth. "Never again," quoth I, and my rear shelf has been clear ever since. 'Nough said? I have heard of children getting a concussion from such flying objects, and I daresay an adult could get one, too.

To get back to the road and what you are watching, I study the cars and consider many of them suspicious. Generally, I pass them, for if my suspicions prove valid, I want them behind me. If a suspicious-looking car did cause a wreck, I wasn't there to see it, but nonetheless, while I can't prove the validity of my suspicions, I still have them.

The car I most prefer to avoid is a huge, four-door sedan driven by a short, elderly person whose head barely comes above the steering wheel. Such cars often wander casually from one side of the lane to the other and can only generously be said to be under control at all. I don't dare honk if such a car offers to displace me from my lane, because honking usually sends the other car jerking toward the lane on its opposite side.

Next, I avoid cars that have been elevated extra-high by their teen-age owners. Such cars are hideously unstable because elevating the car destroys the ability of the suspension to control the weight of the car, and the destruction is exacerbated by the higher center of gravity. Stay clear of such cars.

I also notice the tires on other cars and am astounded at how many I see that are half-inflated; a law to require proper inflation of tires would save several times more fuel than the 55-mph speed limit. Such cars betray their tires long before you see the half-flat tire, for you see them jerking erratically from one side of the lane to the other as the driver makes hasty corrections at the steering wheel.

A car with a severely out-of-balance tire makes a sort of flapping, whacking sound as the car passes, and you can usually see the tire jiggling up and down. Either way, don't hang around in the area; the tire may be half beaten to pieces and could give up anytime. It probably won't, since tires are virtually never the cause of an accident, but "virtually never" isn't good enough odds to stay in the company of such a car.

I don't worry about junky cars unless they are driven by punkish-looking louts, but I do worry about cars that are so heavily loaded in the rear that the hood points skyward. When so loaded, the front wheels have less traction, so the car roadwalks, gets pushed around by the wind, and is only marginally under control.

In the wintertime, I avoid cars with fogged or frosted-over windows and mirrors. I know the driver can't see and does not care to see and I want no such drivers near me.

On the general subject of passing, we should note Jakob Bernoulli (1654–1705), who established that the pressure of a fluid decreases with velocity. What Bernoulli's Law means to you is that when you pass another car, the velocity of the air between your car and the other increases; hence, pressure decreases, and a quasi-vacuum effect draws the two cars together. The effect is greater as the space between the cars is narrower.

So, give the car you're passing a wide berth and get your passing done and *pass*. Don't hang around running closely side-by-side. An irregularity in the road surface could throw the two cars closely enough together for Bernoulli's Law to have disastrous effects.

Note the underlying presumption here: that you are in control of what the car does. You are, indeed, and you may well be more in control than you think. That is, when a collision seems inescapable, we tend to give up and brace for the crash. Yet, with quick thinking and acting, we can often drive our way out of danger, or drive from a greater danger to a lesser one.

Major truths: In terms of its ability to do surprising things, the car is almost always better than you think it is.

Exceptions to major truths: The foregoing rule does not apply on ice or with underinflated tires. In these cases, the car isn't half as good as you think it is.

Given that the car is better than you think, you can often drive your way out of trouble. Unfortunately, people have not been taught to think this way. Public writ, including driver's license handbooks issued by the states, fosters the notion that accidents will not happen if people will simply drive slowly, but after advancing this falsity, the same writ has nothing to say about what to do when a collision is inevitable. When accidents do occur, the newspapers report that "the car went out of control," as if no human agency were involved. Eventually, people come to feel that, indeed, they have no ability (and no responsibility) to assert control in a threatening situation. Furthermore, the national emphasis on driving slowly creates a nation of drivers who do not know how to react quickly when they need to. A nation accustomed to driving 70 mph is accustomed to making quick decisions and taking quick actions; a nation of drones habituated to 55 mph is incapable of either.

In the discussion that follows, keep in mind that at 60 mph you are covering ground at the rate of 88 feet per second; even at a modest 30 mph, you're moving 44 feet per second. The biggest domestic cars are around 18 feet long and the smaller cars, foreign and domestic, are about 12. Thus, at 60 mph, you're moving from five to seven car lengths per second. Now, how much do you think you can accomplish in one second?

Driver's license handbooks often have a table showing "stopping distances" at certain speeds. The distance is usually divided into a "reaction time," when you decide to apply the brakes, and a "braking time," when the brakes are, indeed, applied. Many of these tables were devised back in the 1930s and haven't been revised since, but most are fairly credible within certain limits. Their universal error arises from the fact that they are based on actual tests, but tests wherein the drivers were concentrating on hearing a "stop" signal and getting on the brakes quickly once they heard it. Thus, the reaction times in the tables are much faster than those most people will be capable of in normal circumstances.

Generally, reaction times are given as two- to four-tenths of a second. Now, watch the seconds change on a digital watch and try to convince yourself that you're going to assess a situation and apply the brakes in that fraction of a second. In practice, you'll spend .2 or more seconds simply perceiving and processing information before you even think about stepping on the brakes. Thus, generous as they are, those stopping distances in the handbooks are not something you can depend upon.

As another observation, the car magazines also record a stopping distance in their tests of cars. However, their stopping distances measure the distance the car traveled after the brakes were applied; that is, they measure the performance of the brakes, not that of the driver. In any case, the magazine tests show that most cars can stop in 160 to 175 feet if going 60 mph, and can stop in 275 to 300 feet from 80 mph.

You should always use seat belts, especially on highways, for to take quick action you must be belted securely. For example, a side impact can throw an unbelted driver across a car and, thus, nullify any attempt or hope to control the car.

If you don't freeze up when collision seems imminent, you can avoid or partly dictate your disaster. Suppose another car cuts in front of you so closely that if you hold the wheel straight, you'll run into the car long before you get your foot close to the brake pedal. However, if you don't freeze, if you keep your head working, you may be able to turn quickly enough to avoid a smash. Even if you can't avoid a collision, to turn will get you a side impact rather than a head-on.

Or, suppose you are on a two-lane road when a car in the opposing lane suddenly aims for you. Don't freeze up. Don't hit the brakes, for you'll still get hit. Drive. Steer away. You may escape, and if not, you can move the point of impact from the front to the side or to the rear corner. A corner impact may cause your car to swap ends several times before it stops, but that still beats a head-on.

If you try a few sudden maneuvers of this sort (with properly inflated tires), you will find the car much more able than you thought. Unfortunately, you can't practice this sort of thing without getting cited for reckless driving. Practice aside, don't give up too soon. Drive.

Say a tractor-trailer turns over so it is lying across your lane: Shall you simply smash into it? No; keep a firm grip on the wheel, add a little more power to get the drive wheels to bite a little firmer, and drive around it. If the path takes you off to a deep median ditch, head as straight down the bank as possible rather than across the face of it, and straighten out when you get to the bottom. You may turn over as you do and if the ditch is full of water, you'll most certainly get stuck. Ideally, you can straighten out, proceed along the bottom until you slow down, then climb back onto the road. Stuck or turned over, though, beats running head-on into the truck.

Okay, you've got guardrails on both sides and the truck totally blocks the road: what now? Well, would you rather hit the truck or the guardrails? The guardrail, obviously, so turn. Actually, you probably won't be able to make a full turn, for the car will probably skid somewhat sideways and hit the truck at an angle. It may ricochet off, may slide along the length of the truck and into the guardrail, or may hit the truck broadside (and will probably bounce back several feet). The results of any one of these possibilities will be messy, but any one will certainly improve upon hitting the truck head-on.

One of the more fatuous generalities in the driver's license handbooks is the recommendation to leave one car length for every 10 miles per hour of speed between your car and the one ahead. This recommendation is good, but it simply won't work in the places where it matters the most. If you leave a car length between you and the next car in dense traffic someone else will pull into it. This phenomenon astounded me (in my rustic innocence) when I first encountered it on California freeways, but I have seen it everywhere since. In truly dense traffic, people simply will not tolerate a gap. I have driven the New Jersey Turnpike in absolute bumper-to-bumper traffic, at night and in rain. Any effort to leave a car length between my car and the one ahead of me set off a series of dangerous lane changes as one car moved into the space I left and another moved into the space that one vacated, and so on, in a chain reaction that ran the whole 90 miles from New York to Philadelphia. If you approach South Bend, Indiana, via the Indiana Toll Road on an afternoon when the University of Notre Dame is having a football game, you'll find the same situation; and if something goes wrong with the car up ahead, you won't have a car length to play with.

You have no control over the car up ahead. The driver may feel a heart attack coming on and try to stop suddenly. A bolt may fall out of the differential ring gear carrier, lodge in the ring and pinion gear mesh, and lock up the rear wheels; this is an extremely rare occurrence, but the consequences are a sight to behold when it does happen and you will want acres of room between you and any car it happens to. The car ahead may have a blowout. A bird might hit the windshield and alarm the driver into some wild maneuver. In any case, no one will be following that "one car length per ten miles per hour" rule, so the rule won't help you. You will escape unscathed only if, and to the extent that, you can drive your way out of trouble, and that means constant readiness—and wearing your seat belt, since escape is uncertain.

The same rule applies when you have done something foolish yourself. You find yourself halfway through a curve, going too fast, and the curve gets tighter, as they often do in mountain country. The tendency is to let fright take over, to freeze at the wheel, and skid into the outside guardrail—or over a cliff. Don't. Sit there and drive. Guide the car, *feed it power* to counteract its tendency to slide sideways, hang in there, and drive. Odds are you'll make it (though you may hear the squeal of the tires in your dreams for months afterward).

Or, in suicidal impatience, you pass another car on a hill on a two-lane road and find yourself facing an oncoming car. The tendency is to jam on the brakes—or to throw your hands over your face. Don't. Drive. Head for the ditch and take care to put the car right between the two maple trees there. If you control the steering wheel, you might just pull it off. Much more than you realize, the car will do what you tell it to do.

Obviously, this discussion can't list every conceivable circumstance that can arise, so note the generality: In this country, we have long been taught to get out of trouble by putting on the brakes. We have not been taught to use the steering wheel. Yet, in worst-case conditions, we won't have time for the brakes and the brakes won't help much anyway, so we may as well give the steering wheel a chance. This does not mean arbitrary motions; it means having some notion of what constitutes an escape route and being able to head for it.

TRUCKS: PLAYING WITH THE BIG KIDS

People in cars fear trucks with an irrationality that has the quality of a child's fear of the dark. The fear would be harmless—a child's fear of the dark hurts no one—but for the fact that those burdened with such fear make trouble for themselves and others because their fear gets in the way of their ability to drive.

My personal sympathy for truck drivers arises from having played the game a time or two myself. I began on a bulbous-fendered 6400-series 1949 Chevrolet, what we called a "two-ton" tractor, pulling a 42-foot grain trailer loaded with 36,000 pounds

(600 bushels) of wheat. The truck had a four-speed transmission and a two-speed rear axle—eight gears in all. You started off with the gear lever in first and the rear axle in "low," let the venerable old 83-hp, 216-cubic-inch Chevy six grunt its way up to about 4 mph, then you shifted the axle to "high" with a lever on the dash. After you got up to 6 or 7 mph—a fast walk—you moved the gear lever to second as you shifted the axle back to "low," and so on up to fourth-high and about 45 mph.

Later, I graduated "up" to a 1941 International KB-13, a 2½-ton tractor (big stuff!) that had a five-speed transmission and a three-speed Brown-Lipe auxiliary, or what we called a "Brownie"—15 gears in all. You put both gear levers in first, shifted up 1–2–3 through the "Brownie," then moved the main lever to second as you moved the "Brownie" back to first, and up 1–2–3 through the "Brownie" again, etc.

The object of all this shifting, then and now, is to keep the engine running at its optimum rpm, to avoid "lugging" it so badly that it pounds out its bearings or overrevving it so much that it does the same. The old Chevies and Internationals liked to peak around 3000 rpm; and to stay close to peak all the time meant a down shift at around 2600 rpm—a lot of levering and clutching if the terrain wasn't table flat. Nowadays, tractor-trailer diesels like to run in the 1750–2250 rpm range.

Big trucks do make a noise like the Judgment coming, and they do loom large over the puny cars beside them. They average about 70 feet long and the tandem trailers coming into use make them exceed 100 feet. On the West Coast, they may weigh 110,000 pounds when loaded and will average about 65,000 pounds nationwide. However, the available statistics do not indicate that trucks are in a disproportionate number of wrecks, despite the fact that a long-haul truck averages 100,000 miles per year and so has ten times the exposure of a car that only goes 10,000 miles per year. Actually, the exposure is much higher, since the car spends most of its time in familiar, highly predictable circumstances—going to work, to the grocery store, etc.—while the truck runs everywhere in all weathers. If all the relevant factors are noted, the safety record of trucks is far superior to that of cars.

However, no one is served by a moral scale that plays cars and trucks off against each other according to some ill-defined notion of safety. Car owners and truck drivers are not hostile when they meet in supermarket aisles, so they needn't be hostile when they meet on the road. Personally, I think car drivers have the most to learn about the relationship, as an anecdote may indicate.

The Triumph TR-3 is a low two-seater with a cut-down door and no roll-up windows. When you're beside a truck in one, your eyes are level with the middle of the truck wheel. I used to put my TR-3 right alongside a truck and hold it there for a mile or two at 70 mph because the truck wheel—especially a polished-aluminum Budd wheel—created such an interesting visual effect (check this out sometime).

Once on the Pennsylvania Turnpike, I put my TR-3 beside the front wheel of a truck so Elaine, the political scientist, could enjoy this fascinating visual. We ran along this way, the truck tire moaning its metallic whine, the diesel engine clattering like a cascade of rocks, its radiator fan roaring like a hurricane, the wheel shimmering in the sun, the reflected white pavement stripe seeming to wrap around it like a whirling spiral—while Elaine clutched the "panic bar" in white-knuckled fright. To be brief, the experience scared her half to death and provoked some contumely from her when we pulled into the next service plaza for coffee, some anger being directed at me as much as at dangerous, pushy truck drivers.

As part of declaring that I had not acted unsafely, I said, "Would you assume that truck driver can drive your car?"

"Yes," she said, "he probably can."

"Fine," I said. "Now, can you drive his truck?"

"No, of course not," she said.

"Okay," I said, "then who's the better driver?"

She had never thought of it that way. Few people have. People who have trouble keeping their car in a freeway lane are quick to condemn a trucker who puts 70 feet of truck over 100,000 miles per year. If you think of the matter this way, trucks need not frighten you so much as remind you that you are in the company of experts. Ultimately, trucks (like cars) are as dangerous as their drivers, the difference being that the trucker spends all the time on the road dealing with every conceivable road and traffic condition.

Equally important, people should understand what all those trucks are doing out there. Those truck drivers are not going to the beach or the mountains, are not going to see a relative, nor are they going into the city for a show. They are working. That's how they earn a living. Every time you curse a trucker for some real or imagined offense, remember that the driver (man or woman) is just trying to make a living.

Of course, you would understand better if you drove a truck. In your car, you put the gear lever in "D" and forget it; or you have a manual shift with as many as five gear-lever positions and you use the top one only on the highway.

By contrast, the trucker has 10 to 15 gears to shift through and has a tachometer that defines a narrow 500-rpm range where the engine must run. To climb a long hill may mean four to five gear shifts. This is why truckers pick up all the speed they can when going downhill: if they gain enough speed, they can save a down shift or two when going up.

Consider the number of times someone in a car less than 20 feet long almost clips your fender when moving into your lane (do you, therefore, despise all car drivers?). By contrast, the truck is three or four times as long and the truck driver must look down 60 feet or more of truck and trailer in a rearview mirror to decide when to move in front of you.

If someone cuts in front of you, a light tap on the brake pedal saves the situation, after which you quickly regain speed. By contrast, if someone cuts in front of a truck, the driver has to slow down 65,000 pounds of truck and load, and to lose only 5 mph may cost the driver two gear shifts.

If a car crowds your bumper, you curse the car and forget the matter. If a truck crowds you, you add the incident to the litany of evils you feel you have suffered from truckers. In fact, no one in a car has any good reason to crowd you; by contrast, the trucker may crowd you to keep his tachometer in that 1750–2250-rpm range. If he slows down, he has to downshift and lose 5 mph, despite the fact that his paycheck depends on miles covered. Also, to slow down and let you get ahead invariably leads another car to move into the vacant space, and then that driver will complain that the truck is crowding him.

A large, high-van trailer is, indeed, susceptible to crosswinds, especially if empty. Thus, on windy days, a tractor-trailer combination will wander onto and across the lane-dividing white lines. This does not mean the trucker is careless; rather, it means he's got his hands full and could not (any more than you) anticipate a gust of wind. Some people drive cars with a fingertip on the wheel; by contrast, the trucker uses both hands all the time. When the trucker wanders across the white line on a windy day, the proper response is not a curse but a prayer of sympathy.

Besides being big and noisy, trucks create peculiar eddies of wind. Thus, a car passing a truck experiences a buffet of wind as the hood comes even with the end of the trailer and experiences another buffet as the hood clears the front of the truck cab, the first buffet usually being stronger than the second. This buffeting partly accounts for people's hostility to trucks. They pull close to pass, the buffeting pushes their cars about, and they get scared and back off. Rather than blame their cars or their own driving skill, they follow the truck, fearing to pass and cursing the trucker for their own timidity.

Where the Ohio Turnpike runs close to the western end of Lake Erie, the crosswinds from the lake are notoriously constant and severe. On that stretch, I have encountered literal caravans of cars trailing a single tractor-trailer. One driver would grow bold, change lanes to pass, feel the buffet and fall back, then go through another hassle getting back into the right lane. Then another would try and likewise give up and pull back. The net effect was a line of half a dozen cars weaving in and out like conga dancers. As they did so, I could see their squishy, under-inflated tires or note how some were so vastly overloaded with luggage that their rear bumpers almost dragged the ground.

In those days, I drove the most rusted-out, disreputable-looking 1955 Mercedes-Benz 220a (single carburetor model) imaginable, a car with bad shock absorbers and an unbelievably slopped-out front suspension. I would come tooling up the left lane at 80 mph, toot merrily at the sluggish line of weaving cars, and pass the truck, right hand on the steering wheel, left hand giving the "Gung ho" signal as I passed. The old M-B allowed itself a lurch from the wind currents but never gave the slightest hint of being out of control; in other words, despite age and wear, the thoroughbred suspension underneath gave me full security. The people in the cars I passed gave me hostile looks as I went by, and I think, at that moment, they hated me and my wretched-looking car more than the truck.

To be sure, the M-B was designed to be tractable under such conditions, but any of those domestic cars could have passed that truck, provided the tires were properly inflated and the load decently distributed. My own disgust was aimed less at the soft suspension of the domestic cars and more at the drivers who had never found out how good their cars were. If they had known, they would have passed the truck, would have known that the lurch and buffet amounted to no more than the car's adjusting itself, and would have passed in serene comfort. Since they did not know, they allowed the truck to scare them, and, therefore, they feared and hated trucks.

(The expression "Gung ho," or so it sounded to American ears, was heard among Chinese laborers of the nineteenth century as a signal for a gang of men to work busily or heave together. Eventually, soldiers joined the expression to a trucker's gesture that became known as the "Gung ho" signal. It consists of extending a clasped hand upward and making two downward motions. The motion duplicates that of a steamboat skipper, railroad engineer, or truck driver pulling down on the cord that sounds the whistle/horn. A truck driver traveling by car gives the signal when passing a truck, thus to identify himself as a member of eighteen-wheel society. The trucker normally answers with two toots of the horn. Once taught, children love to give the signal and have a trucker toot for them.)

A car will, indeed, lurch as it passes the rear and front of a tractor-trailer combination, but if the car is in order, the lurch is no more important than a bump in the road. So, know your car, keep it well, and you can trust it to pass trucks for you. Practice, learn how the car responds, and you will be able to keep it under full control and feel completely safe about it.

Exceptions: on glare ice, the buffet can blow you into the ditch, but glare ice calls for special care, anyway.

Since weather has come up, we should note the problem of slush. The dual wheels of a truck throw up incredible gobs of water and slush. Therefore, don't get too close in rain and snow. If the rain or snow has stopped, you may have turned the wipers off even though the road surface is still covered. So, when you look behind and see a truck hauling up to pass, get your hand on the wiper switch and turn on the wipers as soon as the truck wheels hurl that avalanche of slush on your windshield. If you are prepared, you won't be so surprised and frightened and won't feel the trucker has insulted you personally.

However, suppose your windshield-washer fluid has run out

and passing cars throw a dirty mist on your windshield, a mist that dries before your wipers can clear it off, so you are trying to see through a film of dried mud. Well, get up behind a truck and the truck wheels will spray enough moisture that your wipers may be able to do some good.

And, while on the subject of following, a *never, never*: occasionally, you will see a rock lodged between the dual wheels of a truck. When you see this, stay back: *never, never* follow closely behind a truck with a rock stuck in its duals. When that rock gets flung out, it aims for your forehead with the force of a cannonball. Such rocks can (albeit crudely) remove that portion of a human head that stands above the ears, so stay back at least 200 feet; or move into the next lane until you pass the truck. The truck has a legally required "mudflap" hanging behind its wheels to minimize this danger, but that's all the mudflap does—it "minimizes," but doesn't eliminate the danger.

Years ago, before we had four-lane, divided interstate highways, when people met on two-lane roads, they used a system of daytime headlight signals for communication. For example, when meeting another car on a lonely stretch of highway, one flash of the headlights said, "Hello. How are you? Peace unto thee and thine." The signal flash was purely social, equivalent to raising a hand as the cars passed.

Two flashes meant, "Caution, trouble ahead." If a car or truck gave you two flashes, you might find someone off to the side changing a flat or, in the western states, cattle on the road.

Three quick flashes ordered, "Get ready to stop! Quick!" Following three flashes, you were almost certain to find a wreck, a severe washout, or some such problem.

At night, when you wanted to pass, you pulled into the left lane and flashed the headlights. The driver ahead responded by flashing his headlights as a signal that he understood your intentions and was prepared to cooperate, prepared to be on the alert as you passed, prepared to do his share or more to ensure a safe pass. Once you passed, he flashed again to signal that you might freely move back into the right lane ahead of him. These flashes were used even in daylight and a trucker passing a car acknowledged the "All clear" signal by flashing his clearance lights to say, "Thanks for your help."

In the western states, these signals were virtually universal into the early 1960s. People took pride in understanding them and using them. However, as the interstate system developed, people quit using them. For some reason, headlight signals became illegal in most states and driver's license manuals included warnings against them. A huge irony, that—on the old, narrow two-lane road system, the signals were acceptable, but not on the modern, low-hazard interstates.

The legal objection to such signals is that they may be misunderstood, a pathetically lame excuse, considering the carelessness with which people use turn signals, and I have no sympathy for the law on this point. Frankly, I think law enforcement people don't like to see drivers encroaching on law-enforcement turf by helping each other out. (Hence, along with the interstates came injunctions against stopping to assist disabled cars.)

Laws or no, truckers kept light signals and now they are about the only ones who use them—they and a few unrevised oldtimers (like me). Personally, I believe highways would be nicer places if these signals were still in use. First, the signals break down the isolation of drivers and encourage community. In addition, they enhance safety. In any case, since truckers recognize the headlight signals, use them when traveling with trucks.

The most useful signal is multiple flashes, in day or night, after a truck has passed. Your flashing tells the trucker he has cleared your car and may pull over. It further declares that you have assumed the burden of guaranteeing the maneuver, that you are prepared to help out by slackening speed, if need be, to assure that he has room to pull over. Once the trucker sees your flash, he is to understand that he need not worry about you anymore; he need not squint into his rain-fogged rearview mirror, against the glare of headlights, to be sure his trailer has cleared your bumper. When you flash, you tell him he may attend to the traffic ahead of him; you'll take care of things at the rear.

That little bit of help means a lot to the trucker, and for your help, you'll get an answering flash of the clearance lights, provided the trucker isn't too busy with the steering wheel and gear lever(s).

If you pull out to pass a truck, flash a couple of times, too, even in daylight. This warns the trucker of what you're doing.

At night, you'll get an acknowledging flash as the trucker dims his headlights so they don't blind you when you pass, plus another flash to tell you when you may safely pull over.

Since a car doesn't have clearance lights with which to flash a "Thanks," I flash the turn signals—one blink on each side—to show that I appreciate the help.

I have another technique on divided highways with three or four lanes. Say I am in the right lane of a three-lane highway, a truck ahead of me, and traffic whizzing by in the middle lane. The trucker wants to move into the middle lane to pass a car ahead of him but does not have enough acceleration power to merge into the middle lane safely. Since a car maneuvers easily, I move into the center lane, for I can readily fit into a gap between two cars. Once there, I take a position close behind the truck, then flash my lights. Eventually, the trucker realizes that my flash does not mean I am passing, but means he may pull over, means that I am running interference for him in the middle lane. He pulls in front of me, goes on to pass the car, and I go back to the right lane. The maneuver costs me two easy lane changes but gives the trucker a safe merge into the busy center lane.

When I see the trucker trying to make the lane change, or getting ready to pass me, I am conscious of someone at work, someone trying to make the mortgage payments. Trucks are a nuisance, just as steel mills and slaughterhouses are nuisances, but somebody has to do the work. The rest of us can at least try to help.

Once you quit fearing trucks just because they are bigger than you, you will no longer hate them. If you study trucks closely, you will see that they are better controlled than most cars, that the drivers are genuinely skillful. However, much of their skill goes into making sure the truck covers as many miles as it can in one day, for Interstate Commerce Commission regulations limit the number of hours per day a driver may run a truck. The urgency to cover distance means the truck driver is constantly pushing, changing lanes to pass slower-moving cars, and gathering as much speed as possible going downhill, thus to lose less speed going uphill.

People get annoyed because they feel truckers press their luck on lane changes by pulling out in front of cars. I will agree that truckers often do so. However, I wonder why people in cars don't just ease off the gas briefly so the trucker can make the lane change more easily—and give a helping headlight flash. A car will quickly regain lost speed, even on a hill, but the truck will not. If a trucker wants to change lanes, why not fall back and help him do it? That would be safer than making a hostile confrontation about the matter and would help the person who's on the highway to earn a living. Similarly, when you find a truck bearing down on your rear bumper, why not speed up a bit to allow him to make a little time? Or move over to get out of his way, and let him go at his own pace? If we really care about safety, we will do more for safety by being helpful rather than hostile.

TROUBLE ON THE ROAD: SIX CRISES

Our freedom to drive is under constant threat from capricious, evil mechanical failings that can stop us on lonely roads or in the middle of busy intersections. Some of these failings announce themselves with noises that warn us to get the car off the road. Others happen without warning, but yet demand a prompt response.

In the following survey of the more common and more serious mechanical failings, assume the car is on the road when the problem arises. Thus, you must make a quick decision about how to get off the road, even if to do so means crossing several lanes of freeway traffic or driving off into the ditch in a median strip.

Alternator Light/Gauge

The alternator charging light goes on (or the gauge falls to "discharge"). It does not flicker uncertainly, but goes on positively and categorically. Normally, this means the fan belt has broken, and that means the water pump is no longer circulating water, and that means the radiator will shortly be boiling like the *Robert E. Lee* racing the *Natchez*.

Get off the road and shut off the engine. As you do so, put on the four-way flashers so other drivers will know you're having trouble. You've got about two minutes before you overheat; by the third minute, the radiator will be spewing steam like Old Faithful, after which engine damage sets in. If the oil is of good quality, the rings and pistons may tolerate a brief overheating, but to prolong it threatens the cylinder-head gaskets.

If you can't get off the road at once, slow down to about 30 mph, so the engine develops less heat.

Generally, don't stop in a lane of a busy freeway; the danger of being hit from behind is too great. However, choose to stop in the middle of a freeway rather than to enter a tunnel in this condition. Likewise, clog up the entrance to a bridge rather than the bridge itself.

If the problem arises while you're already in a busy tunnel or on a long bridge, keep going at 30 mph, flashers flashing, until you see clouds of steam, for you might get out. Once the steam starts billowing, stop. You are in a dangerous position, but the danger does not justify destroying your engine. When I recall the cars that stall in Boston's Callahan and Sumner Tunnels and Pittsburgh's tunnels, I see no necessity to ruin an engine. If, as in the Callahan/Sumner Tunnel, you have a walkway of sorts along both sides of the tunnel, you can get out (leaving the flashers on) and notify an official or call a tow truck. If you have no walkway, stay put.

If you must stop on a freeway, have children lie down lengthwise on the rear seat. If you get rear-ended, they will be tossed onto the floor ahead of the seat and get bruised a bit, but they won't get a whiplash. Have a front seat passenger keep his/her head firmly against the head rest.

Opinions differ about whether you should get out of the car if you're stalled on a busy freeway. The official attitude is that you should stay in the car. Freeway police don't want people opening car doors and wandering around on foot in the midst of a busy freeway, for the danger of being hit is too great. Furthermore, a person on foot is an aberrant element; drivers don't know what to expect and are likely to make evasive maneuvers that invite collisions with other cars. Generally, the official attitude makes sense: put on flashers and stay put. Once an official vehicle arrives, its flashing lights provide ample warning to other cars that a traffic hazard exists. If, as can happen, you lose your whole electrical system and your flashers don't work, still stay put.

Exceptions to the official attitude might arise if traffic is thin enough for you to safely get out and get off the freeway (e.g., to call a tow truck) or when next to a guardrail where you can get out of the car and on the safe side of the guardrail. Similarly, if you get stuck on a bridge or in a tunnel at two o'clock in the morning, when traffic is light enough to present the minimum danger, you can get out of the car and seek a telephone or bridge/tunnel maintenance office. If you do, swing a light (white) cloth in the hand that is on the traffic side as you walk. The swinging cloth will stand out in headlights much better than a cloth hanging limp. Note that a dark cloth won't show up at all.

The danger, of course, is that of being hit by an approaching car. The situation will call for judgment. In any case, never risk standing beside a car or at the side of a freeway in fast, dense traffic.

If possible, tie a white cloth (but any color will do) to the radio antenna and raise the hood or trunk lid. As the interstate system developed, the cloth and raised hood became a universally recognized distress signal, and it works even with a dead battery.

The charging light may go on for electrical reasons, rather than because of a broken fan belt, though an electrical fault usually creates some flickering before the light goes on. If you have a temperature gauge and if the gauge holds steady even after the charging light goes on, then you may assume that you do not have a broken fan belt. The temperature will respond fairly promptly, so you will know in less than two minutes whether your water pump is working.

If the water pump is working, as shown by a stable temperature gauge, proceed to an exit and then to a service station or shop. En route, turn off every electrical item—radio, heater, etc.—to save your battery.

With a fully charged battery to start with, you can drive 10 to

12 hours in daylight without the alternator working. At night, with headlights on, you can drive about six hours. Either way, you've got ample time to seek help. However, don't turn the car off until you get to a shop, for you may not have enough battery power to crank up again.

Overheating

While the charging light does not always mean overheating is imminent (just most of the time), overheating can happen for other reasons, and it calls for its own response.

First, what are the circumstances: Are you cruising on a cool night or stuck in a traffic jam? Also, does the overheating develop slowly or quickly (with an indicator light instead of a gauge, you can't tell)?

Let's say the event occurs in a downtown traffic jam. The gauge pointer creeps upward slowly and enters the red zone of the gauge. Start easing across lanes to the right. Don't worry about all the honking and cursing you provoke—just start getting the car out of there before it stops completely.

Immediately, turn off the air conditioner, for its heat exchanger is preheating the air to the radiator and making the radiator use extra-hot air to cool the engine.

Next, put the heater on "hot" and turn the blower on full. This amounts to adding a second (smaller) radiator to the system. You will sweat like a summertime jogger, but you will survive; your engine may not without this help.

Also, hold back from the car in front of you so your radiator doesn't have to work with air heated by hot exhaust gasses.

If you're in stop-and-go traffic, put an automatic transmission in "neutral" each time you stop; this slightly reduces the cooling load on the radiator.

Keep the engine at a brisk idle, for the fan will pull more air this way. Even if the fan belt is broken, the car will be less likely to suffer vapor lock and stall because it's moving more fuel through its system.

Keep working to get off the street until you're blowing steam. You will know first by the alarmed looks other drivers cast your way: they can see steam spewing from underneath your car before it bursts out from under the hood. Once you're steaming, give up and shut off the engine, for you have entered the "danger zone" where you can damage your engine.

In the old days, people used to give stalled vehicles a push, despite the fact that different bumper styles and heights made pushing difficult. Nowadays, bumpers are uniform and fit nicely, but "giving a push" has ceased. Those who offer a push will be teen-agers or disreputable-looking fellows in rusty pickups. No matter: to get off a freeway or out of the street, take any push offered. If none is offered, don't hesitate to ask the car behind you. Some people will refuse, but most will help if asked. Obviously, the driver of a Renault Le Car won't feel inclined to push a Cadillac Sedan De Ville, so you have to seek help from a suitable car. Actually, in first gear, a Le Car could move a Sedan De Ville handily—certainly it will move what four people can push by hand—but you probably won't be able to convince the Le Car driver of it, so let it get past you and ask the next car. When being pushed, you can't make tight turns, so make lane changes gradually.

If you're the one called upon to give a push, make bumper contact gently and don't try to go fast.

Gradual overheating implies interference with air flow through the radiator or with water flow through the system. For example, perhaps you've collected so many bugs in your radiator that air can't flow through. Or, as sometimes happens, maybe you've sucked a wind-blown newspaper against it. On the water side, perhaps the thermostat won't open fully or rust has half-clogged the radiator. Except for the wind-blown newspaper, you can't do much about the overheating. You've got to get the car to a specialist.

Loss of Oil Pressure

Overheating is bad. Loss of oil pressure is worse. Serious overheating will damage piston rings, but the engine can survive a while as an "oil burner." Loss of oil pressure, though, leads to a "thrown rod" that entails an overhaul or a new engine. You can fool around awhile with overheating, but when the oil pressure goes, you've got to stop. Right there.

Oil-pressure warning lights come on when the pressure falls from the normal 40 pounds or so to 4 to 12 pounds, depending on the car. However, once the light goes on, you have no way of knowing whether you have as much as 4 pounds of pressure or zero oil pressure, so stop. If the oil-pressure warning light comes on in a tunnel, you're in the same awkward position as when you're overheating in a tunnel, except that loss of oil pressure means more damage quicker. You have to balance the hazards of stopping against the cost of a new engine.

If the oil-pressure warning light only flickers, slow down to reduce the strain on bearings and keep moving as long as the light flickers on and off. If it goes on steadily, stop. Nowadays, traffic jams are so ordinary that your stopping creates nothing unusual, so you may as well stop. If you don't, you'll destroy the engine and stop anyway.

An oil-pressure gauge gives you more warning and more options. Suppose you normally have 40 pounds of pressure at normal speed but as little as 15 pounds when idling; now, suppose the pressure begins fluctuating and falling: slow down and see if the pressure stabilizes. If it does, keep going. As long as you can sustain 5–10 pounds of oil pressure, you may continue for a short while, certainly long enough to get out of a tunnel.

In almost all cases, sudden loss of oil pressure arises from loss of oil, usually from a leaking gasket at the oil filter or drain plug. Unless you are a do-it-yourselfer who carries tools, you can't do anything about it. However, if you can't get repairs, you can keep adding oil to the engine until you get to a shop—provided you can find some oil.

As noted, these latter two problems, overheating and loss of oil pressure, entail the possibility of ruining an engine, which invites a digression to survey the options in such a case.

If the car is a genuine, rusted-out, worn-out junker, admit the fact. Sell it to a junkyard for scrap and buy another car.

If the car is in otherwise good condition, rebuild or replace the engine.

A dealership or independent shop can rebuild the engine for around $1000 to $2500, depending on the quality of the job and the type of car. To find a shop competent to rebuild an engine, ask marque club members and people involved in auto racing. Or, ask the auto parts store clerk about which shops regularly buy internal parts for engines, and ask for a recommendation.

As another approach, buy a brand name rebuilt engine, such as one from Sears. For the same $1000 to $2500, you can get a complete engine, or a "short block." A short block comes without cylinder head(s), manifolds, or ancillaries, and you use those from your old engine.

As the third choice, an independent shop can get a used engine from a wreck. A second-hand engine involves some risk, but many wrecking yards warrant the engines they sell for as much as 90 days. Also, because of the zip-out, zip-in nature of an engine swap, the second-hand engine solution involves the minimum delay. Again, depending on the car, a second-hand engine will cost from $300 to $2500, later model engines being more expensive (and those for expensive foreign cars being most expensive of all).

Brake Failure
Besides temperature and oil-pressure warning lights, cars built since 1968 have a "brake failure" warning light (this light may also serve to indicate that the parking brake is on).

The brake warning light may be activated by excess motion in the brake pedal, by a low level of fluid in the master cylinder reservoir, or by loss of fluid from the brake lines. When it goes on, it means something is wrong: you may have half (two wheels) of your brakes left, or none at all. Test the pedal: if you have some braking left, proceed slowly, anticipate traffic to avoid the need to hit the brakes hard, and you can get to a garage. Drive on the shoulder, with flashers on.

On the other hand, suppose you push the pedal—and nothing happens! Now, how are you going to stop that one to two and a half tons of steel you're captive in?

If the brakes go completely, all you have are your parking brake and your engine. Try the parking brake; if it helps, slow down to a speed where the parking brake can handle the car and proceed carefully.

However, the parking brake will not slow the car down quickly when it is moving fast, so you will need to use your engine. You already know that if you downshift and let up the clutch, the engine will slow the car down somewhat. So, you must downshift as quickly as you can.

Assume a car is going 60 mph in fourth, so the engine is turning around 3000 rpm. At 60 mph in third, the engine would turn around 4500 rpm; in second, around 6000 rpm; in first, around 9000 rpm. At 60 mph, you may not be able to get the car into second, much less first, so you downshift to third, apply the parking brake to give all the help you can, and shift to second as soon as the car slows down a bit, and finally to first. Usually, you have to be down to about 30 mph before you get into first. This method will slow you down, but it may not be fast enough. Despite good sense, you may have to get into second gear at, say, 60 mph or first gear at 40 mph (you'll never get into first at 60 mph).

You do this by "double-clutching," a shifting technique that was standard procedure in the old days when transmissions did not have synchronizers. It involves getting the engine and gears spinning at the right speed for the gear you want and for the road speed you are making. Okay, note the steps closely:

- Depress the clutch, move the gear lever to neutral, and let up the clutch.
- Depress the gas pedal and allow the engine to speed up; you want the engine to achieve the speed, the rpm, that it would have if you were driving at your speed in the gear you want: for example, you want to skip third and go to second at 60 mph; okay, you have to kick the engine up to a 6000 rpm scream.
- Release the gas pedal, depress the clutch, and move the gear lever to the desired gear.

A good race driver can do this in half a second. Without practice, you'll take longer, but with this technique, you can get the car into a low gear even at considerable speed. As you go into the lower gear, give a little gas to reduce the shock when you let up the clutch, then get off the gas. If you can get into second at, say, 60 mph, you will slow down to about 40 mph fairly quickly, then you can go to first.

Let the parking brake off when shifting, but apply it repeatedly and firmly when in gear. Keep a firm hand on the steering wheel, for the parking brake may catch unevenly and cause the car to want to pull to one side.

The downshifting procedure applies to an automatic transmission, too. However, on most, you cannot downshift from "D" to "2" with the lever unless the car is moving slower than 55 mph (the point where the transmission upshifts out of second when second is used as the "passing gear"), and can't shift from second to first until below 30 mph. Also, an automatic won't slow you down as quickly as a manual shift.

Manual or automatic, the gears may not slow you down quickly enough. You may go right under that truck ahead or right into the back of that station wagon wherein the alarmed child is wondering why you are rolling up so close and so fast. You can slow down faster by letting the right wheels (or the whole car) off the pavement onto soft ground, but hang on: a soft shoulder can jerk the steering wheel out of your hands as the right front wheel sinks in. If the road has curbs, let the right wheels scrape the curb. As a last resort (before plowing into the station wagon ahead), let the whole right side of the car scrape a guardrail or the face of a cliff. The shriek of rending sheet metal will haunt you for days afterward, but don't let that scare you off. If you're belted in, all you will do is mess up your car; your passenger will get sprinkled by shattered glass, but the glass in the door window will fragment into pea-size fragments, not dangerous shards. Grit your teeth, hang in, don't be alarmed by the sparks you see flying from your fenders, and you will eventually stop.

Once the car slows to a controllable speed, you can amble along at 5–10 mph until you can get off the road or to a parking place.

Do not—repeat: *do not*—try to improve engine braking by turning off the engine. You may inadvertently lock the steering wheel.

Steering Failure

Though rare, the most dangerous thing (besides brake failure) is loss of steering. Usually, any such loss gives warning via vibration, so you can stop before loss is total, and the loss is rarely total, anyway. However, even a little loss can be disastrous.

Steering loss usually happens because the ball-and-socket part of a tie-rod end wears out and comes apart (which is what you get for not checking on things when the sloppy steering first showed up). Such an event will allow the affected wheel to turn fully inward or outward (usually outward). However, the odds are extremely long against both front wheels' losing their connection at the same time, so when one wheel goes, the other wheel remains to counteract it.

However, the counteraction may not do you much good: the tie rod on the left wheel breaks and the wheel goes to the extreme left; you counteract by turning the right wheel to the extreme right, and the net result is straight-ahead motion—if you're lucky.

If the parking brake acts on the rear wheels, to apply the parking brake firmly (while rolling) will help keep the car in a straight line. If the parking brake acts on the front wheels, as on some front-wheel-drive cars, it will probably make things worse. Since the service (pedal-operated) brakes affect the end with the weight first and most, applying the brakes will also make the wild steering worse, though it will also stop the car—perhaps before it hits something.

Fortunately, loss of a tie-rod end happens rarely. However, loss of a ball joint is not so rare. Depending on whether the upper or lower member of the suspension carries the weight via the spring, a rusted, worn-out ball joint comes apart when hitting a severe bump or when going into a pothole. Indeed, I have seen it happen when a car simply lurched against a curb at 5 mph.

If the upper ball joint goes, the top of the wheel leans out and the bottom tucks 'way under; if the lower one goes, the bottom of the wheel spraddles 'way out. Either way, the remaining wheel will give some control at speeds below about 30 mph. On the potholed streets of Boston and Pittsburgh, I have seen several ball joints go at city speed; in every case, the drivers got the cars to the curb easily, despite their astonishment and alarm.

So, in such a case, hang on and drive. At low speed, e.g., on city streets, you probably won't hurt anything.

I've never seen a ball joint come apart at highway speed and I don't like the thought. Once again, use the remaining wheel to steer as best you can and head for the shoulder. You have your seat belt on, of course, so if you don't make it before you wind up sideways with a tractor-trailer roaring down on you, you're still in fairly good shape. If you don't have your seat belt on, your fate is beyond prediction.

Moral: if you don't keep your front suspension and steering in good order, be sure your life insurance is paid up and your will is made.

Tire Failures

Nowadays, tire failures are rare in the extreme. Twenty years ago, tire advertisements and driver's license manuals were full of references to "blowouts." Nowadays, you hardly hear the word, and few younger drivers have ever experienced a blowout.

A *blowout*, as the word implies, is a sudden loss of air pressure from a tire. However, the sudden loss can come from a fairly small hole, and the hole can come from something as modest as a piece of glass lying on the road. As the tire rotates, it can slam down on a piece of beer bottle with enough force to drive the glass through the tire. As the object goes in, the air goes out.

Two things happen: the car abruptly falls about six inches—the distance from the ground to the rim—at the affected corner, and so lurches; and, the deflated tire puts up considerable resistance to forward motion.

What happens next is determined by whether the weight (engine) is at the front or rear and whether the driving wheels are at the front or rear. In general, nondriving wheels put up the most resistance to motion because no power is going to them. Thus, with front-engine, rear-drive, and a blowout on a front wheel, the steering wheel jerks out of your hands and the car jumps sideways. However, with a blowout on the rear of the same car, the power going to the blown-out tire reduces its resistance to motion and you feel only a lurch.

On a front-wheel-drive car with a blowout on the front, the power to the wheels also reduces the resistance of the flat tire; however, the tendency to pull sideways is accentuated because the wheels that do the steering also have power going to them.

A blowout on the rear of a front-wheel-drive car can be as bad as a blowout on the front of a rear-drive car: the blown tire imposes a tremendous resistance to forward motion, and the power to the front wheels immediately jerks the car sideways in the direction of the blown tire. In sum, the only way a car with a blowout can keep going in a straight line is if all four tires blow out at exactly the same instant (don't count on it to happen).

I have had several blowouts, only one on the front. The first was on the right rear of a 1946 Ford club coupe, at night, on New Mexico State Highway 18, on the notoriously narrow, rough (in 1957) stretch near the town of Taiban. When the tire went, I thought the noise came from hitting one of the numerous bumps. The steering asked for no extra attention but, on that road, it was getting plenty already. Shortly, I heard the tire flopping and stopped, much surprised to discover I had suffered a blowout at 60 mph.

The next two, also rears, happened on the 1200-mile unpaved part of the Alaska Highway from the Alaska border to Fort Nelson, British Columbia, in 1963, the car being a 1957 Plymouth Plaza four-door. In both cases, I heard the "pop" but felt nothing at the steering wheel. However, since I was driving about 50 mph on a washboarded gravel-and-dirt road, the wheel was quite busy, anyway.

My last blowout happened around 60 mph on the Ohio Turnpike, on a heavily loaded 1965 International Travelall station wagon. When the left front tire blew, the lurch and the resistance to rolling jerked the steering wheel from my two hands despite power steering, and the vehicle leaped halfway into the next lane before I was even through hearing the "pop." If another car had been beside me when the tire went, I would not have had the faintest hope of avoiding it: my left-front fender would have plowed right into it.

For years earlier, I had read sugary articles in magazines about how to "hold firmly to the steering wheel" in the case of a blowout and "ease the car off the road." On that day in 1973, I realized that none of the optimists who wrote those articles had ever experienced blowout, at least not on the front of a heavy vehicle. True, after the Travelall had jumped halfway across the next lane, I could assert control and get it off the road, but I learned that when a tire goes, it will do its thing before you know what's happening.

So, if you have a blowout on the *front* of a front-engine, rear-drive car at highway speed, assume the car is immediately going to jump about six feet sideways. As you drive along the interstates, note the cars on either side of you as they pass: if either of you has a blowout right then, you will be very well acquainted in extremely short order. You might even wind up in the same hospital, your cars in the same junkyard.

At lower speeds and with smaller cars, the jump will be less, simply because less energy is involved. On rear-engine, rear-drive cars, the effects will be also less pronounced, but don't depend on these margins to save you.

With front-wheel-drive cars and a blowout on the front, the fact that power is going to the deflated tire somewhat reduces the resistance it imposes to forward motion, so the steering wheel won't jerk so hard. However, if you're driving with only one hand lightly on the wheel (ever notice how many people drive that way?), the resistance will cock the steering wheel and the power to the wheels will help pull you right under the tractor-trailer beside you.

As noted earlier, these grisly events probably won't happen. Blowouts are virtually as rare as the hand crank. Indeed, statistics indicate that tires are involved in less than one half of one percent of accidents and then as a secondary factor, e.g., bald tires that skid in the rain. However, don't depend on statistics to keep you alive; buy good tires and inspect them for damage, e.g., cuts or severe curb scrapes; especially, look on the inside of the wheel.

And keep two hands—at the very least, one hand with a firm grip—on the steering wheel.

Use seat belts. A blowout on the car beside you means a side impact that can throw you across the width of the car. The seat belt will keep you under the steering wheel where you can assert some degree of control.

FLOODS AND DESERTS

Although he wasn't thinking of a car, Geoffrey Chaucer's Pandarus knew whereof he spoke when he declared, "Lord, this is an huge rayn! This were a weder for to slepen inne." You will feel the same way when that great faucet in the sky opens up and makes you wish your car had a rudder and periscope.

Rain

Visibility

Like snow or ice, "an huge rayn" calls for caution, the first rule being to slow down to the limits of visibility. This may mean pulling off the road and stopping—provided you can get off far enough to be sure you won't get hit by an oncoming car. If you can't be sure of that, you're better off to keep moving.

If you're in traffic, study the car ahead and ask yourself, "How visible is it to me?" Once you decide, you know about how visible you are to a car coming up behind you. To improve the margins in daytime, turn on the lights but keep headlights on low beam; if appropriate, turn on the four-way flashers, too.

If you are alone on the road at night, you will, in a sort of hypnotic way, allow your attention to fall on the brightest area illuminated by your headlights. In traffic, you'll find yourself locking your eyes on the car ahead. Neither way is good; try to look a bit down and to the right, for you need to know where the edge of the road is. To know will keep you from going off the road or from wandering across the center line.

In even a light rain in warm weather, your windshield will fog up inside, usually so gradually that you won't notice it. You will blame the deluge outside, not realizing that you have condensation inside. Activate the defroster as soon as you turn on the wipers.

Hydroplaning

Rain presents you with two specific dangers: "hydroplaning" and wet brakes. Either can make you wish you had slept in.

First, a word about tire treads. A smooth tire with no tread pattern at all gives the best traction on a *dry* surface. The tire tread is not there to "grip" the road; rather, it is there to provide channels so that water can escape from under the tire when you are driving on wet pavements. In daylight, you can look in your rearview mirror and see the paths where your tires have displaced the surface water.

How well the tread gets rid of water depends on the tread pattern, the inflation pressure, the weight of the car—and, most of all, the *depth* of the tread. As the tread wears down, the channels get shallower, so less water can escape. If the water on the surface is deep, or if you drive too fast, the tire hydroplanes.

Hydroplaning refers to the phenomenon in which a tire builds up a "bow wave" of water ahead of it, then climbs over the wave to ride *on top of the water* in the manner of a water ski or a flat stone skipped across a pond. Once a tire hydroplanes, of course, it does not touch the pavement. A hydroplaning tire contributes virtually nothing to steering and contributes nothing to braking until it sinks back through the water to the pavement, whereupon it may catch on the pavement hard enough to jerk the car sideways, somewhat like a blowout.

The driving wheels are less affected, since they rather cut through the water, but on a front-engine, rear-drive car, you have probably hydroplaned your front wheels for short distances, say, 10 to 20 feet, without knowing it. The sensation is that of a sudden silkiness in the steering wheel, and it happens often on undular pavements with many shallow puddles. Power steering, unfortunately, obscures the symptom. You hydroplane one or both front tires across a puddle and never know it.

How fast you have to be going to hydroplane depends, obviously, on the weight of the car, the amount of tire surface area, and speed. Generally, assume that you can hydroplane as slowly as 30 mph.

Presumably, a front-wheel-drive car should not hydroplane when power is going to the front wheels. That just means that hydroplaning waits until you let off the gas a bit, then you hydroplane like everybody else (though to apply power will recover the situation). Also, the *rear wheels* of a front-wheel-drive car, like the front wheels of a rear-drive car, may hydroplane any time conditions are right for it. When the rear wheels do hydroplane, a gusty crosswind or a passing car can make the rear end slither. In other words, as long as you are going fast enough, you are vulnerable to hydroplaning.

In any case, a car that is hydroplaning is operating on pure luck. Since both rear wheels of a rear-drive car give equal traction, they keep a hydroplaning car aimed in a straight line. The first attempt to change lanes, or the first gust of wind from the side, can send it skittering across other lanes or into the ditch.

So, be sensitive to your steering wheel and slow down to the speed where you know you have positive control.

Wet Brakes

When rain splashes up from the pavement or when you drive through a puddle, your brake discs/drums get wet. Then, when you apply the brakes, your brake linings must squeeze this water out of the way before they can rub on the disc/drum and slow the car down. The linings need only half a dozen turns of the wheel to clear the water, but those few turns with reduced braking are quite enough to send you through a red light into a busy intersection or into the pedestrians in a crosswalk.

So, when driving in rain, dry your brakes periodically; just push the brake pedal lightly until you feel the brakes beginning to catch, then let off. On an interstate highway with mileposts, I let each milepost remind me to nudge the brake pedal—a light application for just a few seconds is enough.

A rain-filled dip or a flooded intersection requires more drastic action. If you drive through water that is five or six inches deep, apply the brakes lightly before you drive through to keep water out of the brakes, then apply them briefly, but hard enough to make the engine lug, when you get out.

Sometimes, when driving through a puddle, you will stop even when you don't want to because you splash water over your ignition system and the water short-circuits everything. If you enter a puddle running normally and come out with the engine wheezing and gasping like a horse with a straw in its throat, that's what you've done. If so, hold the gas pedal steady—don't let off or try to speed up—and the heat from the engine and the air from the fan will dry things out quickly. If the car stalls completely, you've got to dry off the wiring; a cloth will just spread the water around, so use water-displacing penetrating oil, e.g., WD-40, CRC, LPS, etc.

Diesels, of course, having no electric ignition system, don't have this problem.

To summarize: in rain, slow down, don't hydroplane, keep the brakes dry, and ease your way through deep puddles.

Fog

When fog comes in on Carl Sandburg's "little cat feet," the rule among boatfolk is: "If you don't have to go, don't." In hilly country, you may find fog on the crests or in the valleys, and it will roll up and surround you, not on "cat feet," but on the galloping paws of a cheetah.

The consequence of fog, of course, is that you can't see. The National Highway Traffic Safety Administration, in its Fatal Accident Reporting System (FARS), does not report accidents in the fog as a separate category. However, I conclude from newspaper reports that fog accounts for nearly all those chain-reaction accidents wherein 50 or so cars pile up like dirty laundry in the chute. Fog is dangerous. If you keep moving, you may rear-end a car ahead because you can't see beyond your own hood. If you stop, you are certain to get rear-ended yourself. If you pull over, you may hit a car already off the road or be sideswiped by a passing car. About all you can do is proceed cautiously and try to steer within the limits of visibility. If you can get well off the road, fine; stop and wait for the fog to lift. If not, proceed cautiously, with flashers going.

The usual advice in fog at night is to drive on the low beams, thus to cast your beams on the pavement close to the car; this is good advice. However, do switch to the high beam periodically, just long enough to look farther ahead, for your high beams may pick up another car, a road sign indicating a curve, etc. If the high beams create the visionless "white-out" effect of being inside a white globe, go quickly back to low beams, for the white-out sensation is most disorienting.

A wholesome, well-served pea-souper will make you wish you had bought fog lights instead of landau bars. The main difference between fog lights and headlights is that the filament in a fog light has a hood over it, so that it does not send light rays upward. Rays that go upward illuminate the droplets of water and that's why you see only a white fog in your headlights. With fog lights, you look through unilluminated droplets to the illuminated fog on the road. The illuminated fog at road level doesn't let you see much, so fog lights don't help as much as advertisements suggest, but they do help a little and that amount can be quite enough to keep you out of a wreck. Amber fog lights are no better than clear ones, and neither type helps much in daylight.

Sand/Dust Storms

Irrigation and improved tillage have eliminated the "Dust Bowl" of the Depression era, but in arid lands west of the Mississippi, you can still find yourself in a dust storm so thick you can't see. Such storms usually occur around the equinoxes—in the spring, before fields are planted or the grass has thickened on rangelands, and in the fall, after crops (especially wheat) are harvested and rangelands dry at the end of the summer. The equinoxes seem to set off some unusually strong winds; hence, the seasonal dust storms.

A good, old-fashioned duster will reduce visibility as much as a thick fog does and and leave you just as lost and vulnerable. In addition, the wind will push your car around like a gorilla wrestling a bantamweight. Finally, you can sit in the car and decide on its new color, for when the storm subsides, your car will be sandblasted down to its primer paint, if not its bare metal.

A dust storm does warn you in daylight; you can see it coming miles away as a dirty fringe hanging just above the horizon. People out west know the sign and get the chickens into the coop (a severe dust storm can suffocate a chicken) and the washing in from the clothesline before the storm hits. Tourists won't know; hence, the pileups on Interstate 40, west of Amarillo, Texas, when a "blue norther" hauls dirt all the way down from Saskatoon. If you're a stranger to the plains and you encounter dust and wind, look to the northern or western horizon and listen to a weather forecast (provided your radio will work; the static electricity in a dust storm may give you nothing but crackling). Get off the road if a dust storm is on the way.

Heat

Boston is no hotter than Billings when the temperature in both places reads 100 degrees. Why, then, should the Montana cowboy sweat less than the Boston Irishman (Boston Brahmins, of course, don't sweat at all), while his pickup overheats sooner?

Because, as the adage says, "It's not the heat; it's the humidity." The dry air of the West quickly absorbs moisture, so people don't sweat so much to stay cool. However, the moisture in the air elsewhere in the country enables the air to absorb more heat, so a radiator is more effective in humid air. Hence, all the eastern cars that run well at home but begin to overheat about the time they get west of Salina, Kansas.

Pollution control requires cars to run around 190° F, which isn't far from boiling (212°). However, the cooling system is pressurized, like a pressure cooker, and if your radiator cap is in good order, an engine will run as hot as 230° without causing the coolant to force its way past the radiator cap and boil away.

Also, modern engine oils will tolerate this kind of heat for a short while.

Okay, say you're on Interstate 10, in western Arizona, heading for Blythe, California, where the temperature reaches 125° on a truly hot summer day, and your temperature gauge creeps slowly up to the edge of the red "overheating" zone. The first thing to do is slow down, to reduce the amount of fuel being burned and, thus, the amount of heat being produced.

Alas, this may not change the reading on the gauge: to slow down also reduces the volume of air passing through the radiator, and the gauge may stay the same. Yet, slowing down, say, from 70 mph to 60 mph, or from 60 mph to 50 mph, reduces the loads on the inside parts of the engine and gives the oil more time to carry away some of the heat, so slowing down helps even if the gauge does not respond. In any event, you can keep going as long as the gauge does not go into the red "overheating" zone. If it does, pull over at a convenient place, let the engine run at a fast idle for about two minutes to get rid of some of its highway heat, then shut it off. Let it sit until it cools down to about the middle of the gauge (check by turning on the switch), proceed until it goes into the red again, then stop again. If need be, and if a pleasant resting place be available, just stay put till about 4:00 P.M., when the temperature begins to drop.

If you have only a warning light to indicate overheating, you have less information to work with. Suppose the warning light goes on at 230°. Very well, if the engine gets no hotter, and if you slow down, you can keep going. However, with a warning light and no gauge, you won't know whether the engine is stable at an allowable 230° or if it is getting hotter and hotter. Hence, you will have to apply the stop-and-cool routine until the outside temperature begins to fall. Stop until the light no longer goes on, allow a few more minutes, then drive again.

A car only a year or two old will rarely have a radiator clogged with rust. Hence, a radiator flush is hardly required before a cross-country trip. However, the crisscross meshwork of the radiator may well be clogged with assorted moribund flora (grass, leaves) and fauna (bugs). Have a shop check for such clogging; usually, you can blast the stuff out with water and compressed air, after which you put on a "bug screen" from an auto store before starting on your trip. An outside bug screen will spoil the highly touted aerodynamics of the car, so write the manufacturers and tell them that, next time, you want more radiator, a real temperature gauge, and less aerodynamics.

The shop may find no clogging and advise against a bug screen. The shop is wrong. You can leave South Amboy, New Jersey, and bug-up your radiator before you get beyond Wheeling, West Virginia. Bugs like lights. In cities, they cluster around streetlights and leave cars alone, but on the open road at night, every vagrant bug makes a beeline for headlights and winds up in a radiator.

Older cars need a thorough, thorough cooling-system flushing before going off on a trip and need a thorough de-bugging, too.

Altitude

As you go higher and higher, the air gets thinner and thinner. Like watered soup, the volume is just as great, but you don't get so much good out of it.

In high altitudes, the air, being thinner, has less oxygen, so an engine can burn less fuel. In effect, the engine gets smaller as you go higher. Turbocharged cars may hold their own, but not necessarily.

Accordingly, your car will be getting quite short-winded by the time you get to Colorado's Loveland Pass, where you cross the Continental Divide at 11,992 feet above sea level. Accept the fact. Shift down if you must, but keep the engine running fairly fast. Do not—repeat: *do not*—try any fancy passing maneuvers: you won't have the power you need and will just get yourself into trouble.

Remember, if you didn't know already, that the first car to cross the whole country, in 1903, was a 1903 Winton driven by Dr. H. Nelson Jackson and his chauffeur, Sewall K. Crocker. Jackson and Crocker made the trip from San Francisco to New York in 63 days. Shortly thereafter, Tom Fetch and Marius Krarup one-upped the good physician by driving a Packard the same distance in 61 days. In 1906, L. L. Whitman, driving an air-cooled Franklin, dropped the transcontinental time to 15 days; and in 1908, a 1907 Thomas Flyer took 170 days to win the race from New York to Paris—by way of Siberia!

Nor did the boys have all the fun. In 1909, Alice Huyler

Ramsey (Vassar, '07) made the first transcontinental drive by a woman. Mrs. Ramsey, president of the Women's Motoring Club of New York, was justifiably offended when women were excluded from the New York to Seattle race of 1909. She responded by inviting her two sisters-in-law and a friend to join her in a cross-country excursion. The foursome departed New York on June 9 in a 26-hp Maxwell-Briscoe and arrived 3800 miles later in San Francisco on August 6. The duration of the trip measures neither Alice's driving skill nor the quality of the Maxwell; rather, it measures the public response to the trip: in every city and town along the way, the group had to take time out to be feted by the mayor and be interviewed by the local newspaper.

In other words, cars have been going just about everywhere since the beginning. Don't make a point of going out to challenge nasty weather, but if you get caught in it, proceed with sense and caution and you'll get home all right.

WINTER STORMS

When Europeans began exploring the arctic, they discovered that the Eskimo had words for as many as 15 different types of snow. Nowadays, cross-country skiers separate snow into "new" and "old," and recognize six or seven subclasses of each based on the effects of temperature. By contrast, nonskiers (including most drivers) distinquish "snow" from "slush" or "ice" and end the classifications there.

Whatever its condition and whatever its name, the stuff that falls out of the sky and collects on the road prevents the tires from coming in contact with the road surface. The tires run on something else—fresh snow, packed snow, ice, thawing snow, slush, etc.—and that "something else" does not provide enough traction (e.g., friction) for the tires to control the motion of the car. Thus, wheels spin when getting under way, slide when the brakes go on, and skid sideways when the steering wheel is turned. To further complicate matters, these aberrant behaviors are influenced by the car itself and by its tires.

Mechanical Arrangements

For driving a conventional front-engine, rear-drive car on a slippery surface, the one most important factor is weight distribution. Ideally, each wheel should carry the same amount of weight. If the front is heavier, the rear wheels will spin before they will push the front, and the rear end will offer to trade ends when the brakes go on. If the front is light, the car won't respond to the steering wheel. Obviously, to keep the weight on each wheel equal at all times is nearly impossible; for example, to fill a 15-gallon gas tank adds about 90 pounds to the rear of a car and, thus, affects weight distribution. The generality, though, is that cars carrying near-equal weight front and rear behave the best in adverse circumstances and this rule also applies to four-wheel-drive (4WD) vehicles.

By contrast, front-wheel-drive (FWD) cars carry more weight on the wheels that do the pulling. Generally, they have better traction, but their rear wheels may slither on turns and when braking. Rear-engine, rear-drive cars also get good traction, but their front ends may slither.

No one system, unless it includes 4WD, has an absolute advantage in all conditions. The best front-engine, rear-drive, two-wheel-drive car in snow and on ice that I ever owned (or experienced) was a 1972 Toyota Corona Mark II station wagon. It had Sears steel-belted radial tires with a normal tread that were kept at 27 pounds of pressure and it would plow through eight inches of fresh snow on the parking lot at Charles River Park (Boston) when even the Jeep crowd wouldn't brave it (which, I must add, says more about the crowd than the Jeeps).

The Saab 99, with its front-wheel drive and with conventional tires, does very well, too, but I won't call it better than the Corona. With conventional tires and in deep snow, the Saab pushes a mound of snow up in front of it, then crawls up on the mound until the front (driving) wheels come off the ground. Then they spin, and I must dig the snow from under to let the car back down and either back out or try going forward again. When the Toyota (and other rear-drive cars) would "high-center" in this way, its rear (driving) wheels would pull it backward off the mound.

However, to get slightly ahead of the story, once I put snow tires on the Saab, it became one of the most unstoppable vehicles I've ever driven in snow. I have never driven a car on which the change from conventional to snow tires made such a drastic difference. With conventional tires, it would spin going up a mild incline in a few inches of snow, but with the snow tires, I climbed blithely up such alpine tracks as Ashfield's notorious Brier Hill Road in snow eight inches deep, and plowed through fresh, light snow as deep as 12 inches—snow that stopped some four-wheel-drive vehicles (mostly because of inept driving). I never tried the Toyota wagon with snow tires, but given its performance with conventional treads, I am sure it would do as well as the Saab.

Probably the most helpless cars in snow and ice were the Plymouth Valiant/Dodge Dart models of ten years and more ago. These cars were simply too light at the rear end and would spin their wheels too easily (which does not alter the fact that they were among the most reliable, economical, and long-lived cars ever built in this country).

Improving Your Handicap
Since a front-engine, rear-drive car should have as nearly equal weight at both ends as possible, this may mean adding some weight to the trunk during the winter. So, get about 100 pounds of coarse sand or inert plant-potting material (from a hardware store or nursery), mix in about 10 percent rock salt (the stuff you sprinkle on an icy driveway, likewise from the hardware store) to keep it from caking, then divide it into two manageable 50-pound lots. Put each lot in a garbage bag, put the garbage bags in boxes (a wine or spirits carton from the liquor store), and put the two boxes in the trunk right up against the back seat, or as nearly as possible right over the rear wheels.

This gives you a little more weight. Now, add a small shovel— a child's beach toy will do—to the kit, and you can toss your mixture in front of your rear wheels for more traction if you get stuck.

Sawdust, chain-saw chips, and coarse fireplace or stove ashes will also aid traction, but don't try to use a clay-base "Kitty Litter" to improve traction. The stuff promptly turns to slick mud in the water that forms when your spinning tires melt the ice.

Front-wheel-drive and rear-engine cars won't benefit from added weight, so carry only one 25-pound bag of sand-salt mixture to scatter in front of the wheels when necessary.

Tires and Conditions

To be a purist about it, each distinct snow/ice condition calls for a different tire (just as it calls for a different ski wax). Unfortunately, people can't change tires as often as the road surface changes, so the choices reduce to conventional treads, so-called "all-weather" tires, snow tires, snow tires with studs, and tires with chains. The choice must ultimately be made according to how and where the car is used.

Consider the mechanics of a tire on dry pavement: The tire grips the pavement because pavement-surface asperities dig into the rubber of the tire, just as the asperities on a piece of sandpaper dig into your palm. Accordingly, the smoother the tire, the better traction it has on dry pavement. Hence, the use of smooth "racing slicks" on race cars, and hence, a conventional tire has the best traction on dry pavement because it presents more rubber to the surface. On freshly frozen ice, a conventional or bald tire still gets some traction from asperities on the ice, and the action can be enhanced by lowering the tire pressure to about 20 pounds. This puts more tire surface on the ground and the tire can grip more asperities, or it can gain traction on an irregular surface by pushing against the slopes of the irregularities. I have been stuck many times and on many occasions I got out by dropping tire pressure.

On a firm surface—packed snow or ice—an underinflated tire carries its load at the sides, for the middle of the tread bulges upward where the tire meets the ground. The edges, then, dig in better, somewhat like the edge of a knife, and resist skidding.

To lower tire pressure, of course, contradicts all we've said before about proper tire pressure. However, we lower pressure only as a temporary measure and in circumstances where we expect to drive slowly and maneuver carefully.

Snow tires, with their coarse, knobby tread patterns, don't expect, so to speak, to touch the pavement at all. They expect to run on snow, and so get their traction by packing snow. They amount to a round gear that packs the snow into a firm mass, cuts "teeth" in the packed snow, and then uses the teeth to pull against. To enhance this action, their tread is typically a harder rubber than the tread of a conventional tire. Since the tread is so open, i.e., has less rubber to touch the ground, and the rubber is harder, snow tires do not grip a dry pavement or ice as well as conventional tires. Of course, if the ice is slightly sun-softened, a snow tire can dig in and go. On dry pavement at speed, though, a snow tire is quite noisy and wears out about twice as fast as a conventional tire.

All-weather tires seek the optimum compromise between conventional and snow tires, and I consider Semperit's the most successful. In the absolute sense, they are not as good as snow tires in deep snow (e.g., four to eight inches), but they may be preferred in areas where the snow plows get out promptly after a snow.

Studs are hardened, metal pins, somewhat like short nails, that are inserted into small holes in the tread of a snow tire. At low speeds, the road surface pushes the studs upward and they contribute little or nothing to traction. At higher speeds, centrifugal force flings the studs outward and they dig into the surface to obtain purchase; the action is like that of spiked golf shoes.

On glare ice and on hard-frozen snow, studs are second only to chains. In fresh snow, they are no better than snow tires without studs. On dry pavement at speed, they are precarious because they tend to ride up on the points of the studs and leave little rubber in contact with the road. In any event, they chew up pavement surfaces.

Chains are a pain to put on and take off, but they are categorically superior in deep snow, on packed snow, or on ice. A car with chains will claw its way out of an unbelievable snowdrift, and I have often driven at 50 mph with them in fresh, deep snow. However, on dry pavement, chains shortly grind themselves to pieces. If you use them (and I strongly recommend them), try to keep them running on snow.

Although opinions differ about whether chains should be loose or tight, after two winters in Fairbanks (Alaska), eight winters in Chicago and Pittsburgh, three winters in Boston, and three winters in western Massachusetts (not to mention mud in other places where I also used chains), I put chains on as tightly as possible. A good set costs $50 to $100 nowadays, depending on the size of the tire, but they are your best surety of motion in extreme conditions. If you have chains and still can't go, the next step is four-wheel drive (with chains).

Indeed, no matter what the tire or what the conditions, a 4WD vehicle will enjoy traction vastly superior to that of two-wheel-drive vehicles.

Arguments persist about whether radial tires have inherently superior traction in snow/ice. Theoretically, they should have. In practice, I will allow radials a 5 percent advantage over conventional tires. In other words, the careful driver with conventional tires will still be going when the careless driver with radials is stuck.

The tire you choose should suit the conditions you will encounter. In most parts of the country, snow-plow crews are so expeditious that all-weather tires are quite enough. Where crews can't cover the territory quickly or if you must drive on unplowed roads, choose snow tires. Don't use studs at all unless you have a steep driveway that is always icy (i.e., you would rather destroy your driveway surface with studs than throw sand on it).

As a generality, if all other factors are equal, a larger tire will provide better traction than a smaller one. Thus, the front-wheel-drive Saab, with its 15-inch wheels, is vastly more capable in deep snow than a FWD Volkswagen Rabbit with its 13-inch wheels.

Field Trials

I can fairly say I've driven in virtually every condition with each option. When I bought the Chevrolet Suburban, for example, it had bald tires and I had to make a trip to New York before I could replace them. The trip (January 1982) coincided with a ferocious blizzard, and I drove the 110 miles from Hartford, Connecticut, to New York City with chains—at 25–30 mph in second gear (and, saving a few trucks, had the road all to myself; I didn't see a half-dozen cars the whole distance).

On Christmas Eve of 1962, my ex-dormitory (University of Alaska) roommate, Howard Bowman, his new wife, Letitia, and I drove my '57 Plymouth from Anchorage to Fairbanks via the Richardson Highway in the densest snowstorm I have ever experienced. By the time we got to Tok Junction, the faithful

Plymouth was plowing with its bumper, throwing gobs of snow up on the hood. We ran with chains on snow tires, averaging about 25 mph, the road only faintly marked by humped drifts at the sides. The fresh snow absorbed all sound except the whir of the heater and the swish-flop of the wipers, and the spectral whiteness on all sides obscured our forward motion; I watched the odometer click over tenths of miles to persuade myself that we were actually moving. At daylight on Christmas morning, we reached the lodge at Tok Junction and had breakfast on a bear-skin rug in front of a fireplace six feet wide and as high. The lodge keeper's five-year-old daughter, chortling over what Santa Claus brought down that massive chimney, thought us strange because we spoke so little; in fact, we were re-orienting ourselves to a familiar world after eight hours of watching a cascading kaleidoscope of snowflakes whirling in the headlights.

I drove my Triumph TR-3 from Pittsburgh to Chicago in the December 1968 blizzard. The rear tires were nearly bald, so I dropped pressure to 20 pounds to put more tire surface on the ground and spent 17 hours on a 470-mile trip—counting cars and trucks in the ditch as I counted myself lucky. This was probably the most demanding wintertime haul I've ever made and the one trip that probably should have been postponed.

The nearest I ever came to slithering off the road was east of Adelaide, South Australia, in a Triumph 1200 convertible in 1965, as a slushy, half rain in the lowlands turned to an ice-slick on the crests of the windswept hills. To slow down meant losing the momentum that kept me from spinning my wheels as I climbed the hills, but to go too fast risked skidding in the wind gusts at the crests. To make things worse, Australia's funny labor laws did not (at least then) allow waitresses to work late hours. Hence, no coffee stops along the way, so I drove all night on soft drinks and Cadbury's chocolate (and I swear I have not touched the stuff since).

Once you discover how the car behaves, you can travel quite nicely in deep snow. Everything goes beautifully until you get to the turn or exit you want: you turn the steering wheel—and find you can't! You've got so much snow packed up under the fenders that the front wheels will hardly turn to right or left. This means that instead of making your exit, you run right into the divider that separates freeway from exit.

I first experienced this near Clines Corners, New Mexico, in early 1958, in a 1947 Chevrolet truck. I stopped for a stop sign, signaled my left turn, let up the clutch, and was able to turn the steering wheel just enough to head straight toward a parked car, at which point I discovered I had a second problem: the truck heater had quit long before, so my feet were so numb that I could neither move my right foot quickly to the brake pedal nor push hard when I got it there. Fortunately, the old Chevy truck was so slow in first gear that I did get stopped in time.

Since then, when driving in snow that will pack up, I periodically make gradual lane changes just so the front tires can grind out some of the snow packed up under the fenders. For long wintertime hauls, I also wear thick wool socks and loose shoes; if the heater should quit, my feet will last a little longer if not tightly confined.

The point of these anecdotes is to say that winter driving is not something to fear. A properly prepared car and a sensible driver can handle bad weather, and patience can prevail over poor driving conditions. Note the speeds given: 17 hours, Pittsburgh to Chicago, works out to 27.6 mph. I've driven Interstate 84 several times in snowstorms, and most of the cars I saw in the ditch had passed me several miles back.

The fact that those impatient drivers got into the ditch before they got home underscores the first rule of winter driving. When traction heads toward nil—*slow down!* Reduce the momentum energy that the friction surfaces at the tires must control. When the road is free of other traffic, experiment: Punch the gas pedal and see how quickly the drive wheels break loose. Try the brakes and see how much they will take before the wheels slide. Get an idea of how much room you need to stop. Also, watch the snowbanks and be prepared to head into one if necessary to avoid another car or a pedestrian. Fortunately, snowbanks are fairly soft and don't usually damage a car.

SLIPPING AND SLIDING

Technically, a skid occurs when a tire slides, rather than rolls, over the road surface. Thus, severe braking can cause a tire to slide (and leave a black mark) even though the car continues in a straight line.

Skids of greater or lesser magnitude are just part of the winter scene, along with clean, fresh snow and cars that won't start. First, because a snow-covered or icy road surface does not present a good traction surface; second, because the tires may get warm enough to create a microthin film of water between the tire and an icy surface. Either way, the tire slides easily.

The skids that people worry about are those that happen when they are turning a corner or making an abrupt lane change. When a car goes forward, all its momentum energy is aimed in a straight line ahead. When it makes any sort of lateral maneuver or change of direction, a sideways force arises. The sideways force and the forward force conflict, and the tires and the road surface decide which one wins.

As you round a corner, the front tires must overcome the forward force to get the car to change directions, while a centrifugal force arises that tries to make the car move sideways toward the outside of the curve. Curves are often banked to counteract this force; however, if you go too slowly around an icy curve that is steeply banked, your car may slide down the slope toward the inside of the curve.

If you go into a curve too fast on ice, the lighter end of a car usually slides first. Thus, on a rear-engine Volkswagen Beetle, the car will not respond to the steering and will continue off the road in a straight line. With FWD or a conventional front-engine car, the rear end is lighter and will fail to follow the front end through the curve and will slide sideways off the road; the car may wind up sideways, or the rear end may come all the way around and leave the car facing the other way.

The problem, in any case, is how to reassert control. The only reliable solution is not to get into the situation in the first place.

The only people who can make a car behave predictably on ice are the drivers who compete in winter road rallies in Canada and Europe. The rest of us aren't that good at it and may as well admit it. You can do a little—sometimes—but not much.

Driver's license handbooks and similar publications say that a skid can be corrected by letting off the gas and turning into the direction of the skid. While growing up in arid eastern New Mexico, I had little occasion to test this advice, but the first time I did test it, in Alaska, I found it wouldn't work, because to turn into the direction of the skid aimed me right into a car in the opposing lane. I did the opposite: fed gas and turned the opposite way and, indeed, did recover from the skid. However, I called it luck, not skill or science.

The rule to "turn into a skid" works fairly well and is the proper thing to try first—traffic, schoolchildren, and vertical cliffs permitting. Beyond the easy limits of the rule, however, a car skidding on ice has largely passed beyond the control of the driver and no clever textbook technique will save the situation. Get off the gas, steer as well as you can, and use the brakes lightly or not at all—and smile at the people dodging out of your way.

Therefore, the second wintertime rule, after "slow down," is to use seat belts. A serious skid almost always means a crash of greater or lesser degree, so accept the fact and prepare for it. Don't give up easily, of course, for you may recover the situation, but be prepared.

Next, keep in mind that *if the front wheels begin to slide, they no longer provide steering.* This means staying off the brakes or, at least, being extremely delicate with them. As you apply the brakes, the physics involved effectively shifts the weight of the car forward; too abrupt a shift and the added weight overcomes the traction of the tires and the front wheels slide, nullifying the steering and leaving the car heading somewhere it shouldn't go. The solution is to let off the brakes to restore steering, but this leaves the car rolling toward things it shouldn't hit. However, with the front wheels able to steer, the car can be steered toward the preferable alternative, e.g., a building, guardrail, or ditch rather than people.

Remember: *Wheels that are sliding do not provide steering*, so go easy on the brakes and be prepared to get off the brakes and resort to the steering wheel to resolve an imminent collision, even if the choice simply means a lesser collision.

At milepost 40, near Conway, Massachusetts, southbound Route 116 makes a sharp curve to the left, a curve known as Witch's Corner because the house in the lee of the high prominence on the right is said to be haunted by a witch (I have not met the witch, but I believe what the local people tell me). The prominence, covered with oaks and maples, shades Witch's Corner until the sun is high, which means the curve often has an ice sheet on it even when ice on the rest of the road has melted.

As I casually entered Witch's Corner in the '70 International Travelall one morning, I found a Volkswagen Beetle sideways in my lane, a woman standing beside it. I tapped the brakes just as I entered upon the ice sheet. The Travelall had a dreadful forward weight bias because of its heavy, 900-pound V-8 engine, so the front wheels promptly locked up and slid. I dumbly fought the steering wheel, watching the woman's horrified expression as she saw 4200 pounds of bulk bearing down on her. Eventually, I realized what was happening, got off the brakes, and steered off into the ditch to the right. The exercise was a perfect, classic example of how a car loses its steering when the front wheels slide and was unhappily close to an example of the consequences.

In the Ditch

If you do a lot of winter driving, you should assume you will wind up in the ditch now and again, and if you do it in the right place, you may stay there for several hours, perhaps days. You don't even have to be in an isolated area for that to happen; during the northeastern blizzard of January 1978, so many people abandoned cars on freeways that rescue vehicles could not get to people who were unable to leave their cars. Therefore, every car used in northern climates should have a wintertime survival kit. Cars used in populated areas need only some sand/salt and a set of chains, but cars used for long trips should be equipped to preserve passengers from freezing if halted by a blizzard. The kit should include:

- cheap, fleece-lined rubber boots of the type found in discount stores; the boots should be accompanied by a pair of thick woolen socks (or the equivalent) and should fit well enough to walk in;
- aluminum-faced "space" blanket;
- several cans of Sterno and a one-pound coffee can to burn it in, or a pack of short candles;
- and, of course, a flashlight.

People are usually urged to stay with the car if they go off into deep snow and that is good advice. However, they are also told to "run the car heater until help arrives." People who say things like that presume "help" will arrive in 10 or 15 minutes. Well, on my January 1982 trip to New York, I saw one or two snowplows near Hartford, Connecticut, and another two on the Hutchinson River Parkway outside of New York City, but in the 110 miles between, I saw only a few cars and half a dozen trucks. For four hours, I was virtually alone on the road. Along the way, I saw at least twenty cars on the shoulder, half-buried in snow. I presume no one was in them. In any case, if a major eastern interstate and parkway system can be so empty, think of Interstate 80 in Nebraska or Interstate 94 in Montana. Most of the people who write casually about "waiting for help" have never had to wait for it.

Neither have they noted how long a car will run at idle speed to keep the heater going on, say, 10 gallons of gasoline. Twenty years ago, before drive-in movie theaters provided car heaters, high school couples knew exactly how long their cars would run the heater on, say, a quarter of a tank of gas, but this useful awareness has long since been lost (along with ambition, respect for elders, etc.). In fact, a big V-8 can use up five gallons of gas in less than two hours of idling and a small engine will probably use it in less than four.

If running the car heater is the chosen policy, the engine should be run at intervals, not constantly, to make the fuel last longer.

All this presumes the engine will run, but if the car winds up at a severe sideways or fore-and-aft angle, the engine may not run because of the angle of the carburetor. A fuel-injected engine would run, provided the fuel pump could pick up fuel and provided the oil pump could pump oil. However, the danger of carbon monoxide poisoning is too real to be disregarded. The exhaust system may have been broken as the car went off the road; or if the car winds up in window-deep snow or if blowing snow drifts around it, the exhaust gasses cannot dissipate and will seep into the car. To "run the heater until help arrives" may not work. "Help" may find only dead bodies, as too often happens in such cases.

If you find yourself stranded in a car in deep snow, put on the socks and rubber boots, wrap the space blanket underneath your coat, and curl up. Put the Sterno in the coffee can, put the can on a level surface, open a window a crack to avoid carbon monoxide poisoning from the Sterno, and light the Sterno. Candles will be safer in this respect, for they produce little or no carbon monoxide; however, they do consume oxygen, so the window must still be left open a bit. Make sure the flame is away from combustibles. If the car is at such an angle that gasoline has leaked from the tank and you can smell it, don't light anything. Well huddled and insulated, and sheltered from the wind, a healthy person can tolerate exposure to severe cold for several hours, if not days. As John Coleman, the weatherman from Chicago, once dryly observed, "Many are cold, but few are frozen."

GETTING UNSTUCK

Sometimes, snow conditions will prevent a car from getting out of the driveway. When the traction surface is poor, even a very slight resistance to motion can set the drive wheels spinning.

For example, just to turn the steering enough to pull away from a curb or to stop at a traffic light on a slight hill may be enough to make the drive wheels spin when you try to take off. In these circumstances, the problem is not how to stop motion, but how to institute it.

In general, although exceptions will occur, spinning the wheels faster and faster will only melt depressions under the drive wheels. Also, this action can damage the "spider" gears in the differential.

So, how to get going?

First remove any obstruction to motion; this may mean digging snow/ice away from the paths of the wheels—for only a few feet, because once in motion, momentum will carry the car over a slight obstruction. Next, improve traction; put on chains, drive out of the problem, then remove the chains. The process is a hassle, but it beats a tow truck, especially when none is available. Also you can throw sand or rock salt under the tires at the point where the tire meets the road and in the path of the tire. Coarse sawdust will also help, and chain-saw chips are excellent. In a worst-case situation, jack the car up, if the surface will support the jack, and toss sand/salt directly under the tires. In an even worse case, jack the car up and put boards under the wheels; this is particularly effective when the wheels have dug themselves into a hole—but watch out! The tire may kick the board out. I have thrown boards six feet long and two inches thick halfway across a road this way; a person standing in the way would have been injured, so apply power gently. Again, resort to the board system only when the wheels have dug/melted themselves into a hole.

I have often read and heard the recommendation to "stuff rags" under the wheels to gain traction, but I have never seen it work. Invariably, the tire grabs the rag, jerks it under, and ejects it out behind. I have met people who claim they successfully used rags and I will acknowledge that they used rags and that they got out, but I doubt a necessary connection; I suspect a more skillful driver would have got out without them.

Personally, I have tried burlap bags (what western farmers call "tow sacks" and other people call "gunny sacks"), bathroom rugs, "welcome" mats, car floor mats, and, once, a brand-new, 100 percent virgin wool overcoat, and I never achieved anything except rolling the item into a dirty ball behind the wheel (and losing buttons off the coat). The effort is a waste of time and carrying bathroom rugs for this purpose is a cruel illusion. It won't work.

The other common advice is to rock the car out of a hole. This is good advice. However, most people rock much too brutally. The method succeeds, not on power or on traction, but on momentum. In shifting from forward to reverse gear, the shift should coincide with the rolling of the car and drastic applications of power will not improve on a gently encouraged rocking. A gently encouraged rocking, like the motion of a playground swing, will develop into a motion sufficient to get a car out of a profound depression. Once the car crawls out of its hole, power may be usefully applied in larger doses.

DEAD ENGINES: THAWING THE FROZEN

Obviously, if getting cold prevents a car from starting, then keeping it warm will ensure that it will start. Similarly, once an effort to start a car has failed and the battery has been run down, applying warmth may salvage the situation. Obviously, too, this approach depends on a source of heat. Generally, people have or find heat sources in their houses. Therefore, the person who keeps a car in a garage attached to or near the house can apply warmth to a cold engine more easily than one who parks in a parking lot behind an apartment building, and the person who parks on a lot has an easier time than one who parks on the street.

Note what *warm* means in this context: It does not mean "warm to the touch." Rather, *warm* means "warm enough to make a difference." For example, suppose a car has sat overnight at −10°F; to raise the temperature of the engine 30 degrees to only +20°F will usually be enough to get the engine to start, even though 20°F is hardly what most people mean by "warm."

The most convenient way to apply heat to an engine is with electricity, via either engine heaters or heat lamps. And provided a proper extension cord is used—i.e., the cord should be of 10- or 12-gauge (AWG) wire—electricity can be applied 100 feet or so from the house.

Engine heaters work like electric irons: electricity passes through a wire that has a high resistance to electricity, and as the electricity forces its way through, it heats up the wire. Toasters, hair dryers, and electric space heaters work the same way.

Electric engine heaters come in several types, to wit, *dipstick heaters, block heaters, head bolt heaters,* and *circulating-water heaters.* Prices run from about $8 for the dipstick heater to as much as $40 for the circulating-water heater.

A dipstick heater simply takes the place of the dipstick. It heats the oil, which allows the oil to flow readily, and some of the heat rises to warm the pistons, etc. However, because of its small size, a dipstick heater cannot generate a lot of heat, nor transfer a large amount of heat to an engine. Also, it so localizes the heat in the oil that it hastens degradation of the oil. However, a dipstick heater is the cheapest, most convenient means of heating an engine.

A block heater fits into the engine block, in one of the ports for the so-called "freeze plugs," and heats the coolant in the cooling system. Since heat rises if it can, the warmed-up coolant may flow toward the radiator or toward the car heater, thus warming the whole engine as it goes and allowing the heater to work as soon as the engine is running. Indeed, block heaters are a popular optional item for diesel engines, since diesels normally need help getting started down around 10°F. However, as with a dipstick heater, the small size of a block heater means it must be plugged in a long time to do any good. How long, of course, depends on the size of the engine and on the wattage of the heating element. Also, if installed in a poor location on the engine, it won't spread heat well and if installed poorly, will allow coolant to leak. On many cars, a block heater can't be used at all because other parts of the engine leave no room for it. On others, the electric wire may run so close to the exhaust manifold that it will be burned in two in short order. So, check things out thoroughly before investing in a block heater.

A head-bolt heater takes the place of a cylinder head bolt. It transfers heat to the block and, thence, to the coolant. However, since its heat is localized, it causes the metal in the cylinder head to contract and expand in funny ways and is not a good solution to the problem.

The best system is a circulating-water/coolant heater. These come in 500–1500-watt sizes and connect into the cooling system. They heat the coolant, which rises by convection and sets up a flow that warms the whole engine. In about two hours, a 500-watt unit will bring a small engine of around 1500 cc displacement from 0°F to operating temperature, and a 1500-watt unit will make a big V-8 feel warm to the touch.

The better heaters have a thermostatic control so they do not overheat the engine and so can be left plugged in for long hours. People usually plug them in when they get up in the morning and by the time they have showered, dressed, and got a cup of coffee down, the engine is ready. However, as an equally good approach, though it uses marginally more electricity, the heater can be plugged in after you come home from work or before you retire.

Since a circulating heater depends on convection, it must be mounted low, to create the greatest low-high differences so the coolant will flow. Few mechanics (even in places like Alaska) understand this, so they often mount such a heater wherever they find a place for it, often in locations that are too high and that compromise the effectiveness of the heater. For example, if the heater is connected too near the front of the engine, the heated coolant will open the thermostat and proceed to warm up the radiator, leaving the engine just as cold as it was. Also, if the temperature control for the car heater is left in the "hot" position, the circulating hot water may do no more than warm up the heater, again leaving the engine cold. Installed and used properly, though, circulating heaters are the best way to keep an engine warm.

Circulating-water-coolant heaters are the greatest thing for cars since the electric starter eliminated hand cranking. They make engines run better and last longer, and they save batteries. They prevent the hideous levels of pollution that a cold engine puts out, and they improve the atrocious gas mileage a car gets until its engine warms up. Because they warm the heater, too, they allow the defroster to work right away and guarantee good visibility when a half-asleep driver needs it the most. They prevent stalling in intersections with a cold car.

Obviously, use of an electric heater depends on a source of electricity, and this could mean an extension cord running from a second-story window out to the curb (where raffish boys will steal it or where a vexatious litigant will carefully trip over it and sue).

All the above applies doubly or triply to diesel cars. Manufacturers like to say that diesels start "easily" in cold weather because they have glow plugs, and if everything is in perfect order, a diesel will start fairly readily down to about 20°F. However, "easily" means one thing to a public relations agent in an office and quite another to a motorist, and if the battery is weak or the oil heavily sludged up, a diesel needs heat much more than a gasoline engine. The first option to specify for a diesel car is an engine heater; it will do the car much more good than a rallye stripe or electric windows.

Absent a proper engine heater, a light bulb under the hood will help cars parked in sheltered places. However, if the car is parked where it is exposed to wind, a light bulb is useless. Its minimal benefit can be enhanced by covering the engine with a reflective aluminum space blanket or perhaps with strips of aluminum foil, but even these help little when a car is exposed to a cold wind.

A 100-watt light bulb simply does not put out enough heat to warm up most engines, although such a bulb will help a Volkswagen Beetle if shut up in the engine compartment. Furthermore, a light bulb radiates its heat in all directions, so most of the heat is not aimed where you need it.

A better way is to use a 150-watt heat-lamp bulb. However, such a bulb *must* be used with a ceramic socket and *must* be used with an aluminum reflector so that it does not come into physical contact with rubber hoses, plastic wiring insulation, etc.

The technique is to place the lamp so that its heat is aimed on the engine block, rather than on the valve covers or air cleaner. Then, with the heat lamp in place, cover the whole engine with a heat-reflective space blanket and lower the hood. The hood needn't be shut tightly; just bring it down to keep the space blanket in place.

Unfortunately, you may not find enough room under the hood for a heat lamp, even if you use a small-diameter reflector. In this case, you have to go underneath and aim the heat lamp at the bulbous part of the oil pan. Cover the engine with the space blanket, too, and the heat that rises will be contained and reflected back into the engine compartment.

On the Chevrolet Suburban engine, an in-line six, I put the heat lamp at the rear, sort of behind the exhaust pipe, so that the lamp bulb was only a few inches from the block. If I drove the car home in the evening, I put the heat lamp in place with the engine warm. Otherwise, I put it in place about 10:00 P.M. and left it on all night. In weather of −10° to 0°F the one lamp made a marked difference in how well the engine started. Reasoning that "If some is good, more is better (and too much is just right)," I added a second heat lamp to the other side, just aft of the distributor.

After a night with two 250-watt lamps, the engine would start as promptly as in summer. If I pulled the dipstick, the oil was almost warm to the touch. The heater would deliver warm air by the time I was half a mile from the house. By contrast, without the heat lamps, I would drive three miles before the heater began to deliver slightly warm air.

Natalie's Chevrolet Malibu with the V-6 engine did not provide room under the hood for a heat lamp, so she aimed the lamp at the bottom of the oil pan. Obviously, this did not heat the engine so well, but it certainly made a marked difference. In sum, if you can't afford a proper engine heater or can't afford the cost of having one installed, a heat lamp will keep your engine warm.

Note, however, that the engine needs several hours under a heat lamp to benefit. You won't do any good in only an hour or two with a heat lamp.

Do not—repeat: *do not*—park a heat lamp where it can burn wiring insulation, hoses, or fuel lines.

DEAD BATTERIES: JUMP STARTING

When a car won't start, people first seek a "jump," i.e., help from another battery via cables with big "alligator" clips on the ends. In most cases, especially above about 15°F, a jump is enough to start a car.

Before we jump, though, consider what we are trying to do: we want to transfer energy from a strong battery to a weak battery. If we look, we will see that the battery cables are as big as a man's finger. If we look at the battery cable connections, we will see that they have at least a full square inch of contact surface.

Now, look at a pair of jumper cables. They are (or should be) as big as a finger. So far, so good. But now look at the contact surfaces at the alligator clips. These surfaces are the only avenue whereby the jumper cable can transfer energy. Yet, the contact surface consists of a piece of copper hardly as thick as a penny. This is not much surface area whereby to transfer the energy the starter on the dead car will require. If the battery in the dead car is truly dead, you will never get enough power through those clips to start it.

In most successful jump starts, the jumper battery only gives the quasi-dead battery a boost, and the power to start actually comes from the apparently dead battery. That is, the power to do the cranking does not have to come through those little clips on the ends of the jumper cables.

So what do we do with a genuinely dead battery, assuming we're attacking the problem with jumper cables?

Quite simple: Hook up the cables, start the good car, and let it run as long as 15 or 20 minutes—half an hour, if need be— and charge up the dead battery. Having given the dead battery a sizable charge, you then crank with both batteries. This virtually guarantees success.

On recent General Motors cars, this is the only way you can do it. The battery cables on these newer GM cars mount on the side of the battery and are held in place with small bolts. Those little bolts are the only place where you can connect the jumper cables, and you can never get enough power through them to crank the car. However, you can get enough power through to charge the battery.

To be technical about it, you can by-pass the battery completely and go straight to the terminal at the starter. However, this still leaves you with the problem of trying to move a great deal of energy through a very small contact surface. Furthermore, if you don't know what you are doing, you can create all kinds of sparks, so you're better off to patiently charge the battery on the newer GM cars before trying to jump start them.

Okay, now that all the qualifications have been stated, time to "give a jump." One jumper cable will have red ends and one will have black ends. Red goes to the "positive" or "+" side of the battery. Look on the top of the battery for an inscription. If you don't see an inscription, the larger post is the positive one. However, look carefully: don't let your astigmatism or a parallax error mislead you. Okay, red goes to positive and black goes to "negative" or "−."

Primary warning: in the midst of fiddling with the cables, do not—repeat: *do not*—let the two unoccupied ends touch each other while the other ends are connected to a battery. If you do, you will knock off some big sparks. Also, note that you shut off the good car before attaching the jumper cables.

You should connect to the dead battery first, and herein a problem arises. Most manufacturers say to connect the black cable, not directly to the dead battery but to some piece of body or engine metal. The point of this recommendation is to by-pass the dead battery. That way, the dead battery does not soak up energy from the good battery; also, you eliminate the danger of the good battery delivering such a jolt of power to the dead battery that the dead battery explodes when the water in it turns into steam due to the charge from the good battery.

Unfortunately, unless you know all about that stuff under the hood and unless you recognize a good contact surface, you can't apply the above good advice. Furthermore, you will often find that your connection to the engine or the body won't transfer enough energy to crank the dead car. So, you may as well do what everybody else does: connect directly to the cable ends of the dead battery. Connect the cables, carefully keeping the other ends apart, and work the clips back and forth a bit so the teeth in the alligator clips dig into the battery cable terminals and make a good contact.

Now, go over to the good battery. Since you have moved away from the dead battery, you are in no danger if the good battery causes it to explode. The possibility of explosion is remote in the extreme, but just to be sure, advise all bystanders to stand back. Connect the cables to the good battery.

Many car manufacturers say not to run the engine when giving a jump because the alternator will sense an excessive load and burn itself up trying to supply it. Okay, try to start the dead car once with jumpers connected. If it doesn't start, start the good car and let it charge the dead car for a few minutes, then leave the good car running and try the dead car again.

Don't grind on the starter of the dead car for more than 10 seconds at a try. Most owner's manuals will allow up to 30 seconds, but those manuals are wrong. Don't overwork the starter: it costs too much to replace if overworking it melts the soldered connections inside.

A word about the words of caution in the foregoing: safety has become a national mania in recent years, one consequence whereof being that remote hazards require warning far out of proportion to their probability. Hence, the warning about exploding batteries. I have watched innumerable times as the most impossibly inept amateurs set about to jump start a car and I have never seen any of them explode a battery. I once blew the caps off a battery with a battery charger, and once blew the top out of a 6-volt battery while jumping it with a 12-volt battery. In both cases, the event occurred because I created a condition of intermittent contact. The connections between the battery and the charger and between the two batteries were not constant, and the circuit was "making" and "breaking" repeatedly while the jumping was going on. The surges of power caused the blowups. In sum, if you proceed as outlined, which is the standard way of jumping, with my addition of using the good car to first charge the dead car (an excellent addition to standard practice), you will have no problems.

To review. The good way to jump a car is to:

- shut off the good car;
- connect jumper cables;
- start the good car and let it run for several minutes at a fast idle; it will recharge the battery of the dead car a little (actually, in a couple of hours, the good car would fully charge the dead car);
- shut off the good car;
- and, crank the dead car.

If this doesn't work, start up the good car, run it at a fast idle, and crank the dead car some more.

Don't crank for more than 10–15 seconds continuously, lest the starter on the dead car overheat.

If the dead car still won't start, give up and apply heat.

Summary

- Don't try to jump to battery terminals that are so corroded that power can't get into them.
- Don't try to jump with shabby, cheapo cables.
- Be sure to get red-to-red, etc.
- Let the good car charge the dead car for a while before cranking the dead car.
- Don't be mulish; if the dead car won't start, don't burn up its starter or the alternator on the good car in futile efforts; stop and apply heat to the dead car.

Note that we are dealing with a car that has a dead battery due to cold weather, not one that refuses to start because of serious mechanical defects.

ACCIDENTS

Given the plague, pestilence, and war that lashed the era, people of the Middle Ages knew death or dismemberment could come at virtually any time. Nowadays, we are less familiar with violence. When it does occur, we let specialists deal with it, for most of us know nothing about such things.

Yet, we are not immune from human experience of the less-desirable kind. On any highway, at any given moment, you could be the second to arrive at the scene of an accident, right after those who got there first because they are the ones involved. You will find yourself responsible and will find yourself unprepared for it. Yet you must do something and must make good decisions quickly.

Think about it: Do you know how to stop someone from bleeding to death? How to get someone out of a burning car despite the mangled seat-belt latch that won't open? Can you practice *triage*—can you analyze injuries and say, "That one, though still alive, is hopeless, so I will save this other one instead?" This will be a hard decision, but you may have to make it. Or you will have to decide whether to race to the nearest telephone or to stay on the scene and render immediate aid. Do you anticipate another car soon? Indeed, will an approaching car have adequate warning, or is it likely to plow into the whole mess and add to it? What will you do?

Since you have neither special training nor special equipment, and since every wreck is different, you have no clear rules to follow. You will have to make judgments.

Alternatively, suppose you are in a subsequent car; when you arrive, you find carnage and a moil of people. Should you stop? What will you add to the situation—one more onlooker gawking at someone else's misfortune, or competent help? If you can't help, don't stop to leer at the dead and maimed.

I have no special wisdom in such matters, for I have had little experience with this sort of thing. Late one night on the Ohio Turnpike, I came upon a car and camper-trailer jackknifed in the median ditch, the trailer upside-down and the car on its side. Several other cars had already stopped. The family from the wrecked car were lying on their backs on the grassy bank awaiting the ambulance that had already been summoned, a baby of about 18 months whimpering quietly in the arms of a woman from one of the cars that had stopped. Those standing around consulted their watches often, indicating that the ambulance was expected any minute.

I could add little to the situation. Since no one else had done so, I set up three "fusee" flares farther back down the road to warn approaching traffic and to guide it over to the right lane, and went my way.

Check that: carry flares or reflectors. From a distance, car lights may be such a jumble that approaching drivers can't tell what's going on. Your flares/reflectors will give them some orientation.

On another occasion, I was in a roadside rest on Interstate 80, west of Sidney, Nebraska, with the carburetor of the contemporaneous International Travelall (a noble beast, that one, a '65 model) spread out on the hood. Thus, I was immobile when two Harley-Davidson motorcycles of the "Hawg" type, each bearing a couple in black leather jackets, came roaring by. As the Hawgs passed the roadside rest, the sleeping bag on the luggage rack of one cycle slipped and got wedged in the rear wheel. The rear wheel locked up and the bike went skittering into the ditch, the rider struggling valiantly and futilely to keep it under control as it fell and sent the passenger—someone's daughter—cartwheeling down the side of the road like a gymnast gone berserk.

Coincidentally, a single motorcyclist was leaving the rest and so roared to the fallen bike. Those on the companion Hawg also stopped, as did a CB-equipped car. The crew of the fallen bike were hustled into an ambulance that arrived almost immediately (from God knows where) and the passenger on the second Hawg (someone else's daughter) righted the fallen bike, kicked it into action, and the caravan departed the scene. Here again, I could add nothing, so didn't leave my carburetor, and this has been my experience with wrecks (except the one I was in, and that is another story; I was not hurt, but my firewagon-red TR-3 was a mess).

Whether you arrive early or late at the scene of a wreck, the questions that matter are "What's to be done?" and "Who's in charge?" In such situations, someone always seems to take charge. That person may be you, and you have to decide what to do. If someone else is in charge, you have to decide whether he knows what he is doing and either assume control of the situation or counter his erroneous directives. The situation can be awkward, but usually it is not. If the person who has assumed control does not fully know what is best to do, that person knows it better than anyone else.

If you end up in charge, you have to make decisions right away. If no one has a CB radio, someone must hasten to a telephone. Give the job to someone in a Mercedes-Benz or a BMW. However, if you are the one directed to go to a phone, remember that people who are hurt are depending on you. You are not allowed the luxury of wrecking your own car on the way, and when you get to the phone, you are not allowed the pleasure of babbling incoherently. Give the relevant particulars: Where the wreck is, east-, west-, north-, or southbound on what route, near what exit or overpass, just beyond which billboard or cornfield, etc. Give the nature of the wreck and the number of people involved, but don't fool around with such declamations as, "Oh, it's just terrible!" Leave that sort of thing to the newspaper reporters.

If children are involved and if they are not injured, nominate someone to gather them to one side (or put them in a car) and calm them. If the person you pick for this duty says, "I'm a nurse"—or, better yet, says, "I'm a doctor"—assign the children to someone else and help the nurse/doctor organize the first-aid program. Become a sort of gang-boss to get others to carry out her/his orders.

Meanwhile, loudly tell people not to light cigarettes: gasoline vapors may be floating around. Detail someone to go back down the highway with flares, a flashlight, or even a white cloth and warn approaching traffic. If the wreck victims are out of their cars and on foot, gather them together. They'll huddle together in shock and will feel better by the imposition of some control, by evidence that someone cares and that they are not alone in their tragedy.

If a fire has started, you may have to drag someone out of a burning car—if you can. In the presence of fire, anyone with a fire extinguisher will come running with it, but they may not always know how to use it. Generally, aim for the source of the fire—a broken fuel line, the carburetor, upholstery, etc. Or you may decide to aim at the passengers themselves, if fire is licking around their feet and you can't get them out of the car. That is, use the fire extinguisher to keep the fire at bay until you can pry a door open with a lug wrench. You may commandeer someone's six-pack of beer or soda—an excellent fire suppressant—and slosh it over a burning car seat. Don't pour it on the people though, unless clothing is burning and in that case, shake the container to create the maximum amount of carbon dioxide foam.

We need not review first aid here, though we should note that a nodding acquaintance with first aid might well be part of driver's license examinations. The counter-argument is that poorly trained people cause more damage than they prevent; hence, we should depend on modern communications rather than on the lay person's competence at first aid. The counter-argument has merit and reminds you that you shouldn't move anyone unless you absolutely must, lest your joggling sever a spinal cord or puncture lungs with broken ribs.

Last, if a distraught woman keeps crying, "Where's my baby?" and no baby can be seen, start searching. The baby may be under the front seat or may be a toddler (or even a 10-year-old) who has wandered off in a daze. Well-swaddled babies have been found calmly sucking their thumbs a hundred feet from a wreck, and toddlers have been found wandering in roadside fields. Accordingly, even if you don't see a baby, credit the mother's cry and look.

If the "baby" turns out to be a Pekinese, tell her to shut up.

REFLECTIONS

Our examination of owning and operating automobiles has concluded not with the pleasures but the perils of driving. While the perils are real, they do not define the position of the automobile in the cosmic perspective.

Rather than peril, the proper question is what the automobile *is, has been,* or *may be,* and whether those things have been good or not. To answer, the automobile has been *freedom,* more than anything else, and so it will continue to be (unless, or until, the Luddites prevail). Freedom has never come cheap and the freedom made possible by the automobile has certainly imposed its cost in scrap iron and carnage. However, only freedom presents a challenge worthy of the human spirit. Agreed, freedom may be the freedom to live in a tract house, but it is also the freedom to escape.

In 1350, following the decimation of the laboring classes by plague and pestilence, various nobles appealed to Edward III to correct the "insolence" of servants who took advantage of their reduced numbers to demand higher wages. The good King, of course, innocent of economics, imposed wage controls. The so-called insolence of the servant class persisted, though, so under the guise of laws to prevent the unemployed from moving to wealthier parishes, thus to enjoy higher levels of Restoration "welfare," Charles II instituted "poor laws" that effectively prevented unemployed or poorly paid laborers from seeking work, or better-paid work, in another parish. A laborer had no freedom to move and, thus, no choice but to accept whatever wage was offered in his own parish. The implications of such a policy can be pursued in several directions, one of which was aptly noted by Adam Smith in *The Wealth of Nations* (1776):

> Slaves...are very seldom inventive; and all the most important improvements, either in machinery, or in the arrangement and distri-

bution of work, which facilitate and abridge labour, have been the discoveries of freemen.

The American colonies and colonists spread beyond easy reach of the King's bureaucracy, and the frontier offered an escape where even the bureaucracy could exercise itself. Thus, the United States has always been a place of freedom, particularly freedom of motion. The folk songs the colonists brought from England involved unrequited loves, often between serf and noble; the songs the colonists and their descendants wrote for themselves involved "long, lonesome roads," "leaving on a midnight train," and similar themes of freedom of motion, and a wanderer who returned via the "backroads" of memory did so by choice.

Henry Ford did not invent the automobile. He did not even invent the assembly line. Henry Ford's great success arose from selling the most freedom at the cheapest price. So Isotta-Fraschini could sell a custom-coachwork brougham for $8000 in 1927; in the same year, Henry Ford sold Model T Fords for $380. The American patrician certainly went faster—the $9000 1928 Cunningham would go 100 mph to the Model T's 45 mph—but the significant fact is that the plebian got to go at all. Henry Ford's contribution to civilization was to provide emancipation from age-old constraints of space so the notion of freedom inherent in the American ethos could be expressed.

Ford's fame as a commercial, enterpreneurial genius often obscures his (and our) debt to the cut-and-try scientists of the previous two centuries, the experimenters who wrought without textbooks of physics, machinist's tools, or even pocket calculators to develop the elements of the modern automobile—Christiaan Huygens trying gunpowder as a fuel in 1673; Samuel Morey, of New Hampshire, devising an engine and carburetor in 1829; Nicolaus Otto harmonizing the impulses of a four-cycle engine in 1876; Karl Benz "inventing" the automobile in 1886 and going into production with his dictum, *Der beste oder nichts*—"The best or nothing"—and many, many more who literally made up the sciences of metallurgy, thermodynamics, and electricity as they went along.

Here lies a circular (or spiral?) teleology: people free to create, creating the means for other people to exercise freedom. Agreed, people use that freedom to regiment themselves into freeway ranks and to create the world Nahum (2:4) predicted where:

The chariots shall rage in the streets, they shall justle one against another in the broad ways...they shall run like the lightnings.

Nahum, obviously, did not know half the truth of his own prophecy—but now we are back to carnage and peril again.

We could, of course, reduce our peril by reducing the freedom to own a car. The Europeans, more by habit than intention, followed this policy for the first fifty years, using price as a means of restricting car ownership to properly deserving aristocrats, but Henry Ford ruined that approach over here. We could, of course, seek more and more impositions on the use of cars, as latter-day disciples of Edward III and Charles II have attempted with the 55-mph speed limit, but for their efforts we have the same (or more) carnage but with less freedom, and the free people have, sensibly, ignored such impositions as much as radar detectors will allow.

We cannot seem to escape the fact that the freedom to drive entails risk of carnage. Security, then, lies not in annihilating risk by annihilating freedom, but in reducing risk and fear by knowledge and understanding. Hence, this book: what we understand, we do well, and what we do well, we do with fewer risks.

PART IV

How It Works

ENGINE

Engine: from the Latin *ingenium*, or the product of a clever mind; apostrophically, *gin*, as in Omar Khayyam's "...who didst with pitfall and with gin / Beset the road I was to wander in."

By now, we have driven a car all over the place and under all circumstances, so we may as well find out what's been happening under the hood and under the floorboards to make it all possible.

Let us approach the matter, though, as from the very beginning: open the car door—but watch out that the upper corner doesn't hit you in the eye and that the lower corner doesn't hit you in the shins. Some car doors seem deliberately designed to get you that way.

Sit down in the car. Now, put your left foot in the place where it will spend its idle time. Is it comfortable? If not, adjust the seat. Now, try the right foot on the brake and gas pedal in turn. Can you move from one to the other quickly? Does the motion require conscious thought, or is it automatic? If not automatic, try to find a position for the seat that gives you the best motion possible.

Next, adjust the rearview mirror. We went over this before (pages 251–52), so just a reminder that the inside mirror should show you what's *behind* the car, while the outside mirror should show you what's *beside* the car.

As soon as you shove the key into the ignition switch, you're going to set off some buzzers and flashing lights that are there to remind you to fasten your seat belt. To avoid these reminders, fasten the seat belt first. Yes, it is a bother, especially in hot weather or when you're wearing a freshly pressed suit, but do it anyway. The seat belt is a nuisance, just as a smallpox vaccination is a nuisance, but the two serve the same purpose. You might get by without it, but remember that most accidents happen at speeds below 30 miles per hour and within 25 miles of home. The seat belt is the cheapest insurance you can buy.

Seat belt fastened, turn the key to the first notch. This usually brings on more lights. Some cars will wink a light to tell you that you haven't closed the door; on some, a recorded voice tells you. Most cars, though, have only a standardized set of lights to report on various engine functions. The usual two are the oil-pressure warning light and the alternator (battery) -charging light. As soon as you start the car, the engine will build up oil pressure in its system and the alternator will begin charging the battery, and these lights will go out.

On virtually all cars, the first click of the key unlocks the steering wheel so you can turn it. On many Saab and Porsche

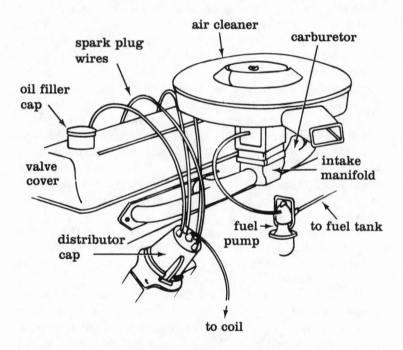

Basic external engine components

Whether the engine mounts fore-and-aft or athwartships, its external components will be arranged much like this. The air cleaner dominates the scene when you raise the hood, with the carburetor under it and spark plugs typically on the other side.

models, the key locks the gear lever instead of the steering wheel. The first click may also allow the accessories to work. It may energize the *ignition system*, though many cars reserve this for the second click.

You will know the ignition system is energized when those lights in the instrument cluster go on or when the pointers of gauges move. The fuel-gauge pointer will move to its proper position to tell you how much gas you have in the tank.

You are now ready to provoke great events. Remember the Michelangelo painting of "The Creation of Adam," the one that shows God touching Adam's hand to pass to him the spark of life? You are now involved in enterprise of that sort. You are ready to unleash energies that have puzzled the brains of the world's best scientists.

First, as the owner's manual says, depress the gas pedal one time and let it back up. On an older car, you may depress it two times, if need be. Likewise, in wintertime, you may depress it twice if you find that the car starts quicker that way. Now, move your foot completely aside and leave it there. That is, stay completely away from the gas pedal while applying the starter.

Now, what have you done? We are assuming a "cold" car that sat in the garage overnight. When you pushed the gas pedal down, you released a catch on the *carburetor*. The carburetor itself is a sort of atomizer. When the engine sucks in air, the air flows through the carburetor and picks up a fine mist of gasoline. When you released the catch, the *choke* closed. This choke is a little trap door in the top of the carburetor. When it is closed, the carburetor cannot suck in as much air as usual and this makes the air-to-gasoline ratio richer. When the car is cold, it likes that.

The other thing you did when you pushed the gas pedal was to pump the *accelerator pump*, a little pump inside the carburetor that works like those that people spray houseplants with. It squirts a measure of raw, liquid gasoline down the mouth of the engine, providing the engine a very rich mixture for starting.

Of course, if you have an *electronic fuel-injection* (EFI) system, such as that on the Volkswagen Rabbit, your owner's manual may tell you not to push the gas pedal for cold starting. On older cars with mechanical fuel injection, such as the earlier Mercedes-Benz SE models and some Alfa-Romeos, pushing the gas pedal simply allows assorted linkages to get into position for starting.

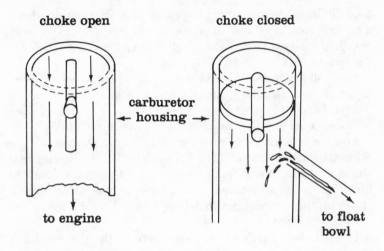

choke open   choke closed

carburetor
← housing →

to engine   to float
bowl

Choke action

The choke is a little trap door in the top of the carburetor. When open, it permits an unimpeded flow of air. When it is closed, the restricted air flow creates a vacuum, and the vacuum sucks gasoline from the float bowl. Once the engine is running, the air flow is fast enough to sustain continuous fuel flow.

A fuel-injection system doesn't squirt any gas until you apply the starter.

Diesel cars, e.g., the Mercedes-Benz, Oldsmobile, Peugeot, Datsun, Isuzu, etc. diesels, have fuel injection, too, so pressing the pedal on them doesn't pump anything, either. Also, before you even push the accelerator pedal (the "diesel pedal"?) on a diesel, you have to pull a little knob or push a button to let the *glow plugs* heat up. Glow plugs are like that electrical device that gets the fire started in an oil furnace. More on diesel, later.

Other exceptions are the Stromberg "constant depression" (CD) carburetors that are used on some foreign cars (such as the Saab), and the SU (Skinner Union) carburetors used on the old MG and Triumph roadsters. These carburetors don't have accelerator pumps, so don't bother pumping on them.

Last, on some older cars, you work the choke by hand. You pull a knob on the dashboard: a long way if the engine is cold, none if it is hot.

Back to mission control: key turned to the second notch, indicator lights glowing, and gas pedal pushed once. Now, turn the key to the next notch. You will hear great busy-ness under the hood. A "grunch-clunk" followed by a "whirrr and grrrind," then the full-throated rumble of your Eclat Eight bursting into life.

Release the key. It will spring back from the starting notch. Do this quickly, so the starter doesn't try to turn an engine that is already running, for that sort of thing ruins starters.

Now, when you turned the key and brought on all those lights, you did nothing particularly magical. You did, however, allow electricity to flow from the battery to the *ignition system*; that is, to the *coil*, thence to the *distributor*, and thence to the *spark plugs*.

When you turned the key to the second position to activate the starter, you let electricity flow to the *starter solenoid*. Technically, a solenoid is a device that converts electricity into motion. Think of it as just a big switch that you work with electricity instead of by hand. When your solenoid got into motion, it did two things: First it pushed a little gear (*pinion*) on the end of the starter motor into mesh with a big gear (*ring*) on the *flywheel* of the engine; second, the solenoid closed a switch that allowed battery power to go to the starter.

The starter is just an electric motor. When it got the power, it began to turn and its pinion gear turned the engine flywheel round and round.

The flywheel is bolted to the *crankshaft* and the crankshaft is connected to the other moving parts of the engine.

Inside, the engine has a series of *pistons* that move up and down in *cylinders*. These pistons and cylinders resemble the plunger (piston) and barrel (cylinder) of a bicycle pump, and they connect, via *connecting rods*, to the crankshaft, which itself resembles the pedal crank on a bicycle; that is, the crankshaft makes one piston go up as another comes down, and vice versa.

To help them seal off pressure, the pistons are surrounded by piston rings. When piston rings wear out, the pistons can't hold pressure, so the engine gets hard to start and does not develop full power.

Now, at the top of the cylinder is a pair of *valves* that resemble the entrance doors at an airport. That is, one is "enter" and the other is "exit." The "enter" valve lets air and fuel into the cyl-

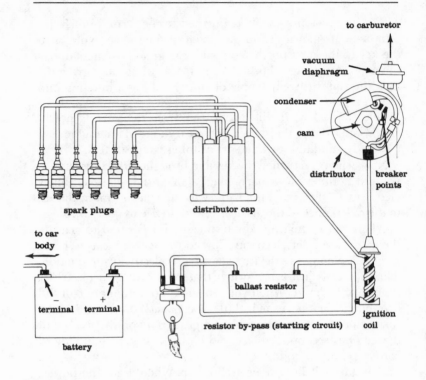

to carburetor

vacuum diaphragm

condenser

cam

distributor

breaker points

spark plugs

distributor cap

to car body

terminal — terminal +

battery

ballast resistor

resistor by-pass (starting circuit)

ignition coil

Conventional ignition system

Here are the basic elements of the conventional, breaker-point ignition system that served the past 75 years. Don't take the wiring here too literally, for some of the wires—e.g., the ones that involve the starter—aren't shown. Also, the wiring cannot indicate that the coil works more by inductance than by conductance.

The important detail here is the manner whereby the cam opens the breaker points as it turns. The rotor, not shown, sits on top of the cam. As it rotates in the distributor cap, the rotor conducts a spark to a spark plug each time the cam opens the points. The vacuum diaphragm regulates spark timing according to engine speed.

inder. After the fuel burns and the pressure it creates has pushed the piston down (and turned the crankshaft, to make the wheels go 'round), the "exit" valve opens and the burned gasses go out. The proper words for these valves are *intake* and *exhaust*.

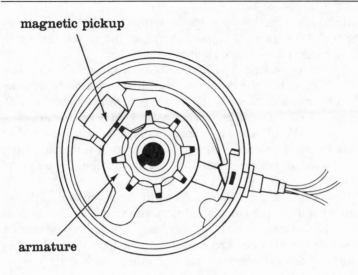

magnetic pickup

armature

Distributor for electronic ignition

The first improvement in ignition systems in about fifty years came in the early 1970s when Chrysler Corporation pioneered electronic ignition. In the system illustrated, the armature and magnetic pickup take the place of the breaker points. The "points" break, and the spark jumps each time a tip of the armature passes the middle of the magnetic pickup.

The airport has security guards to make sure nobody comes in the "exit" door or goes out the "enter" door. To do this same job, the engine has a *camshaft* that is connected to the crankshaft by gears or by a chain similar to a bicycle chain. Springs hold the valves closed, and *cams* on the camshaft push the valves down to open them and let them up so springs can close them again. These valves must open and close at the right moment relative to the up-and-down motion of the pistons. Since the pistons are connected to the crankshaft, and since the crankshaft also drives the camshaft, all the pieces work together.

The coil in the ignition system is, technically, a transformer. It takes the 12 *volts* of power from the car battery and transforms it to around 25,000 volts so the electricity will jump across a gap in the spark plug. When the spark jumps across the gap, it ignites the fuel. Like the opening and closing of the valves, this spark must jump at exactly the right time.

A word *en passant*: The 25,000 volts in the spark plug wire won't kill you, because by the time the coil transforms the original 12 volts into 25,000 volts, the *amperage* is so low that it will do no more than give you an alarming shock. However, spark plug voltage could kill a sickly infant, perhaps, or someone with a weak heart. If you see a baby messing around with spark plug wires while an engine is running, give it something else to play with.

From the coil, the 25,000 volts go to the distributor, a device somewhat like a person at an airport who stands there and says, "Gate 17 this way, gate 21 that way," etc. The 25,000 volts comes from the coil via one wire, and the distributor routes the electricity to each cylinder in turn by a wire to each spark plug— "There a spark, you go to number one; here a spark, you go to number three," etc.

The spark jumps the gap in the spark plug after the piston has first moved down to suck in air and fuel and then moved back up to squeeze (compress) the air-fuel mixture. Now, what tells the distributor when to send the sparks? Well, that same security guard, the camshaft. The camshaft turns the distributor via gear teeth, and since the crankshaft (which is connected to pistons) is also connected to the camshaft, the pistons, valves, and sparks are all coordinated.

We must digress briefly for an exception, namely, the *rotary* engine used in the Mazda RX-7 (and in the old NSU Ro80 and a few outboard motors of about 15 years ago). A rotary engine does not have pistons and cylinders. It has a triangle-shaped thing that spins around inside an irregular chamber shaped as an epitrochoid. As it spins, the apexes of the triangle trap air and fuel in a little space, just as a piston contains air and fuel in a cylinder. When the fuel burns and creates pressure, the pressure pushes the triangle thing around. To a degree, the action somewhat resembles a stream of water turning a water wheel.

Of the dozens of experimental rotary engines built right after World War II, the one designed by Felix Wankel, an Austrian, made it into cars. Rotary engines got a lot of good press about a dozen years ago because they were smooth and quiet. Then, around 1972, they flunked all the emission tests and almost disappeared completely. The Mazda people, in Japan, managed to sanitize the engine and now use it in their sporty RX-7 model. A rotary engine is an interesting alternative to a piston engine, but it is not better in every way. If it were, every car manufacturer would be using it.

All of this engine machinery has but one purpose; to wit, to burn fuel and convert heat energy into the rotary motion of the crankshaft. The fuel burns and produces heat, and the heat causes the molecules in the air-fuel mixture to spread out, to get as far away from each other as possible. As the molecules squeeze outward in every direction, the piston is the only thing that can move, so the pressure pushes the piston down—just as a cyclist's foot pushes a pedal down. After the air-fuel mixture has burned, the camshaft opens the exhaust valve, and the combustion residues—the "ashes," so to speak—go out the exhaust valve and down the exhaust pipe.

The fuel started out in the fuel tank, got sucked up by the *fuel pump* (which is also worked by the camshaft), and was dumped into the carburetor. The carburetor has a *float* and a *needle* valve, which work like the float valve in a flush toilet. Just as the float and valve in the flush toilet shut off the water when the toilet tank is full, the carburetor float and needle valve shut off the gasoline when the *float chamber* is full. Tiny passages, or *jets*, let the liquid gasoline flow from the float chamber into the stream of air that is sucked in when the piston moves down as the intake valve is open. This mixes the air and fuel in the proper proportions.

A fuel-injection system, whether gasoline or diesel, has no carburetor. In a diesel system, the fuel pump delivers fuel to a *fuel-injection pump*, and the injection pump delivers fuel to the *fuel injectors*—one per cylinder—in turn. A gasoline fuel-injection system does not require an extra injection pump because it doesn't work at pressures as high as a diesel system, so in a modern gasoline system the fuel pump delivers gasoline directly to the injectors. The fuel injectors, one at each cylinder, amount to little squirt guns, which, as with the sparks and the valves, give each cylinder a squirt of gasoline or diesel fuel at the right time. In the old days, a camshaft within the fuel-injection pump set off the squirts, but modern electronic fuel-injection (EFI) systems use electronically controlled solenoids to do the squirting (diesels still have injection pumps).

The latest system for mixing air with gasoline is *throttle body injection* (TBI), a sort of cross between a carburetor and a fuel-injection system. TBI uses only one injector, which gives a squirt of gas each time an intake valve opens.

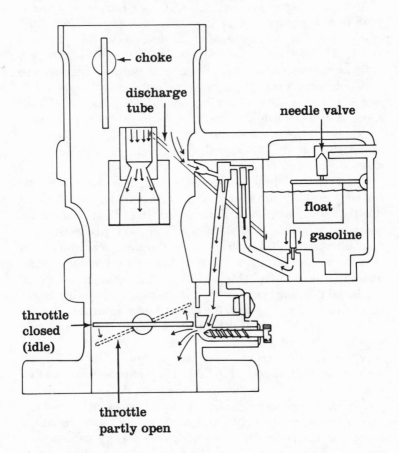

Carburetor

This rather resembles a maze for training rats, which is what a modern carburetor is like inside. Note the convoluted path of the air and fuel at idle speed, as in this carburetor. At cruising speed, most of the fuel will come through the discharge tube.

A cold engine wants less air, so the choke closes when the engine is cold and opens as it warms up. After a cold engine has run about half a minute, you give the gas pedal a little tap. This eases up on the linkage and lets the choke off a little, and the engine slows down.

Review all the commotion going on inside the engine: a series of shafts spinning, pistons and valves going up and down, the coil pumping up the juice, the distributor sending sparks to the plugs, the sparks jumping across the gaps in the plugs and setting off fires, and air rushing through the carburetor at hurricane speed, drawing gasoline with it to supply the fires that generate the heat that creates the pressure that moves the pistons that, ultimately, turn the wheels.

All this you set off with no more than the turn of a key.

ENGINE WORDS

Before proceeding, we ought to pause to define some terms. The terms will matter little to our discussion of engines. However, you will hear them bandied about on the showroom floor, so best we note them.

To illustrate these terms, consider the 1983 edition of Ford's Mustang coupe: Ford considered the weight of the car and the performance that would suit most buyers, and chose a four-cylinder engine as the *standard engine* for the car. However, for people who want more power, Ford will build a Mustang with a six-cylinder, a small V-8, or a large V-8 engine. All four engines are *stock* engines, in the respect that they come right off the shelf, so to speak; but while all are stock, only the four-cylinder is standard with the Mustangs. The larger engines are *optional*.

A stock engine comes right off a manufacturer's production line and hasn't been modified in any way, e.g., for racing. A standard engine is the engine the manufacturer reckons will suit most buyers of a particular car. Most domestic manufacturers offer several engine choices, but foreign manufacturers rarely offer optional engines; if you want a bigger engine, you buy a bigger car. However, foreign manufacturers do offer *turbocharged* engines as an extra-power option. Of turbochargers, more anon.

Our survey so far has treated all engines as if they were alike. Obviously, all engines are not alike, so we must consider whether the differences among them matter and, if they do, to whom.

The question of whether an engine is "good" or "bad" hardly needs to be asked. We have no "bad" engines today. Back before 1950, Fords had weak piston rings, Chevrolets had weak connecting-rod bearings, and Plymouths were hard to start in damp weather. No matter which one you bought, you knew from gossip, etc., where the weaknesses lay. Nowadays, these differences have disappeared. However, the reputations have been handed down from thirty years ago, and you still hear Fords criticized as "oil burners" when they are not (since 1949) and Chevrolets condemned as having "weak rod bearings" despite the fact that Chevrolet fixed the bearings in 1953.

We have seen two "bad" engines in recent years, one being the aluminum-block engine in the Chevrolet Vega. Generally, when you cast an aluminum-block engine, you must put ferrous-metal liners in the cylinders. General Motors tried to get by without the cylinder liners, the aluminum cylinders wore badly, and the Vegas became oil guzzlers in short order. Eventually, General Motors put one of their good, cast-iron engines in the Vega (then promptly discontinued it).

Note, in passing, that metals technology has advanced to the point that Mercedes-Benz now has an aluminum-block engine without ferrous cylinder liners; generally, if Mercedes-Benz says they can do it, you may believe them.

The other "bad" engine of recent years was the Cadillac V-8-6-4 engine that ran on four, six, or eight cylinders as conditions required. The first engines of this type gave trouble, and General Motors effectively pulled the engine off the market when the first lawsuits hit, reworked the system, and brought it back in improved form. Eventually, they discontinued it.

Note what is said here: We have no bad engines *that we know of* right now. Unfortunately, an engine can prove bad once it is in use awhile. For example, burned valves, wherein the perimeter of the exhaust valve erodes due to heat, was a common failing thirty years ago. By 1970, engines had so improved that burned valves were virtually unheard of except in unusual circumstances, such as when a car overheated badly. However, pollution control devices increased the temperatures inside the engine, and in 1973 burned valves began turning up with embarrassing frequency in the big V-8s, which had thitherto been immune to such problems. To be sure, the problems didn't turn up for about 50,000 miles, so the owners got considerable use before the repair bill; and to be sure, not every engine suffered burned valves. Yet, here was an inherent weakness that took a long time to show up.

Changes since 1973 have, once again, virtually eliminated burned valves. However, any of the new engines that have appeared in the past year or two could exhibit a flaw after a few more years. For example, the Volkswagen Rabbits of 1975–76 were good. Then VW modified the valve seals in a way that was not good. Thus, many of the next Rabbits—the '77, '78, and '79 models—suffered severe oil consumption after about 20,000 miles. VW finally did a recall on the bad seals (and used better seals on subsequent models). In both of these cases, burned valves and Rabbit seals, an inherent flaw did not show up until the engine was in use awhile.

The inherent goodness or badness of an engine is a raw matter of how much money is spent building it. In Europe, people drive up to 140 mph, so the Europeans build engines for sustained speeds of that sort. For example, the original, German-made Volkswagen Rabbit owner's manual gave the maximum cruising speed as 100 mph.

By contrast, domestic car manufacturers build engines to cruise about 70 mph fairly continuously and take great comfort from the fact that few of their engines are ever driven that fast for any length of time (now you see who benefits from the 55-mph speed limit).

However, the question of absolute quality is academic for most people. Domestic engines normally last for 100,000 miles and more of domestic-style driving and at the national average of about 10,000 miles per year, that's about 10 years' worth, by which time the rest of the car has crumbled into rust.

One qualification: Big engines don't work as hard as small engines and those domestic engines that go over 100,000 miles are mostly the bigger engines. Smaller engines, such as those in Toyotas, Datsuns, VW Rabbits, Chevettes, etc., are probably good for about 70,000 miles, by which time they will be loose in the bearings and worn in the piston rings (though they may well go much farther with optimum care). That's still about seven years of driving. If the rest of the car is still good after seven years, a $1200 to $2000 overhaul (at current prices) will give the engine another 50,000 miles, and a more expensive overhaul will give it more.

Another qualification: How long an engine lasts is a matter of how hard it works during its lifetime, and few car engines work hard. But if you keep a car so heavily loaded that you must drive with the gas pedal on the floor or near the floor all the time, your engine will wear out quicker, especially if it's a domestic engine rather than a European one.

Another relevant thought: The engine itself rarely gives problems; problems come mostly from the ancillary stuff—starter, water pump, etc.—and nowadays that generally means the carburetion and ignition systems, both of which are burdened with pollution-control devices.

To deny the importance of differences among engines is not to deny that differences exist, and when you go car buying or when the in-house car freak corners you at work, you'll hear a lot of numbers and terms thrown about. To pursue those numbers, the most-familiar one is for engine *displacement*, which refers to how much air the pistons suck in (i.e., displace) as they move up and down. For example, think of a piston at the top of its cycle, so that it's right up near the valves. For all practical purposes (or, at least, for purposes of definition), the piston has no space above it. Now, let the piston go to the very bottom of its up-and-down cycle, and measure the volume of the space that is above the piston. That volume is the displacement of that one cyclinder; the displacement for the whole engine will be the displacement of one cylinder multiplied by the number of cylinders. For example, General Motors' 305-cubic-inch V-8 engine has eight cylinders of 38 cubic inches each. When GM needed a smaller engine, they just whacked two cylinders off the 305 V-8, and had themselves a nice 229-cubic-inch V-6 ($38 \times 6 = 229$ cubic inches).

The diameter of the pistons is defined by the *bore* of the cylinder. The 305 V-8, for example, has pistons 3.736 inches in diameter. The distance the pistons move up and down is their *stroke*. In the case of the 305, the stroke is 3.480 inches. The next time GM wanted a smaller engine, they just redesigned the engine block of the 305 V-8 to reduce the bore to an even 3.500 inches, and this gave them the 267-cubic-inch V-8 but with the same 3.480-inch stroke.

We hedged a few lines above, because at the top of its stroke, the piston will have some space above it. Call the volume of that space equal to one. Now, bring the piston all the way down and measure the space: call it eight. Thus, the engine we're measuring has a *compression ratio* of 8:1; that is, it squeezes the fuel-air mixture that would normally occupy eight spaces down into one space.

Displacement is usually stated in cubic inches, cubic centimeters, or liters (the metric uses being a foreign influence) and is the measure of whether an engine is "big" or "little." About the biggest stock engine of recent years was the 500-cubic-inch Cadillac engine of a few years ago and one of the smallest was the Fiat 850-cubic-centimeter (about 52 cubic inches) engine of the late 1960s. Nowadays, the biggest stock engines run around 350 cubic inches and the smallest around 75 cubic inches.

A small engine working hard is more fuel-efficient than a big engine that is loafing. However, a car with a small engine will not accelerate as fast and will slow down more on hills and when carrying several people. Thus, use and preference should dictate the size of the engine. When engine options are available, a sound policy is to choose an engine one size bigger than the standard engine. If the standard engine proves too sluggish, you cannot change it conveniently. However, a larger engine will impose no significant loss of fuel economy and will give you the advantage of more power when you want it. You will pay slightly more money, but if you bargain hard enough, it needn't be much.

Note, in passing, that the size of the engine is only marginally important to fuel economy. The most important factor in gas mileage is the weight of the car.

The other common numbers that refer to engines indicate the number of cylinders and pistons. For most purposes, the number of cylinders also defines the "size" of the engine, but not always. For example, Ford's 300-cubic-inch six-cylinder engine is bigger in displacement than Mercedes-Benz's 234-cubic-inch V-8 of eight cylinders.

If the cylinders are in a row, one after the other, the engine is an *in-line engine*. Virtually all four-cylinder engines are in-line. If the engine has two rows that connect at the bottom, it is a V-type engine, as in V-6 and V-8. If the cylinders point away from each other, the engine is a *flat*, *opposed*, or *horizontal* engine. The old Volkswagen Beetle made this type of engine familiar, and it remains today in the Subaru and the Porsche 911.

An in-line engine is cheap to make and fairly easy to repair. A V-type engine costs more to make but gets a lot of power into a small space. Technically, an opposed engine has the least vibration, but the advantage may be too slight to notice. All types have been used in dozens of different cars, and no one type must apologize for its record.

Recall the security guard who tells the valves when to open? If the security guard, the camshaft, is up on top, the engine is an *overhead-camshaft* (OHC) engine; and if it has two camshafts up there, it is a *double-overhead-camshaft* (DOHC) engine. Conventional engines have the camshaft down in the middle. OHC and DOHC engines are very peppy and capable of high speeds. However, they are expensive to build and often impose tune-up difficulties in the matter of valve adjustments. Technically, they are superior to the conventional system; but in practice, a conventional engine works very well, and you are not missing much if you don't have an OHC engine.

A much more significant difference is between a carbureted engine and a fuel-injected (FI) engine, which nowadays means *electronic fuel injection* (EFI). Fuel injection is better in every respect. In practice, the difference is that fuel-injection systems are more compatible with pollution control. That is, FI/EFI systems do not need as many extra little control devices for pollution control and the chances of trouble from a faulty pollution-control device are reduced to almost nothing. FI/EFI does cost a bit more, but is well worth it.

These are the terms/concepts that come up most often in car

talk. Others also occur, such as *cross-flow cylinder head, hemispherical combustion chamber*, but none of these features is absolutely better than any other. If any one were superior in every respect, every car would have it, just as every car has round wheels. Don't let such phrases influence your choice of car—unless you are a true car freak and these things mean something to you. When the salesman says, "Now, this car has our special overhead camshaft," in a tone that implies you should buy the car for that reason alone, just raise an eyebrow and say, "Ah, yes—and is that how they did it on the old 1937 Talbot-Lago?" That will turn the salesman's attention to the upholstery.

If the salesman casually says, "No, the '37 Talbot-Lago had conventional overhead valves," then you know you are in the presence of a maestro—one who probably deserves listening to.

HORSEPOWER

The current concern for fuel economy has reduced the public consciousness of *horsepower* (hp). Manufacturers who were bragging about 300-hp engines a few years back don't want to admit that they are now building cars with only 100 hp, so the whole topic is a bit muted.

Horsepower is one standard way of defining the ability of an engine to do work. The concept arose around 1780 when James Watt, of steam engine fame, was trying to sell steam engines to coal-mine operators. In those days, miners used horses to hoist coal or ore up a shaft and Watt was constantly asked, "How many horses will your engine replace?" To answer the question, Watt literally invented the concept of horsepower, defining one horsepower as the ability to lift 33,000 pounds one foot in one minute.

The notion of comparing a horse and an engine never worked well, and it provoked many a guffaw amongst the bib-overall set back around 1905, when a lone mule would be called upon to extract an 18-hp Jeffrey Rambler from a mudhole (given its weight, you needed a four-horse team to get a 30-hp Locomobile out of the same mudhole). Today, engineers are discarding the notion of hp and using the Watt as a measure of work.

The performance of a car—acceleration, top speed, hill-climbing and load-carrying ability—is a raw matter of how much hp is available to move how much weight. A ratio of 40 pounds per hp implies sedate performance, 24 pounds per hp is brisk enough for most people, and 15 pounds per hp indicates a real tire-screecher.

When I read road tests in car magazines, I pay more attention to acceleration times than to hp, and like to see acceleration times of 0 to 60 mph in 12 to 15 seconds. If less than 12, the car has more power than I need; if more than 15, the car may be a bit sluggish—but so what? The Volkswagen Beetle of the early 1960s had a 0–60 time of 23 seconds—and how many people were bothered by it? In those days, the only car that *would not* beat a Beetle from 0 to 60 was a Mercedes-Benz 190 D diesel, which needed 30 seconds to poke its way up to 60 mph—but no 190 D went unsold because of its leisurely acceleration. In sum, choose to be a trifle overpowered rather than underpowered, but don't worry about hp numbers if they don't mean much to you.

To give some identity to some current numbers, a 74-hp VW Rabbit weighs 1980 pounds (26.75 lbs/hp); a Cadillac Eldorado diesel uses 105 hp to move its 4100 pounds (39 lbs/hp); a Mercedes-Benz 240 D diesel, though, has only 67 hp for its 3250 pounds (48.6 lbs/hp). The Chrysler Imperial, 4035 pounds and 140 hp (28.8 lbs/hp), seems to enjoy a distinct advantage over the Lincoln Continental Mark VI, 4050 pounds and 134 hp (30 lbs/hp). However, the current hp numbers for the larger gasoline engines are misleading because they are a sort of falsehood-by-understatement.

As noted earlier, the manufacturers hardly speak of horsepower at all anymore, and they rarely put hp numbers in their advertisements. They have three reasons for this policy: First, they don't want to be sued by an aggrieved buyer if an engine fails to deliver exactly its advertised hp; second, they don't want to appear to encourage wasteful use of fuel; and, third, they are "fudging" numbers with the Environmental Protection Agency (EPA).

A high hp rating puts an engine at a disadvantage in EPA certification procedures. To minimize the disadvantage, the manufacturers "de-rate" their engines by simply taking the hp rating at a lower speed. Thus, in 1969, Ford rated its 302-cubic-inch V-8 as 210 hp at 4400 turns, or revolutions per minute, or *rpm*. Now, they rate the same engine as 134 hp at 3600 rpm. However, if run at 4400 rpm, the current Ford 302 will develop close to the same 210 hp of years ago. Thus, with the larger domestic engines, you buy more hp than the manufacturer actually claims.

DIESEL

European cynics regard Americans as an innocent, childlike lot who will endorse any idea—even an old idea—if it seems new. The diesel car business exemplifies what the cynics mean. Peugeot built diesel cars as early as 1922, Mercedes-Benz put them into production in 1936, and Peugeot and Mercedes-Benz diesels became the world's taxicabs virtually everywhere but in North America. In America, though, few people wanted diesel cars until the shock of the "fuel crisis" of 1973. General Motors seized the initiative, and the Oldsmobile diesels appeared in 1977 (1978 model year) to the accompaniment of advertising that suggested that no one had ever thought of a diesel car before. Olds planned a first-year production run of 110,000 diesel cars and found they could have sold three times as many. General Motors announced more diesels to come, and Cadillac, the fundamental symbol of *nouveau riche* plutocracy, issued a diesel. "Surely," everyone said as diesel buyers lined up, "the diesel millennium is at hand—our salvation from the fuel crisis."

Like the millennia announced by broadcast evangelists, the diesel millennium somewhat resembles the Hadacol tonic business of thirty-odd years ago: Once people got a taste of the stuff, they found the claims a bit overstated.

A diesel car costs more—usually about $1000 more. Fifteen years ago, when gasoline cost 30 cents per gallon and diesel fuel cost 15 to 20 cents, fuel savings were claimed as the reason for buying a diesel. The same claim is made now when gasoline and diesel cost the same. In fact, the arithmetic wouldn't support the claim then and it won't support it now. The much-touted economy of diesels is true in terms of miles per gallon but, in the long run, not in miles per dollar.

Note that we are not condemning diesels here; rather, we are denying the exaggerated claims made for them. Mechanically, diesels are good pieces of machinery. They work like gasoline engines, the main difference being that diesels squeeze the air they suck in very tightly before they get any fuel. That is, they have a very high compression ratio. So high, in fact, that the heat they generate by compression sets the fuel on fire (note how the bicycle pump gets hot as you pump up a tire), and they don't need an electrical ignition system with spark plugs. However, if you burn gasoline in a *compression ignition* engine (as opposed to *spark ignition*), the gasoline explodes instantaneously and the explosions can destroy the engine. Therefore, if you want to ignite the fuel with the heat from compression, you have to use a slow-burning fuel, and that means diesel fuel, which is effectively the same thing as #2 household heating oil.

To squeeze tightly before igniting the fuel also causes the fire to release more heat energy when it burns. Thus, a high-compression engine gets more heat and, consequently, more work out of a gallon of fuel. This was Rudolph Diesel's purpose when he developed the engine that bears his name in 1897—to build a highly fuel-efficient engine. Also, the oily fuel necessary to control combustion in a high-compression engine has more heat energy per gallon than gasoline. These two factors—high compression before combustion and a high-energy fuel—give a diesel car its fuel mileage.

That fuel economy must be balanced against the negatives. An oily fuel does not vaporize readily when going through a carburetor, so the fuel must be squirted directly into the cylinders against the high compression pressure. This entails an expensive injection system. And, since diesels work at higher pressures, they must be built stronger, which means more-expensive—and heavier—internal components. For example, the 71-hp diesel engine in a Peugeot 505 weighs around 500 pounds, or about as much as the nominally 134-hp, but effectively 200-hp, V-8 gasoline engine in a Ford pickup. As an interesting contrast, the gasoline and diesel engines in the Volkswagen Rabbit weigh close to the same because the Rabbit diesel engine is simply the basic gasoline engine with a different cylinder head. The diesel cognoscenti consider the engine a bit of a lightweight for a diesel, but the engine does not seem to suffer for it, partly because automobile use doesn't tax an engine that much.

Stronger should also mean "long-lived," and truck and marine diesels do outlast automotive gasoline engines by wide margins. However, the differences between automotive diesel engines and automotive gasoline engines are not so striking. So what, if somebody's Mercedes-Benz or Peugeot diesel ran 150,000 miles before needing an overhaul? The world is full of job-lot domestic gasoline engines that have run as far. Alternatively, so what if a diesel might go 500,000 miles (as a truck engine does)? For people who drive 10,000 miles per year, that would be fifty years, and how many people want to drive the same car that long?

Due to peculiarities of their nature, a diesel of a given physical size develops about half the horsepower of a gasoline engine of the same physical size. Despite the burdens of pollution control, the General Motors 350-cubic-inch V-8 develops as much as 230 hp as a gasoline engine, but only 125 hp as a diesel. This characteristically reduced horsepower of a diesel means reduced performance—slower acceleration, loss of speed going uphill, and less power to tow a trailer. For example, the gasoline-powered Volkswagen Rabbit accelerates from 0 to 60 mph in about 13 seconds, while the diesel Rabbit takes about 20 seconds.

Also, because of their combustion characteristics, diesels are noisy. The noise can be subdued, but the fact remains that diesels are noisy and no one, not even Mercedes-Benz, can deny it (although M-B is very good in this respect). Automotive writers try to dodge the noise issue by such evasions as "Such-and-such a car is not noisy—for a diesel" or "The noise was not oppressive." Agreed, but some people are more oppressed by noise than others, so study this factor if you are considering a diesel.

Also, diesels stink, just as the kerosene lantern in the mountain cabin stinks. That's the smell you get when sitting behind a diesel at a traffic light. If its windows are open, the smell sometimes comes inside the diesel car, too. Diesel cars smoke, too, but shouldn't. When a diesel smokes continuously, it is getting too much fuel for its air supply and needs its fuel-injection system adjusted.

Under present circumstances, you can't always find a service station with diesel fuel when you want it, and in some states, you must have a special fuel user's permit for a diesel car.

The one single, undeniable advantage diesels can claim is fuel economy. By EPA estimates, the gain is around 30 percent. For example, in city driving, the gasoline-powered Peugeot 505 gets around 20 mpg, the diesel sibling around 27 mpg.

Given the juggling that can be done with numbers in a car-buying deal, the exact extra cost for diesel power is hard to tie down. However, assume an extra $1000 for the diesel option in the Peugeot and assume both gasoline and diesel cost $1.25 per gallon. Assuming 10,000 miles per year, the fuel bill for the gasoline car will be $625. The fuel bill for the diesel will be $463, for an annual saving of $162. So, you need six years to pay the extra cost for the diesel out of fuel savings—and you suffer the reduced performance in the meantime.

The diesel advocates will quickly rejoin that fuel cost is only part of the story, that the diesel owner saves money because diesels don't require periodic tune-ups, this being another egregious falsehood. Agreed, diesel cars don't get regular tune-ups of the fuel-injection system, and that's one reason they smoke when they shouldn't. A diesel injection system ought to be checked at least once a year to assure that its injection timing is right and that each injector is delivering the proper quantity of fuel.

Agreed, though, that diesels don't need spark plugs once or twice per year. However, they do require changes of larger, more-expensive oil filters, and changes or servicing of fuel filters. In addition, the battery in a diesel is more vulnerable to terminal abuse because of cold weather cranking demands, and the cost of the larger diesel car battery will pay for the battery in a gasoline-powered car and leave enough change for several sets of spark plugs.

The "sleeper" in the diesel deal is a detail that no one mentions in the advertisements and that has been sorely neglected by the automotive press; namely, that down around zero degrees and colder, the paraffin wax that is a constituent of diesel fuel settles out and congeals. Once the paraffin congeals, it usually clogs up the fuel filter and the car promptly stops. You can dodge this wintertime problem by switching from #2 diesel fuel to #1 fuel, but not all manufacturers approve of #1 fuel (because it doesn't lubricate the injection pump enough) and even #1 turns to jelly around 20 degrees below zero.

The problem rarely arises when driving around town, partly because the engine radiates sufficient heat to keep the fuel filter warm enough to ensure fuel flow. The problem arises more on the highway when a cold spell degenerates into a total, arctic blizzard. Wind rushing under the car cools the fuel filter to as low as 50 degrees below zero. The fuel turns to jelly and won't flow to the engine. Then, the car stops. No matter about dark of night, snowstorm, lonely road, or sick child—the car stops right there, and it won't go again until you drag it to a garage and warm it up.

Many diesel owners escape this problem by adding about one gallon of gasoline to every ten gallons of diesel fuel during the winter months and this seems to work, even though it is not endorsed by the manufacturers. Other diesel owners install fuel filter heaters or fuel-line heaters, such as trucks use, wherein radiator coolant or electric heating elements warm the fuel.

Before you buy a diesel, ask the dealer how you are supposed to deal with the sub-zero problem of semi-solid fuel. If the car has a built-in fuel heater, demand a strict accounting of its capability. If you are lucky, you won't have the problem. However, one of the saddest sights of the winter is to see rusty, old, dilapidated casualties of a blizzard beside an interstate highway—and, right beside those wretched hulks, the most elegant collection of diesel-powered Oldsmobiles, Cadillacs, Mercedes-Benz "D" models, Peugeots, etc.

TURBOCHARGERS

Another device that gets a lot of plumpery nowadays is the *turbocharger*. Teen-age boys say, "Gee whiz" (or the current equivalent in adolescent patois), when a "turbo" car passes, and advertisements suggest that a turbocharger automatically qualifies a car for a Le Mans race.

This is all nonsense, of course. The facts are much less exciting.

Think of an engine as a stove. If we want more heat out of the stove, we have to make it burn more fuel, but to get it to burn more fuel, we have to give it more air.

To give an engine more air, we just bolt a turbocharger to it. The turbocharger force-feeds the engine with more air than the pistons can suck in by themselves, and this extra air allows the engine to burn more fuel and, thus, to develop more power.

The late 1960s were Detroit's most wasteful time in terms of extravagant uses of body sheet metal. If you raised the hood of a 1969 Pontiac Bonneville, you saw that you could easily put two engines into the space. In that era, if you wanted a bigger engine in a car, you had ample room for it.

Nowadays, fuel economy dictates car design and cars have less useless sheet metal. Look under the hood of a recent Chevrolet Malibu V-6, and you won't find enough extra room to stick your hand in beside the engine.

So, if you want a bigger, more-powerful engine but don't have space for it, you have to make the engine effectively bigger without increasing its physical size. You can do this by force-feeding it more air and enabling it to burn more fuel. Hence, a turbocharger.

A turbocharger consists of two fans, or more precisely, two *turbines*, one an *impeller* and the other a *compressor*. The two are integrated into a unit that connects to the exhaust system and provides a convenient route for air going into the engine. Exhaust gasses drive the impeller, the impeller turns the compressor, and the compressor blows air into the engine.

A turbocharged engine gives you two things. First, the snappier performance of a bigger engine. If you want performance, check out the "turbo" cars. Second, higher price—up to $5000—and higher repair costs if the turbo system fails. Check your pocketbook before deciding how much you value that higher performance. You'll find that you can spend as much as $5000 to add about 30 hp. By contrast, while the Ford Futura was in production you could get a Futura with the optional V-8 engine and thus increase its hp from the standard 90 hp to an effective 150 hp for only $300.

A turbocharger does cause the gasoline to mix with the air more thoroughly, and this thorough mixing is claimed to improve fuel economy. Theoretically, the claim ought to be true. In practice, the difference is negligible, if it exists at all.

As noted, a diesel engine of a given physical size usually develops considerably less horsepower than a gasoline engine of the same size. For this reason, a turbocharger makes much more sense on a diesel; indeed, turbochargers are rapidly becoming standard equipment on diesel cars. The cost considerations, of course, remain.

In summary, a turbocharger improves acceleration, hill-climbing, and top speed. If you can't get these qualities by ordering a larger engine, you can get them from a turbocharged engine— if available, and if you're willing to pay the price.

TRANSMISSIONS

After all this technical stuff, you will be relieved to recall that, so far, you're just sitting in the car with the engine running. Okay, time for the next step: Release the parking brake.

What? It wasn't set? For shame!

"But the car was just sitting in the garage," you rejoin. "Why should I have the parking brake on?"

Answer: to keep you in the habit of using the parking brake, so much so that reaching for the parking brake is as routine as opening or closing the door. The parking brake has several purposes, one of which is to prevent damage to your gear systems if you get bashed from behind when parked. Wherefore, to preserve the gears, maintain the habit of setting the parking brake. If it doesn't hold, get it fixed.

Okay, for practice, just pretend you released the parking brake.

At the same time, put your foot on the brake pedal. Then, uphill, downhill, or sideways, the car will not go anywhere when you let off the parking brake. A car with an automatic transmission that has been left in "Park" will not roll and put its weight against the *pawl* that holds it when in "Park," and the gear lever will move easily.

Presume our Eclat Eight is a "four-on-the-floor" model with a gear lever sticking up by your right knee and a *clutch* pedal down there to the left of the brake pedal. Okay, depress the clutch pedal.

Now, what did we do this time?

Let us back up to a prior question: What do we want to do? Well, we have motion at the engine and we want to transmit that motion to the rear wheels. Clearly, we must have some sort of transition between the stage of no motion and the stage of beginning motion. The clutch provides us with this transition: it allows us to gradually and gently connect the engine to the wheels.

Ordinary household existence provides no analogy for a clutch, but skiers will be familiar with the rope-tow ski-lifts at the less-elaborate lodges. At the top of the hill, an engine or electric motor turns a large pulley. Another pulley is at the bottom of the hill. A large rope passes around both pulleys, just like the fan belt on a car. The skier (no motion) stands beside the moving rope (motion) and confronts the problem of getting into motion along with the rope. The technique is to grasp the rope loosely, to let it slip through the hands somewhat, so that the skier moves

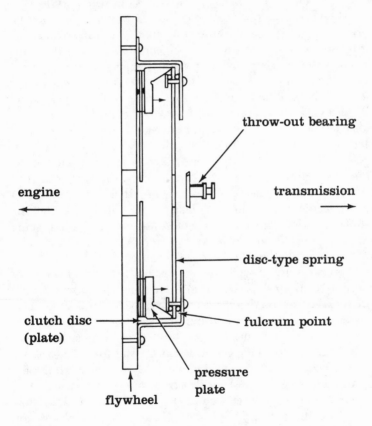

throw-out bearing

engine

transmission

disc-type spring

clutch disc (plate)

fulcrum point

pressure plate

flywheel

Clutch

The vertical cross section here obscures the roundness of the clutch and its related parts, so concentrate on the vertical relationships: the throw-out bearing presses forward on the disc-type spring, and the spring works at the fulcrum point to lift the pressure plate. As the pressure plate moves away from the clutch disc, it stops turning.

only two feet as the rope moves ten feet; next, to grasp the rope more firmly so that the skier moves five feet to the rope's ten; and, finally, to hold tightly so the rope does not slip at all and make ten feet along with the rope. In this example, the skier's hands constitute the clutch.

The clutch in a car likewise provides a means for gradually bringing the wheels into motion along with the engine. Stated crudely and a bit too simply, the clutch is rather like a cheese sandwich. The engine turns the two slices of bread and the slice of cheese turns the shaft that goes into the *transmission*. The first piece of bread is bolted to the crankshaft, and the second slice of bread has a hole for the transmission shaft to pass through.

When the clutch pedal is up (clutch engaged), springs hold the two slices of bread together so they squeeze the cheese tightly between them. When you push the clutch pedal down, you pull the slices of bread apart, which leaves the cheese sitting still. Since the cheese is not moving, it doesn't turn the transmission shaft and gears. Therefore, you can move the gears into engagement without making them crash. When you put the car into gear and ease up on the clutch pedal, the slices of bread begin to turn the cheese, first slowly and then faster as you let off the pedal. By the time you take your foot off the pedal, the whole sandwich is turning as one piece and engine power is going into the transmission to make the gears go 'round and, ultimately, to make the wheels go 'round, too.

This transmission whereof we speak is a "transmission" because it "transmits" power from the engine to the wheels that provide the traction that makes the car move. Here again, everyday experience includes nothing that looks or acts like a transmission. If you have used a hand-turned eggbeater, you know how the handle on a big gear transmits power to each beater via smaller gears. Okay, so you understand how gear teeth mesh.

Well, a lot of gears mesh inside a transmission. However, when you move the gear lever to and fro, you do not actually slide gears into and out of mesh (except for reverse gear, where you actually slide a gear). Rather, the lever moves *synchronizers*, that are actually small, specialized *cone clutches* that connect one gear to another. The analogy is imperfect, but think of a 10-speed bicycle: The lever does not move the gears; rather, it moves the chain from one gear to another.

No matter what the arrangement, you can't shift from one gear to another unless you take the power off of them. In a transmission, when you push the clutch, you prevent the engine from sending power to the gears, and the gears, being under no strain, can be shifted easily.

You may well wonder why you need the transmission at all. After all, if the engine is powerful enough to propel the car up to 100 mph or so, why does it need a transmission to get away from a traffic light?

The proper answer involves the concept of "torque multiplication," but rather than get into that, just think of the red wagon you had as a child. After you put Little Sister and the neighbor kid in the wagon, you had to strain and grunt to get the load moving, but once you got it rolling down the sidewalk, maintaining speed was easy. That's sort of how torque multiplication works. You use a low, powerful gear to get the car moving or to go up a steep hill, but once you're moving along on the level, the engine can maintain its speed easily.

We should note in passing that a 200-hp car will use all its 200 hp to move the car 100 mph, but at 50 mph or so, it uses only about 30 hp of its 200-hp potential.

We may digress here, too, to speak further of *rpm*, or engine speed. If you take something and rotate it one full turn, the object makes one revolution, e.g., as the earth does in 24 hours. When an engine idles at a traffic light, its crankshaft makes about 800 turns, or revolutions, per minute, or 800 rpm.

Engines have a maximum speed of rotation, a certain rpm they should not exceed. The racing types call this rpm the "*redline*" because an rpm-counter, a *tachometer*, has a red line at that point. Generally, the redline falls at 5000 rpm up to about 6500 rpm, depending on the engine, smaller engines typically being faster than big engines, and diesels having about a 4000-rpm redline.

Engines also have an optimum speed, or rpm, where they like to run the most. This speed is at the level of power output known as *maximum torque*. Generally, maximum torque occurs around 3000 rpm on smaller engines but as low as 1500 rpm on larger engines.

Now, let's experiment with our "four-on-the-floor." Watch the tachometer as we speed up to 30 mph in each gear in turn. Okay, ready? At 30 mph in first gear, our tachometer reads 6000 rpm. In second, it shows only 3000 rpm; in third, it goes only to 2000 rpm, and in fourth, it goes just to 1500 rpm—and in each case the ground speed is 30 mph. If we had a five-speed transmission with an *overdrive* (OD) gear, engine speed in fifth/OD would be down to about 1200 rpm at 30 mph.

These numbers illustrate *gear ratio*; the gears in the transmission control the ratio of engine speed to ground speed.

Gear ratios must suit the engine and the car. The above numbers are close to true of the Triumph TR-3, a rough-riding, open British two-seater of twenty years ago. (The TR-3 will crop up now and again, so get used to it. I've owned and loved three, the third of which is in the garage undergoing restoration.)

A Volkswagen Rabbit engine makes about 2600 rpm in fourth at 60 mph, as does a Porsche 911 (actually, the Porsche makes 2590 rpm), and about 2600 rpm at 60 mph is fairly typical. The International Travelall, a wonderful truck-like station wagon once made by International Harvester but discontinued in 1975, also made 2600 rpm at 60 mph. (Get used to this Travelall, too. I've owned five, most of which had run over 100,000 miles before I got them and worked them like galley slaves for a year or two. The fifth and last, alas, is now in the local junkyard, a victim of its swinish appetite for fuel. A fair trade, though; the current Saab 99 came *from* the junkyard).

The importance of knowing about rpm and gear ratio is to better understand what your engine is doing. Perhaps you've noticed that people who are inexperienced with a manual shift often let the car slow down too far before they shift to the next lower gear and the car either starts bucking or stalls. Or they wait too long before they shift, and allow the engine to speed up until it roars like a dump truck climbing a hill. The important thing about gear ratios is to shift at the right point so that you don't over-rev, but come out with the right engine speed for the next gear. Some speedometers have little marks to tell you when to shift, and some new cars have little lights that tell you. Traditionalists like me prefer tachometers.

Also, as noted, your engine has a certain rpm where it develops the most *torque*—the "maximum torque" area. Your engine is happiest and most efficient when running in this area. A small engine will have a narrow—say, 500 rpm—maximum torque area, while a big engine will develop maximum torque across a broad rpm range.

If the notion of gear ratio does not make sense, borrow a bicycle with gears—whether a 3-speed Sturmey-Archer or a 10-speed derailleur—and ride a bit. You'll see why you have gears and why you need to change gears for various conditions.

All of the above applies to manual transmissions, but virtually none of the above is true of an automatic transmission, except the part about gears turning or not turning and the part about gear ratios.

First of all, an automatic doesn't have a foot-operated clutch. All right, so it doesn't; but how does it connect the engine to the wheels without making a jerk?

Easy. It doesn't mechanically connect the engine to the wheels at all. Instead of a clutch, an automatic has a *torque converter*.

If you put two electric fans face to face and turn one on, the "on" fan will make the other one turn, too. In this case, the torque, or power, in the "on" fan has been converted to motion in the "off" fan.

That's how a torque converter works. One fan—actually, a turbine—on the back of the engine blows oil toward another fan (turbine) on the front of the transmission, both fans being enclosed in a housing to contain the oil. At idle speed at a traffic light, the engine turbine doesn't blow hard enough to turn the transmission turbine against the resistance of the brakes. Even with the brakes off, the car will only creep slowly, but push the gas pedal and the engine turbine blows quite hard and sets the transmission turbine to turning and the car takes off smoothly.

Once the power gets into the transmission, it turns gears. To avoid bogging down in the intricacies of a *planetary gear* system, let's just say that a series of small clutches cause one or another set of gears to transmit the power. One set does first gear, another does second, perhaps both together do third or fourth (where applicable), and another does reverse.

Clutches? Don't we need a pedal to work them?

No. In this case, an oil pump in the transmission pumps oil to the clutches and oil pressure engages or disengages them. We also use *bands*, which work like a hand grabbing the lid of a mayonnaise jar. Oil pressure makes the bands squeeze or not squeeze and the bands help change the gears.

All you do when you move the gear lever on an automatic transmission is open one valve or another. The open valve lets oil under pressure flow to either the "R," "L," "2," or "D" circuit, and other little valves in the *valve body* and *governor* take care of everything else.

When you shift into "Park," you move a single gear tooth, a *pawl*, into one of the gears so that nothing can move, and that locks the wheels that move the car.

Generally, a manual transmission gets better gas mileage because it loses less energy between engine and wheels. However, while an automatic loses energy in its torque converter and oil pump, it may be preferable in a car used in stop-and-go city traffic. Also, an automatic can be put into motion very gently and its torque converter provides a sort of shock absorber between the engine and the drive wheels, so an automatic gives better traction on ice. This same shock-absorbing capacity also protects the gears from shocks and, in consequence, an automatic transmission normally outlasts a manual and it obviates clutch adjustments/replacement in the meantime. It does, however, require an annual change of transmission oil.

People, some of whom write for the automotive press, still condemn automatics as trouble-prone. This is because when these writers were children, they heard grizzled old mechanics who grew up on the sliding-mesh car transmissions of 1920 criticize the first General Motors Hydramatics of 1940. I know. I heard all those fatuous and ill-informed stories, too. However, the writers I criticize believed the stories and never looked into the matter afterward, much less ever overhauled a Borg-Warner T-28, a Chrysler TorqueFlite, or any other automatic transmission.

We all have things we will have to answer for in the next world. I will have to answer for the abusive things I have done to automatic transmissions. The '57 Plymouth Plaza I owned in Alaska twenty years ago had the Chrysler push-button automatic. I would run the engine up to about 2500 rpm and punch from "R" to "D" without letting off the gas when rocking out of a snow bank. The transmission would grunt like a weight lifter and the whole car would rock as the gears caught with a jerk— but I never tore up that transmission.

Though loathe to do so, I will further admit that I treated the

Borg-Warner T-35 in my Saab 99 the same way and, upon inspecting its bands and clutch discs at the end of the winter, found no evidence of harm from it. Likewise with several Borg-Warner transmissions in various International Travelalls and several Chrysler units in small trucks. I have not practiced these improper exercises on General Motors automatics, but I do not doubt that they will take considerable abuse, too.

Besides the myth that automatic transmissions are weak, another old notion persists, viz., that you can start an automatic transmission car by pushing it. Well, you can't. As recently as fifteen years ago, many automatics had two oil pumps, one at the front and one at the rear. The engine turned the front pump and the drive shaft turned the rear one. If the engine was not running, you could push the car and the drive shaft would turn the rear pump, which would engage the gears, which would start the engine. Nowadays, virtually all automatics have only the front, engine-driven oil pump. You can push the car all day and never start the engine.

The control system in an automatic transmission decides when to shift, though you can (within limits) override the control system with the gear lever. If you are going too fast or too slow for the gear you are in, the system will automatically shift to the next higher or lower gear.

Generally, the system may be relied upon; put the lever in "D" and forget it. However, to bring up rpm again, you can improve on the system a bit.

A torque converter has a certain speed known as "stall speed." We'll skip the technicalities; the important point is that an automatic will be happier if it is kept above its stall speed when it is working hard, such as when climbing a long hill or when towing a load.

On the Saab 99, stall speed occurs around 2000 rpm. As I climb the steepness of Massachusetts Route 116 toward Ashfield when towing the boat, I watch the tachometer. If I find the engine speed hanging around 2000 rpm—right at "stall speed" for the torque converter—I either speed up to, say, 2500 rpm or I downshift to second (which increases the rpm) to ease the load on the torque converter. If you always haul a lot of weight with an automatic, find out your "stall speed" and try to avoid running right at or right below it when loaded heavily.

Now, to explicate an earlier point: Your car is in a parking lot or at the curb, with the engine off and in gear or in "Park," when some ham-handed lummox trying to park bashes your front or rear bumper hard enough to rock your car. The force of that bashing could break off gear teeth in a manual transmission, and most certainly will break off the pawl that holds an automatic transmission in "Park." However, if your parking brake is in good order and is firmly set, the bashing may bend your bumper or slide your wheels, but it won't damage your transmission. That's why you maintain the habit of using the parking brake.

Likewise, suppose you come to a stop on a steep hill: You bring the car to a stop, hold the foot brake, and shift to "Park." Then, when you let off the foot brake, the car rolls downhill an inch or two and its weight goes against the pawl that holds the car in "Park." When you go to leave, you find the pawl locked so tightly that you can't move the lever from "Park" at all; or you jerk on it and break off the gear lever. So, when you come to a stop on a hill, shift to "N" and set the parking brake firmly enough that it holds the car. Then shift to "Park." Do it this way, and you'll never find yourself yanking at the gear lever with both hands to get the car out of "Park."

DIFFERENTIAL

The transmission alone is not enough to get the power to the wheels. Hence, we must run a *drive shaft* from the transmission to the *differential* and from there out to the wheels. The drive shaft connects the transmission to the differential, and the differential is the link between the drive shaft and the rear wheels.

Alas for simplicity, the transmission is bolted firmly to the car but the differential and rear axle are on springs that allow the car to bounce up and down. The bouncing would bend the drive shaft, so we put a flexible *universal joint* at each end of the shaft. Then, the car can bounce all it wants to as the rear wheels stay on the ground, and without bending the drive shaft.

Front-wheel-drive and rear-engine cars do not have drive shafts in the usual sense of the expression, because the engine, transmission, and differential are integrated into a single unit, the *transaxle*. The drive shaft is eliminated.

Differential? Oh, that. Well, a differential is something that makes a difference. Push a tricycle around a corner. Notice that the inside rear wheel doesn't make as many turns as the outside wheel. See the difference? Okay, the rear wheels of a car do that, too, when going around a corner, and the differential allows one to make fewer turns than the other. The differential is that big, round lumpy-looking thing right between the rear wheels of most cars. On trucks, you can see it easily. It also has gears, which take the power from the drive shaft, divide it into two, and send half that power out to each rear wheel via the axle shafts.

A differential has one serious weakness: It divides the power in half only if both wheels have equal traction. If one wheel is on mud or ice and the other on a good surface, the differential sends all the power to the wheel with less traction. Hence, the apparently illogical sight of a car trying to pull away from an icy curb, the wheel on ice spinning madly and the one on dry pavement not turning at all.

Obviously, you will never get anywhere with one wheel spinning and the other doing nothing. You can get out of the problem with a so-called "limited-slip" or "positive-traction" differential. These differentials won't allow one wheel to spin while the other does not. They came on the market as optional equipment about twenty years ago, and so remain.

Every time I see some useless styling detail that cost a lot of money, I wish the money had been used to put a limited-slip differential in the car. A limited-slip keeps you from getting stuck, reduces the tendency to skid on corners, and may reduce tire and transmission wear to some minimal extent. In sum, a limited-slip differential is one of the most worthwhile options.

FRONT-WHEEL DRIVE

Nowadays, the phrase in automotive vogue is *front-wheel drive*, or FWD. On a conventional car, such as your garden-variety Ford or Mercedes-Benz, the engine is up in front with the wheels that swivel right and left to steer, and the rear wheels transmit the power to the ground to propel the car. Well, with FWD, the front wheels also take the power to the ground to propel the car (and the rear wheels just sit there and roll along).

As noted, in a front-wheel-drive system, the engine, transmission, and differential comprise a single unit known as the transaxle. The arrangement packages the power system into a compact unit that reduces the total amount of metal in the whole car.

The current popularity of FWD is a product of the effort to reduce weight in the search for optimum fuel economy. It is not some new discovery. In fact, FWD enjoys the cachet that, in the absolute sense, it is the oldest automotive drive system. In 1771, Nicholas Cugnot built a tricycle-like wagon with a steam engine driving the front wheel. Cugnot tried to sell the vehicle to the French army (who should have paid more attention to its possibilities), but it got away from him in a demonstration and smashed itself against a stone wall (perhaps the world's first car wreck).

Cugnot was not the only one. From the earliest, designers have sought to exploit the space- and materials-efficiency of FWD. The Cord L-20 of 1931 might be the first production FWD car, though the Cord reputation rests more on the elegant 812 Phaeton of 1937. Citroen, of France, committed itself to FWD in 1934 and has never built anything else. General Motors broke ground of a sort with the FWD Oldsmobile Toronado of 1965 ('66 model year), which proved that FWD would work on a large, heavy car. In short, the mechanical excellence of FWD systems is not a matter of doubt.

Just as the automatic transmission became virtually standard a few years ago, FWD is becoming virtually standard on smaller cars. And, as with every other automotive feature, FWD has become the subject of much mythology and misinformation. FWD does impose peculiar engineering problems because the same pair of wheels must apply traction to the road, must provide steering, and must support the weight of the engine. That is a lot to ask and car salesmen who sell conventional front-engine, rear-drive cars often invoke the engineering problems of FWD in an effort to condemn it unfairly.

If you like a certain FWD car, don't let anyone talk you out of it. Remember, every Saab built since the original one in 1947 has been FWD. The fantastic old Citroen DS 19/21 models had FWD, too, and when Volkswagen decided to put the engine up front in the Rabbit, they also went to FWD.

From an engineering point of view, FWD saves some weight and reduces the lump in the floorboard that would otherwise contain the drive shaft. Also, FWD cars generally have better traction because the weight is over the wheels that drive and steer. However, this rule is not absolute. In reverse in deep snow, FWD cars can be helpless because they can't get their rear (non-driving) wheels to back out of deep ruts. As with virtually every other detail on a car, no one particular way of doing things—including FWD—is absolutely superior to all other ways.

FOUR-WHEEL DRIVE

So, some cars drive from the rear wheels, some from the front—and some from both. For example, if you put a differential between the front wheels and run another drive shaft forward from the transmission, then you have *four-wheel drive*, or 4WD.

In 4WD systems, all wheels can apply traction to the road surface. The system became familiar after WW II when soldiers came home with fond memories of the wonderful "Jeep." After the war, Jeeps went civilian, and assorted look-alikes—Chevrolet Blazer, GMC Jimmy, Ford Bronco, and the late International Scout—appeared to compete for 4WD eminence.

The 4WD system has not been limited to off-road vehicles. Four-wheel-drive cars raced in the Indianapolis 500 in the early 1930s, and more recently, Subaru, Datsun, American Motors, and Toyota have made 4WD passenger cars. Indeed, a veritable plethora of 4WD cars are under development by other companies and will be available in a few years. In some instances the 4WD works all the time and in others the additional two driving wheels can be engaged/disengaged at will.

The absolute advantage of 4WD is traction, an advantage, obviously, that shows up most in the winter. On snow and ice, a 4WD vehicle makes a two-wheel-drive car look pathetic and gives the 4WD driver (and passengers) incredible security. The system provides a vast oversupply of traction in normal conditions and imposes a fuel penalty because of its extra weight and gears, but the fuel penalty is certainly worth its cost to people who drive in all weathers.

BRAKES

Having got the engine running, got into gear, and got the car out of the driveway, away we go! Life being as it is, though, the first thing we encounter is a STOP sign. Now, we have 2000–4000 pounds of scrap iron and sheet metal hurtling along at 30 mph or so, and we've got to stop it.

So, we push the brake pedal, which activates the *service brakes*; that is, the brakes that stop the car. (The other one is the *parking brake*, which some people call the "emergency brake," for that was its original purpose.) If all is well in the system, we stop promptly. Even the frailest driver can easily bring a 5000-pound car to a halt. Now, what is afoot here?

The engine burns a fuel to generate heat and converts the heat energy into motion. The brakes reverse the process; they convert motion into heat by friction, then dissipate the heat into the air.

The stove-in-reverse principle by which brakes work seems peculiarly hard for people to grasp. People say, "The brakes work by rubbing." True enough, but that rubbing produces heat and the heat must be able to escape, for if the heat could not escape, the car would not stop. Race cars, for example, have special air scoops to cool the brakes.

As with the engine, the brakes involve pistons that work in cylinders. As with the torque converter, the brakes involve an oily liquid (*brake fluid*) that is used to transfer energy. And, as with the clutch and the transmission, familiar experience provides nothing that works like a braking system, although the brakes on a bicycle replicate part of the system.

Perhaps a good place to start is with a water pistol, one made of the clearest plastic possible, so you can see what's going on inside. You will see a round chamber (cylinder) that fills up with water from the reservoir in the handle. You will also see a little plunger (piston) in this cylinder that moves when you pull the trigger. When you pull the trigger, you close off an aperture so you don't just squirt the water back into the reservoir. Rather, the piston forces the water out of the cylinder and through the little brass nozzle in the end of the pistol barrel.

Now, get a second water pistol and a piece of small hose. Stick the hose over the two brass nozzles so the pistols are shooting each other. Squirt the one on the right until you see the cylinder on the left fill up (from being shot by the right). After the left cylinder is full, hold the right trigger and pull the left trigger. The force in the left trigger finger will be transmitted through the water and will push the right piston outward. You will feel the force at your right trigger finger.

That's how hydraulic brakes work. They have one major water pistol (*master cylinder*) that is connected via tubing and hoses to

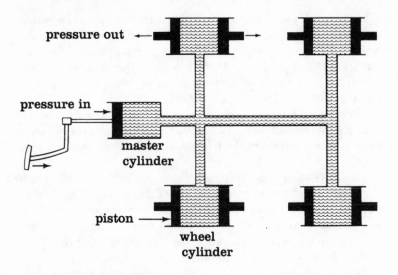

pressure out ←

pressure in →

master
cylinder

piston →

wheel
cylinder

Hydraulic system

Here are all those "water pistols" connected to form a single system.
Note that this is an old way of doing things: a leak anywhere in the
system will nullify the whole system.

a water pistol (*wheel cylinder*) at each wheel. When you push on
the brake pedal, you push a plunger (piston) in the master cylinder and squirt brake fluid out to the cylinders at each wheel.

So far, all we have are some "triggers" at the wheels that move
outward when we push the brake pedal. We have to get that
trigger motion to do something to stop the wheels.

We will start with a *disc* (rather than *drum*) brake because disc
brakes have *calipers* (rather than *brake shoes*), and to find out what
a caliper is we again examine a 10-speed bicycle. Work the lever
on the handlebars and watch what happens at the front wheel:
A pair of levers that work like bread tongs come in from the
sides and squeeze rubber pads against the rim of the bicycle
wheel. Those little levers at the wheel are a caliper and the rim
plays the role of the disc. The major difference between the
bicycle and the car is that on the car you use hydraulic pressure
to squeeze the caliper, rather than a cable and a lever.

On a car, the disc itself is just that—a metal disc about 10 inches in diameter and about half an inch thick that fits on the same bolts that hold the wheel on the car. Squeeze the caliper together, it stops the disc, and the disc (obviously) stops the wheel.

If you see a motorcyclist (who seems friendly), ask for a demonstration of the motorcycle disc brake. On a motorcycle, the master cylinder is up on the handlebar, and the caliper and disc are out in plain sight where you can see them.

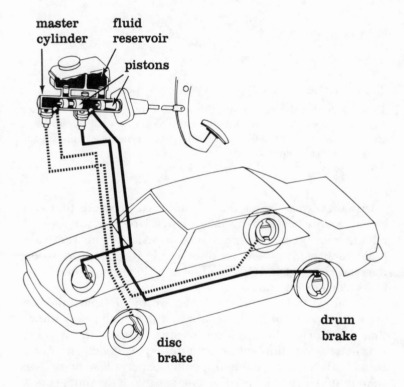

Divided braking system

Since 1968, all domestic cars use a braking system wherein the master cylinder is divided into two parts, each of which serves two wheels. A leak at one wheel leaves two wheels for braking. The broken lines show one two-wheel system, and the solid lines the other.

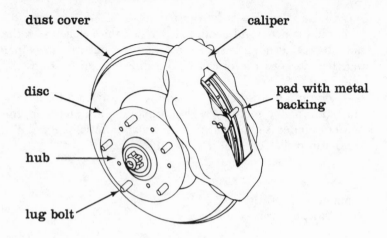

Disc brake

In a disc brake, the pistons are contained in the caliper. The caliper fits over the disc in a way that allows the piston on each side to force the pads against both sides of the disc. Some systems accomplish the purpose with a single piston.

Disc brakes are better than drum brakes because they can generate more heat and dissipate it faster. However, for assorted reasons, mostly economy in production, many cars still use drum brakes and many others use discs on the front and drums on the rear. Here again, you won't find anything in your house that looks like a drum brake.

For an example of a drum brake, we will do something we are not supposed to do. If we are careful, we will get by with it (but we shan't let the children see us). Suppose the washing machine has just finished its "spin-dry" cycle, gone "click," and turned off, leaving the tub inside the washer still spinning. We want to stop it right away so we can take the clothes out at once. So, we lift the lid, put our hands inside the rim of the tub, on opposite sides, and hold against the rim. Soon, the friction we thus develop brings the tub to a stop. (Careful, though. If you stick a hand in too far, the spinning tub will grab it and rip your arm off at the shoulder.)

In this case, the tub is a brake drum and our hands are a pair of *brake shoes.* The piston in the wheel cylinder pushes the brake shoes outward against the inner surface of the brake drum and makes the drum stop, just as our hands stopped the tub.

For a parking brake, we connect cables to the brake shoes or to the calipers (à la bicycle) so we can set the brakes.

The bigger the car or the faster it goes, the harder you have to push the brake pedal to stop it. To give you some help, the manufacturers made *power brakes.* In the original systems, an engine-driven pump provided hydraulic pressure to work the

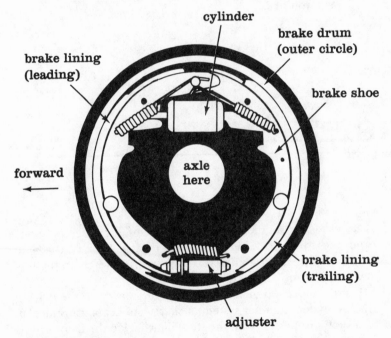

Drum brake

A drum brake resembles a cake pan wherein the wheel cylinder forces the linings, mounted on brake "shoes," outward against the inner lip of the drum. Note that the leading brake lining is slightly shorter (at the top); this is to prevent the leading lining from grabbing abruptly when the brakes are applied. The parking brake linkage and the self-adjustment system, which acts on the adjuster at the bottom, are omitted here.

master cylinder. Of course, if the pump quit, you lost your brakes, so current systems are not full "power" brakes; rather, they are "power-assisted."

Present-day Fords use a variant of the original hydraulically actuated master cylinder, while most other cars use *vacuum boosters*. The engine sucks and creates a vacuum, the vacuum moves a large diaphragm, and the diaphragm pushes on the master cylinder (along with your foot).

Power-assisted brakes are virtually standard on all cars now. If not standard equipment, they are among the most worthwhile options. Don't pass up power-assisted brakes if you can get them on the car you like.

STEERING

Robert Frost was more right than he knew, for a "yellow wood" is not the only place where two roads diverge. In fact, roads do it all the time, and we must turn our steering wheel to the way "less traveled by" or to the other.

Just as shafts and gears conduct engine power to the driving wheels, so does another system of shafts and gears transmit arm and shoulder power from the steering wheel to the front wheels for steering. The shaft from the steering wheel goes to what is, technically, a transmission. However, because of its narrow, specialized role, this transmission is the *steering box*. This steering box contains two gears. The one on the end of the steering wheel shaft is a *worm* gear and looks rather like the threads on a screw. The other gear is really only about two teeth of a *cog* gear, a cog gear being what you normally think of as a gear. This portion of a cog gear is the *sector* gear because it consists of only a sector of a circle. The sector teeth fit into the worm-gear thread. As the steering wheel turns the worm, the sector teeth follow the worm-gear thread up and down, depending on which way you turn the steering wheel. As the sector-gear shaft turns, it works a lever that connects to *tie rods*, which connect to the wheels.

Tie rods are "tie rods" because they tie things together. Tie rods have *tie-rod ends* that wear out and make the steering sloppy.

The system usually includes an *idler arm* that keeps the tie rods lined up so they work right. Idler arms also wear out and make the steering sloppy. Indeed, the steering box wears out, too, but it can usually be adjusted, although nobody ever seems to do it.

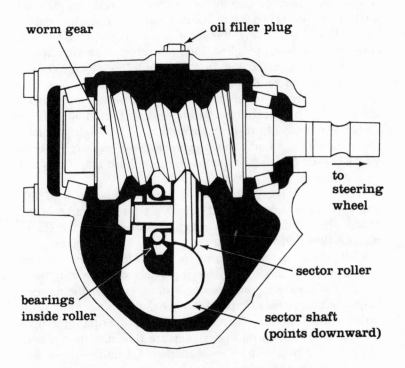

Worm (gear) - and-sector (gear) steering

Innards of worm-and-sector steering box. Note that the teeth of the sector gear are actually rollers that turn on bearings. The plug is where you check the oil.

Since the wheels must turn to right and left, we need some sort of hinge where the wheel connects to the car. In the old days, this "hinge" did, indeed, resemble a door hinge and the wheel swung left or right on the *kingpin* of the hinge mechanism. After 1952, following the example set by the Ford Motor Company's Lincoln, everybody switched from the kingpin to the *ball-joint* system. Ball joints come in pairs, one upper and one lower. They wear out, too—sometimes so badly that a front wheel literally falls off the car.

Karl Benz's (as in Mercedes-Benz) first automobile of 1886, a powered tricycle, used a tiller, like that on a sailboat, for steering. The first steering wheel was on the 1891 DeDion-Bouton, a most progressive French car, but did not become universal until around 1910. In those early days, of course, many cars weighed only a ton or less. To pick one obscure example, the 1912 Union 25 two-seater (at $650) weighed 1300 pounds; for an equally obscure second example, the 1912 Touraine Six (at $2250) was heavy enough at 2800 pounds to qualify as a "luxury" car.

Up to around 1930, cars ran on tall, narrow tires that looked like overgrown bicycle tires and ran on a rock-hard 50 to 70 or even 100 pounds of pressure. Given their light weight and narrow tires with high inflation pressures, these cars were easy to steer. Too easy, in fact; a mere trifling of loose gravel or sheet ice would send them skittering into the ditch.

Wider tires inflated to about 35 pounds came in the 1930s and even wider tires, inflated to only 24 pounds, came in the 1950s. Meanwhile, cars grew to behemoth extremes, for example, the 1952 Oldsmobile 98, which weighed over 5000 pounds.

With cars of this sort running on soft wide tires, even strong men needed help with the steering wheel when getting away from a curb. Hence, *power steering*, wherein the engine drives a hydraulic pump that pumps oil to a hydraulic cylinder that helps turn the wheels. With power steering, all the steering wheel does is open a valve to let oil under pressure flow into the cylinder and push the piston one way or another. Of course, if you lose oil pressure in the system for any reason, the manual system remains so you don't lose control of the car.

As with many good things, power steering has been taken to absurd extremes. It is hardly needed at all on cars that weigh less than, say, 3000 pounds; yet, it is installed on cars as small and light as a Datsun 310 coupe.

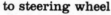

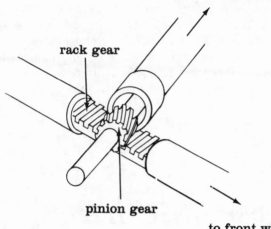

Rack-and-pinion steering

Rack-and-pinion steering is a simpler way to convert steering wheel motion to sideways motion.

All of the above applies to the worm-and-sector system and its variants, such as *worm-and-peg* or *recirculating ball*. However, the *rack-and-pinion* system differs. In a worm-and-sector system, you take power from the steering-wheel shaft and point it downward to swing a lever from side to side. In rack-and-pinion, you take power from the steering shaft and point it directly out to both sides at once. This reduces the number of tie rods and idlers, which makes the system cheaper and reduces the number of parts to wear out.

A *pinion* is a small, round gear. A *rack* is a gear that is flat instead of round. If you take a length of bicycle chain and staple it along the length of a broomstick, it constitutes a rack. The steering wheel turns the pinion, which moves the rack from side to side, and the ends of the rack connect to the wheels and turn them.

Despite a lot of exaggerated advertising, rack-and-pinion steering is nothing extraordinary. It is simply a cheap, simple way out of certain engineering problems. That's why it first became popular on smaller, cheaper cars. So what, if a BMW has rack-and-pinion steering? So did the 1959 Triumph Herald, one of the most cheaply built cars anybody ever produced. Nowadays, Mercedes-Benz uses the recirculating-ball form of worm-and-sector, while Jaguar uses rack-and-pinion. When marques of such engineering distinction differ, you know that neither system is absolutely better than the other.

SUSPENSION

We are in command of our fate. We can go, stop, and turn. However, life being as it is, we do not find magnificent boulevards bordered by rosebushes. Rather, we encounter twisty paths beset with bumps, potholes, and vagrant, existentialist dogs that we must, perforce, avoid, not to mention careening idiots in other cars and massive, smoke-belching trucks that threaten to bully us off the road.

The steering system helps us proceed amid such hazards without getting into trouble, but the *suspension system* helps a great deal, too.

The steering allows the car to maneuver, but the suspension system keeps the wheels on the ground. In this function, it is one of the most misunderstood systems on a car, "misunderstood" in the respect that most people think the suspension system is there to give the car a "soft ride." This is not true, despite the fact that car manufacturers and car salesmen have fostered this egregious fallacy. In most cases, the softer the ride, the less the system is able to keep the wheels on the ground.

The suspension system consists of the springs and shock absorbers, plus an array of arms and linkages that work through hinge-like joints to allow the wheels to stay in contact with the road as they go over bumps or through potholes. If the system were not there, the car would most definitely have a harsh ride, but more important, the wheels would bounce completely off the ground just as a marble bounces on concrete. The system also controls whether and to what extent the body of the car leans as it goes around curves, and the degree of leaning influences how well the tires adhere to the road.

Besides keeping the wheels on the ground, the suspension

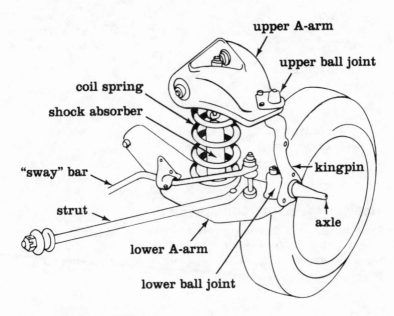

Front suspension

Elements of a typical independent front suspension system. The coil spring meets the car body at a point under the upper A-arm and, thus, carries the weight of the car via the lower A-arm, lower ball joint, and axle. The "sway" bar allows the spring on the opposite side to share the load when going over bumps, and the strut keeps the lower A-arm from being forced forward or backward by the effects of bumps and braking. Alternate systems use a torsion bar that runs lengthwise and connects to the pivot of one A-arm, and other systems use the Mac-Pherson Strut that incorporates the shock absorber and spring into one unit and eliminates the upper A-arm.

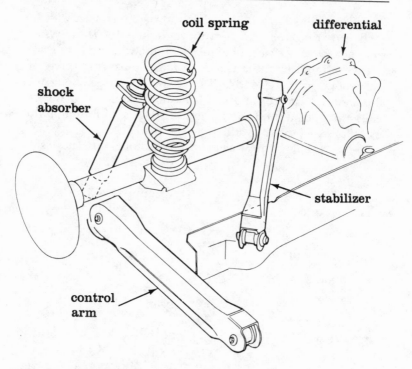

coil spring

differential

shock
absorber

stabilizer

control
arm

Rear suspension, coil springs

Coil springs can be used at the rear, too. The stabilizer keeps the rear axle from moving from side to side, and the control arm holds it in place fore-and-aft, plus transfers the motion of the wheel to the car body.

system helps the car follow the path dictated by the position of the steering wheel. Compare the front wheel of a bicycle to the front wheels of a shopping cart: On the bicycle, the weight of the rider is carried behind the center of the front wheel; on the shopping cart, the wheels carry the weight ahead of their centers (that is, they are casters). The shopping cart is relatively easy to keep straight but relatively hard to make turn; a bicycle, relatively, is the opposite. Similarly, whether the weight is ahead of or behind the center of the front wheels affects the way a car handles.

Besides this "caster angle," engineers have to worry about toe-in, camber angle, kingpin inclination, steering axis, roll center, and much more. They may choose to use *MacPherson Struts*, or unequal-length *A-arms*, longitudinal struts, or trailing arms, and may use *coil springs, leaf springs,* or *torsion bars.*

For most people's uses, the technical stuff hardly matters. Agreed, *independent rear suspension* (IRS) is better, but how good does your rear suspension have to be? My Saab 99 does not have IRS, yet its rear suspension is good enough to keep the rear wheels on the road at much faster speeds than I drive, and I normally take 40 mph curves at 50 mph and take them at 60 mph when I'm feeling frisky (I also wear out my tires fast, too). Do I have any genuine need for the ultra-sophisticated rear suspension of a Mercedes-Benz? No (but I do wish I had another 1962 model 190 SL).

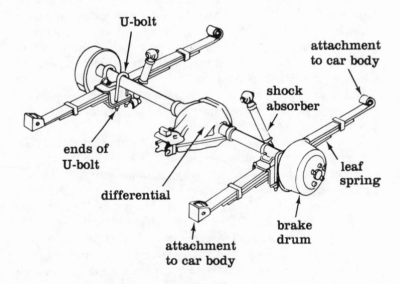

Rear Suspension, leaf springs

Leaf springs were the norm on all wheels fifty years ago and are still commonly used on rear wheels. The axle attaches to the springs via the U-bolts, and the springs transfer motion to the car body.

Note those U-bolts carefully; they become important on p. 216 when you're changing a tire.

The point here is that a car salesman will try to convince you that the car he is selling has a suspension system superior to that of the car in the dealership across the street. It may, indeed, have a superior suspension system, but does that superiority matter in your driving? All modern cars are quite good and are certainly much better than the cars of even twenty years ago, so don't worry about the jargon. In terms of what you actually experience with the car, the tires will make as much difference as the suspension.

To put some of the jargon into context, a Porsche 911SC ($26,000) and a BMW 528e ($23,000) both have a MacPherson Strut front suspension—as do a Pontiac J2000 ($7000) and a Volkswagen Rabbit ($6000). So what does this tell us about MacPherson Struts? Similarly, a Jaguar XJ-S at $30,000 and a Mercedes-Benz 380 SEC at $50,000 both have unequal-length A-arms, as do the Saab 900 ($11,000) and the American Motors four-wheel-drive Eagle ($9000). In general, MacPherson Struts dominate now, partly for reasons of weight and economy of manufacturing, but the current Rolls-Royce Silver Spur at around $120,000 has unequal-length A-arms up front, just as the 1934 Chrysler did ($1245 at the time).

In summary: As a cat may be flayed or a fish filleted in diverse ways, so do suspension systems vary, but all current ones do the job well enough for most people.

This does not, of course, mean that all systems are alike. To me, any mid- or full-size domestic car feels as if it is mounted on sponge rubber: I find the steering ambiguous and the suspension squishy. However, many people do not react as I do. I can condemn such systems all I want, but my raving makes no difference to people who are comfortable with such cars.

By contrast, virtually all foreign cars and the smaller domestics have a firm suspension and precise steering, but my praise of such systems means nothing to people who don't like cars of this latter sort.

Testdrive as many cars as you can, and include rough, twisty roads in your test. Let your road test dictate what you buy—not some hypertechnical phrase in an advertising brochure.

WHEEL BEARINGS

A "bearing" is anything that "bears" a load. That little metal pad under the leg of a desk is, technically, a bearing.

Cars have all kinds of bearings. The ones on the crankshaft are called "shell bearings" and look like strips of metal bent into half-circles. Those at the piston end of the connecting rod look like a piece of bronze pipe and are called "bushings."

The bearings that matter to the driver are the ones at the wheels, particularly the wheels that do the steering.

Front-wheel bearings are either *tapered-roller bearings* or *ball bearings*. In cars, neither type has an absolute advantage. The crucial difference to the car owner is whether the bearings require periodic adjustment and lubrication, or whether they are sealed. Sealed bearings are used in a number of new cars because they are more compatible with FWD systems. However, when a sealed bearing loses its seal and, thus, its grease, nothing can save it. After a sealed bearing goes, the thing that comes next is a tow truck. By contrast, you can sometimes patch an adjustable bearing together well enough to drive slowly to a shop.

However, sealed bearings are quite reliable. I know of sealed front-wheel bearings on Saab 99s that have outlasted two engines and are still going after 240,000 miles.

Most front-engine, rear-drive cars have tapered roller bearings on the front wheels, and these bearings require periodic lubrication and adjustment. When they get loose from wear, they create sloppiness in the steering and peculiar effects in the brakes. If they need grease and don't get it, they overheat, turn blue, and crack into little pieces. Then, the wheel comes off. If you're inclined to neglect your adjustable front-wheel bearings, please don't get close to me on an interstate highway.

Major truths: If you have adjustable wheel bearings, make sure they get greased and adjusted at least once a year or every 10,000 miles.

ELECTRICALS

Virtually everything on the car works by electricity. You use electricity to start up and to feed the spark plugs and you may use electricity to open the windows or the trunk lid.

The electricity originates in the *battery*, but while you're driving along it comes from the *alternator*. If you need more power than the alternator can supply—for example, if you honk your horn—the battery supplies the extra power and then the alternator recharges the battery.

Most books that attempt to simplify electricity compare it to a water system, but that analogy hangs up in relating *volts* and *amperage* (amps) to pressure and volume. Rather, I prefer the simpler analogy of a bucket with a faucet in the side. Accept, *per dicta*, that the water in the bucket is 12-volt water (whereas the bucket that supplies your house is full of 110-volt water). However, while the water is always 12-volts, the faucet can run at a gush or a trickle, and this rate of flow represents amperage.

So, you turn on the key and let a trickle of water flow to the instruments and to the ignition system. At that rate, the electrical trickle will run about 30 hours before the battery-bucket goes dry. If you turn on the headlights, you open the faucet more, so the battery will last about 12 hours. If you sound the horn, the battery will run down in less than an hour.

If you apply the starter and just hold it on (assuming the car doesn't start), you will empty the battery in less than five minutes (and half-melt your starter, too).

Say you apply the starter and crank up: that consumes a quart from your bucket in five seconds. Once the engine is running, though, the alternator takes 15 minutes to replace that quart. Also, it supplies the trickle that feeds the ignition system. Once the alternator has filled the battery up again, the battery just sits there waiting to be called on to supply a ration of electricity in a hurry.

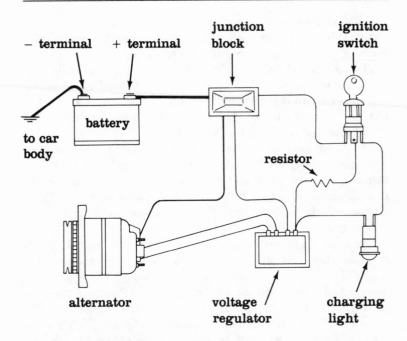

Electrical system

The foundations of the electrical system are the battery and the system that keeps it charged. The wires that supply the lights, horn, etc. typically "tap into" the system at the ignition switch or at the junction block.

The alternator also has a faucet on it, viz., the *regulator*. The regulator works like a skillful horse jockey: it doesn't allow the alternator to work so hard that it burns itself up.

"Look," yells the battery-bucket, "I'm two quarts short and I want two quarts—right now!"

"Patience, patience," says the regulator. "We're filling you up as fast as we can—but we aren't going to kill ourselves over it. Indeed, where would you be then, if we did?"

A modern car keeps its regulator busy. You move the turn signal lever and the regulator opens the faucet a bit to supply the flashing lights, opening and closing with every flash. Likewise when you use the cigarette lighter, horn, etc. However, modern alternators mostly have solid-state ("transistorized") regulating elements that are immensely reliable. Cars often go over 100,000 miles on the original alternator and regulator.

Virtually all the lights on a car are bulbs just like those in your living room lamps. A few instrument lights are light-emitting diodes (LEDs) or liquid-crystal displays (LCDs). These are pretty, but they are expensive. However, they require less electricity than bulbs and are highly reliable.

The headlights are specialized bulbs in the respect that they have a built-in reflector and two filaments (except four-headlight systems, wherein only two of the four lights have dual filaments). One filament reflects its light low and to the right for the "low" beam, and the other filament reflects higher and farther for "high" beam.

The brake lights are connected to a switch that the brake pedal flips on when you put on the brakes, and this matter deserves study. That is, you should know how hard you have to push your pedal to turn on the brake lights. If your car requires a heavy pedal pressure to turn them on, you won't be warning cars behind you when you apply the brakes lightly. Watch when backing up at night and note when you see the brake lights go on.

As an aside, sometimes you can apply the brakes lightly and use the brake lights to augment back-up lights.

A switch somewhere in the shift linkage turns on the back-up lights, and this switch goes bad more often than it should. Hence, you may be driving at night with your back-up lights on—most annoying to the driver behind you.

On older cars, the bulb for the tail light and brake light (on each side) is also a dual-filament bulb. One filament, the dim one, serves as the tail light and the bright one as a brake light. The brake-light wires are routed through the turn-signal switch so that the brake light also serves as a turn signal. When you apply the brakes as you signal a right turn, the left side works as a brake light while the right serves as a turn signal.

This older system saves the cost of some wire and a couple of bulbs and so was adopted in America. By contrast, European cars kept the functions separate—one bulb to each purpose. In the past few years, domestic cars have shifted to this superior system. If a turn signal goes out on older cars, you can't readily tell whether the fault is in the brake part of the wiring or in the turn-signal part; the newer system simplifies diagnosis.

The turn-signal system has a *flasher*, too, which is simply an intermittent switch, i.e., one that goes off and on by itself.

The windshield wipers are run by an electric motor that is linked to the wipers by levers or cables, and the heater blower is also an electric motor. Electric motors may also be used in power-window systems. Electrically, your car is a fairly complex system.

To clarify a point *en passant*: the heater gets its heat from the engine, not from the battery. The actual heat exchanger, the "heater core" as mechanics call it, resembles a small radiator. It receives hot coolant from the engine as a fan driven by a small electric motor blows air through it.

Of course, an exception: on air-cooled cars like the Volkswagen Beetle, the heater gets its heat from shrouds that cover the exhaust manifolds, and the same blower that cools the engine forces warm air into the car.

An air conditioner gets its "cold" the same way a refrigerator does, by alternately compressing and releasing Freon gas.

When a water pipe in the basement freezes and bursts, you turn off a valve to prevent a flood, so we'd better have some valves like that in our electrical system. Electrically, our broken pipe is a *short circuit*; that is, a place where the electricity can escape from the wire before it gets to the bulb or motor it's supposed to work. In electricity, a short circuit allows more power to rush through the wire than the wire can handle, so the wire gets hot and melts its insulation. Then, the hot wire may start a fire. Even if it doesn't cause damage, a short circuit will empty the bucket, leaving you with a dead battery. To prevent such evils, we put automatic "shut-off valves" in the system.

These valves are *fuses* or *circuit breakers*, and they work just like those in your house. Sometimes, fuses blow or circuit breakers trip just because they are feeling old and tired. Usually, though, they don't blow/trip unless you have a broken pipe—a short circuit—somewhere. If you replace a blown fuse and it immediately blows again, don't bridge the fuse with wire or aluminum foil; have a mechanic find the short circuit and fix it.

POLLUTION CONTROLS

You activated all that stuff under the hood and put those wheels in motion because you wanted to go somewhere. Of course, you had no intention of fouling the atmosphere. Yet, in the nature of the way it burns a petroleum-based fuel, an engine spews out considerable foul stuff—carbon monoxide (CO), unburned hydrocarbon compounds (HC), and oxides of nitrogen (NO_x).

Everybody knows that when you expose a piece of camera film to light, the light causes chemical changes on the surface of the film. Well, if you let sunlight fall on a mixture of CO, HC, and NO_x, you create "smog," a sort of catch-all term that includes both the products of combustion and the products of photochemical reactions among such combustion products.

Smog was a recognized problem in the Los Angeles valley even before 1940, but no one knew quite what to do about it. By 1960, the problem had appeared in every major city and the automobile had been identified as the villain. California required minimal pollution control in 1963, and by 1967 (model year 1968), pollution control went national. Since 1968, the standards have grown progressively more stringent.

Pollution controls do their job by controlling the combustion event and by treating the exhaust gasses. One part of the system deals with the carburetor, another with the ignition system, and a third with the exhaust. A modern car may have as many as two dozen little gadgets under the hood for pollution control.

You may think an engine itself is complicated. Well, the overall pollution-control system—stuff bolted onto the outside of the engine to control pollution—is actually more complex than the engine itself.

Some devices, such as *thermostatic air cleaners, exhaust-recircu-*

lation valves, and *catalytic converters* (in the exhaust system), are used by virtually all car manufacturers, but each manufacturer has its own particularities. Chrysler has an *air-aspirator system*, General Motors uses *pulse-air injection*, Ford uses a *vacuum-diverter valve*—and the list goes on.

Perhaps you have seen a workshop manual by *Chilton* or *Motor* in a shop. Including electronic ignition, itself a part of pollution control, the 1981 *Chilton* devotes 65 pages to pollution-control systems—over twice the 31 pages it gives to brakes and more than three times the 18 pages on steering systems. This gives you some notion of how messy pollution-control systems can be.

You would think that after fifteen years pollution control would have done some good. Yet, in 1979, the Los Angeles area had its worst "smog alert" in 24 years, and when Ronald Reagan won the 1980 election, various people in the Environmental Protection Agency (EPA) declared that we were losing more ground all the time and that Reagan must not be allowed to reduce pollution standards. In sum, the results have been ambiguous.

If the results have been uncertain, the costs have not: they have been astronomical, both in the increased cost of cars and in reduced efficiency and, thus, reduced gas mileage.

I have always felt that pollution-control efforts should aim at traffic patterns rather than the vehicles. That is, my (drastic) approach would be to simply keep private cars out of the downtown areas of large cities. Indeed, Richard J. Daley, the late mayor of Chicago, was developing a plan of this sort when he died. Only a mayor of Daley's political will power could have done it, and Daley has not been given the credit he deserves for his plan to "give the city back to the people."

The car manufacturers have represented the EPA as dictatorial bureaucrats with no comprehension of technical problems, and the EPA people have represented Detroit as evil troglodytes willing to destroy the earth in the name of profits. Perhaps both accusations are true. However, in my more cynical moments, I think the whole thing was a "put-up" job. When the clever detective seeks to determine who bashed the master's head in, he asks, in legalese, the question "*Cui bono?*" That is, "Who benefits?" Well, whatever all those little gadgets may have done for the environment, every little one of them made some profit for the manufacturer.

Of more immediate interest, those little gadgets destroyed a piece of Americana, a piece as fond as apple pie. They eliminated the clever youth who could fix any defunct car with a piece of baling wire and the mythical ancient who could diagnose any engine ailment with a geriatric ear. Nowadays, mechanics need diagnostic equipment to figure out what ails an engine, a step pioneered in 1971 when Volkswagen added some wiring that could be plugged into a special engine analyzer. Most current cars now have similar built-in diagnostic systems.

This is all good. However, if your car stalls beside the road, you'll need the analyzer—and an electrical outlet to plug it into—to figure out what's wrong.

POSTSCRIPT
GLOSSARY
INDEX

POSTSCRIPT: THE 55-MPH SPEED LIMIT

We noted that buying a car becomes an ontological act in the respect that the purchase involves a personal sense of values. Similarly, we showed that our style of driving expresses our sense of social values.

We have, however, rather neglected the fact that driving a car is also a political act in the respect that driving confronts us constantly with the force of law and requires that we respond in accordance with our attitude toward the law.

Driving has become much more political in recent years because of the national 55-mph speed limit. While people either accept or reject it, few remember how and why we got it, nor are they aware of the official falsehoods that have been offered to justify it. Accordingly, we might well examine the matter as an afterthought.

History and Background

Up to about 1960, most highways in the United States were two-lane roads of unlimited access; that is, a driveway or side road could meet the highway virtually anywhere. Only a few turnpikes (mostly toll roads) and local freeways had four lanes, median strips, and limited-access. In that era, speed limits ranged from 50 mph to 65 mph, often with one limit for daytime and another (lower) one for night.

The big national road-building scheme, the interstate highway program, began in 1956. The interstates were designed for a 70-mph cruising speed (outside of cities), and people promptly began using them that way. States found themselves issuing numerous speeding tickets, and a strong movement grew up to raise speed limits to the speed that would include 85 percent of the drivers (the "85th percentile" rule). Around 1960, old 55- to 65-mph speed limits fell like ninepins before the 70-mph limit, and several Western states allowed speeds up to 75 mph.

Thus, people were surprised in the summer of 1973 when a major oil company sponsored singer Johnny Cash in commercials that warned of an impending fuel shortage. When Cash urged people to drive 50 mph, rather than 60 mph, they didn't know what he was talking about. They'd been driving 70 mph for a dozen years.

The sponsoring oil company knew its business, though, for a fuel shortage had been a-borning since 1959, when President Dwight D. Eisenhower vetoed a plan to deregulate interstate prices of natural gas. Because producers could not sell natural gas at profitable prices, they quit looking for it, and since oil and natural gas commonly occur together, they effectively stopped looking for oil, too.

Next, the zeal of the Environmental Protection Agency in the late 1960s frightened many people into shifting from coal to oil for heat. This shift created a stronger demand for petroleum fuels. Even so, the gestating fuel crisis offered to produce no viable result.

Richard M. Nixon came into office in 1969 determined to assure the fuel crisis. His first relevant act was to impose wage and price controls in 1971; since oil producers could not sell their products at profitable margins, they quit bringing them to market at all. Many people who owned only one or two oil wells— the producers who account for the bulk of domestic petroleum— shut their wells down completely, and the big oil companies closed many domestic wells and bought crude oil overseas. To further assure the fuel shortage, Nixon also altered national policy to allow more oil imports from the tinderbox of the Middle East (thus to make up for the oil not being produced at home). Last, to cover all possibilities, in late 1973, Nixon (and the Congress) took the wage-price controls off everything *except* oil.

The rest is well known. Local shortages (such as those singer Cash warned about) had occurred by midsummer 1973. The Arab oil embargo after the Yom Kippur War spread them nationwide. Eventually, under the persuasive influence of successive price increases from around $3 per barrel in 1973 to a high of $42 on the "spot" market in 1979, the Arabs agreed that money was more important than politics, and oil supplies flowed again.

Throughout the 1970s, economists like Milton Friedman urged the removal of price controls on oil, the point being that market forces would regulate fuel consumption and, thus, preclude a national shortage. After Friedman's ideas were put into practice in a qualified way, fuel prices went up and the shortages disappeared along with the crisis.

Meanwhile, having produced the "fuel crisis" somewhat in the spirit of children who wreck the playroom, Nixon and the Congress began searching for a solution to it. They chose the 55-mph speed limit. The federal government, through the Department of Transportation, promised to withhold highway money from the states if they failed to comply with the limit; however, the government also promised handsome grants to the states to assist them in enforcing the limit. The states, anticipating a windfall of grant money, plus more from speeding tickets, literally fell over themselves bringing their speed limits into compliance. By January 1974, the whole program was in place.

Safety

Once the program was in place, the NHTSA branch of the Department of Transportation began claiming the lower speed limit "saved lives." Critics of these claims promptly pointed out that the traffic fatality rate had begun falling in October 1973, three months before the lower speed limit went into effect. The critics suggested that both fuel shortages and the modest price increases that had been allowed had resulted in reduced driving, and reduced driving resulted in fewer fatalities. In any case, the critics said, the 55-mph speed limit could not be given credit for a trend that developed well before the limit went into effect. NHTSA never responded to these critics in any substantive way.

The decline in the accident rate, continuing downward as it had been doing for fifty years, did accelerate from 1974 to 1977. NHTSA gave the 55-mph speed limit all the credit, while the critics pointed to reduced driving, improvements in roads and cars, more use of seat belts, and the retirement of older cars that lacked safety features. The critics also pointed out that traffic on rural roads, roads already posted below 55 mph, accounted for much of the reduction in traffic fatalities, and so concluded that the 55-mph limit could not be entirely responsible for the decrease. Traffic authorities in some states noted that traffic flow and traffic density, more than any high or low speed limit, were the two factors that correlated most directly with traffic fatalities. Yet other critics pointed out that one-third to one-half the deaths, on all roads and at all speeds, involved drivers who were legally drunk and hardly under the influence of the 55-mph speed limit at all. NHTSA never responded to these critics, either.

In 1978, the fatality rate began rising again and for no apparent reason. Many advocates of the new speed limit immediately blamed the increase on stiff-necked, recalcitrant drivers who exceeded the 55-mph limit, but various public officials quickly replied that such was not the case. The officials had no choice: the states had to report compliance with the speed limit to get their federal highway money, and to blame speeders for the fatality increase would be to admit that their compliance reports were false.

Indeed, critics had long said as much and had pointed to various "numbers games" provoked by the law. For example, the federal government put up $15,000,000 in "bonus" money for states that could report significant reductions in traffic fatalities, which prompted state officials to revise the causes of traffic fatalities in their reports so their states would qualify for a bonus.

The compliance standard itself provoked some friction between the federal government and the states over the issue of how much compliance was required. The figure was eventually set at 50 percent. In other words, the states and the federal government acknowledged that half the drivers (voters?) would reject the 55-speed limit.

Once they had a number to aim for, the states began juggling their numbers to achieve the desired figure. Since they had the answer already, all they had to do was to manipulate the numbers until they produced the right answer. Most states did a convincing job of it, but Massachusetts, a state notorious for crude forms of political expediency, overstated a correction factor in its 1982 numbers and produced a compliance figure of 52.9 percent. Alas, the federal government used a less generous correction factor and came up with only 43.7 percent compliance, enough to require cutting off the federal grant money. At this writing, the state and federal officials are in a huddle, trying to cook the numbers enough to salvage the grant money and the illusion that the public endorses the 55-mph speed limit.

We should note two more factors relevant to the compliance numbers. First, speed is mostly checked on freeways and interstate highways—that is, on the very highways where the fewest accidents occur.

Second, the speeds of the cars are not usually checked with radar guns, apparently because the states and the federal government know that police radar isn't good enough to produce competent data. Of course, radar is considered good enough to justify speeding fines.

Traffic fatalities rose to a peak in 1980, then began a marked decline. Throughout, the states have claimed compliance, and the federal government has committed millions in aid for enforcement—$20,000,000 authorized in 1980, with long-run estimates of about $650,000,000 over the next decade, for an average of $65,000,000 per year. In addition, independent observers estimate that nationwide, state and local jurisdictions spend as much as $2,500,000,000 of their own money in enforcement.

Given the money spent on enforcement, the 55-mph speed should do some good. Unfortunately, no one can prove it. NHTSA claims it "saves lives" and has offered figures ranging from 4000 to 6000 lives per year. These figures put NHTSA in the position of having to enumerate events that did not happen, and so can hardly be enumerated. In other words, NHTSA pulled the numbers out of a hat. Statisticians have (arguable) ways to predict the number of events that do not happen, but that still leaves the question of what, in fact, caused the events not to happen. So far, NHTSA has not made the case for the 55 mph speed limit.

Grant, *arguendo*, that NHTSA could make its case, and accept 6000 lives and an extreme figure of $2,565,000,000 per year for enforcement; the cost comes to $427,500 to save one life. However, economists who attempt to put a value on lost time believe the 55-mph limit actually costs the nation closer to $6,000,000,000 per year, which works out to $1,000,000 per life.

To begrudge a measly $1,000,000 or $427,500 to save one life seems cruelly venal. On the other hand, if kidney dialysis machines cost $25,000 each, the $2,565,000,000 spent directly on enforcement alone would save 102,600 lives, and this is granting the dubious claim that the 55-mph speed limit saves lives at all. The $6,000,000,000 figure would provide 240,000 dialysis machines. Poured into cancer research, the same money would ultimately save even more lives. In sum, if the government genuinely desires to save lives, the 55-mph speed limit is about the most expensive, most inefficient way of doing it that can be found.

On the other hand, one body of opinion believes the 55-mph limit actually causes accidents and, thus, fatalities because it interferes with traffic flow and provokes much more lane-changing, bumper-riding, etc. This group cannot *prove* its position, though the available evidence is on its side.

The one thing everybody does agree on is that universal use of seat belts would reduce fatalities by one-fourth to one-half. The absence of a law requiring the use of seat belts raises questions concerning the official sincerity about saving lives.

Saving Fuel

To move a car faster unarguably consumes more fuel. The relevant questions become, "How much?" and "At what cost?"

Here again, DOT officials have offered inconsistent estimates about how much fuel the 55-mph limit saves, the inconsistency arising from the fact that no one knows. As with lives, the problem requires knowing the cause of incidents that did not happen, and in a context of many possible causes.

Generally, the 55-mph limit applies only on limited-access highways because secondary highways already have lower speed limits. Such highways carry about one-third of all vehicle miles, so any fuel saving from the 55-mph limit can come only from that one-third.

But many, perhaps most, of the drivers in that third would not exceed 55 mph anyway. The usual estimate is that 50 percent of the drivers on limited-access highways would normally drive

55 mph or slower. Thus, any saving can come only from the remaining half of that original one-third, or from the one-sixth of all drivers who would normally exceed 55 mph. Furthermore, the saving will be limited to the difference in fuel consumption between driving, say, 55 mph and driving 70 mph. The saving will be greater with big cars and less with small cars, which are becoming more numerous here of late. Once these factors enter the equation, the 55-mph speed limit might possibly reduce vehicular fuel consumption by 2 percent, and thus save about 2,200,000,000 gallons per year. Depending on the estimates used, the cost to save fuel by this method runs from about 85 cents to $2.72 per gallon—a losing proposition in any case, considering how enforcement diverts police manpower from more useful activities.

The earlier generality, that speed requires energy, overlooks differences in the efficiencies of energy-conversion systems, i.e., engines. Due to some high-order complexities of combustion science that involve the phenomenon of the *brake mean effective pressure* (BMEP) imposed on the top of the piston and the *brake specific fuel consumption* (BSFC) that produces that pressure, a small engine working hard is more efficient than a big engine that is loafing. In consequence, a small engine may get its best gas mileage at a speed well above 55 mph. My Saab 99 approaches 29 mpg at 60 mph, but doesn't exceed 27 mpg at 55 mph. I've met other people who have had similar experience; one fellow reported that his Honda Accord gets its best mileage with the cruise control set at 64 mph.

The 55-mph limit, if followed scrupulously, will keep all those small car owners from finding out that their cars may be more economical when exceeding 55 mph, but as the numbers of small cars increase, more people will discover this fallacy in the 55-mph limit. Of course, under the law, they will be penalized for doing the very thing the law claims as its purpose: saving fuel.

Negative Effects

If the 55-mph limit has done no verifiable good, it has certainly done immense harm. It has diverted highway police from secondary, high-hazard roads to the low-hazard highways for the sake of establishing compliance (or for the sake of filling state coffers with money from fines). By raising speed to such importance, it has led to the use of cheap, inaccurate radar guns (bought with federal grant money) and has thus made practicing liars and thieves out of many police (some police officers know this and some don't). It has created unnecessary tension between police officers and drivers and taught drivers contempt for the law (deservedly so, given the nature of the law). It has made speeding fines a basic source of revenue for many small towns and thus negated one of the original motives for the interstate system.

However, the future looks more honest. Several states have reduced the fine for exceeding 55 mph to a token. Other states have proposed dropping it entirely. For a short time, the Reagan administration considered repeal of the national speed-limit law. Eventually, as the effort to balance the federal budget continues, the country may discover it can't afford to spend so much money to force people to drive so slowly.

GLOSSARY

A-arm: a framework shaped like a capital A used in some suspension systems. The legs of the A hinge to the car body and the apex hinges to the kingpin.

accelerator: the proper name for what people usually call the "gas pedal"; sometimes called the "throttle."

accelerator pump: a tiny pump in the carburetor that squirts a shot of liquid gasoline into the engine when you push the accelerator pedal all the way down.

alternator: an electrical generator that produces alternating current; on a car, the alternating current passes through a rectifier that changes it into the direct current that runs the electrical things on the car and keeps the battery fully charged.

amperage/amperes: a characteristic of electrical energy; the more work done at a given voltage, the more amperes (amps) required.

antifreeze. See *ethylene glycol.*

API: American Petroleum Institute, an organization that develops performance specifications for petroleum products, particularly lubricating oils.

ATF: automatic transmission fluid; an oil specially compounded for heat resistance and for compatibility with rubber-like seals.

ball joint: a link between two pieces that allows the two pieces to work in several directions at once, e.g., a human hip joint; on a car, ball joints allow the front wheels to turn for steering even as they bounce up and down over bumps.

band: a metal strap that surrounds a circular case containing gears in an automatic transmission; the bands hold or release gear cases to accomplish gear changes.

battery: a device that generates electricity from chemical action; in a car battery, the chemical action arises between sulfuric acid and lead; hence, a "lead-acid" battery.

bearing: an object placed between two other objects to transmit a load from one to the other, e.g., from the wheel to the axle of a car; ball bearings are metal balls, and tapered-roller bearings look like a cone with the tip cut off.

bias-belted: a bias-ply tire that has a belt of reinforcing cord immediately under the tread.

bias-ply: a form of tire construction wherein the layers of reinforcing cord run from one side to the other and cross each other at an angle of about 45 degrees.

"book": common expression for monthly and quarterly handbooks published by the National Auto Dealers Association; the "book" amounts to a market report and lists the average value of a used car for five years back.

brake: a device for arresting or preventing motion; on a car, the brakes act on the wheels.

brake drum: an item that resembles a circular cake pan; brake shoes rub against the inside of its raised edge to develop friction to stop the car.

brake fluid: an oily liquid with an extremely high boiling point that is used to transfer energy, via metal tubing, from the driver's foot to the brakes.

brake pad: a piece of asbestos or similar heat-resistant material mounted on a metal backing: in a disc-brake system, the pads are contained by the caliper and grip both sides of the disc.

brake shoe: a curved piece of metal with asbestos on the convex (outer) side that contacts the inner (concave) surface of a drum brake.

caliper: in a disc-brake system, the piece that contains the hydraulic cylinders and pistons and the brake pads and fits over the disc so the pads can squeeze against it.

cam: a piece of metal, usually on a shaft, that impinges on an object and causes it to move.

camber angle: the degree to which a tire leans outward at the top.

camshaft: a shaft, with cams, which opens the valves in an engine; a spring closes the valve after the camshaft rotates the cam away from the valves.

carburetor: a device for mixing gasoline and air in the right proportions so the mixture will burn.

caster angle: the degree to which a wheel carries its weight ahead of or behind its center.

catalytic converter: a device in the exhaust system that neutralizes pollutants in the exhaust.

choke: a device within the carburetor on an engine to reduce the quantity of air and create a more fuel-rich mixture for starting the engine when it is cold.

circuit breaker: a switch that flips to "off" when too much amperage passes through the electrical circuit that the switch completes.

clutch: the device that connects the engine to a manual transmission and allows the connection to be broken at will, e.g., for gear changes, etc.

cog: a circular gear with teeth around its perimeter.

coil: technically, a transformer; it changes the 12 volts from the battery into about 25,000 volts for the spark plugs.

coil spring: a spring that looks like a corkscrew; commonly used with front wheels.

combustion chamber: the area at the top of the cylinder where the fuel-air mixture is ignited by the spark plug; usually contained in the cylinder head.

compression ignition: setting the air-fuel mixture on fire with heat generated by compression rather than with a spark, i.e., a diesel.

compressor: in an air-conditioning system, a device that uses a piston in a cylinder to compress Freon gas; in a turbocharger, a turbine that forces air into the engine.

connecting rod: the piece that connects the piston to the crankshaft in order to transmit the pressure developed above the piston to the crankshaft.

constant-velocity (CV) joint: a variation on the universal-joint theme that experiences fewer cyclic vibrations.

coolant: the liquid that circulates through the radiator and engine block (and heater) of a liquid-cooled car to cool the engine; ideally, consists of a 50-50 mixture of antifreeze and water.

countershaft: a shaft in a manual transmission that turns opposite from the way the engine does and that is necessary to produce first, second, third, and reverse, but not fourth, gears.

crankshaft: the shaft, which works like a bicycle pedal crank, that converts the up-and-down motion of the pistons and connecting rods into rotary motion.

cylinder: a deep round hole in the engine wherein a piston moves up and down.

cylinder head: a piece of metal that bolts to the top of the engine block and covers the cylinders: it contains the valves and has passages for air-fuel to enter and for exhaust to escape.

diesel engine: an engine that uses the heat generated by compression to ignite its fuel.

diesel fuel: an oily fuel, virtually identical to household furnace oil, used in diesel engines; has high heat value per gallon.

differential: the device that receives power from the engine via the drive shaft, divides it in two, and sends half to the driving wheel on each side of the car to propel the car.

dipstick: a long, thin, narrow piece of metal that sticks through a hole to measure the level of oil in an engine, an automatic transmission, or a power-steering reservoir.

disc brake: a brake that uses the two faces of a disc as a friction surface.

displacement: the volume of each cylinder with the piston at the bottom of its downstroke, multiplied by the number of cylinders; displacement is a general measure of the size of an engine and is usually given in cubic inches, cubic centimeters, or liters.

distributor: a device that receives high-voltage electricity from the coil and distributes it to each spark plug in turn.

drag coefficient (given as C_d or C_x): a measure of the resistance the surrounding air imposes on the forward motion of a car; hardly a useful number, since a 4000-pound car with a low C_d will still use more fuel than a 2500-pound car with a high C_d.

drive shaft: the shaft that conducts power from the transmission to the differential.

drum brake: a brake that uses the inside of a raised edge, e.g., such as the raised edge of a cake pan, as a friction surface.

electronic fuel injection (EFI): a system of using electronic devices to inject precise quantities of fuel into the engine, as an alternative to a carburetor; precise fuel metering improves fuel economy and reduces pollutants.

engine block: the basic foundation of the engine; it is a large metal casting that contains the cylinder holes, passages for oil and coolants, and a means of mounting the crankshaft. The cylinder head bolts on top of the block.

ethylene glycol (CH_2 OHCH$_2$ OH): a liquid with an extremely low freezing point; mixed with water in a 50–50 ratio for use in the cooling system of a water-cooled engine.

exhaust: vaporous and carbonous residues of air-fuel mixture combustion; the primary source of air pollution caused by a car.

exhaust gas recirculation (EGR) valve: a valve that allows some exhaust gas to dilute the air-fuel mixture for the purpose of reducing combustion temperatures and, therefore, pollutants in the exhaust.

exhaust manifold: an antechamber that collects exhaust gasses from several cylinders and ducts them to the exhaust pipe.

exhaust pipe: a pipe that connects to the exhaust manifold to conduct exhaust gasses to the rear of the car.

exhaust valve: the valve that lets the exhaust gasses out of the cylinder.

firewall: the sheet-metal bulkhead that separates the engine from the passenger compartment.

firing order: the sequence in which sparks go to each spark plug.

flasher: a switch that goes on and off by itself; used to make turn signals flash, rather than shine continuously.

flat engine. See *horizontal engine.*

float: a buoyant object in a carburetor that floats upward to close the needle valve and stop fuel flow to the carburetor when the carburetor is full of fuel.

float chamber: the fuel reservoir in the carburetor, where the float fits.

flywheel: a heavy, solid metal disc bolted onto the crankshaft; its inertia smooths out the jerkiness in the operating cycles of the engine and it provides a convenient place to put the ring gear. The clutch is bolted onto the flywheel.

four-wheel drive (4WD): a system for enabling all four wheels to propel the car; provides extremely good traction in adverse conditions, e.g., mud, snow, etc.

front-wheel drive (FWD): a system for using the front wheels to propel the car; the system simplifies the car overall, but complicates the steering and front suspension.

fuel pump: the pump that moves fuel from the tank to the carburetor or fuel-injection system.

fuse: an electrical circuit link that melts in two if amperage in the circuit is too high; an alternative to a circuit breaker.

fusee: a type of flare that burns with an intense red flame.

gear ratio: the relationship of the rotative speed of one gear to the gear it meshes with; in first gear, for example, the gear driven by the engine makes about three turns while the gear it meshes with and that turns the drive shaft makes only one turn, for a 3:1 ratio.

glow plug: an electrical device, similar to a tiny burner on an electric range, that is contained in the combustion chamber of a diesel engine and is used to ignite the fuel when the engine is cold.

governor: any device that regulates or responds to speed; in an automatic transmission, the governor causes the transmission to shift at the right speed.

half-shaft: the short drive shaft that connects the differential to the front wheel of a front-wheel-drive car.

"handling package": optional-equipment suspension components used to give a domestic car a "European-style" suspension.

horizontal engine: a type of engine in which the cylinders are mounted 180 degrees apart, as on the current Subaru; also called "flat" or "opposed."

horsepower (hp): a concept established by James Watt (1736–1819) to measure work; one hp equals the work to raise 33,000 pounds one foot in one minute; equivalent to .746 kilowatts.

hydraulic valve lifter: a link in the valve-actuating system that automatically compensates for wear and, thus, needs no routine adjustment.

hydroplaning: a phenomenon whereby a tire rides up on the surface of water that has collected on the road; when hydroplaning, tires cannot control a car.

idler arm: part of the steering that keeps the tie rods lined up properly.

ignition system: the whole apparatus for igniting the air-fuel mixture; usually refers to the coil, distributor, and spark plugs, but also includes the battery, ignition switch, and, perhaps, various pollution-control devices.

impeller: the turbine in a turbocharger that is turned by the exhaust gas and turns the compressor.

independent suspension (front or rear): a system that allows a wheel on one side of the car to respond to a bump without affecting the corresponding wheel on the opposite side; improves road holding and comfort.

in-line engine: a type of engine in which the cylinders stand in a row, with their axes in one plane.

intake manifold: an antechamber under the carburetor that conducts the air-fuel mixture to the cylinders; injectors for gasoline fuel-injection (but not for diesel fuel-injection) systems commonly fit into the intake manifold.

intake valve: the valve that lets the air-fuel mixture into the cylinder.

jet: a tiny passage in a carburetor that conducts liquid gasoline from the float chamber into the air stream sucked through the carburetor by the pistons and thence into the cylinders.

kingpin: on earlier cars, the equivalent of a hinge pin that allows the front wheels to swivel to the left or right.

leaf spring: a type of spring resembling laminated strips that didn't get glued together; commonly used at the rear.

lexicographer: *vide* Johnson, a harmless drudge.

MacPherson Strut: a form of front suspension wherein a shock absorber and coil spring are integrated into a single unit; invented by Earle Steele MacPherson (1891–1960), who also invented the ball joint while he was an engineer at the Ford Motor Company.

mainshaft: the shaft in a manual transmission that rotates in the same direction as the engine does.

marque: the aficionado's way of designating the manufacturer of a car; what peasants mean by the word *make*.

master cylinder: receives pressure from the driver's foot and transmits it to the wheels for braking; the brake pedal pushes a piston in the master cylinder, and the master cylinder piston forces brake fluid to the wheel cylinders/calipers.

maximum torque: the engine speed at which the engine is happiest and closest to optimum efficiency.

needle valve: the valve the carburetor float impinges upon to shut off the flow of fuel from the fuel pump.

oil pan: the reservoir for lubricating oil, at the bottom of the engine.

oil-pressure gauge: an instrument that registers oil pressure.

oil-pressure indicator light: a warning light that goes on if the oil pressure is too low.

oil pump: a device in the engine that pumps oil under pressure to all the moving parts to reduce friction (and the damage friction would cause).

opposed engine. See *horizontal engine.*

optional: not standard, i.e., not included in the "base price" of the car.

overdrive: a gear ratio allowing the engine to make fewer turns than the drive shaft; allows a slow, economical engine speed for highway cruising.

parking brake: the brake, actuated by hand or foot, which keeps the car from rolling when it is parked; can be used as an emergency brake, though it is not highly effective in that function.

pawl: any metal protuberance fitted into an aperture to prevent an object from moving; in an automatic transmission, a pawl locks the drive shaft when the car is in "Park."

pinion: a small gear, usually a cog type, found in the differential, in rack-and-pinion steering, and on the starter.

piston: a metal item that resembles a short tin can (i.e., is hollow inside) that has been opened; the piston receives the pressure generated by the burning fuel and transmits it to the connecting rod.

piston rings: metal rings that surround the piston to assure a tight gas seal in the cylinder.

planetary gear system: the type of gear system used in an automatic transmission.

positive crankcase ventilation (PCV): a system for sucking crankcase vapors into the engine and burning them, rather than venting them directly into the air. Crankcase vapors were identified as a major source of smog, and the first step in national pollution control was mandatory PCV in California in 1963.

power-assisted brakes: a system of augmenting the force of the driver's foot via vacuum or hydraulic pressure developed by the engine.

power steering: a system that uses the engine to supply the power to steer.

rack: a gear that resembles gear teeth cut into a straight piece of material.

rack-and-pinion steering: a simple, expedient way of transmitting steering-wheel motion to the front wheels; a pinion gear on the end of the steering shaft is used to move a rack gear from side to side.

radial tire: a form of tire construction wherein the reinforcing cords in the body of the tire run sideways, while the reinforcement immediately under the tread runs in the direction of travel.

radiator: a slablike gridwork with little tubes running one way and thin metal fins running the other; hot engine coolant runs through the tubes as air flows through the gridwork to remove heat from the coolant and, thus, cool the engine. Since its purpose is not to supply heat (as in a home heating system) but to get rid of it, technically, it is a "heat exchanger."

recap: (verb) to put a new tread on an old tire; (noun) an old tire that has been given a new tread.

ring gear: a gear that surrounds the flywheel and is turned by the starter pinion gear.

rocker arm: a link in the valve system; in many engines it serves as the valve lifter.

roll bar: a reinforcing bar that passes above the passengers in an open car to prevent them from being crushed if the car overturns.

rotary engine. See *Wankel engine.*

rpm (conventional abbreviation for "revolutions per minute"): the way of indicating how fast the crankshaft of an engine is turning.

SAE: Society of Automobile Engineers, the professional society of engineers, organized in 1905, that develops standards used in the automobile industry.

sector gear: a gear in worm-and-sector steering that transmits steering-wheel motion to the tie rods.

service brakes: the foot-actuated brakes used in normal driving.

shock absorber: the American term for what the British more precisely call a *damper*; it damps (or retards) the bouncing of the car body when going over bumps.

short circuit: a circumstance of defective electrical wiring wherein electricity from the battery can return to the battery without passing through (or activating) an electrical device.

slave cylinder: any hydraulic cylinder that receives force from a master cylinder and applies it to a task; technically, brake wheel cylinders are "slaves," but the term is generally restricted to the slave cylinder that disengages the clutch.

solenoid: a device that converts electrical energy into linear motion; on a car, the solenoid pushes the starter pinion gear into mesh with the flywheel ring gear and, at the same time, routes electricity to the starter motor so it will turn the engine.

space frame: a metal framework resembling a ladder on which the car body mounts; a heavier form of construction, now rendered obsolescent by unit-body construction.

spark ignition: the system for using an electric spark to ignite an air-fuel mixture.

spark plug: the device that ignites the air-fuel mixture in a gasoline engine; one end of the plug extends into the combustion chamber; an electrical spark jumps across a gap in this end to ignite the air-fuel mixture.

standard engine: the engine a manufacturer recommends for a particular car.

starter: an electric motor that turns an engine to get it started.

steering box: a housing for the worm-and-sector gears of a worm-and-sector steering system.

stock engine: an engine straight from the factory and with no modifications made to the manufacturer's specifications.

suspension: the system interposed between the car body and the wheels; includes the springs, shock absorbers, and assorted linkages.

sway bar: a suspension member that links the two front or two rear wheels together to reduce excess sway when taking a curve.

synchronizer: a type of clutch between gears in a manual transmission that eases shifting.

tachometer: a gauge that registers rpm, or engine speed.

tappet: technically, the item the cams on the camshaft impinge upon; sometimes called a "valve lifter."

thermostat: a heat-sensitive valve that restricts the flow of coolant through the radiator until the engine gets warm.

throttle body injection: (TBI): a technical middle ground between a carburetor and electronic fuel injection; uses a single injector mounted in what amounts to the body of a carburetor.

tie rod: the final link between the steering wheel and the wheels that steer.

tie-rod end: a small ball joint that connects a tie rod to the wheel.

toe-in: the degree to which the front wheels point inward.

torque: a twisting force; the engine applies torque to, e.g., the drive shaft; torque applied to the axles makes the wheels turn to propel the car.

torque converter: an element of an automatic transmission that converts torque from the engine into torque on the transmission shaft.

torsion bar: a stiff, springy rod used in lieu of a coil or leaf spring.

transaxle: in front-wheel-drive or rear-engine cars, the unit that incorporates the transmission and differential; sometimes, the engine is also considered as part of the transaxle.

transmission: a device that transmits power from a source to a receiver, e.g., from an engine to wheels; the transmission in a car uses gears and shafts to transmit power.

turbine: a type of sophisticated fan that either develops pressure in, or receives pressure from, a fluid; found in torque converters and turbochargers.

turbocharger: a device for using the pressure developed by the hot exhaust gasses to force-feed an engine with extra air.

U-bolt: a bolt formed in a U shape that attaches a leaf spring to an axle.

unit-body: a type of automobile construction that eliminates the space frame by strengthening the whole car body.

universal joint (U-joint): a mechanism that connects two rotating shafts and allows them to form an angle even as they rotate; a U-joint transmits power around a corner, so to speak.

vacuum booster: a part of the power-assisted braking system; uses vacuum developed by the engine to increase the force the driver applies to the brake pedal.

valve body: the part of an automatic transmission that controls gear shifting by the opening and closing of valves and the consequent completion or nullification of circuits of oil under pressure.

valve lifter: technically, the piece that actually pushes a valve open; sometimes referred to as a "rocker arm" or "tappet."

V-belt: a cord-and-rubber belt that is endless (forms a complete circle) and transmits rotation from the crankshaft to the fan and water pump, to an air-conditioner compressor, etc.; in cross section, the belt resembles a trapezoid with a narrow top, but "trapezoidal belt" seems cumbersome, so people use "V-belt."

V-engine: a type of engine in which the cylinders lie in two planes that form a V, with the crankshaft at the bottom.

volt: a unit of electrical energy that remains constant within a single system; a car has a 12-volt system.

voltage regulator: a device that varies the charging rate of the alternator according to whether the battery needs more or less recharging.

Wankel engine: an engine developed by Felix Wankel, an Austrian; sometimes called a "rotary engine" because it uses a triangular rotor turning in an epitrochoid chamber, rather than a piston in a cylinder.

wheel cylinder: the hydraulic brake cylinder at each wheel that receives pressure from the master cylinder and transfers it to brake shoes or brake pads.

worm-and-sector: a steering system that uses a worm gear to rotate a sector gear to transfer motion from the steering wheel to the front wheel.

worm gear: a gear that resembles a screw thread, i.e., forms a spiral around the longitudinal axis of the gear.

INDEX

locating, 228; Skinner Union (SU), 322; Stromberg "constant depression" (CD), 322
Car Prices for 1983, 48
Carter, Jimmy, 53
Cash, Johnny, 382
Cassidy, Christine, 180, 181
Cassidy, Raymond, 10–11, 96–97, 132
Caster angle (wheel), 135, 368–69
Catalytic converter, 128–29, 138, 232, 377
Cathode-ray tube (CRT), 129, 149–50
Charles II, 314, 316
Chevrolet, Louis and Gaston, 29
Chevrolet, 294, 330; reputation of and differences in, 8–9, 10, 12
Chevrolet models: Blazer, 207, 356; Camaro, 39–40; Celebrity, 3, 42; Chevelle, 249; Chevette, 4, 5, 10, 14, 18, 79; Chevy II, 29–31; Citation, 14, 30–31, 52–53, 66; Corvette, 39–40; GMC light trucks, 113; Malibu, 12, 30, 305, 342; Nova, 29; Suburban, 14, 139, 195, 201–2, 207–8, 249, 292, 305; Vega, 10, 14, 330
Chilton's workshop manual, 170, 226, 377
Chocks/blocks, for changing flat tire, 214, 218, 221, 225
Choke, 321, 322, 329;

automatic, 160–61
Chrysler, 40, 132, 370; options offered by, 59; pollution controls of 377; reputation of and differences in, 8–9, 10, 12; transmission, 171–72
Chrysler models: Imperial, 336; LeBaron, 54; Town and Country coupe, 35–36
Circuit breakers, 375
Citroen, 354; model DS 19/21, 27, 33–34, 355
Classified ads, 52
Claybrook, Joan, *The Car Book*, 53–54
Clicking, from under hood, 191–92
"Clunking," 89–90, 196
Clutch, 87, 90, 133, 344–46; cone, 346; fluid level, 233; hot, 198–99
Clymer's workshop manual, 226
Cog gear, 362
Coil (ignition system), 323, 325–26
Coil springs, 216, 369
Cold-weather packages, 70–71
Coleman, John, 299
Combustion knock, 193
Compression ignition (CI), 338
Compression ratio (CR), 333
Compressor (turbocharger), 342–43
Cone clutches, 346
Connecting rods, 192–93, 323

Sound systems, 69–70
Spark ignition (SI), 338
Spark plugs, 84, 124, 129, 323, 326; defective, 191, 192
Speed limit, 384–85, 388
Sport package, 66
Sports cars, prices of, 39–40
Stall speed (automatic transmission), 351
Standard engine, 329, 330, 333
Standard Oil Company, 124
Starter, 323
Start-up, noises at, 194
Station wagons, 61; prices of, 45–47
Steering, 362–66; checking, on used cars, 81–82; failure, 275–76; power, 66–67, 88, 231, 364; system adjustments, 134
Steering box, 85, 134, 362, 363
Steinbeck, John, *The Grapes of Wrath*, 20
Stock engine, 329–30, 333
Studded tires, 210–11, 290, 291, 292
Studebaker Land Cruiser, 35
Stutz Bearcat, 36
Style, 16–17, 37
Subaru, 13, 31, 42, 334, 356
Sullivan, Louis, 40
Sunbeam-Talbot, 15
Sun roof, 64
Suspension system, 5, 6–7, 32, 366–70
Sway bars, 65; rear, 66

Synchronizers (transmission), 346

Tachometer, 347–48
Tailpipe, 86
Talbot-Lago, 335
Tapered-roller bearings, 371
Thatcher, Margaret, 45
Thermostatic air cleaners, 376
Throttle body injection (TBI), 328
Tie-rod ends, 134, 363
Tie rods, 85, 363
Timing chain, 192
Tire(s), 203; all-weather, 290, 291, 292; bias-belted, 203, 204, 207, 208; bias-ply, 203–5, 207, 208, 209–10; with chains, 290, 291–92; changing flat, 213–25; checking, on used cars, 81; checking pressure of, 74–75, 90, 237–39; failures, 276–79; mixing types of, 209–10; quality of, 205–8; radial, 62, 203–5, 206–10, 292; recapped, 211–12; rotation, 136; snow, 290, 291, 292; spare, 211, 222; studded, 210–11, 290, 291, 292; and suspension, noises from, 197; tread, 280; types of, 203–5; used, 212–13; in winter storms, 290–92
Tire manufacturers and/or types of tires: Armstrong